Culturally Responsive Counseling *With* Latinas/os

Patricia Arredondo
Maritza Gallardo-Cooper
Edward A. Delgado-Romero
Angela L. Zapata

AMERICAN COUNSELING
ASSOCIATION
5999 Stevenson Avenue
Alexandria, VA 22304
www.counseling.org

Culturally Responsive Counseling With Latinas/os

10   9   8   7   6   5   4   3   2   1

American Counseling Association
5999 Stevenson Avenue
Alexandria, VA 22304

Director of Publications   Carolyn C. Baker

Production Manager   Bonny E. Gaston

Editorial Assistant   Catherine A. Brumley

Copy Editor   Beth Ciha

Cover and text design by Bonny E. Gaston.

Library of Congress Cataloging-in-Publication Data

Arredondo, Patricia.
  Culturally responsive counseling with Latinas/os / Patricia Arredondo, Maritza Gallardo-Cooper, Edward A. Delgado-Romero, Angela L. Zapata.
    pages cm
  Includes bibliographical references and index.
  ISBN 978-1-55620-241-4 (alk. paper)
  1. Hispanic Americans—Social conditions.   2. Hispanic Americans—Economic conditions.   3. Hispanic Americans—Population.   I. Gallardo-Cooper, Maritza. II. Delgado-Romero, Edward A.   III. Zapata, Angela L.   IV. Title.
  E184.S75A875 2014
  305.868'073—dc23   2013010821

Dedication

To the millions of Latinas/os who will shape the future of the United States and to my Association for Multicultural Counseling and Development, Latino Network, and National Latina/o Psychological Association *familias*.

—Patricia Arredondo

• • •

To George, Nisa Pilar, and Jonathan, who affirm and transform my Puerto Rican roots.

—Maritza Gallardo-Cooper

• • •

Dedicated to my professional *familia* (National Latina/o Psychological Association) and my children, Javi, Isa, and Gil.

—Edward A. Delgado-Romero

• • •

I'd like to dedicate this to my dad, Emiliano Zapata, for instilling in me my Latino family values; my mom, Deborah Cornell, for always supporting and encouraging me; my sister, Elena Castellano, for being my rock; my nieces Lexus and Chloe for being my inspiration; and my partner in life, Brian Hicks, for believing in me and honoring my dedication to my work. Thank you for being an important part of my life—*Te quiero mucho para siempre!*

—Angela L. Zapata

• • •

Muchisimas gracias to our *"hija"* Marisela López Flores, a doctoral student in Counseling Psychology at the University of Wisconsin-Milwaukee. She made all of the *detalles* fall into place with great *orgullo* (pride).

Table of Contents

Preface

Estimates indicate that in the year 2050 the Latino population will be 30% of the U.S. population, a demographic shift driven primarily by births and not immigration (Passel & Cohn, 2008). Census projections also indicate that ethnic minority individuals (persons of Black/African, Asian, Pacific Islander, Latino/Hispanic, and Native American heritage) will be the majority, surpassing the White population. Many readers of this text may find that with each passing year, they are working with, teaching, counseling, advising, being taught by, and being led by Latina/o professionals in the workplace and perhaps have family members of Latino heritage. In a phenomenon sometimes referred to as the "browning" of America, Latinos are transforming the United States demographically, culturally, and politically. As reported in 2012, 1 out of every 4 children younger than age 18 in the United States is of Latino heritage, and 93% of these are U.S. citizens (P. Taylor, Gonzalez-Barrera, Passel, & Lopez, 2012).Thus, the future of the country is guaranteed to be Latina/o American.

School counselors are already on the front lines, working with children born in the United States to immigrant and second- and third-generation American-born parents. The parents of their students may be of different ethnic heritages, not speakers of Spanish, and, like others, trying to live out the American Dream. Thus, to be effective and client-centered, school counselors must have a breadth of knowledge about Latino families, cultural and bicultural values, gender roles and rules, and parents' expectations for their children's educational future. Counselors must be mindful of the trends in academic achievement for Latina/o students from kindergarten through Grade 12. Although the high school dropout rate for Latino students has historically been about 50%, with more children born in the United States, there will likely come to be less attrition and more individuals pursuing some form of postsecondary education.

Those who work on college campuses providing counseling, career counseling, or advising to students or military veterans need to appreciate how to promote Latina/o student achievement. The majority of new students will be the first in their families to attend college, and they will often be attending local institutions. Therefore, counseling professionals will need to be creative to engage commuters, residential students, honors students, less prepared students, and even parents. Consider that in 2012, Latinos became the largest ethnic minority group on 4-year campuses (Fry & Lopez, 2012) and that Hispanic-Serving Institutions educate more than 50% of Latino students in the United States. These are just the current data; imagine the future data.

Some 20–25 years ago, counselors attending the conferences of the American Counseling Association lamented the fact that Latino families were "traditional," monolingual Spanish speakers and immigrants, fatalistic, and otherwise resistant to counseling. This text challenges all of these myths about Latinos and Latino families. With roots in the territories of the U.S. southwest for centuries, contemporary Latinas/os have achieved bicultural socialization and reflect the multidimensional diversity of all other Americans in terms of sexual orientation, religious and political preferences, work ethic, desire to get ahead, and so forth.

The amount of information available on Latinos has never been greater. Our sources for this text are other authors, primarily Latinas/os who have published on topics such as educational trends, health beliefs and disparities, machismo, spirituality, acculturative stress, economic mobility, DREAMERS (young adults, most of whom are unauthorized, who would be positively affected by the passage of the Development, Relief, and Education for Alien Minors Act), immigration, gender role change, the academic achievement of first-generation college students, international counseling, and so forth. Then there are the scholars from multidisciplinary backgrounds—health and health care; community studies; elementary, higher, bilingual, and other dimensions of education; sociology; political science; history; international relationships; counseling and psychology, particularly from multicultural and Latino-specific perspectives; economics and consumerism; media; and so forth.

The Pew Hispanic Center is one of the most reliable sources of research on a range of topics relative to Latinos, including religion, politics, aspirations for life change, and demographic shifts in the country initiated by Latino mobility. The Southern Poverty Law Center is a social advocacy organization that champions the rights of all groups and individuals who experience discrimination and various forms of hate crimes. The National Institute for Latino Policy provides daily updates on matters involving and affecting Latinos on the mainland and in Puerto Rico. For example, the topic of pro-statehood versus remaining a commonwealth is discussed from multiple angles.

Finally, Latinos have not only increasingly become part of the mainstream media but have established their own media as well. NBC, Fox, and CNN have Spanish-language programming. NBC Universal produces daily human interest reports, news, and other updates targeting the U.S. Latino viewer. Today, most online networks have Spanish-language versions. Yet Univisión has a worldwide audience that outshines any U.S. mainstream network in terms of viewership. We are beginning to see cultural shifts in the country. For example, soccer (or *fútbol,* as it is called in Spanish-speaking countries) broke the barrier with the World Cup in the early 1990s. Magazines such as *People en Español, Latina,* and *Latino* are popular and widely available. In academia there is the *Hispanic Outlook on Education, Hispanic Business,* and two academic journals with a Latino focus: *Journal of Hispanic Higher Education* and *Journal of Latina/o Psychology.* The American Counseling Association's *Journal of Multicultural Counseling and Development* is also an excellent multicultural resource that often reports on Latino-centered research. If all professional disciplines and forms of media are covering and coveting the burgeoning Latino population, it is essential that counseling professionals in all contexts become fully prepared through Latino-centered awareness, knowledge, and skills. It has always been our contention that when counselors focus on specialty issues or groups not typically addressed in training, they learn about theories, beliefs, and practices that can then be applied to other cultural groups. The Latino-based worldviews, child-rearing practices, beliefs about health and mental health, beliefs about identity development, and response to counseling discussed in this book will seem similar to, and a little different from, those of other individuals and cultural groups (e.g., White Americans, Asian Americans, Pacific Islanders). Regardless of the setting or the population being served, context and culture matter when it comes to being a culturally competent counselor. It is our hope that the knowledge provided in these chapters will inform and be adapted to counselor education, research, practice, and community engagement with Latinos and non-Latino groups as well. It has heuristic value.

Overview of the Book

This book applies Latino counseling competencies (Santiago-Rivera, Arredondo, & Gallardo-Cooper, 2002) adapted from the Multicultural Counseling Competencies (D. W. Sue, Arredondo, & McDavis, 1992) paradigm. Each chapter begins with a *dicho* (proverb) to illustrate a way of giving advice or guidance as it relates to a particular time in life or circumstance one is trying to manage. We attempt to use *dichos* that speak to the topic of each chapter and its content. Chapters 1–8 provide knowledge necessary for culturally responsive and ethical practices with individuals and families. Chapters 9 and 10 give more attention to interventions, although each chapter introduces case scenarios that are designed to stimulate analysis and considerations from multiple perspectives. Chapters 11 and 12 focus on the counseling profession. In Chapter 11, we discuss the role of the *ACA Code of Ethics* (American Counseling Association, 2005) in informing culturally competent practice informed by the Multicultural Counseling Competencies (D. W. Sue et al., 1992) and Latino-specific competencies. In Chapter 12, we provide a rationale for an intentional focus on Latino-centered counseling so that counseling professionals will be better prepared for this reality based on projected demographics. The case scenarios and examples throughout invite counselors to think about situations from a Latino lens and then use the knowledge they acquire to conceptualize the cases and hopefully discuss them in classroom or supervision settings. Each case study is based on real experiences but is deidentified and changed slightly to protect anonymity. Throughout the text we use Spanish words and terms as appropriate, and because Spanish is a romance language, the term *Latina/o* is used. Readers may walk away with increased personal knowledge of commonly used words that can facilitate relationship building or simply greater confidence in their cross-cultural counseling repertoire. Finally, Appendix A contains the Culture-Centered Clinical Interview–Revised, a tool for more inclusive and culture-centered data gathering with Latinas/os, and Appendix B provides a list of resources that can inform Latino-centered knowledge building.

Changes in the overall Latino demographic since 1990 and 2000 censuses have been dramatic. Annual updates from the Community Population Survey, published by the U.S. Census Bureau, have captured these population trends. Thus, in Chapter 1, "Who Are Latinos?" we go beyond data from the 2010 Census report to regular updates on various indicators—age, national heritage, geographic distribution, health and health risks, military service, fertility rates, and so forth. In 2013, individuals of Latino heritage, from 1st to 10th generation, made up 16.5% of the U.S. population. In Chapter 1 we discuss how the birth rate—not immigration—is the contributing factor to these demographic changes, with implications for education, economics, and employment discussed in later chapters. Chapter 1 also addresses historic and contemporary immigration and relevant legislation affecting immigrants and children of immigrants. A mindset of empowerment has emerged and is energizing Latino and other ethnic youth to advocate for self-determination and inclusion in the country they consider to be theirs.

The uniqueness of Latinos, their similarities to other cultural groups, as well as their within-group differences are discussed in Chapter 2, "Latino Worldviews and Cultural Values." The contemporary Latino multicultural worldview has evolved from historical intersections of indigenous (e.g., Aztec, Mayan, Mixtec), African, and European beliefs and practices. Culture as a way of life was shaped in the New World by religious and spiritual beliefs, family and community values and practices, economics, work ethic, and environmental factors. *La raza cósmica* (Vasconcelos, 1925), or the "cosmic/universal race," best describes the complex Latino culture. Latinos have drawn from many sources of influence over the centuries, throughout eras of conquest and diasporas, to core beliefs about family-centeredness, interdependence, the role of a higher power, cultural pride through the arts and literature, and many manifestations of self-determination. This chapter discusses core values as anchors but not limitations; with each generation, values and beliefs are modified and lived out differently.

Chapter 3, "Acculturation and Enculturation Processes," builds on the first two chapters with further discussion of the shaping of individuals based on beliefs and value orientations as well as the role of acculturation as a phenomenon of change for individuals and *familias* (families). For too long acculturation has been viewed as a process of Americanization. Scholars now admit that acculturation is not an A equals B phenomenon but rather a complex process involving cognitive, emotional, and behavioral changes. Enculturation, or the process of becoming more knowledgeable about one's Latino heritage, can also lead to identity change and renewed worldviews. Because acculturation is a form of socialization and change, stressors are always part of the journey. For example, a Latina and a Caucasian first-generation college student will experience acculturation in the new college environment in similar and different ways. On a predominantly White campus, the Latina is in the minority, which adds stress to her acculturation process. The White student will likely experience stressors, but not necessarily because of her national heritage. Thus, what we learn about Latinas/os from concepts typically applied to them, like acculturation, will be useful for counselors working with heterogeneous populations.

A plethora of research has addressed identity development among Latino adolescents, which is often coupled with processes of behavioral acculturation, ethnic pride, and intergenerational conflict. Chapter 4, "The Complexity of Latina/o Multidimensional Identity," provides many examples of the intersections of different dimensions of identity for Latinas/os as well as the heterogeneity of Latino identity across different natural/cultural groups (i.e., Cubans, Puerto Ricans, those of Mexican heritage). There is a discussion of how color, economics, citizenship, immigrant status, geographic residence, and other individual differences influence self-identity. In a color-conscious society, there are more challenges for acceptance and inclusion for Latinos who are brown and black. Speaking with an accent in a country where there are political arguments for English-only policies and anti-bilingual education, individuals experience further marginalization, confusion, and self-doubt. A further conundrum is that of gender, sexual orientation, and religion. The Latino worldview tends to be conservative and traditional on these three dimensions of identity. Thus, knowledge about these biases will be useful for counselors working with clients who are examining their identity concerns and relationships with family members in particular.

Education has long been the determinant for advancement for immigrant and low-income families. In Chapter 5, "Education," we discuss the presence of Latinos in record numbers in K–12 schools and higher education. For example, it was reported that in 2012 approximately 1 in 4 elementary students (24.7%) were Latino and that among prekindergartners through 12th graders, 23.9% were Latino (Fry & Lopez, 2012). For the first time in history, Latinos have become the largest ethnic minority group on 4-year campuses (Fry & Lopez, 2012). This chapter focuses on examples from across the United States, where counselors make a difference in educational settings.

Drawing on empirical research studies, we report on interventions with students, parents, and counselors that can guide the work of all counselors. Furthermore, with the number of first-generation college students increasing, it is important to examine factors that enable and limit academic success. Fortunately, research is under way in universities on intersecting issues such as marginalization, the power of identity groups such as fraternities and sororities, and the effects of high school achievement on college performance. Attention to research-based data will be of great value to practitioners.

Chapter 6, "Employment, Economics, and the Psychology of Working," introduces interrelated topics related to the advancement of Latino families in U.S. society and Latinos' historical contributions to the country's economy in some of the lowest paying yet necessary work roles. Latinos are represented in the agricultural, service, and construction industries, more so than other cultural groups. Low wages and the exploitation of undocumented immigrants have led to approximately 47.1% of Latino families earning less than $20,000 a year, according to the 2010 American Community Survey (U.S. Census Bureau, 2010a). In spite of obstacles introduced by legislation, discrimination, and other structural barriers, the need for self-determination is a psychological driver for Latinas/os in the workforce. In fact, in 2012 Latinos expressed confidence in their personal finances and the direction the country was moving. They too are pursuing the American Dream.

Currently, many Latinos are confronted with multiple life challenges. Immigrants in particular, both authorized and unauthorized, have more barriers to negotiate on a daily basis. Thus, Chapter 7, "Situational Stressors and Their Effects," addresses the types of stressors faced by Latinos, including negative portrayals in the media, stereotype threat, and acculturative stress. The Latino paradox as it relates to health is discussed as one example of resilience. Freedom University is introduced as a collective resource for unauthorized students and an example of how concerned educators can help to combat unjust legislation, ensure social justice, and model resilience.

Chapter 8, "*La Familia Latina:* Strengths and Transformations," includes multiple discussions about the evolution of Latino families over the centuries. Counselors need to learn about the Latino life cycle across the life span; the transformation of families because of individual differences; mobility, forced and chosen; stressors; plans; and the persistence of the value of *familismo* across generations. Latinos need to be recognized as people of strength, constancy, and persistence. After all, who else could do the back-breaking work of agricultural workers, toil in the kitchens of the best restaurants, and work two or three jobs to make ends meet? Latinos are goal-oriented, and parents transmit this expectation as they apply the *dicho* (proverb) *De padres sanos, hijos honrados* (From well-centered parents emerge honorable children).

Chapter 9, "Planning for Culture-Centered Assessment and Practice," is very instructive and pragmatic. Examples describe the role of Latino perspectives in making clinical assessments and the cultural syndromes most applicable to

Latino groups. Furthermore, there is discussion about the role of interpreters and culture-bound diagnoses. Finally, readers are reminded how to apply Latino cultural values sensitively, effectively, and ethically when they work with children and families.

Building on the previous chapters, Chapter 10, "Latinas/os in Counseling," addresses various scenarios that may occur when Latino individuals and families engage in Western-style counseling. The focus on spirituality is noteworthy insomuch as immigrants and second-generation Latinos may seek solutions to difficult life situations in their belief system and also with indigenous spiritual support. The use of language in counseling is examined as well, and readers are reminded that ethnic match is not a factor in successful counseling. Discussions of strengths-based models that acknowledge resilience and other demonstrations of self-determination are woven throughout the chapter. Counseling with Latinas/os is a growing specialty area within the profession, and counselors must be prepared to deliver culturally appropriate and ethical services.

Chapter 11, "Ethics and Organizational Cultural Competencies," examines the ethical basis for multicultural competence with Latino populations. In this chapter, we also identity professional associations and other resources counselors can turn to to expand their awareness, knowledge, and skills related to Latinos.

Throughout the text, considerable data are reported about the increasing Latino-heritage population in the United States, particularly children. Given these facts and other data about the multidimensional Latino population and its impact on education, the workplace, the economy, and other systems in the country, it seems reasonable to conjecture about the implications for the counseling profession. Chapter 12, "The Future of Latina/o-Centered Counseling," considers how the profession will shift and adapt to Latinos through teaching, research, service, and clinical practice. Moreover, there will be opportunities for international educational collaborations with Spanish-speaking nations to the south, enriching the practices of individuals and educational institutions from Colombia, Guatemala, Venezuela, and other countries. Comas-Díaz (2012) speculated that the new generation of Latinos will be *futuristas,* a group that synthesizes Latino and U.S. values into a community-focused society. The 2012 Presidential elections underscored this sentiment.

We hope that this comprehensive volume about Latinos will inspire and propel counselors to embrace the multifaceted, changing, and complex reality of Latinos in the United States. The future of the United States is tied to the future of the Latino people as they grow in number and influence, and counselors, guided by the ideal of social justice, can help to ensure that this future is inclusive and promotes the well-being of all people. *Adelante siempre*—always moving forward, *porque "Sí se puede"*—because yes we can.

About the Authors

Dr. Patricia Arredondo has contributed to the counseling profession for more than 35 years through her extensive scholarship and leadership in multicultural counseling competencies, counseling Latinas/os, organizational diversity, women's leadership, and social justice advocacy. Her scholarship, leadership in professional associations, and mentorship of hundreds of students and emerging professionals are extensive. She is a past-president of the American Counseling Association (ACA), the National Latina/o Psychological Association, the Society for the Psychological Study of Ethnic Minority Issues (Division 45) of the American Psychological Association, and the Association for Multicultural Counseling and Development. Dr. Arredondo was named an ACA Living Legend and an American Psychological Association Fellow. She received her EdD in counseling from Boston University. Dr. Arredondo is the president of The Chicago School of Professional Psychology, Chicago Campus.

• • •

Dr. Maritza Gallardo-Cooper has been a mental health practitioner for the past 35 years in the private and public sector. She has been a clinician, a director of outpatient and residential treatment programs, and a coordinator of school-based consultation and treatment programs. Her practice has focused on marriage and family therapy, school psychology, clinical supervision, training, program development, and the effectiveness of service delivery. Her involvement with Latino mental health issues began in 1978 when she was a member of the Hispanic Task Force of the President's Commission of Mental Health. She is an active member of the American Counseling Association and the Association for Multicultural Counseling and Development and is a past-vice-president of the Latino Concern Group. She is also a member of the National Latina/o Psychological Association and the Society for the Psychological Study of Ethnic Minority Issues (Division 45) of the American Psychological Association. Dr. Gallardo-Cooper teaches graduate courses in clinical supervision at the Universidad del Valle de Guatemala and is a respected author in the areas of bilingual counseling and multicultural family therapy. Dr. Gallardo-Cooper holds a doctorate from the University of Florida.

• • •

Dr. Edward A. Delgado-Romero is a professor and director of training for the counseling psychology PhD program at the University of Georgia. He is a founding member and past-president of the National Latina/o Psychological Association and a Fellow of the American Psychological Association through the Society for the Psychological Study of Ethnic Minority Issues (Division 45) and the Society of Counseling Psychology (Division 17). His doctoral degree is from the University of Notre Dame. He is the proud father of Javier, Isabel, and Guillermo.

• • •

Dr. Angela L. Zapata is a therapist and the diversity coordinator at the Marquette University Counseling Center. She earned her doctorate in counseling psychology from Arizona State University with an emphasis in multiculturalism and diversity. Angela is a member of the American Counseling Association, the Association for Multicultural Counseling and Development, and Counselors for Social Justice. She teaches a social justice course for students housed in the Inclusive Leadership Learning Community, is the cochair of the Division of Student Affairs Diversity Committee, and is the cofacilitator of the Lesbian, Gay, Bisexual, Transgender, and Queer-Questioning and Ally Student Discussion Night. As an adjunct faculty member in the College of Education, Dr. Zapata teaches classes in the counselor education, counseling psychology, and educational policy and leadership programs. She has a passion for social justice and encourages her students to become future leaders in diversity and social justice.

• • •

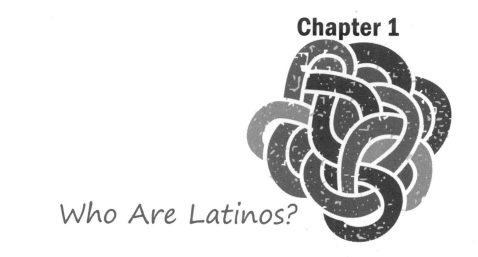

Chapter 1

Who Are Latinos?

Una raza mestiza, una mezcla de razas afines, una raza de color—
la primera raza síntesis del globo.

The cosmic race, a fifth race embracing the four major races of the world.
(Vasconcelos, as cited in Anzaldúa, 1987, p. 75)

• • •

Objectives

- Provide 2010–2012 data on persons of Latino heritage in the United States.
- Discuss multiple variables that describe Latinos.
- Familiarize the reader with legislation of relevance to work with persons of Latino heritage, particularly immigrants.

Sabías que/Did you know that . . .

- According to the 2010 Census, the Hispanic population grew 43% between 2000 and 2010 and contributed to 56% of the growth in the overall U.S. population (Passel, Cohn, & Lopez, 2011).
- The Latino population is projected to increase to 29% of the overall U.S. population by the middle of the 21st century, an increase driven primarily by births and not immigration (Passel & Cohn, 2008).
- Puerto Ricans are American citizens but cannot vote in Presidential elections if living in Puerto Rico.
- Of Latino youth younger than 18, a total of 93% were born in the United States. Approximately 800,000 Latinas/os turn 18 each year (P. Taylor, Gonzalez-Barrera, Passel, & Lopez, 2012).
- The Deferred Action for Childhood Arrivals Program is based on a policy enacted June 15, 2012, that allows unauthorized Latinas/os younger than age 30 to remain in the country.

• • •

Case Scenario

Alice, a former middle school math teacher, was now a high school counselor in a primarily White and African American community. She had grown up in a small town in a historically White community in the Midwest. When she had graduated from college, Alice had decided to move to the state capital to launch her teaching career. She had always enjoyed helping others, and in college and high school she had volunteered at the Boys and Girls Club tutoring African American students. For her, this was a way of giving back to her community. She said that her decision to become a school counselor was an extension of her desire to make a difference in the lives of young people. Alice's school counseling practicum had been in Lincoln, Nebraska, and her new position as a high school counselor was in Omaha. The cities were very different in terms of their industries and community demographics.

An immigration policy in a neighboring state had led many immigrant families, primarily of Guatemalan and Mexican heritage, to move into Omaha and its school district. Local churches, Catholic Charities, and other civic groups supported the family settlement. Alice heard that many families contended that they had their citizenship documents, but the local police and U.S. Immigration and Customs Enforcement profiled them as being illegal. The children enrolled in the high school were highly diverse, much to Alice's surprise. That is, some spoke English fairly well, others were monolingual Spanish speakers, and yet others needed someone to translate from their Mayan language into Spanish. Alice also noted that these students dressed like most other teenagers.

Several students had visited Alice's office to establish a school schedule. She was surprised to learn that at least 10 sophomores had been born in the United States and had lived in multiple states, according to their families' work journey. Most had parents in the agricultural industry, moving across the Midwest following the crop season and/or working in the dairy industry. Omaha was known for meatpacking, and some students shared that their families had found employment in this industry. Although students in the first group Alice met with, who were from Guatemala and Mexico, seemed to have the paperwork they needed to enroll, they exuded a cautionary and somewhat timid demeanor. Alice considered herself to be open and helpful, but the students responded with terse responses. She wondered whether they were being rude, withholding information, or just nervous.

Alice had never worked with Latino children and families and confided to her colleagues that she felt out of her league. Some of the teachers had been at the high school a while and had had Mexican, Guatemalan, and other Latino-heritage students in their classrooms. They warned Alice that the children may be gone by the end of the semester, depending on the work situation in town and their parents' legal status.

The arrival of the new immigrants was front-page news. Alice listened to national coverage of the legislation in the nearby state and was shocked at what she now characterized as inhumane. Families could not rent if they did not have proof that they were in the United States legally. Employers had to report their unauthorized employees. Public hospitals were required to check residency, and even schools had been asked to check whether students were living in the school district legally. Alice had prepared to become a school counselor in a program that had prided itself on social justice advocacy but was beginning to feel confused and powerless. Reports on current state demographics also surprised her. She had no idea Latinos were the fastest growing population in the United States.

Framing the Data

It is often said that numbers don't lie, so it behooves counselors and other helping professionals and administrators to know the data and projections on the largest ethnic group in the United States and the implications these data have on their work. The diversity among Latinas/os, as among any other ethnic group, is complex and often challenging, and Vasconcelos's (1925) quote about Latinos being the cosmic race is illustrative of this complexity. The rainbow metaphor often used to describe the ethnic/racial panorama of people in the United States can also be applied to individuals who fall under the umbrella term *Latina/o*. Stereotypes of Latinos in terms of visible or physical markers often fall short. Consider that Latinas/os hail from more than 19 Spanish-speaking countries in the Northern and Southern Hemispheres, Central America, and the Caribbean and that such a national heritage may still signal a multiracial heritage (mestizo, *mulato*) because of conquest, slavery, and transnational relocations. Thus, it is reasonable to understand why knowledge about the within-group differences and collective or shared cultural factors of Latinas/os is a starting point for counseling professionals. In this book, the focus is on Latinos in the United States with ancestry in Spanish-speaking countries, including Puerto Rico, a commonwealth of the United States. Individuals of Brazilian heritage are not discussed in this book. Although they may consider themselves Latinos, their mother tongue is Portuguese. In addition, Spaniards from Spain are not included in U.S. Census data.

The 2010 Census provided a definition for Hispanic or Latino origin people: "'Hispanic or Latino' refers to a person of Cuban, Mexican, Puerto Rican, South or Central American or other Spanish culture or origin regardless of race" (Ennis, Ríos-Vargas, & Albert, 2011, p. 2). Specific to the definition, the 2010 Census categories were as follows:

1. No, not of Hispanic, Latino, or Spanish origin
2. Yes, Mexican, Mexican American, Chicano
3. Yes, Puerto Rican
4. Yes, Cuban
5. Yes, another Hispanic, Latino, or Spanish origin

For Selection 5, individuals were invited to specify that origin, with prompts for Colombian Dominican, Salvadoran, Spaniard, and so on.

National Origin Reporting

Of the approximately 50.5 million respondents to the 2010 Census (16% of the U.S. population), three quarters self-reported being of Mexican, Puerto Rican, or Cuban heritage, in that order. There was an increase from the 2000 Census in the number of individuals from Central America, primarily El Salvador (152%) and Guatemala (180%), and the Caribbean, notably the Dominican Republic (85%). A recent report indicated that 1,827,200 people are of Salvadoran heritage, slightly less than the number of people of Cuban heritage, 1,888,599 (Humes, Jones, & Ramírez, 2011). The number of individuals from South America grew by 105%, from 1.4 million in 2000 to 2.8 million in 2010 (Humes et al., 2011).

Hispanic or Latino is not a racial category because Latinos have multiple ethnic and racial heritages. Thus, another question in the 2010 Census inquired about origin and race. The majority (53%) of respondents selected White (26,735,713) or some other race (18,503,103). The other categories selected, in descending order, were Black or African American, American Indian and Alaska native, Asian, Native Hawaiian and other Pacific Islander, and some other race (Humes et al., 2011).

Within-group differences account for the self-reporting about race, with 85% of persons of Cuban heritage specifying White alone versus Black alone (5%) or multiple races (4%). Persons of Dominican heritage had a contrasting reporting profile: White alone (30%), Black alone (13%), "some other race" alone (46%), and multiple races (10%; Ennis et al., 2011).

Many Census 2010 reports are available for review from the U.S. Census Bureau. In addition, updated demographics are published by the Community Population Survey. Another valuable source for specific reports on segments of the Latino population is the Pew Hispanic Center.

In addition to national heritage data, other demographic factors to consider when working with Latinas/os include geographic distribution, age, gender, family size, motherhood and fertility, marital status, intermarriage and divorce, citizenship, English proficiency, military service, and health indicators. More detailed data on education, employment, classism, careers, Latinos and the criminal justice system, and religion and political affiliation are discussed in subsequent chapters. References to immigrants are included in all chapters, from demographic data to other considerations, such as immigrants as first-generation college students and as clients in therapy.

Chapter 4 provides a holistic view of Latinas/os and their various dimensions of identity (e.g., sexual orientation, religion). These data are essential to counselors and other helping professionals in various work settings because they provide context and possible starting points for engagement with individuals and families. Acquiring this information can inform culturally responsive and ethical practice.

National Geographic Data

The Latino population increased in all 50 states and the District of Columbia from 2000 to 2010, and Latinos accounted for more than 58% of the growth in 33 states (Passel & Cohn, 2011). (The remaining 27 states are home to 8.7 million Latinos.) Significant population growth in the border states of Arizona, California, and Texas is not entirely surprising because these three states were part of Mexico until 1846, when the Treaty of Guadalupe Hidalgo was signed.

Moreover, in 2010 roughly 75% of all Latinos (37.6 million people) lived predominantly in eight states with populations of 1 million or more: Arizona, California, Colorado, Florida, Illinois, New Jersey, New York, and Texas. Arizona, Colorado, California, New Jersey, Illinois, and Texas had a combined Latino population of about 30 million, constituting 31% of the Latino population in the United States (Passel & Cohn, 2011).

Regional Growth

Between 2000 and 2010, the Latino population doubled in eight southern states: Alabama, Arkansas, Kentucky, Maryland, Mississippi, North Carolina, South Carolina, and Tennessee. South Carolina's Latino population grew the most, from 95,000 in 2000 to 236,000 in 2010, a 148% increase (Ennis et al., 2011). This population growth is not accidental. Employment continued in the agricultural, manufacturing, service, and health care industries in these states. However, the majority of work was entry-level or unskilled work that paid little. A state-by-state analysis reveals specific types of employment for Latinos. For example, in Kentucky Latinos work in horse-breeding and horse-racing businesses. Alabama and Arkansas have extensive food-packing and poultry industries that require employees willing to do hard work for long hours and often in undesirable conditions.

Hawaii has also witnessed a growth in its Latino population. Puerto Ricans historically arrived to the islands to work on sugar plantations, similar to work opportunities on the island of Puerto Rico. Maui and the Big Island of Hawaii have experienced the greatest growth, with more and more newcomers being of Mexican descent (Essoyan, 2012). The draw has been the service industry. Because the islands are a holiday destination, there has been growth in the number of hotels and golf courses. In addition, on the Big Island there are coffee plantations and other agricultural businesses.

There are also regional differences in the distribution of highly diverse Latino-heritage groups. Some of the distribution follows historic settlement patterns, such as the distribution of Mexicans in the Southwest and West. Puerto Ricans have been in the Northeast for many years and have been joined primarily by Dominicans and Ecuadorans. Nearly 100,000 Ecuadorans live in Queens County, New York, and 241,000 Dominicans live in Bronx County, New York. The largest settlement of Cubans (48%) in the United States is concentrated in Miami-Dade County, as are the largest communities of Colombians, Hondurans, and Peruvians. Individuals of Salvadoran and Guatemalan heritage reside primarily in Los Angeles County, California. However, the largest Latino-heritage group in Washington, DC, is the Salvadorans (Ennis et al., 2011).

Clearly, all of these demographic changes across the country have implications for counselors in K–12 settings, college counseling centers, counselor training programs, and community health and mental health centers as well. How can these new population scenarios be conceptualized for best practices?

Gender and Age

To inform reading and analysis of cases in future chapters, here we introduce data on gender and age distributions. Men represent 50.7% of the Latino population in the United States (25,722,250) and women, 49.3% (25,007,020). The data on age are more compelling when compared to the data for White non-Hispanics, as reported by the Pew Hispanic Center based on the 2010 American Community Survey. Whereas 33.6% of the Latino population is aged 18–90, 39.65% of the White non-Hispanic population is in that age group. According to Motel (2012), among 55- to 59-year-olds, 2,443,693 are Latino and 15,263,487 are White non-Hispanic. Among 20- to 24-year-olds, 4,356,125 are Latino and 12,491,370 are White non-Hispanic, The largest distribution is in the under-18 age group: 17,181,535 are Latino and 39,637,206 are White non-Hispanic. Latinos 18 and younger make up 16.9% of the U.S. population; White non-Hispanics 18 and younger make up 10.05% of the population. These are remarkable statistics with implications for future generations of Americans. According to Passel et al. (2011), it is children and grandchildren of immigrants, primarily born in the United States, who will fuel the population growth in the country.

According to the Pew Hispanic Center, the median age of the U.S. population is 37.3 years. The median age of Latinos is 27.6 years; Whites, 42.3 years; Blacks, 32.9 years; and Asians, 35.9 years. There are also within-group differences with respect to age. Persons of Mexican heritage have the lowest median age, 25 years, whereas persons of Cuban origin have the highest median age, 40 years (Motel & Patten, 2012b).

Implications of Population Growth

Some of these trends may be surprising; however, these data are very instructive for planning in different counseling contexts and regions of the country. For example, counselor educators in the eight southern states in which the Latino population has doubled need to be mindful of their geographic location and the opportunities for counselors-in-training to have real-life experiences with Latinos in those areas. Because of the significant increase in the percentage of Latinos over a 10-year period in South Carolina, many more immigrant Latino families may reside there and someday seek counseling services. Furthermore, counselor educators need to know the national origin of the Latino families they work with and how long they have been in the community. Alternatively, they should know whether they are long-term residents, as is the case in many California, Texas, and Arizona border towns and in the 30 largest metropolitan areas where Latinos reside. The growth in the Latino population, particularly in the number of children and youth, suggests the need for strategic planning in all counseling settings. Planning will have to take into account different strategies for families with longer histories in the United States, immigrant parents and children born in the United States, and multiple-heritage couples and families. There are more involved discussions of counseling approaches in Chapters 9 and 10.

Fertility and Motherhood

Overall, the number of ethnic minority births surpasses that of White births. In fact, on July 1, 2011, 50.4% of the country's population was children aged 1. Of this total, Latinos accounted for 26.3% of the population aged 1 and younger; Whites, 49.6%; Blacks, 13.7%; and Asians, 4.4% (Passel, Livingston, & Cohn, 2012).

Whereas in the past, immigration was the primary reason for the growth of the Latino population, today it is childbirth, principally by women of Mexican and Mexican American heritage. According to Passel et al. (2012), the fertility rate is 2.4 among Hispanics, 2.1 among Blacks, and 1.8 among Whites. The youthfulness of the Latino population is a factor. The percentage of Latinas between the primary childbearing ages of 15 and 44 is 4%, whereas for White non-Hispanics it is 3.1%.

Within-group differences found in a 2009 Pew survey are also noteworthy:

- Nearly two thirds (64%) of Puerto Rican women aged 15 to 44 who had given birth in the 12 months prior to the study were unmarried. That was greater than the rate for all Hispanic women (45%) and the overall rate for U.S. women (38%; Motel & Patten, 2012a).
- More than one half (53%) of native-born Latinas, less than three fourths (73%) of Black women, and more than one fourth (29%) of White women who had given birth in the 12 months prior to the study were unmarried.
- Less than 1 in 10 (6%) of Cuban women aged 15 to 44 had given birth in the 12 months prior to the survey. That was less than the rate for all Hispanic women (8%) and the overall rate for U.S. women (7%; Motel & Patten, 2012b).
- For women of Mexican heritage, the rates of childbirth are far higher. "From 2006–2010 alone, more than half (53%) of all Mexican-American births were to Mexican immigrant parents" (Pew Hispanic Center, 2011). Also, consider that immigrant women are younger than native-born Mexican Americans.
- Interracial relationships lead to multiracial babies: In 2010, 9% of Whites married someone who was Latino or of another race (Wang, 2012).
- Most Asian and White mothers are college educated.

- The size of the Latino family is decreasing. The average family size is 3.14 persons (U.S. Census Bureau, 2010c), down from 3.93 in 2000.

English Proficiency

A persisting perception is that Latinas/os do not speak English or speak it poorly. With the number of native (U.S.) births now higher than the number of foreign births (62.9% vs. 37.1%, respectively; U.S. Census Bureau, n.d.), a greater percentage of Latinos will be proficient in English or bilingual at best. According to a report from the Pew Hispanic Center, "Nearly two-thirds (65%) of U.S. Hispanics, ages five and older either speak only English at home or speak English very well" (Motel & Patten, 2012b, p. 1). Alternatively, foreign-born Latinos will speak primarily Spanish at home.

There are also within-group differences with respect to language proficiency. Data from the American Community Survey (Motel & Patten, 2012a) indicate that the groups with the highest rates of English proficiency are Puerto Ricans (82%), Mexicans (64%), Colombians (59%), and Peruvians (59%). Groups with the lowest English proficiency are Guatemalans (41%), Hondurans (42%), and Salvadorans (46%). Also, less than 50% of the population aged 5 and older is proficient in English. Various explanations can be considered. First, Latinas/os from these Central American countries have a shorter history in the United States, certainly in comparison to persons of Mexican and Puerto Rican heritages. Second, the greatest percentage of immigrants is from agricultural or rural backgrounds. Guatemalans may speak Spanish as their second language and their native or tribal language as their primary language. Finally, many of these newcomers live in ethnic, Spanish-speaking enclaves and work in settings with other immigrants, reducing their need and opportunity to master English.

Citizenship

Another common perception about Latinas/os has to do with their citizenship status. This of course will change in the next 20 years with the increase in the number of native versus foreign births. The 2010 Census reported that 74% of Latinos, or three out of four, are citizens compared to "93% of the entire U.S. population" (Motel & Patten, 2012b, p. 10). Within-group differences also parallel historic and political relations with the United States. For Puerto Ricans, citizenship is a birthright. There is a 1% difference between Cubans (74%) and Mexicans (73%) with respect to citizenship status. Similar to data regarding English proficiency, Hondurans (47%), Guatemalans (49%), and Salvadorans (55%) have lower rates of U.S. citizenship. Again, their eligibility is affected by the number of years they have been in the United States.

Latinos in the Military

"Latinos in the Military, 1946-Present" (Jones, 2004) provides a comprehensive report on the participation of Latinos in major wars: World War II, the Korean War, the Vietnam War, Operation Desert Storm, and, more recently, the conflict in Iraq and other 21st-century wars. Latina/o veterans have historically been overlooked in media accounts. In 2007, the National Council of La Raza, the largest Latino civil rights group in the United States, took Ken Burns to task for overlooking the role of Latinos in World War II in his documentary *The War* (Burns, Novick, & Ward, 2007). The omission of the voices of Native Americans and female veterans was also noted by other advocacy groups. Few know that nine Mexican Americans and one Puerto Rican soldier were awarded the Congressional Medal of Honor for their service in the Korean War. Moreover, 13 Mexican Americans and 2 Puerto Ricans were recipients of the recognition for their role in the Vietnam War. All together, Latinos received the highest proportion of Medals of Honor than any other ethnic minority group.

Since 9/11 there has been a deliberate focus on the military recruitment of Latinos, and with the promise of education and good salaries, their numbers have increased. Another motivator is the opportunity for immigrants to become naturalized citizens. The first U.S. soldier to die in the 2003 Iraq war was José Gutierrez, a Guatemalan immigrant, and another early casualty was José Angel Garibay, an undocumented immigrant. The projected increase in the Latino population (1 out of every 4 Americans in 2050) suggests that more Latinos will become part of the armed forces. The Deferred Action for Childhood Arrivals Program allows individuals who serve in the military to provide evidence of their service as another pathway to becoming authorized to stay in the United States. This legislation is discussed in the section on Latino immigrants later in this chapter.

With the return of more military personnel from the wars in Iraq and Afghanistan, counselors will find themselves treating active military personnel, veterans, and/ or their families in different contexts, from college campuses to mental health centers. How Latinos in the military cope with trauma or other issues may be related to their cultural values and religion and to other circumstances, such as dropping out of school. On being discharged, and emotionally burdened with the experiences they witnessed, veterans have a difficult transition reentering civilian life. Gone is the structure of military life with its clear roles, rules, and responsibilities. Latino men are expected to be strong and exude macho behavior. In other words, the expectation is that Latinos assume responsibility for their families and/or contribute to their parents' needs and not ask for help. Because the majority of military veterans are men, counselors must appreciate the masculine attitude toward help seeking and how this might prevent Latinos from receiving the health care and mental health care benefits they deserve.

Latino Health and Health Risks

Among Latinos, heart disease, cancer, unintentional injuries (accidents), stroke, and diabetes are among the leading causes of illness and death. Asthma, chronic obstructive pulmonary disease, HIV/AIDS, obesity, suicide, and liver disease are other health conditions and risk factors for Latinos. Unfortunately, Latinos also have higher rates of obesity than non-Hispanics, particularly among second- and third-generation groups (Office of Minority Health, 2012d). One figure that stands out is the obesity rate among women. According to the Office of Minority Health (2012d), "From 2007–2010, Mexican American women were 40% more likely to be overweight, as compared to Non-Hispanic Whites."

The incidence of heart disease is lower among Latinos than White non-Hispanics (5.2% vs. 6.6%, respectively), and Latinos are less likely than White non-Hispanics to die of heart disease. The percentage of Mexican American men with high cholesterol is almost the same as the percentage of White non-Hispanic men with this condition. Also noteworthy is the lower incidence of cigarette smoking among Latinos compared to White non-Hispanics (see Table 1.1).

Health disparities affect Latino subgroups differently. For example, "While the rate of low birth weight infants is lower for the total Hispanic population in comparison to non-Hispanic Caucasians, Puerto Ricans have a low birth weight rate that is 60 percent higher than the rate for non-Hispanic Caucasians" (Office of Minority Health, 2012c). Puerto Ricans also have higher incidences than other Latino groups of asthma, HIV/AIDS, and infant mortality, and Mexican Americans

Table 1.1

Age-Adjusted Percentage of Persons Aged 18 and Older Who Are Current Cigarette Smokers, 2008–2010

Gender	Hispanic	Non-Hispanic White	Hispanic/Non-Hispanic White Ratio
Male	17.3	23.9	0.7
Female	9.6	20.9	0.5

Source. Centers for Disease Control and Prevention (2012b).

"suffer disproportionately from diabetes" (Office of Minority Health, 2012b). The incidence of Type II diabetes among Mexican Americans has been well documented for the past 20–30 years (see Table 1.2).

The data on the incidence of HIV/AIDS among ethnic minority groups in the United States are alarming, as these groups accounted for "almost 71 percent of the newly diagnosed cases of HIV infection in 2010" (Office of Minority Health, 2012b). In 2010, "84 percent of children born with HIV infection belonged to minority groups" (Office of Minority Health, 2012b). Among Latinos, HIV/AIDS has spread at a rapid rate, with Latinos accounting for 20% of AIDS cases but representing only 16% of the U.S. population. More specific findings indicate that Latinos

> are almost three times more likely to be diagnosed with AIDS than Whites. Hispanic males were also 2.3 times more likely to die of AIDS than their non-Hispanic White counterparts, and Hispanic women were 3.4 times more likely to die from AIDS. (Office of Minority Health, 2012a)

These data are particularly noteworthy for counselors working in community-based health centers and correctional institutions. Counselors will also have to be mindful of reasons for contracting HIV/AIDS and the shame associated with HIV/AIDS in the Latino community as a whole.

Health care disparities are compounded by a lack of access to preventive health care and health insurance, language and cultural barriers, and a lack of proximity to health care services. Counselors are encouraged to refer to the Surgeon General's report on health and mental health disparities of 2001 (U.S. Department of Health and Human Services, 2001). Although it seems dated, it was the first compilation of health care disparities for ethnic minority groups.

Latino Immigrants

The topic of the immigration of Latinos, especially from Mexico, has become a battleground for many politicians and activists in favor of and against the historic stream of immigrants from Spanish-speaking countries. As consumers

Table 1.2

Age-Adjusted Percentage of Persons Diagnosed With Diabetes Per 100 Population, 2010

Gender	Hispanic/Latino	White	Hispanic/White Ratio
Male	9.3	6.8	1.4
Female	9.3	5.4	1.7
Total	9.3	6.0	1.6

Source. Centers for Disease Control and Prevention (2012a).

of information from many forms of media, counselors need to have an informed understanding of Latina/o immigrants across the life span, for, as the previous sections on demographics indicate, it is likely that counselors will engage with Latino individuals and families at some point in their careers. In this section, we discuss historic and contemporary data as well as terminology for categorizing immigrants.

Historic Events That Made Latinas/os Foreigners on Their Own Land

In Chapter 4 we discuss *mestizaje* and *mulato* identity and other self-attributed descriptors of national identity as a result of colonization and oppression and how colonization and oppression resulted in the diversity of those who are today considered Latinas/os. There are many historic starting points for the continuous and contemporary status of Latino immigration, and we discuss a few of these here.

In 1846, Mexico and the United States signed the Treaty of Guadalupe Hidalgo, whereby Mexico ceded territory to the United States that included the states of Arizona, California, Colorado, Nevada, New Mexico, Texas, and Utah. As a result, Mexican nationals became foreigners on their own land, losing property rights and other benefits of their Mexican citizenship.

The Spanish-American War between Spain and the United States in 1898 led to another change in political autonomy and affiliation for Cubans and Puerto Ricans. As a result of this war, Cuba gained its independence from Spain and Puerto Rico became a commonwealth, not a state. This status continues to this day, giving Puerto Ricans the right to vote in U.S. Presidential elections when they live in the United States, join the military, pay taxes, and so forth. However, Puerto Ricans do not have representatives in Congress. Their status as U.S. citizens opened the doors to a steady flow of Puerto Ricans from the island to the mainland for educational and economic opportunities following World War II. Other Spanish-speaking countries, such as Cuba, have a different storyline that is described further in Chapter 5.

Contemporary Demographics

Latinos make up nearly half (47%) of the country's 40 million immigrants (Motel & Patten, 2012a). However, between 2000 and 2010, there was a decrease in the number of new arrivals, and today births of Latino-origin children outnumber arrivals due to immigration. For example, as a result of births, the Mexican-origin population grew by 7.2 million between 2000 and 2010, and "from 2006–2010, 53% of all Mexican-American births were born to immigrants" (Jordan, 2011, p. A3). As the demographics evolve, both increasing and decreasing in different regions of the country, it is predicted that Latino-origin immigrants and their children will contribute to the projected population growth through 2050.

Nine countries are cited as contributing the most to U.S. immigration from Spanish-speaking countries: Mexico, Cuba, El Salvador, Dominican Republic, Guatemala, Colombia, Honduras, Ecuador, and Peru (Motel & Patten, 2012b). All are considered democracies, except Cuba. Although Puerto Rico is the second greatest contributor to the overall Latino population in the United States, it is important to keep in mind that Puerto Ricans are American citizens, even though they may be seen as immigrants because their experiences in the United States may be more like those of other immigrants.

Children of Unauthorized Immigrants

Immigrants, both legal and unauthorized, are younger than the population in general and made up 15.7% of the adult population in 2009 (Passel & Taylor, 2010).

Younger people are associated with higher fertility rates, and indeed data indicate that immigrant adults are more likely to have children younger than age 18. In fact, unauthorized immigrants are parents of 23% of all children younger than age 17, and 85% of the children are born in the United States (Passel & Taylor, 2010). Disaggregating the data further reveals differences in fertility rates for various groups of unauthorized immigrants. Latinas/os in the United States are on average younger than members of other ethnic groups and also have higher fertility rates.

Unaccompanied Minors

To leave violent conditions in their homeland and/or to reunite with parents in the United States, many children make the journey *al norte* (up north). In a heart-breaking biographical account, Nazario (2007) followed the travails of Enrique, who rode on the rooftops of the dangerous train cars from Honduras to find his mother in the United States. More recently, as reported in *The New York Times* (Preston, 2012), there have been many complications and hardships relating to the legal situations faced by unauthorized children who are caught by U.S. Immigration and Customs Enforcement. Preston (2012) described the story of Juan, age 6, alone in the United States without a parent or a lawyer and facing deportation on his own. Juan and other children generally do not comprehend what is going on and yet must appear in court, sometimes with legal representation and other times with court-appointed public defenders. The problem is that no parent or family member is present, indicated Preston. There is also double jeopardy for the parents of the children if they are unauthorized as well. In the case of Liliana, who arrived in the United States with someone else's documents and was detained, her parents were of no help. Furthermore, as Preston reported, lawyers are reluctant to take Liliana's case because of her parents' status. Counselors need to be aware of the existence of these children because they may end up requiring court-ordered assessments or perhaps even make it into a classroom because they somehow dodged the immigration net. Rather than affixing blame, counselors need to do some role play: *How would it be if I had been on my own in a foreign country at age 10?*

Immigrant-Related Terminology and Legal Positions

Immigrants in the United States are individuals who were born in another nation and on their arrival in this country are ascribed that nationality (e.g., Korean, Jamaican, Irish, Mexican, Romanian). For example, someone may be called an *Irish national.* A label of *Irish American* signals that the individual was born in the United States and is of Irish heritage. The same applies to Mexican Americans.

Lawful U.S. residency is evidenced by a United States Permanent Resident Card, formerly termed an *Alien Registration Card* and informally known as a *green card.* This signals permanent residency. Unlike U.S.-born citizens, immigrants are expected to carry their green cards to show evidence of their lawful or legal status.

Many labels, often inflammatory, are ascribed to unauthorized Latino immigrants. These include *illegal* and *illegal alien.* Although the term *undocumented* is also used, among social justice advocates the term *unauthorized* is preferred. When unauthorized immigrants stay in the country to seek or maintain employment, they take on unauthorized status. Individuals hold unauthorized status because they have entered the country without the proper documents or have overstayed their tourist, work, and/or student visa(s). Although Mexican-heritage workers have historically been brought to the United States on work permits, it is expected that when these expire they will leave the country. When they stay to seek further employment without the proper papers, they take on unauthorized status. Further discussion about contract workers can be found in Chapter 6.

Refugee-Related Legislation

Protection for individuals seeking asylum is granted in international human rights standards promulgated by the 1951 United Nations Convention and the 1967 Protocol Relating to the Status of Refugees (Gzesh, 2006). Refugee status is granted to individuals to protect their safety and lives, in general. The Refugee Act, "a humanitarian law intended to expand eligibility for political asylum in the United States" (Gzesh, 2006), was enacted in the late 1970s at the end of the Jimmy Carter Administration.

For Latinos, the most vivid example of refugee-related legislation begins with the Cuban Refugee Program, initially authorized in 1961 in response to the flight of Cuban people from Castro's communist regime. The programs established by this legislation provided child welfare services, medical care, loans for education, and adult education. After the creation of these programs, Cuban refugees continued to arrive via boatlifts (in 1963 and 1965), the most notable being the Mariel boatlift, which brought more than 125,000 individuals to the United States in 1980. Because of its proximity to their homeland, most Cubans settled in Florida (see Chapters 4 and 5).

Two terms often used interchangeably, *asylum* and *refugee status,* refer to protections granted to individuals who must leave or have left their home country for their own safety. According to U.S. immigration law, an individual's status depends on where he or she is at the time the petition is made: Specifically, one must be outside the United States to apply for refugee status and already in the United States to apply for asylum. To be eligible for this protection, individuals must demonstrate that they are unable or unwilling to return to their home country because of past persecution or a well-grounded fear that persecution will happen again if they go back. Grounds for possible persecution include one of the following: race, religion, nationality, membership in a particular social group, or political opinion (Bray, n.d.).

Examples of refugees are Russian Jews who were allowed entrance into the United States in the mid-1970s and Vietnamese people who fled the war in their home country. As a result of civil wars in El Salvador and Guatemala in the 1980s, many individuals and families fled through Mexico to the United States and petitioned for asylum based on human rights violations in their respective countries. Returning to their homeland meant certain death. The controversy around granting these individuals asylum status dragged on for nearly 15 years because the Ronald Reagan Administration wanted to classify them as economic migrants and denied that their home governments were violating their rights. Another confounding issue was U.S. support of governments that were indeed oppressing their own people. Finally, in 1990, Congress passed legislation and President George H. W. Bush granted Temporary Protected Status for groups "in need of a temporary safe haven" (Gzesh, 2006, p. 5).

Unfortunately, criminalization of the refugees was at the center of the debate because of their unauthorized status. However, it was religious groups, the activism of the Sanctuary Movement, primarily in the Southwest, and litigation by the American Baptist Churches on behalf of the asylum seekers that led to a fair and humane outcome for the refugees from El Salvador and Guatemala.

However, for counselors working with Latinos from El Salvador or Guatemala and other Central American countries (e.g., Honduras, Nicaragua), this historical context may be relevant because of the legacy of loss, trauma, and other psychological fears that was imprinted on their parents or on them.

Immigrants and Immigrant-Related Legislation

Legislation dating back to 1924 was designed to control immigration and the rights of immigrants, both authorized and unauthorized. In this section, we address more recent federal and state legislation of the past 10 years.

Two months after the horror of September 11, 2001, terrorist acts, President George W. Bush signed into law the USA PATRIOT Act, commonly known as the Patriot Act; President Barack Obama extended the law by 4 years in May 2011. Though it is well-intended legislation meant to protect Americans, it has proven controversial. According to Roberta Baxter (n.d.),

> The Patriot Act remains to control, change and restrict American life as never before September 11, 2001 activities happened. Some law enforcement actions are given more breadth because of the Patriot Act while citizens and visitors alike are scrutinized in many areas.

Following 9/11, Latino immigrants, U.S. citizens, and others perceived to be of Middle Eastern heritage became targets of hate crimes. See Chapter 9 for more information on stressors such as discrimination and hate crimes against Latinos.

Senate Bill 1070, enacted in Arizona in 2010, became the lightning rod for anti-Latino behavior, and other states, most notably Alabama and Georgia, also enacted legislation modeled after Arizona's. Many restrictions were applied to unauthorized immigrants, including making it a crime not to have legal documents in one's possession if stopped by law enforcement officers. Furthermore, the law allowed officers to stop individuals they perceived as being illegal. Although many sections of the legislation were overturned by the Supreme Court in July 2012, appeals persist. In support of the Supreme Court rule, the California Senate passed what became known as the anti-Arizona immigrant legislation.

New immigration policy signed on June 15, 2012, by President Obama allows unauthorized immigrants younger than age 30 to remain in the country and work legally, go to school, and apply for a driver's license (Jordan & Kesling, 2012). Thousands of young people were brought to the United States as infants and are not aware that they were born in Mexico or elsewhere. For them, the United States has always been their homeland. The Deferred Action for Childhood Arrivals Program allows unauthorized Latinas/os younger than age 30 to apply for driver's licenses, get work permits, and otherwise come out of the shadow of un-authorization to more fully participate in their country. The shortcoming of this legislation is that it is not a pathway to citizenship. With the reelection of President Obama in 2012, it is possible that this limitation will be lifted.

Proposed bipartisan legislation that has waned for two Presidential cycles is the Development, Relief, and Education for Alien Minors (DREAM) Act. It was first introduced in the Senate on August 1, 2001, but has failed to receive the support of the full Congress. The act provides a pathway to citizenship by granting conditional permanent residency to individuals who satisfy certain criteria. These include being of good moral character, graduating from a U.S. high school, having arrived in the country as a minor (younger than age 16), and having 5 years of continuous residence in the country. There are other provisions for individuals who have served in the military or graduated from a 4-year institution; further details are provided in "DREAM Act" (n.d.). Critics argue that the act would create an amnesty program and would give social and economic benefits to those who are here illegally. In other words, critics contend that unauthorized immigrants would be rewarded.

Concluding Thoughts

Let's go back to Alice with more knowledge in hand about Latinas/os in general, immigration laws, and the conditions that have put individuals and families in jeopardy. Put yourself in Alice's shoes. She is in a new role as a high school counselor working with Latina/o students, a role that is not part of her previous personal or professional experience. The *ACA Code of Ethics* (American Counseling Association, 2005) states, "Association members recognize diversity and embrace a cross-cultural approach in support of the worth, dignity, potential, and uniqueness of people within their social and cultural contexts" (p. 3). Working from this broad statement, how will Alice be able to bridge relationships with her students, their families, and community groups?

According to the Multicultural Counseling Competencies (P. Arredondo et al., 1996; D. W. Sue, Arredondo, & McDavis, 1992), to be culturally responsive counselors must know themselves, their values and assumptions about others, and the worldview that informs their assessment of others' behavior as well as their own. Consider the following inquiries, paraphrased from "Operationalization of the Multicultural Counseling Competencies" (P. Arredondo et al., 1996):

- Can Alice identify the culture(s) to which she belongs and the significance of these memberships on her relations with others of different groups or even of her own heritage groups?
- Does Alice have a positive assessment of her own heritage, and, if so, how might this affirmatively or negatively affect her assessment of the Latino students and families she has never known before?
- How will Alice gather the resources and data about the new students to whom she needs to be culturally responsive? Who will be her Latino-specific informants, coaches, and guides?
- It is quite possible that Alice is experiencing both cognitive and emotional dissonance. Her counselor training and practicum did not provide her with the live knowledge and contact that would lessen the surprise of working with Latina/o students and their families. Is she having a cultural freeze, or is she able to readily adapt to the population in a nonjudgmental way? One should not assume that Alice will not be culturally sensitive or responsive; however, the Multicultural Counseling Competencies cited regarding personal biases, assumptions, and knowledge cannot be taken for granted. Ultimately, it is these factors as well as Alice's sense of emotional confidence that will influence her decisions about how to be an advocate for and educational support to her students. Consider the Latino-centered competencies that apply in this situation: "Culturally skilled counselors can identify biases and assumptions, both positive and negative, they have about Latino clients and their families that may affect a counseling relationship" (Santiago-Rivera, Arredondo, & Gallardo-Cooper, 2002, p. 19).
- Culturally skilled counselors have an understanding of "regional, situational and sociopolitical contexts that have influenced Latino clients" (Santiago-Rivera et al., 2002, p. 20).
- Culturally skilled counselors seek knowledge and resources to inform their engagement with Latino populations in specific contexts.

• • •

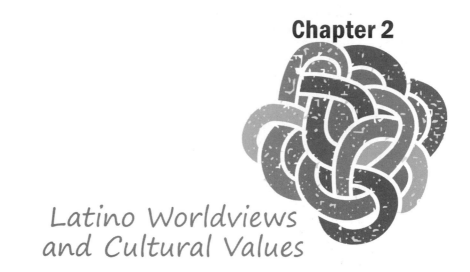

Chapter 2

Latino Worldviews and Cultural Values

De médico, poeta, músico y loco todos tenemos un poco.

Of doctor, poet, musician, and madman, we each have a trace.

(Sellers, Nelson, & Soto, 1994, p. 69)

• • •

Objectives

- To review the etiology of Latino cultural/multicultural worldviews.
- To examine beliefs, values, traditions, and practices embedded in the Latino worldview and how they persist and evolve across generations.
- To examine the role of values as anchors, buffers, and guideposts for individuals and families.

Sabías que/Did you know that . . .

- The goal of parenting is to raise children who are *bien educados* (well mannered).
- Family-centeredness persists with third- and fourth-generation families, who prefer to provide care for elderly parents rather than place them in a nursing home.
- Latino upbringing is influenced by religion and spirituality.

• • •

Case Scenario

Nancy had the good fortune to be offered admission to a small Ivy League college. Although she grew up on the Lower East Side of New York City, less than 3 hours from the college, she felt as though she was in a new world, one very different from her neighborhood life in the city. Now in a small-town university environment, she felt self-conscious and conspicuous. She was darker than most of her classmates, was dressed well, but did not particularly care for the preppy look so popular with classmates; she had all White professors, quite different from teachers in the city; and lived with a roommate who preferred to spend time with friends from boarding school. Although Nancy had participated in a summer bridge program for incoming scholars of color, she was only one of six Latinas in the class and one of two in the residence hall. The other student was from Texas and of Mexican heritage; Nancy was of Puerto Rican/Dominican heritage and had grown up in the Bronx.

The university's celebrations of Hispanic Heritage kicked off a few weeks after school began. Nancy hardly noticed until she learned that the author of *When I Was Puerto Rican*, Esmeralda Santiago, was going to speak on campus. Nancy just knew this book would speak to her. Nancy's roommate declined the invitation to attend the lecture, stating that she would not find it personally interesting. Loneliness set in again. Had Nancy made a mistake by coming to this university? Maybe staying in New York where more people looked like her, shared her interests, and liked Latino arts would have been smarter. Everywhere she went on campus, she felt that she stood out. She remembered what her mother and *madrina* (godmother) had always said: "Be proud of your *cultura*; respect yourself and others will respect you. You are an intelligent young woman and *Si Díos quiere* [If God permits], you will achieve our dreams. We love you very much." When Nancy came out of her self-reflection, she thought of Yolanda, the student from Texas, and decided to invite her to the lecture. Yolanda accepted.

You are a counselor at the university counseling center. When Nancy arrives to talk about her disinterest in her studies and her sadness, how might you learn more about her and what underlies her sadness? Although you have been at the counseling center for 3 years, you have seen perhaps only one Latino student. Latina/o students typically do not seek services. Thinking back to your multicultural counseling course, a couple of points stick out. One is that Latinos typically drop out of counseling almost immediately because of trust issues and embarrassment about talking with strangers about personal matters. Nancy admits that she has never seen a counselor to talk about problems. In high school she was an A student and met with her counselor only for scheduling.

Counselor: Please tell me a little bit about how your transition to college has gone.

Nancy: It's been okay. Pretty different from my high school. I've met a couple of nice students and professors.

Counselor: I am glad to know that you have met some nice professors. On the intake form you wrote that you are disinterested in your studies. Can you tell me a little more about why you are disinterested?

Nancy: I like my classes alright. I just don't know if I belong here. No one in my family went to college, so I don't know if this is what it should be like. I'm confused.

Counselor: First, you can be proud about being the first in your family to go to college. It is a big deal. I was the first one in my family to go to college, too.

Nancy: Really? Were you confused and sad sometimes? Did you feel pressure to do well for your parents?

What do you hear in Nancy's narrative that may speak to her values and values conflict? Is her confusion similar to or different than that of other new college students or first-generation college students? How might her examples be relevant to discussions with other underrepresented students on college campuses? How does a sense of not belonging potentially affect academic performance and retention? Do you believe the counselor should have revealed she was a first-generation college student? In this chapter, we address Latino values and beliefs and how these influence individuals' thinking, emotions, and behaviors. Though the Latino worldview is deeply embedded in the past histories of people from different ethnic, racial, and cultural origins, it continues to be a force of socialization for contemporary Latinos. In addition, we examine situations in which values conflict and provide culture-centered perspectives for counselors.

Latino Value Orientations and Worldview

De padres sanos, hijos honrados (From well-grounded parents, honorable children; Rovira, 1984, p. 68). To engage in a discussion of Latino-centered value orientations and worldviews, one must consider historical events, because these are the antecedents and reference points for what is described today as Latina/o culture. After all, Latinos as a collective are heterogeneous peoples, diverse in their origins, traditions, and historic evolution, as are other cultural groups. For example, the term *Asian* is used to describe persons of Chinese, Korean, Japanese, and Vietnamese heritage, but each group has its own history and unique cultural attributes and languages. Latinos include multiple ethnic groups signified by their nation of origin, but they share unifying factors, including a history of colonization, common values, and the use of the Spanish language. In this section, we discuss the evolution of contemporary Latino culture, with multiple themes that contribute to shared beliefs, views, and practices that persist over generations, providing further evidence of why it is a unique branch within psychology. That is, traditional psychology models emphasize the individual versus the collective experience, the intrapsychic versus the environmental and sociological, and deficit perspectives versus a focus on resilience and strengths from the family and community. These are attributes of Latino-centered psychology.

The Mestizo/Latino Polyculture

Latino culture dates back more than 500 years in North, Central, and South America. Latino is a polyculture or a multicultural culture influenced by European conquerors, primarily from Spain; African slaves brought to the New World; the indigenous peoples who resided throughout these continents at the time of the European conquests; and persons from Asia, who emigrated or were also brought as slaves to the South American continent. Specific terms describe the progeny of the conquerors. *Mestiza/o* or *mestizaje* has been used to refer to the progeny of Spanish and indigenous peoples and *mulata/o* to the progeny of Spanish, indigenous, and African peoples in particular. Keep in mind that what is today Guatemala, Mexico, the southwestern United States, and the Caribbean Islands were the entry points for the colonizers. Thus, today's Latinas/os have deep roots in the New World, roots that precede the formation of the United States, a multicultural, multiracial nation.

Mestizos, or *la raza cosmica* (the cosmic race; Vasconcelos, 1925), are a fascinating confluence of peoples of wide-ranging historic, geographic, and cultural origins. In his writings, Vasconcelos consistently referred to mestizos (contemporary Latinos) as a synthesis of other races and *una raza de color* (a race of people of color). When used by Latinos, the term *race* may not have the same meaning as has been artificially constructed in the social sciences. For example, von Blumenbach theorized four racial classifications—Caucasian, Mongolian, Ethiopian, and Malay—based on geography and people's physical appearance (Gould, 1994). This embodiment of different cultural origins is what makes it impossible to refer to *Latino* or *Hispanic* as a racial category. On the one hand, there is geographical location, albeit quite extensive; on the other hand, the intermarriage of colonizers and colonized has yielded a multicultural/multiracial mosaic of peoples.

An interesting footnote in this discussion of cultural origins concerns October 12, celebrated as Columbus Day in the United States. In Spanish-speaking countries, *día de la raza* is celebrated as a day of unity and pride, signaling a collective personhood and pluralism. In the United States, National Hispanic Heritage month, from September 15 to October 15, originally began as Hispanic Heritage Week in 1968. During this period, independence days are celebrated in Chile, Costa Rica, El Salvador, Guatemala, Honduras, Mexico, and Nicaragua.

The historic origins speak to a mestizo worldview or personality (M. Ramírez, 1998) grounded in the people themselves, colonization, and forced religious conversion and the simultaneous maintenance of indigenous spiritual beliefs and practices. Environmental, social, and political conditions also affected lifestyle changes and adaptations, whether forced or as survival strategies. In practice, Latinos/mestizos have led lives of adaptation and resiliency for centuries. Similarly, the *mulata/o* also endured oppression because of their African ancestry. The descendants of Africans learned the cultural, spiritual, and social beliefs and practices of their ancestors that influence their worldview. For example, *LatiNegra/o* refers to Latinos with African ancestry. Rather than use the term *African Latina*, Comas-Díaz (1996), stated that she wanted to "avoid the partial or total negation of the Latinness in African Latinas by the Latino community" (p. 170).

The discussion thus far provides an accounting of historically lived experiences by the survivors of European colonization and the contexts in which this took place. Thus, we are learning about the development of a new macro-, polyculture culture, referred to as *Latino*, and many nation-specific cultures as well. Multicultural counseling specialists have spent considerable time discussing the concept of culture and what it means for individuals and groups. There are well over 100 definitions of culture, but the majority of definitions have common denominators. Parham, White, and Ajamu (1999) described culture as "a complex constellation of mores, values, customs, traditions and practices that guide a people's cognitive, affective and behavioral response to life circumstances" (p. 14). For Latinas/os, beliefs, values, traditions, and other practices passed on across generations represent a synthesis of many different cultures. "Culture is to human collectivity what personality is to an individual" (Hofstede, 1980, p. 21). Hofstede also indicated that *culture* is a term usually used to refer to societies, as we discussed with indigenous societies, and one that can also be applied to ethnic groups or regional groups. Thus, at times there are circuitous discussions about Latinos as a cultural collective and Mexican Americans or Puerto Ricans as ethnic groups or cultural groups. This consideration will become particularly relevant as discussions of value orientations, family constellations, and acculturation processes ensue in the chapters that follow.

The Latino Multicultural Worldview

Worldviews have been discussed by social scientists and cultural anthropologists as representing or embodying behaviors that are rooted in cultural values and beliefs and how people live their lives. Kluckhohn and Stodtbeck (1961) organized worldviews along five dimensions: how cultures/people view (a) relationships (i.e., hierarchical, collectivist, individualist), (b) time (here and now, future, past orientation), (c) nature (embrace or live in harmony with it, try to dominate it, fear it), (d) activity (doing, being, being-in-becoming), and (e) people (basically good, basically bad, both good and bad). Their research with non-U.S. cultures gave a glimpse into other ways of living shaped by environmental and geographic conditions (e.g., island vs. mountainous settings); social structures, such as tribal networks and a collectivist relationship orientation; and influences of nature and its effects on planting, harvesting, and other life practices for well-being. Research measures have been developed to tap the worldviews of individuals and organizations (Ibrahim & Goodwin, 1986), and the global work of Hofstede (1980) on national values is another approach to identifying worldviews.

Although the discussions of worldview may seem old-fashioned to contemporary counselors or counselors-in-training, each one of us has to examine the various types of influences and experiences on our own values and beliefs. The Multicultural Counseling Competencies suggest that culturally skilled counselors identify the specific cultural group(s) from which they derive their fundamental cultural heritage and the significant beliefs and attitudes held by those cultures that they assimilate into their own attitudes and beliefs (P. Arredondo et al., 1996). Students in counselor training at times have described themselves as "Heinz 57" or of mixed heritage or as "White," without any realization that "White" has an origin somewhere. When students are encouraged to think about their grandparents or great-grandparents, there may be an awakening to a history and heritage from a European country of historic origin. Another way to encourage awareness is to inquire about family traditions or family sayings. The following question can be posed: Did you ever stop to think about family expressions, perhaps sayings your grandparents or even your parents often repeat? *Dichos* (proverbs), or lessons about life, can generally incite discussion and lead naturally to other proverbs as examples of culture. The *dicho* used in the introduction to this section is a values statement about expectations of parents. Another *dicho* of relevance to this discussion is *Dime con quien andas y te dire quien eres* (You are known by the company you keep). Many influences on worldview and values are expressed in *dichos* (sayings), traditions and attitudes for Latinos and non-Latinos alike.

Relational Values

Family-centeredness, concern for others' well-being, interdependence, and *graciousness* are some of the words that speak to Latinos' prioritization of relational values. *Familismo,* or the valuing of the extended family, is an anchor for individuals who have been socialized in traditional beliefs about the importance of the family. Perhaps this focus derives from indigenous roots and village or small-town beginnings, where everyone knew one another and looked out for one another. M. Ramírez (1998) asserted that survival in the midst of European conquest drove indigenous people to maintain strong connections. *Familismo,* therefore, may be seen as a buffer for individuals like Nancy, who feel lost and isolated in the midst of new surroundings and people. When meeting with college students who are sad about being separated from their family, counselors need to understand that this emotion is normal and that Nancy is not overly dependent or from an enmeshed family. Enmeshment is a stereotype ascribed to Latino families for being close and concerned about one another (Falicov, 1998; Montilla & Medina, 2006; Santiago-Rivera, Arredondo, & Gallardo-Cooper, 2002), and often independence and autonomy from family are touted as superior values for college students. For Nancy and others, ongoing engagement with *familia* is primary to their identity and a natural expression of loyalty, interdependence, and collectivism.

Familismo may also have counterpoints. It is fair to point out that for some individuals, *familismo* may be smothering and controlling, leading to feelings of guilt if they declare or desire to move away or not to attend all extended family functions. For contemporary families, social mobility may mean that children may move away for college or work after college. Acculturation processes may change or challenge beliefs in *familismo,* and this may be disruptive to family dynamics and may even result in intergenerational conflict. Once again, the burden would fall on the individual who steps away from an overinvolved or controlling family network. Guilt is a natural reaction when one makes an unpopular choice to move away, even for good reasons. However, it is best that a counselor check out the reality of family influence for a client and not assume closeness based on the client's *familismo* experiences.

A manifestation of *familismo* is *compadrazgo,* or extended family relations. The Catholic rituals of baptism, First Communion, and even marriage introduce *comadres* and *compadres* (coparents), *madrinas* (godmothers), and *padrinos* (godfathers) into the family structure. *Comadres* and *compadres* assume a special relationship to the parents of the children. However, these titles may also be attributed to one's close friends, signifying a special relationship to the family. Nancy's *madrina* seems to play an important role in the family, as Nancy recalled her encouragement when she was feeling blue. Family friends may be considered family regardless of a lack of biological relationship. *Tias* and *tios* (aunts and uncles) and *abuelos* and *abuelas* (grandparents) are also part of the nuclear (instead of extended) family, and *abuelos* in particular hold special status. In the historical Latino hierarchical family structure, elders have always been treated with special regard and respect. Depending on their age and physical mobility, they may be deferred to and accommodated in special ways.

Family is family, and this also signals making family visitors feel at home when they visit, especially from their home country. Tourist visas generally allow family members to stay up to 6 weeks. This leads to extended stays in the home of a son or daughter and, of course, adaptation by everyone. If the children do not speak Spanish, there may be a strain in the household, putting more demands on the adult children. Extended visits can be a sort of honeymoon for the entire family, but over time, and depending on the personalities and needs of the visitors, they can put strain on family relationships. Family loyalty, pride, and a sense of belonging are also fostered by *familismo.* According to Falicov (1998), family rituals strengthen the bonds among individuals, create a sense of intimacy and caring, and symbolize a "communitarian worldview" (p. 105). Another example of the enactment of *familismo* is found in professional Latino counseling associations. At annual conferences, students and professionals of all ages readily hug, kiss, and become very expressive emotionally when seeing one another, as it is traditional to do. It is like one big family reunion where a sense of belonging is unmistakable. If Latinos forget to code switch and greet White colleagues in this way, embarrassment or awkwardness may ensue!

La Familia

Insomuch as Latino families are organizations with hierarchies and roles, there are scripts to follow based on birth order and gender. Parents are the authorities, and in keeping with expectations about *respeto* (respect) for elders and seniors, they have unquestioned authority (Falicov, 1998). This is particularly important for non-Latino counselors to realize, even if children are involved as interpreters in a school situation. The children likely know their roles and rules and may resist asking their parents certain questions because it may come across as disrespectful. Parents are more than a figurehead, and even if they do not speak sufficient English in school-based settings, they still hold authority in the family. The structure defines roles, rules, responsibilities, and, for children, compliance to said roles and rules.

Falicov (1998) provided a very detailed explanation of assignments and expectations for mothers, fathers, sons, and daughters. A few examples follow:

- Latina mothers are revered for their commitment to *la familia* and the sacrifices they make for their *hijos* and *hijas* (sons and daughters). It is quite common for mothers to work outside of the home to bring in a second income, but they still place their family first, and if they subscribe to the messages of *marianismo* (self-sacrifice in the manner of the Virgin Mary), they will do for children first rather than for themselves. Respect and reverence for mothers and motherhood persists. Career-oriented Latinas are often reminded by their parents about the importance of motherhood, thus creating a double-bind for lesbians and/or women who prefer not to have children. With more college-educated women remaining single longer, there are shifting self-expectations among these women about motherhood. A forthcoming case scenario in this chapter is illustrative of this point.
- "Nowhere are parent-child closeness and devotion greater than in the relationship between mother and an oldest, and an only or favorite son" (Falicov, 1998, p. 170). This is an example of family connectedness and also a way of pointing to the status of males in Latino families. If the father is not present, the mother has another man to rely on. Of course, there can be a negative dimension to this bond if the mother uses the son as a way to maintain distance from her spouse or to create an alliance that marginalizes the son from his father. A humorous statement seems appropriate to underscore this mother–son bond. In the book *Loving Pedro Infante* (D. Chávez, 2001), the protagonist, Tere, frustrated with her relationship with noncommittal men, quips about what a *madre* (mother) is and should be: "You place her up on the altar where all Mejicanos (men) place their mothers, next to God" (p. 229).
- Fatherhood is a responsibility that comes with high expectations for Latino men. There are stereotypical images of Latino fathers as strict disciplinarians and bossy with their wives. Alternatively, there are many examples of men who share decision making with their wives (Y. M. Sanchez, 1997; Toth & Xu, 1999), enjoy playing with their children, and believe in the sanctity of marriage. In a study of Mexican immigrant first-time homeowners, couples reported that they engaged in shared decision making; they underscored respect for the other's opinion and that this was important for their children to learn as well. As might be expected, a man's father is his model for the role of fatherhood, positively and negatively.
- Birth order does matter in Latino families. The oldest child is expected to do more, especially as it relates to younger siblings. If the oldest child is a daughter, she will be given many more domestic assignments to support her mother. As in many homes, the division of labor among children may fall along gender lines. That is, girls will have more in-house chores and boys outdoor chores, or perhaps none at all. There is the stereotype of the Latin Prince, a boy who has been spoiled by his mother and expects other women to spoil him in the same way. However, as times have changed, so have the roles of boys and men. They too are expected to contribute to self-maintenance, cooking, and other formerly typical female tasks.
- Closeness and interdependence among Latino siblings is expected. And although children may go away to school, there is still an expectation that they will return home and claim their own room or shared room. Latino children are socialized that siblings have much more value than peers or friends, and this is exactly the opposite for many White children, who are taught to socialize mainly with their same-age peers. Thus, Latinos may see a lack of closeness with siblings as abnormal. Siblings may share the same parents, but this does not mean that as adults they will raise their children similarly or that they will maintain the family values practiced when they were growing up. Many contributing factors to the ways in which *familias* evolve are also common to non-Latino families.

Respeto, Obligación, y Lealtad (Respect, Obligation, and Loyalty)

Respeto is the cornerstone of Latino relationships. As might be evident through the previous discussions, many Latino families are hierarchical, delineating clear lines of authority and decision making. Children are socialized to be *bien educados*, or well-mannered and respectful, and to represent the family honorably. Thus the *dicho De padres sanos, hijos honrados.*

The hierarchal nature of the family structure has implications for roles, rules, and rituals, including communication patterns within and outside of the family, particularly with authority figures—the supervisor, teacher, police officer, minister or priest, and so forth. Where there is *confianza* (trust), as it appears for Nancy, her mother, and her *madrina,* there is also a sense of intimacy and vulnerability. As stated by Montilla and Medina (2006), "Family is not merely a decorative establishment; it fulfills several practical functions that help in the survival task of its individuals" (p. 104).

The priority on interpersonal values outside of the family begins with the term *personalismo* (preference for personal interactions). Latinos have often been characterized as party people or as very social and friendly compared to some Caucasians. However, quite likely individuals are enacting *personalismo* through qualities such as *simpatía* (sympathy), *caridad* (caring), and *confianza.* Being congenial, caring, and trusting correspond to this value. Nancy has likely had this type of experience with friends and even other adults; however, she does not seem to have it with her roommate. When individuals extend their goodwill and it is not reciprocated or perhaps the gesture is diminished or ignored, Latinos might say that *fulano/a me faltó el respeto* ("so-and-so" disrespected me). Interpersonal breeches in counseling situations can actually drive Latinos away. For example, Nancy might have visited with a counselor to speak about her loneliness, the lack of friendliness of her roommate, and homesickness. If the counselor was not culturally aware, he or she might describe Nancy as overly dependent on her family, exaggerating homesickness (after all, she is only 3 hours away from home), and socially immature. A counselor not prepared to be culturally competent might recommend that Nancy try to be friendlier to her roommate or join a social skills group. If this were to be a counselor's response, it would be easy to understand why Nancy would not return to counseling and why she might feel even more isolated. A culture-centered counselor would appreciate that he or she has to extend *personalismo* if he or she expects to work effectively with Nancy.

Amabilidad (friendliness, caring, warmth) and politeness are further characteristics of *respeto* (Falicov, 1998). Because of the highly relational Latino worldview, many terms can be used to describe positive attributes of relationships. "Niceness" has also been attributed to Latinas for what may come across as politeness (Alemán, 2009; Alemán & Alemán, 2010) or acquiescence. When a woman does not question or disagree with what is presented, the behavior can be interpreted as acceptance.

Gender Socialization

In a hierarchical, multigenerational, and complex culture, there are many nuances to the discussion of gender socialization for Latinas/os. There is the influence of religion, historical cross-cultural patterns for raising women as second-class citizens globally (P. Arredondo, Psalti, & Cella, 1993), generational differences, education and socioeconomic factors, and the microculture of a given family. The historical meaning of *marianismo,* machismo, and *caballerismo* (gentlemanly behavior), culture-based, gender-related phenomena, should be appreciated, and these terms should not be used in stereotyped ways. As with all concepts and theories, there is always some relative truth to their meaning and application, but with the highly diverse Latino populous, counselors must learn about these concepts with an open mind and without judgment. Counselors may react emotionally when reading about *marianismo* and machismo, but it is their responsibility to examine their attitudes and/or discomfort should these emotions emerge. The Multicultural Counseling Competencies state that culturally skilled counselors "identify how general emotional reactions observed in [themselves] could influence effectiveness in a counseling relationship" (P. Arredondo et al., 1996, p. 63).

Marianismo

The framework of *marianismo,* associated with Catholicism and the Virgin Mary, provides both the conscious and unconscious mindset learned by both boys and girls as often modeled by their parents and grandparents. In any household, children observe their parents' behavior and often emulate it as they grow up and become adults. The same can be said about Latino households. The enactment of sex role behavior has many precursors, but nothing is clearer than how boys and girls learn from their parents.

According to the Ten Commandments of *marianismo* (M. R. Gil & Vázquez, 1996), women are to be self-sacrificing, submissive, and pure, in the image of the Virgin Mary. In families that perpetuate examples of *marianismo,* young girls are taught indirectly or overtly the following messages:

1. Do not forget a woman's place.
2. Do not forsake tradition.
3. Do not be single, self-supporting, and independent minded.
4. Do not put your own needs first.
5. Do not wish for more from life than being a housewife.
6. Do not forget that sex is for making babies—not for pleasure.
7. Do not be unhappy with your man or criticize him for infidelity, gambling, verbal and physical abuse, or alcohol or drug abuse.
8. Do not ask for help.
9. Do not discuss personal problems outside the home.
10. Do not change those things that make you unhappy that you can realistically change. (p. 8)

Context matters, and in the development of the Ten Commandments, this needs to be acknowledged. The authors of *The Maria Paradox* (M. R. Gil & Vázquez, 1996), in which the Ten Commandments of *marianismo* was first published, developed their list of commandments based on qualitative research with therapy clients in New York City. Their clients were of different ages and Latino heritage, and all described experiences that both celebrated and minimized their womanhood. As presented here, the Ten Commandments all seem negative and suggest that women learn to put up with situations that are not in their best interest. *Aguantar* means "to put up with or suppress." Unfortunately, *aguantar* is thematic in the commandments, suggesting that women have learned disempowerment.

As with all concepts or theories, however, these cannot be all-or-nothing propositions. Anecdotal feedback from Latinas of different generations varies. Some women have reported that they recognize the commandments from their own family experiences but never had a name for what they were seeing. For example, one woman mentioned how her father always expected to be waited on by his wife and daughters at the dinner table, to the point of their putting food on his plate. In time, this practice was applied to the sons in the family by the sisters. The women were conscious of the sexist treatment but followed the family script. More recently, in 2011, some women in graduate school disputed the Ten Commandments, indicating that they did not play out in their homes. As women of Latina heritage assume greater self-sufficiency, attend college and graduate school, become employed in professional positions, and become heads of households, these messages may become less relevant. However, counselors need to exercise caution and not assume that new-generation Latinas are less influenced by *familismo, respeto,* and *marianismo* than were their mothers and grandmothers. After all, values and traditions passed on across generations are not readily erased from one's mindset.

Latinas on the Margins

Women of Latina heritage are increasingly outpacing men as high school and college graduates, mirroring national trends. The National Center for Education Statistics reported that 88% of native-born Latinas and 85% of native-born Latinos have completed high school, and 4% of Latinas and 5% of Latinos have completed a general equivalency diploma. Data from the 2010 U.S. Census indicate that 61.4% of Latinos and 64.4% of Latinas have completed high school. For college graduates, the rates are exceedingly low: 12.9% of Latinos and 14.9% of Latinas (Fry, 2010).

These achievements can be celebrated, but they are also of concern. In her poetry, Anzaldúa (1987) wrote about how women like her had to survive the "Borderlands" or *Entre Fronteras* experiences in the United States. She underscored the multidimensionality of Latinas and how this can be a blessing and a burden. An acclaimed feminist writer from southern Texas, Anzaldúa promoted women's strengths as mothers, workers, and social activists and also lamented discrimination and racism because of one's ethnicity. She also reminded readers that being a lesbian in a Mexican community was a risk. Today, Latina lesbians can be open about their sexual identity in many places, but like Anzaldúa cautioned, it may put a woman on the margins in her family. Parents still desire that Latinas marry and have children, which puts lesbians and women who elect to remain childless in the proverbial double-bind.

Latinas are moving into careers in greater numbers than their male counterparts. Although data are not well documented in this regard, this phenomenon raises other issues for expectations that Latinas become mothers. Even in contemporary *familias,* Latinas are still expected to marry and become mothers. Of course, this is not so different from societal expectations and pressures on women in general; however, given the value of *familismo,* women feel more pressure to please their parents, *abuelos* and *abuelas,* and extended family members.

Case Scenario

Claudia was 35 years old, was single, and had been born in Chicago of Mexican immigrant parents. She lived with her male partner, an issue of consternation to her parents and other family members. She went to counseling to sort out the confusion she felt about letting others down and her chosen lifestyle. Claudia admitted to the counselor that she was not interested in having children and had never had this desire; however, it made her feel enormously guilty and selfish. Her partner, a professional like her, of Peruvian heritage, agreed with Claudia's preference. His parents were not in the United States and were proud of his accomplishments from a distance. They also had grandchildren in Peru. Although Claudia's parents had grandchildren, they had been born to their sons and their wives. They claimed that a child by their daughter was something special. Claudia's goal was to come to terms with her guilt, accept her decision, and have a conversation with her parents about her appreciation for them. She wanted to be empathic but did not have the right words to speak with them respectfully.

Claudia's counselor was of Polish immigrant heritage and appreciated the dilemma. Through discussions and role plays, and by bringing in her partner, the counselor gave Claudia the support she needed to accept her decision—but it was not easy. In this situation, the counselor demonstrated Latino-centered competence by recognizing family-of-origin structure and functioning as one of many possible types of family organization without imposing a standard for Claudia. She also inquired about other family members who had not had children. In this way she drew Claudia out of an issue that may have seemed like hers alone, not one that perhaps she had in common with other family members.

Machismo y Caballerismo

In the popular press and academic literature, machismo has typically been associated with an expectation of behavior for men of Latino heritage. It is referred to as "the masculine force, which to one degree or another drives all masculine behavior" (Andrade, 1992, p. 33) and Mexican men's manifestation of perceived male characteristics, both positive and negative (Arciniega, Tovar-Gamero, & Sand, 2004). However, it is generally presented more negatively and associated with attributes of sexism, chauvinism, womanizing, and hypermasculinity (Arciniega, Anderson, Tovar-Blank, & Tracey, 2008). This all-or-nothing portrayal of Latinos leaves a less than positive image for counselors who are not knowledgeable about the positive aspects of machismo.

Latino researchers have argued that there must be a bidimensional view of machismo that recognizes the positive aspects of men's behavior. For example, machismo also means that men nurture, protect their family, are breadwinners, and are responsible for their family's well-being. Other attributes of machismo include dignity, hard work, spirituality, and emotional connectedness (J. M. Casas, Wagenheim, Banchero, & Mendoza-Romero, 1994; Mirandé, 1988, 1997). Anecdotally speaking, Latino men attending conference presentations at which machismo is introduced are always quick to point out the positive aspects of the concept. They report feeling offended when others insensitively ask them whether they are "*machos.*" Counselors need to be aware that the terms *macho* or *machista* (macho man) are more slang and crude and are viewed as a microaggression if attributed to a man indiscriminately.

In their research, Arciniega et al. (2008) introduced the concept of *caballerismo*, associating it with the more positive qualities of machismo. The term emanates from the words *caballo* (horse) and *caballero* (horseman, or man with gentlemanly qualities). Because it is an old term, *caballerismo* also refers to chivalry and to men of a higher status that show respectful behavior toward others, quite the opposite of the negative associations of machismo. In their studies with Mexican men, Arciniega and his colleagues (2008) found support for the "two-dimensional representation of machismo" (p. 19).

Case Scenario

Jaime, an engineering graduate, was about to enter a premier engineering firm in Boston. A graduate of a local prestigious university, he felt fortunate to be selected for the position, which would likely take him to the company's global sites in Latin America. Originally from Colombia, Jaime had grown up in New Jersey, the youngest of three children. His older siblings were also college graduates, as were his parents. In Boston, Jaime became active in an association for Latino professionals, finding validation for his identity and also a place to connect with a few other Colombianos.

At a gathering he confided to his friends that his new supervisor had made comments about his Colombian heritage. First he had stated that he had not known that Colombians were Black, had asked whether Jaime was a macho, and had off-handedly joked rhetorically that he had hoped Jaime "was not involved with drug cartels." Shaken that the person he was going to report to was making these quips, Jaime wondered about his possible success with the company. Although one of his friends suggested that he speak to a human resources manager, Jaime knew that as a newcomer he would do no such thing. Another friend told him to document the experience in a safe place and that he would back up Jaime if the situation ever warranted it.

Although this scenario does not involve a counseling situation, it is used to illustrate a few culture-specific considerations for counselors. First, persons of Latino heritage who grow up in the United States are bicultural and are attuned to the cultural ignorance of others who are not used to working with Latinos. Second, according to research by Solórzano, Ceja, and Yosso (2000) and D. W. Sue et al. (2007), underrepresented individuals like Jaime are likely to experience microaggressions, unintentional or intentional insults, and disrespectful comments. Third, Jaime is a Black Hispanic (Afro-Colombian), according to U.S. Census categories, and likely the recipient of prejudicial comments because of his multiracial, multicultural heritage. The comment about Jaime's association in drug cartels is also indicative of stereotypes that continue to be held by professionals with power and privilege in different education and work settings. The comment is highly inappropriate and likely a reminder to Jaime that he has to maintain a formal, professional relationship with his boss. Fourth, Jaime may have to be hypervigilant at work, which may distract him from the tasks at hand.

Summary

Although *marianismo* and machismo are grounded in Latino cultural socialization, they have different meanings in specific families and for specific individuals. After all, all families are microcultures, and no two Latinas or Latinos are alike. Counselors cannot assume that Latinas/os are well versed in these terms and need to be cautious about introducing them into counseling sessions because they may come off sounding too academic or culturally inappropriate. Gender socialization is complex and must be understood as it relates to an individual's entire upbringing and other dimensions of his or her identity (i.e., geographic origins, parents' education, generational and socioeconomic status, religious affiliation, and status as an immigrant or non-immigrant). Consider this Latino cultural competency: "Culturally skilled counselors can understand and appreciate the diversity and heterogeneity within the Latino population" (Santiago-Rivera et al., 2002, p. 55).

Religion and Spirituality

The detribalization of the native populations of the Americas had many implications. One relates to the role of religion, Catholicism, as a tool of oppression and conversion among indigenous groups in which spirituality based on different beliefs, rituals, and values was pervasive. Latino religious or spiritual worldviews are similar to those of Native Americans in terms of ceremonies, relationships with nature, and sacrifices to invoke wellness or other positive outcomes for the people. For example, in Catholicism there are rituals to celebrate births and deaths; indigenous people also have ceremonies for these life events. Whereas Catholics pray to saints, indigenous people invoke the gods associated with the forces of nature—the sun, the moon, water, and earth.

Catholic priests or missionaries were part of all European conquests, enacting their role as spiritual caretakers and spreading their faith. The rules prescribed by Catholicism were very clear and the prejudices toward non-Europeans and non-Catholics were dogmatic, regardless of the country of conquest. One's life and soul were saved through baptism, and where this was not accepted, death was certain. It is important to remember that in the 15th century Spain was a Catholic country, and at that time there was no separation of church and state (or church and royalty). Alliances between the Catholic Church and the governments of Mexico and other Latin American countries are not as pronounced now as they once were, but for a period of time mistrust persisted. For example, secular lines blurred with religious lines, and throughout the 30-year presidential dictatorship of Porfírio Díaz in Mexico, the Catholic Church was the handmaiden of the government. Often this meant that the poorest people lost their lands or otherwise were coerced into bequeathing their lands to the Church.

For Catholics of Mexican heritage, La Virgen de Guadalupe is revered and celebrated each year on December 12. The story of the *Virgen's* appearance is full of symbolism and an example of life in 17th-century Mexico. The *Virgen* appeared to Juan Diego, an indigenous man who worked around the church. Although the priest did not initially believe he saw the apparition, the truth came out when Juan Diego opened the poncho-style wrap he was wearing. There on the front of his poncho was the image of an indigenous Virgin Mary surrounded by angels and stars. Furthermore, roses fell from his poncho, additional evidence of a miracle in the cold month of December. Today, La Virgen de Guadalupe is recognized as the patron saint of North America, and men and women alike are named Guadalupe (Lupe) in honor of *La Virgen*.

Indigenous Healers and Practices

"In North America, religion among African Americans, Latinos and Native Americans is a product of the cultural mestizoization process" (M. Ramírez, 1998, p. 36). In other words, the historic intersections of indigenous and Catholic beliefs and practices in particular have led to cross-cultural practices of support, healing, and beliefs in higher powers (supernatural beings, gods and goddesses, and God).

The worldview of healers is grounded in beliefs about supernatural forces, the restoration of balance and harmony in the body, and harmony for family and community. Many of these beliefs and practices emanate from a preindustrial time when Western medicine was practiced and individuals lived off the land (i.e., hunting, harvesting crops, and building homes from nature's resources), prior to the arrival of the conquistadors. An example of cultural mestizoization in Latin America and the Caribbean Islands is the use of indigenous rituals and artifacts. Leading these ceremonies are *curanderos* (folk healers) and, in the case of Puerto Rico and Cuba, *espiritistas* and *santeros* (folk healers), who introduce African beliefs and practices along with the Catholic and indigenous.

As healers *curanderas/os* address problems with physical health, love, and home life. They may address issues of *susto* (fear or fright), often a symptom for children.

Psychologist Brian McNeill stated that *susto* is a manifestation of posttraumatic stress (personal communication, October 12, 2012). The *curandero* might introduce herbs into the treatment to cleanse and to heal. In Latin America, the *bótanica* is the place to find different remedies to alleviate pain or illnesses. *Limpieza* (cleansing) is another practice that drives away evil spirits and restores balance. The *curandero* may sing or chant, use plants, involve the individual in breathing and meditation exercises, and go into a trance-like state himself or herself. Also used for cleansing is the *temazcal* (sweat lodge). The indigenous people consider the *temazcal* to be a house of prayer and a space for purification. The shape of the structure is seen as the womb of mother earth.

The practice of Santería in Puerto Rico and Cuba is grounded in African Yoruban beliefs and practices. A *babalao*/(babalawo) is the Yoruban high priest who presides at ceremonies that also incorporate practices from Christianity. According to spiritual beliefs, at birth one acquires an *orisha,* or a protective guide for life. *Ashe,* also referred to as a force of energy, is uttered in rituals that recognize and give thanks to predecessors. *Espiritístas* are healers who combine indigenous practices with more modern Latino practices. As the term signifies, *espiritistas* communicate with spirits in the afterlife and/or the supernatural world to find guidance and healing for contemporary concerns.

Curanderas/os, santeros, and *espiritístas* are often sought out in lieu of a practitioner of Western medicine for physical and mental health reasons, depending on the region of the United States. *Curanderos* may be more accessible in the Southwest and California, whereas *espiritístas* and *santeros* may be more typically found in the Caribbean. Counselors need to be aware that for some individuals, there is shame associated with seeking out *curanderos,* and inquiring about this in therapy requires sensitivity. It is also important to note that *espiritismo* and Santería are not religious belief systems or affiliated with an institution such as the Catholic Church. As was stated earlier, the practices are grounded in beliefs that date back more than two centuries. Furthermore, although individuals may identify with different faiths, they may still seek alternatives for health and mental health treatment and turn to *curanderas/os, sobadores* (massage therapists), and *espiritistas.*

Case Scenario

Esteban and Amalia fled El Salvador during the bloody civil wars of the 1980s, having witnessed the merciless murders of friends and family. They came with two small children, Rosa and Julio, grateful to have their children safe at hand. All seemed fine. Little Rosa started first grade and Julio went to nursery school while the parents worked in day jobs. One day Esteban and Amalia were called by the school nurse because Rosa had an epileptic seizure. They were advised to take her to the doctor and they did so dutifully, uncertain what might have precipitated the seizure. A few weeks later, Rosa had another seizure, this time at home. Startled and clearly afraid, Esteban approached his Mexican American employer for help, confiding that he believed that Rosa had been given the *mal ojo* (evil eye) by a family from El Salvador who were of the opposite political party. Esteban and Amalia wanted to take Rosa to a *curandera* who might remove the curse. They were convinced that the pills the doctor had given were of no use.

Counselors working in community health centers or even schools may face requests like the one made by Amalia and Esteban. When working in communities with a critical number of Latino families, it behooves counselors to learn about faith-based services as well as alternative health practices. Latino-centered competencies remind counselors to be prepared to respond to cultural beliefs involving folk remedies and ones requesting traditional religious interventions, such as meeting with a priest or minister: "Culturally skilled counselors can identify specific cultural beliefs and practices such as the use of health-related folk remedies that help a family cope with illness" (Santiago-Rivera et al., 2002, p. 35).

Latinos and Religion Today

In 2006, one third of Catholics in the United States were Latinos, and with the number of Latinos in the United States at 50.5 million and growing (Ennis, Ríos-Vargas, & Albert, 2011), it is predicted that this number will also increase. In fact, Latinos are transforming American religion and becoming the mainstays of many Catholic churches, which are losing non-Latino parishioners who are aging, move away, or simply no longer choose to participate. It should be noted that although Latinos are of all religious affiliations—Muslim, Jewish, Pentecostal, Catholic, and other Christian faiths—Catholicism continues to dominate.

A 2006 study by the Pew Hispanic Center and the Pew Forum on Religion & Public Life of 4,016 adults (Catholic and non-Catholic) and surveys with 650 Catholics uncovered beliefs and practices that may prove of interest to religious communities, political leaders, and policy makers (Pew Hispanic Center, 2007). For example, "More than half of the Hispanic Catholics identify themselves as charismatics, compared with only one-eighth of non-Hispanic Catholics" (p. 3). Charismatics are generally associated with the evangelical churches grounded in beliefs of spirit-filled or renewalist movements, "including divine healing and direct revelations from God" (p. 1) Furthermore, the data showed that Catholics likely convert (18% in the study) to evangelical faiths in which spirit-filled religion can be experienced. More specifically, among evangelical converts (51%), 43% were former Catholics. One explanation for leaving the traditional Catholic Church is its dull service, which leaves little room for the more emotional participation that is possible in evangelical and charismatic services.

The study also revealed that both immigrants and English-speaking Latinos are drawn to ethnic or Spanish-speaking churches. Once again, the bond of culture, language, and a place to be yourself draws a cross-section of Latinos. Respondents also spoke of God as an active power in their lives and of their rituals of engaging in daily prayer, attending church services at least once a month, and having religious objects in their homes (Pew Hispanic Center, 2007). It is common for Latino Catholics to have small altars with La Virgin de Guadalupe as the centerpiece or crucifixes and statues of favorite or patron saints visible throughout their homes. The Latino devotion to the Virgin Mary, Jesus, and God, in general, is also an expression of relying on a higher power, sometimes referred to as *fatalism*. If one were to go to churches in Mexico, one would find many petitions at the church altars, supplicating for favors to heal an illness or expressing thanks because a loved one is now improved. The expression *Si Díos quiere* (If it is God's will), has often been misperceived as fatalistic or as a sign of giving up one's control. However, it is more of an acknowledgment or worldview that some things in life cannot be controlled.

Another representation of religious or spiritual affiliation involves names. Catholic Latinos are often named for the Virgin Mary (María), for Jesus Christ (Jesús), or for La Virgen de Guadalupe (Guadalupe). If one is born on the birth date of a particular saint, that name might be given (e.g., Teresa, José). Of course, individuals may be named after parents and/or grandparents as well. Latino Evangelicals tend to name children after biblical personages, particularly those from the Old Testament (e.g., Jacóbo or Ester). Names such as Yanelli, Cuatemoc, or Monteczuma recognize indigenous roots and express affirmation of Aztec roots.

Another interesting finding in the Pew Hispanic Center (2007) study concerns the intersection of religion and politics. The respondents indicated that their religious beliefs do influence their political opinions and that churches should do more to address social and political matters. Those who were more involved churchgoers tended to have more conservative views on matters such as gay marriage and increases in government-supported services. Another distinction was found with respect to political party preference. "Latino evangelicals are twice as likely as Latino Catholics to be Republicans" (p. 77), which is a larger percentage than non-Latino Whites proportionately. Alternatively, Latino Catholic conservatives prefer Democrats. Even more interesting were data on the percentage of Catholic Latinos eligible to vote—71% of eligible Latino Catholic voters were Democrats and 21% were Republicans. In general, the Latino electorate is overwhelmingly Catholic (63%) and Democrat. Among evangelicals there is a more even split for Republicans versus Democrats, although there is a slight favor toward Republicans.

Concluding Thoughts

Culture is transmitted across generations in explicable and often inexplicable ways. Values, beliefs, and traditions have grounded Latino families for centuries, serving as guidelines for desirable behavior and anchors during times of change. But value conflicts are not uncommon for Latinos, as external forces in the mainstream U.S. society affect individuals in different ways. The challenge for counselors is to go beyond stereotypes and portrayals of Latinos in popular media and on *telenovelas* (soap operas). They must meet their clients or client families in the here and now and not make assumptions about their traditional values.

• • •

Chapter 3

Acculturation and Enculturation Processes

Cuando joven, de ilusiones; cuando viejo, de recuerdos.

While young, it's all dreams; when old, all memories.

(Sellers, Nelson, & Soto, 1994, p. 60)

• • •

Objectives

- To review acculturation and enculturation models.
- To recognize the role of acculturative stressors on immigrants and other Latinos going through change processes and their effects on mental well-being.
- To learn about the intersection of changes related to acculturation and ethnic identity.

Sabías que/Did you know that . . .

- Acculturation is about multidimensional processes of cognitive, emotional, and behavioral change.
- Measuring acculturation levels is complex because of the internal and external factors that affect individuals in transition.
- Acculturative stressors typically affect mental and even physical well-being.

• • •

In an op-ed column published by the National Institute for Latino Policy, Janet Murguía (2011), chief executive officer of the National Council of La Raza, declared, "Hispanic values are American values." She pointed out that although many were surprised at 2010 Census reports indicating continued growth in the Latino-heritage population, Latinos have been a dynamic and contributing part of the fabric of the United States for many years. However, the history books do not account for the myriad ways Latinos have contributed to U.S. culture. She noted that Latinos have participated in all wars in which the United States has taken part and that the "first Medal of Honor given to a Hispanic soldier was during the Civil War" (p. A11). Murguía went on to say that Latinos share the same values as all other Americans—good schools, safe neighborhoods, jobs commensurate with abilities and need, religious practices, and respect and love for the country. In all likelihood, the 1 in 4 children who are Latina/o (Pew Hispanic Center, 2011) are being socialized by the American culture as well as their home culture. In some cases, the latter may already be more American than bicultural, depending on their parents' generational status.

Acculturation Models and Processes

How does the acculturation phenomenon manifest for Latino immigrants and their children and for third- and fourth-generation Latinos or Latinos of multiple-heritage parents? Acculturation-related research has been based on premises of change and adaptation for immigrants that go from Culture A to Culture B in a new host country. Some of the research, however, has included Latinas/os born in the United States, a methodological error. Latinas/os born in the United States know that they are citizens, even if they are categorized as minorities. Moreover, their socialization process in the United States is different from that of immigrants born and raised in a Spanish-speaking country. Yet even Latinos born in the United States go through acculturation processes for several reasons: For example, they are the first in their family to go to college; they marry outside of the culture and into another family's cultural milieu; or they move from, say, a Cuban-centered community in Miami to a Mexican-oriented locale in San Diego. These examples are not unusual and are provided here so that counselors may stretch their thinking about the concept of acculturation. Although the focus herein is the Latino population, the acculturation phenomenon can explain the behavior of non-Hispanics as well.

This section introduces evolving thinking about acculturation processes for Latinas/os. The discussion in Chapter 2 informs this discussion and underscores the many ways in which cultural worldviews—values, beliefs, traditions, and other Latino-informed rituals and practices—need to be factored into understanding the complexity of the acculturation process and its effects on individuals' self-efficacy, identity development, and mental and physical well-being.

Acculturation was originally positioned as a unidirectional process reflecting primarily behavioral preferences for food, music, language use, and so forth (Cuéllar, Harris, & Jasso, 1980), that is, moving from a Latino-centered worldview and cultural ethos to a new American worldview. However, continuing research on the phenomenon indicates that acculturation for Latinas/os is not an all-or-nothing event or outcome but rather one involving cognitive challenges (e.g., Does this make sense? Why do they think that show is funny?), emotional dissonance (e.g., confusion, loss, discomfort), and decision making about choices one can make (e.g., Will this school be good for my child so that she can go to college?). That is, acculturation is multicontextual (Cano & Castillo, 2010; M. Ramírez, 1998). Individuals go through acculturation processes in relation to their environment or location, societal messages about inclusion or exclusion, relationships, and recognition of their personal self-worth. In the following scenario, differences in worldviews between a father and a son illustrate how the father has made adaptations in the way he responds to those in authority and how the son recognizes the double standards that Latinos face even if they are born in the United States. Is the son resisting acculturation, or is he just like any other teenager who is resisting authority that is based on unfounded prejudices?

Case Scenario

David was a high school senior with an independent spirit. Born in Youngstown, Ohio, to parents originally from Puerto Rico, he took pride in playing on the football team. He was also an above-average student. A run-in with a history teacher landed David in the principal's office. She accused him of disrupting the class by talking to his friends. When he denied it, she sent him out of class. David contended that it was someone else who was doing the talking and that the teacher was always on his case. "She doesn't like football players," he stated. "I also think she doesn't like Latinos; she always seems to accuse us of doing something wrong but lets the White kids off the hook."

In a counseling session with a bilingual counselor, David's father expressed his displeasure with David's behavior:

Father: Why do you always have to talk back? The teacher is usually right.

David: I am not going to let people push me around like you do at work. You are always so willing to help out even when your boss does not give you a raise. You are just too nice.

Father: Haven't I taught you that you must respect your superiors? They might not always be right, but she is still your teacher. *Tienes que tenerle respeto* [you have to show her respect].

David: This is the problem; you have your old-world ideas. I was born here, I know about racism and discrimination toward Latinos, and I know my rights. People are always taking advantage of you and *mamá*. I won't let that happen to me.

Father: Pero hijo (but son), I am proud of being Puerto Rican and I want you to be, too. We have worked hard to have you achieve what we could not and don't want you to lose it.

David: Papi, I understand. I am proud of being Puerto Rican too, but I also want people to see me as an American, because I am.

The scenario illustrates intergenerational worldviews influenced by different socialization experiences and how these may affect family relationships. David sees himself as both American and Puerto Rican, and the bilingual exchanges are perhaps indicative of communication in the family home. His father also owns his Puerto Rican identity but engages with people such as his boss in a hierarchical manner of *respeto* (respect). He does not rock the boat, as David did in defending himself when wrongly accused by his teacher. Furthermore, David is also cognizant of racism toward Latinos, having likely experienced and witnessed it throughout his schooling in the football locker room and in other social settings. Although David seems to be challenging his father by pointing out that others take advantage of him and his *mamá*, he actually seems to be saying that he is aware of and does not like the fact that others disrespect his parents. A culturally responsive counselor will readily see the common denominators between David and his father. Their mutual caring and respect comes through, as does the sense of hope for David's success. A counselor might pick up on the emotions of pride, frustration, and helplessness embedded in their comments. Both are at different places in the acculturation process—or are they? David's father plays by the rules. Does this make him less acculturated? In the United States, individualism and assertiveness are valued and promoted in the human development process. To say that David's father is at a low level of acculturation because he does not challenge authority would be to overlook his valuing of respect for authority and his approach to managing interpersonal relationships from the value of *personalismo* (a valuing of interpersonal relationships).

David shows more bravado because he feels wronged. His indignation may be masking his awareness of being marginalized because of his Latino identity. David's behavior may seem to reflect a high level of acculturation—he can speak for himself and point to the teacher's lack of fairness, but his approach certainly is not respectful of communication protocols in the school. Researchers have suggested that ethnic pride (Castillo et al., 2006) is a buffer in challenging situations and can also suggest a higher level of acculturation. However, in the case of David and his father, the counselor must be aware of the emotional costs associated with acculturation processes. At what point does acculturative stress or stress related to racism, overwork, and poor salary need an outlet, and if it does, how will it be channeled? Are these different manifestations of acculturative stress based on generational worldviews and the context in which each individual was socialized?

Perspectives on the Acculturation Process

For many years social scientists have tackled questions and definitions about the meaning of acculturation. The work of John Berry (1980) is often cited as seminal to the evolution of the field of study and, more specifically, how it relates to cultural worldviews and behaviors. Berry conducted some of his research with Aboriginal communities, particularly in Canada, attempting to understand their issues of marginality, stress, and ethnic identification.

Early models of acculturation pointed to inclusion and exclusion options. That is, individuals supposedly went through processes of cultural change moving from marginalization to assimilation independent of environmental and social conditions; they just sort of became acculturated (Falicov, 1998; M. Ramírez, 1998). An early measure specific to persons of Mexican heritage was the Acculturation Rating Scale for Mexican Americans (ARSMA), published in 1980 (Cuéllar et al., 1980). It was well received at the time and the primary tool for measuring acculturation among Mexican Americans. However, it was criticized by Mexican American researchers because it was unidirectional, implying that culture change went from the "mestizo culture to identification with White culture" (M. Ramírez, 1998, p. 116). By following this paradigm, there was no way to assess *enculturation*, a construct that measures an individual's "process of socialization (or resocialization) into and maintenance of the heritage culture norms" (Cano & Castillo, 2010, p. 222). The ARSMA-II (Cuellar, Arnold, & Maldonado, 1995) meant to be more inclusive but still fell short according to many Mexican American researchers. Their criticism was that it did not account for bicognitive and bicultural development or other expressions of multicultural adaptability and personality development. M. Ramírez (1998), a proponent of mestizo psychology, the bicognitive development of Mexican Americans (M. Ramírez & Castañeda, 1974), and the power of biculturalism (M. Ramírez, Cox, & Castañeda, 1977), believed that it was possible to have multicultural orientations via different socialization processes. Specific to this discussion on acculturation from a holistic perspective for Latinas/os is the Multicultural/Multiracial Experience Inventory (M. Ramírez, 1998), a tool for assessing behavior based on worldview and accounting for differing values, attitudes, and behaviors among family members. He labeled this an *expansionist model*.

Items from the Multicultural/Multiracial Experience Inventory were based on premises of life-span development, inclusionary experiences of family and societal relations, and assumed multicultural and multiracial orientations to life. M. Ramírez's (1998) items inquired about early life experiences, cross-cultural comfort and discomfort, personal development goals, self-awareness, influential adults, school environments, and so forth. Inherent in the items was attention to barriers to multicultural/multiracial development and orientations, which were often overlooked in acculturation scales.

Case Scenario Analysis

Using David as an example, we might learn that he grew up in multicultural and multiracial neighborhoods and attended schools that had a multicultural mix of students but likely primarily White teachers and administrators. As a 17-year old adolescent, David is at another optimal point of human development—cognitively, emotionally, and in relation to his identity formation. He is aware of how he has seen discrimination and racism against his parents and in society, and by extension against himself. In the brief scenario, David's parents emerge as likely influential adults, but he is also frustrated by their giving in to others who disrespect them. If not examined fully, this frustration could be turned outward and result in David separating himself from White adults (a marginalization strategy); lashing out at them, as he did in the classroom; and even disrespecting his parents.

The scenario also illustrates that David and his parents are maintaining their cultural heritage and working within the larger society but with different behaviors based on some differences in values, attitudes, and life experiences. It is impossible for ethnic and racial minorities not to engage in the larger White society even though they are not overtly welcomed or appreciated. To this end, Berry's model of acculturation strategies is most appropriate to the scenario. The framework includes attitudinal and behavioral strategies toward integration, assimilation, marginalization, and segregation (Berry, 1997, 2003) toward one's group and toward the larger society. Generally speaking, the expected behavior is for the other, be this an immigrant or ethnic minority individual, to engage in assimilation or integration strategies. The individuals manage their transition and fit in.

There may be another way of viewing David's acculturation process. Because he was born in the United States, he is bicultural. Now consider David's acculturation options and strategies. David could choose to enculturate himself into his Puerto Rican family culture by only hanging out with other Puerto Ricans, reverting to speaking primarily Spanish, and choosing to attend a university on the island of Puerto Rico. In so doing, he would intentionally be responding to messages of the larger White society of exclusion versus multiculturalism. Over time, David might have different experiences that cause him to see the larger society as truly multicultural and his cultural heritage and upbringing as assets at work and in relationships. He would continue to be proud of his Puerto Rican identity; understand the dilemma his parents faced as marginalized, underappreciated individuals; and perhaps marry someone not Puerto Rican.

Assessing Acculturation

The review *Acculturation* addresses acculturation theory, measurement, and applied research (Chung, Organista, & Marín, 2003). Research findings were reported for acculturation status as it relates to ethnic identity, changes in cultural values, differences in acculturation processes for same-family members, mental health and physical well-being or distress, depression, alcohol use, and other health risks. Individual researchers work from different acculturation constructs and methodological approaches and perhaps categorize Latinas/os in broad strokes. Conceptualizing acculturation for Latinas/os as a unidimensional versus multidimensional and multilinear process ignores the complexity of the ecological framework that informs change and personal development across differing geographical settings and life experiences.

In spite of the plethora of studies examining acculturation as a multidimensional process of change, Zane and Mak (2003) concluded that more work is required to deconstruct the concept into "specific psychological elements" (p. 58). They wondered how help seeking or the preponderance of severe mental health disorders may relate to acculturation status. Like M. Ramírez (1998), Zane and Mak acknowledged the importance of context, value changes, preferences, and other behavioral changes resulting from contact, length of time in the United States, the generation status of one's parents, and so forth.

Many psychologists have investigated the relation between acculturation and ethnic identity, sex role attitudes, and the role of language in multigenerational homes, particularly for immigrant and U.S.-born individuals. Specific to the focus on identity is the Multigroup Ethnic Identity Measure developed by Phinney (1992) and used with many immigrant and U.S.-born adolescents and adults. Similar to acculturation, ethnic identity involves change from retaining and identifying with one's identity of heritage to adapting to or identifying with the dominant culture or evolving a new culture (Phinney, 2003) and sense of identity. Of course, this is not a unidirectional process; developing a culturally congruent identity for Latinos has many pitfalls along the way. Latino identity in all of its complexities is discussed more fully in Chapter 4.

Acculturative Stress

Adapting to change; learning how to navigate a new context and culture; and negotiating new and unfamiliar circumstances, language, relationships, and economics all contribute to personal and family stress. Discussions about the intersections between acculturative stressors and the acculturation process (Arredondo-Dowd, 1981; Miranda, Bilot, Peluso, Berman, & Van Meek, 2006; Santiago-Rivera, Arredondo, & Gallardo-Cooper, 2002; Smart & Smart, 1995) have introduced various considerations, particularly in reference to an immigrant or an immigrant family facing multiple life changes simultaneously.

Stressors can be emotional, psychological, or physical. Immigrants experience loss and grief (Arredondo-Dowd, 1981) related to three phases of the immigration experience: premigration, when one has plans, expectations, and goals; migration as it relates to the journey of leaving one's home country and traveling to the United States, which is not always a safe journey; and postmigration, the period in which acculturative stressors will manifest. Inherent in the loss and grief process are emotions of loss and mourning. Borrowing from stage models of loss and grief, Arredondo-Dowd (1981) also suggested the following:

- Immigrants are in shock initially about their life change even if they have anticipated making it; individual differences can be anticipated for children, adolescents, and adults, particularly if not everyone wanted to leave the home country. In Latino families, as has been discussed, parents make decisions for the collective. Unfamiliarity with the environment and limitations on accessing familiar foods and seeing family and friends begin to introduce emotional stress and confusion.
- Immigrants struggle to fit in and speak the language. Adolescents struggle to make friends, and parents experience pressures to find well-paying employment and relocate to a safe neighborhood. In this phase there are multiple stressors for children and parents alike, at times leading to emotional reactions such as frustration, fear, and anger within the family that cannot be soothed.

- Immigrants accept that the family is here to stay. Although families encounter discrimination, less than ideal living conditions, demands to work two jobs, and so forth, it is generally less desirable or perhaps even impossible to return to their country of origin. Thus, adaptation or some form of acculturation ensues.

Scholars have also indicated that acculturative stress may be mediated by the premigration experience in the home country, education level, and the response of the host country (P. Arredondo, 1986; Arredondo-Dowd, 1981; Miranda et al., 2006). Berry's (2003) conceptualization of dynamics in the acculturation process indicates that strategies from the receiving culture that provide an ambiance of multiculturalism, melting pot (assimilation), segregation, or exclusion will influence the newcomer's adaptation strategies of integration, assimilation, separation, or marginalization.

Inherent in this discussion is the need for counselors to pay attention to the different types of stressors that may affect family members. For children, it may be bullying or difficulty learning; for adolescents, it may be peer pressure by other Latino adolescents who look down on them because of their outsider status; and for adults, situations will vary, but day-to-day anxiety and dissonance has to be expected. Many adult immigrants experience pressure to support family in their home country as well as themselves and the family members who came with them. The amount of *remesas* (remittances) sent by Latinos to families in their home country has slowly declined as the economic situation in the United States has declined, disproportionately affecting Latinos (M. H. López, Livingston, & Kochhar, 2009). M. H. López et al. (2009) reported that "among Hispanic immigrants who sent remittances in the last two years, more than seven-in-ten (71%) say they sent less in the past year compared with the prior year" (p. 2). The primary reason for this had to do with their financial situation. This is discussed more fully in Chapter 6 on employment and economics.

Acculturative Stress With New Experiences

Changes in environments—from country to country, home community to college, home to a work assignment in another state, home to a new neighborhood, one's own home to a rental—are all stressors that affect individuals and the unity of the entire family. Keeping in mind that Latinos have a collectivist worldview reflected in values of *familismo* (interdependence with, closeness to, and loyalty to family), counselors need to anticipate that what may seem like normative developmental experiences for adolescents, young adults, and adults may still introduce feelings of upset, unhappiness, and distress. A few examples follow, and managing and guiding individuals' experiences and transitions as a result of acculturative stress is discussed in the later chapters on counseling interventions.

Case Scenario

Rosa graduated from the University of Arizona in her hometown of Tucson and accepted admission to Harvard Medical School. Clearly a talented student, she successfully navigated her first year, but after returning from a 6-week visit with her *familia* she was second-guessing her situation. Yes, the classes were demanding and she worked hard, but the academics were not her real concern. Rosa, an attractive, light-skinned, fair-haired, blue-eyed woman, was reexperiencing the stress of not fitting in among primarily White medical peers. She found herself once again explaining why she wanted a field experience in a Latino agency. "People don't believe I am Mexican American and bilingual," she reported to her private practice counselor. Rosa also felt guilty and selfish about being so far away from home and not available to assist with child-rearing responsibilities as she once had. She expressed concerns about not fulfilling her role as the oldest daughter and of neglecting the *familia*. Rosa's stress initially manifested as vague stomachaches, and with no clear medical explanation indicated, the physician recommended that she speak to a psychologist. Rosa was aware of the clinic setting at the university but did not want her peers and professors to know that she was asking for help. Rather, she networked with new colleagues at community-based Latino clinics and connected with a Latina therapist.

Ethnic minority scholars indicate that ethnic match in counseling is not generally necessary, and in some situations (Maramba & Nagayama Hall, 2002; Shin et al., 2005) ethnic minority clients prefer a White counselor (Alvarez & Helms, 2001). However, socially and culturally aware individuals such as Rosa recognize barriers in the environment. She is in a unique life circumstance and going through an acculturation process.

With respect to different forms of acculturative stress, a culturally responsive counselor needs to take into account the multiple adjustments Rosa is experiencing. She has moved from a familiar geographical area and its desert warmth to the cold Northeast; is experiencing the loss of family connectedness and the ensuing guilt about not doing enough for the *familia*; is perhaps seeing people who may look like her but do not have the day-to-day Mexican and Native American familiarity she is used to seeing in Tucson; is hearing Spanish being spoken, but not regularly, and does not have other cultural comforts close by; and is experiencing pressures to succeed academically in a White world in which few Latinas/os can be found. Rosa is a member of an underrepresented group in medical school, and as with other students, managing the culture of this educational context and the pressure to succeed is demanding and perhaps a strain on her physical and mental well-being.

This analysis is in no way meant to portray Rosa as helpless or to say that she faces the same challenges of Latina immigrants with few resources and children to worry about as well; rather, the objective is to point out that counselors need to consider the different situations in which the framework of acculturation can be used to assist a Latina managing multiple life transitions. Counselors also need to recognize that the family is often considered the primary buffer (Saldaina, 1994) in situations of stress, but given the distance between Rosa and her nuclear family, the counselor and Rosa will have to identify other coping resources that can contribute to more equilibrium for her.

Concluding Thoughts

One goal of this chapter has been to describe the dynamics introduced by acculturation processes and how these differentially affect individuals in the same family. Throughout, the scenarios have illustrated the complexity of thought and emotions and acculturative stressors for Latinos in different contexts. It is possible that individuals move in and out of one of the four acculturation strategies—integration, assimilation, marginalization, and segregation—depending on their life situations. It might seem easier for Rosa and David to assimilate and "be American," but from what was described in the case scenarios, this seems unlikely. It behooves counselors to learn more about the benefits of enculturation processes and how these may facilitate individual Latinos' sense of self-esteem and identity congruence.

Culturally responsive counselors

- are aware of circumstances that put families at risk and the "different forms and degrees of stress they experience (e.g., psychosocial, acculturation, trauma)" (Santiago-Rivera et al., 2002, p. 68)
- recognize situations of acculturative stress
- recognize that acculturation is not a short-term process but can be a life-changing experience.

• • •

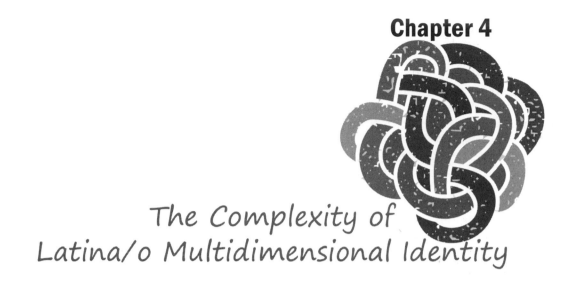

Chapter 4

The Complexity of Latina/o Multidimensional Identity

A más riesgo, más provecho.

The greater the risk, the greater the gain.

(Rovira, 1984, p. 159)

• • •

Objectives

- To review Latina/o identity development models and the impact on one's sense of self.
- To examine self-referent labels of identity and recognize the diversity inherent between and within groups of Latinas/os.
- To understand the complexity and multidimensionality of Latina/o identity.

Sabías que/Did you know that . . .

- Latina/o identity development is an integral process that includes the individual, family, group, and community.
- Latina/o identity is inextricably linked to religion, spirituality, and faith.
- The intersectionality of dimensions of Latino identity is complex and multifaceted.
- Acculturation plays a role in Latinas/os' concept of self.
- Political consciousness is important in Latina/o gender and sexuality identity development.

• • •

Case Scenario

Julia was a 22-year-old first-generation Latina college student in the Southwest who was about to graduate from college with a bachelor's degree in nursing. She identified her ethnic heritage as Mexican American. She stated that the primary language spoken at home was Spanish, and although she preferred to speak English outside of the home, Julia often would switch to speaking Spanish in session when she was experiencing particularly difficult emotions. She further identified as lesbian and as a feminist as well as reported a strong Catholic identity. She shared with the counselor that she had recently come to terms with her own sexual identity and was in a committed relationship, though she still struggled with how this identity fit within her Catholic beliefs and those of her church. She also shared that she was in the process of coming out to family. Julia described how she had told her mother about her sexuality about 2 months prior to attending counseling, sharing that her mother "broke down and cried" when Julia had come out to her as a lesbian. Julia expressed sadness and disappointment that her mother was struggling with Julia's sexuality as well as expressed pain that her mother would consistently mention their Catholic beliefs and her fear that Julia would not go to heaven. Her mother had requested that Julia not come out to other family members, which caused Julia to feel a sense of rejection and isolation. Julia shared that her partner, whom she identified as Caucasian, was having difficulty understanding how Julia's mother could react in such a way, as her own parents had known for years about her sexual identity and had been very accepting. Julia reported that she had not yet told her mother about her partner but was worried that her mother would react negatively to her having not only a female partner but a White one. Julia feared that her mother would not accept her partner.

Counselor Dilemma

You are a counselor at a local community center. When you hear Julia's narrative, what more do you feel you need to learn about her situation and concerns? What values seem to impact her presenting concerns? How do Julia's intersecting identities play a role in her internal conflict? In her conflict with family? With her partner? In what ways does this narrative speak to identity concerns? How do her conflicts impact her sense of self and her sense of empowerment? In what ways might she be able to resolve these identity conflicts?

Latina/o Identity

Latina/o identity is complex and multidimensional. When counselors are working with this population, they need to have a thorough understanding of the evolution of Latina/o identity, as well as the intersectionality of ethnic identity and other categories of identification, including race, gender, sexual orientation, religion/spirituality, social class, and so forth. Not only do Latinas/os use various terms to self-identify, but these terms emerge from sociocultural and historical contexts and have an impact on one's sense of self. Furthermore, the Latina/o population is not homogenous; rather, it is very heterogeneous, with many differences both between and within groups. As was mentioned in Chapter 3, acculturation plays a role in Latina/o identity as identities are merged with the dominant culture. Keep in mind this acculturation process as we discuss identity models and dimensions of identity in the chapter.

Culturally Sensitive Identity Models

To begin to understand the complexity of Latina/o identity it is first necessary to have knowledge of various culturally sensitive identity development models. Traditional identity models, such as Erik Erikson's (1963) psychosocial development model, which proposes stages in which identity task-related events occur throughout the lifetime, have been found to be sexist (Chrisler & Smith, 2004; Messer & McWilliams, 2003) and to lack cultural sensitivity (McGoldrick & Carter, 1998). The use of culturally sensitive identity models allows counselors to more readily consider the complex and dynamic systems in which Latina/o identity develops. These models also help to convey the importance of culture, ethnicity, and race in Latina/o identity, as well as other identity statuses that contribute to one's dynamic understanding of self.

Dimensions of Personal Identity Model

P. Arredondo and Glauner (1992) presented the dimensions of personal identity model as a way to view individuals holistically and to acknowledge the interconnection between various identity statuses (see Figure 4.1). This model includes three domains under which multiple identity constructs fall, thus allowing an individual to determine which identities hold the most salience and importance at any one place and time. Thus, context is important when considering which identities may play a more explicit role.

Dimension A includes those identities into which one is born or that remain fairly constant. It includes age, culture, ethnicity, gender, race, language, physical disability, social class, and sexual orientation. Many of these identities are visible and are often the center of bias, stereotypes, prejudice, discrimination, and oppression. People may hold positive and negative attitudes and beliefs about these identities, which can impact how they view themselves and may affect their self-esteem and sense of

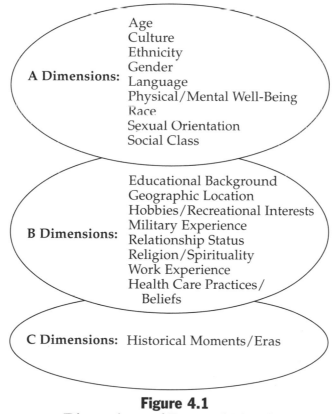

A Dimensions:
Age
Culture
Ethnicity
Gender
Language
Physical/Mental Well-Being
Race
Sexual Orientation
Social Class

B Dimensions:
Educational Background
Geographic Location
Hobbies/Recreational Interests
Military Experience
Relationship Status
Religion/Spirituality
Work Experience
Health Care Practices/Beliefs

C Dimensions: Historical Moments/Eras

Figure 4.1
Dimensions of Personal Identity

Source. P. Arredondo and Glauner (1992).

personal empowerment. Counselors must become aware of their biases and stereo-types around these identities, as they can impact the services provided to clients. For example, a counselor may hold a stereotype of Latinas/os as having a darker pheno-type, speaking Spanish, being from a lower socioeconomic status, and being Catho-lic. Although this description may fit some Latinas/os, there is great variability both within and between groups, and it definitely does not fit all Latinas/os. Thus, this stereotype could negatively impact the therapeutic relationship.

Dimension B consists of less visible identities that could be conceptualized as developmental, as they are much more fluid and allow for more choice. This do-main includes educational background, income, geographic location, marital sta-tus, religion, work history, military experience, citizenship status, and hobbies/recreational interests. It is incumbent on the counselor to thoroughly assess these, as they could be ignored if the counselor focuses primarily on the A dimensions. Furthermore, the identities in this dimension appear to result from interaction of the A dimensions and the C dimensions. For example, a Latina born in the late 1980s might view her career options and resources quite differently than a Latina born in the early 1950s, especially as a result of the civil rights and women's rights movements. The Latina born in the late 1980s may not only see higher education as a real possibility but recognize the many educational resources in place that she might access to make this possibility a reality.

The impact of the C dimension clearly has importance for how one's identities are lived. The C dimension includes historical moments or eras that occur through-out the lifetime. This dimension clearly speaks to the context of and external influ-ences on one's life experiences. Thus, the individual's environment or context in-fluences how he or she identifies. For example, immigration is a historical moment that impacts individuals and families on many levels, including in terms of their sense of identity and self-confidence. This model encourages counselors to view their clients within multiple contexts, allowing for the identification of strengths as well as challenges. Understanding the many factors that affect an immigrant from Chile, including race and a unique Spanish dialect, might help the counselor to provide appropriate services, understand reasons behind the decision to immi-grate (which might include historical, social, political, and economic reasons), and reinforce and enhance coping techniques.

Latino Dimensions of Personal Identity Model
P. Arredondo and Santiago-Rivera (2000) built on the personal identity model in re-sponse to the need for counselors to be mindful of the heterogeneity of the Latina/o population. They contended that this model can help counselors refrain from engag-ing in the stereotyping of various Latina/o groups by acknowledging varying so-ciopolitical histories and relationships as well as different socioeconomic conditions and resources. This model provides another way to conceptualize Latinas/os and their families. In the A dimension are included the following identity concepts: age/generational status, culture/Euro/mestizo/indigenous, gender/machismo/*mari-anismo*, language/regional accents, physical/mental status, phenotype, sexual ori-entation, and social class. In the B dimension are included acculturation status, citi-zen status, educational background, geographic location, family relationship status/*familismo*, religion/spirituality/folk beliefs, work experience, health care practices/beliefs, identity status (self-referent labels), and economic status. Personal/familial/historical eras/events and sociopolitical forces are included in the C dimension.

As can be seen, additional culturally specific concepts are included to encourage counselors to think more broadly and holistically when working with Latinas/os. P. Arredondo and Santiago-Rivera (2000) suggested that counselors can facilitate discussion and understanding of these aspects of identity among Latino families. Furthermore, considering these multiple identities can raise counselors' awareness of working with both the individual and the family unit at the same time. Counselors need to recognize that different identities may be prevalent and important depending on when clients present for counseling and the context in which they do so; thus, ethnicity should not be the only factor that counselors address. For example, a 15-year-old Latino adolescent with a mother of Mexican descent and a father of Puerto Rican descent may present with issues associated with acculturation level, gender expectations, language preference, phenotype, and generational status. Another concern this teenager may present with is a biracial/bicultural identity. Counselors may need to respond to the entire Latino family to best meet the adolescent's needs.

The Bioecological Approach

Bronfenbrenner and Morris's (1998) bioecological approach poses five systems in the environment that influence a person's development and suggests that one cannot fully understand development without considering how each level impacts a person. The five systems Bronfenbrenner and Morris (1998) discuss are the microsystem, mesosystem, exosystem, macrosystem, and the chronosystem. Although this model is not specific to Latina/o culture, it does have implications for Latino identity development. One's microsystem is made up of the immediate environment, including one's family, school or work, peers, church group, and neighborhood gathering places. Most important to understand about this level is that a person helps to construct the microsystem, actively shaping his or her world. For Latinas/os, this system might include not only the immediate family with which they live but also the extended family, which might further include *compadres* and *comadres* (coparents). The mesosystem acts to connect the different aspects of the microsystem, and it recognizes the direct and indirect factors that bind people to one another. Among the Latina/o population, the mesosystem might work to connect the family with those from their religious or spiritual community. The exosystem consists of broader societal institutions, for example social welfare services, mass media, legal services, and friends of family. The exosystem can immediately impact personal development and influences how the microsystem and mesosystem function. For example, Latinas/os may utilize social services to gain access to medical care for their families. The macrosystem consists of the larger cultural context and its influence on the individual. This includes the government, political value systems, and religious value systems. The chronosystem involves the relationship of time and environmental events on one's development. This might include historical events, such as immigration, or more gradual historical alterations or changes, such as changes in the numbers of Latinas/os attending institutions of higher education. Using this model helps the counselor understand the context in which the client functions and the various influences on Latina/o identity development. For instance, not only is *la familia* (the family) a vital part of the lives of Latinas/os, but so too is the neighborhood in which one lives and grows up; access to quality education and health care; utilization of community resources; and the cultural context, which may or may not be welcoming and inclusive. Such influences can impact how Latinas/os view themselves in their world, having myriad effects on their self-esteem and self-efficacy as well as their quality of life.

Mestizo Identity Development Model

Mestizo models of identity development address the impact of the colonization of indigenous populations of Latin America, South America, and the Caribbean by

European conquistadors. *Mestizo* is a term denoting the confluence of indigenous and European cultural heritages. This identity is marked by the positive manner in which diversity and pluralism are viewed (M. Ramírez, 1998). The dominant belief is that many cultures can coexist and be synthesized into one's identity and personality. This pluralistic identity is seen as ideal, one in which loyalty can be maintained not only to the original culture but also to other cultures and lifestyles. M. Ramírez's theory makes many assumptions, including that (a) ecology influences personality and impacts how a person develops and functions through physical and social environments; (b) personality is influenced by culture and history; (c) physiology and genetics are important in personality development and functioning; (d) spirituality plays a large role in identity development, influencing the individual's search for purpose in life; (e) family and community influence the development of identity and personality; (f) development and functioning are affected by economic and political forces; and (g) the process of coping with life's challenges and problems impacts the person's identity development and establishes the person's orientation toward diversity.

M. Ramírez (1998) posited four developmental stages of mestizo identity development: the early childhood years, the middle childhood years, adulthood, and maturity. In early childhood, children are encouraged to develop strong family connections and a strong family identity. It is expected that children will inherit various talents, abilities, and characteristics from both of their parents' families and will carry on the historical stories of the families of their parents. Children in this stage are expected to take on gender-appropriate characteristics and roles. In this stage, biracial or multiracial children may experience difficulties in terms of racial ambivalence, as they may be attempting to merge racial and ethnic identity labels that are much more complex than the labels their parents may use. M. Ramírez argued that ethnic and national cultural identification is important to both the family and the community; thus, children are taught that rejecting national and cultural identities is similar to rejecting the self. During middle childhood, peer groups play an important role in continued explorations of ethnic/racial identity, with peer groups becoming an extension of the family. Acceptance by the peer group is a key part of this stage. Thus, group identity continues to grow. It is during this stage that older peers and relatives often become role models.

During adulthood, peer groups and the community continue to play a role in identity development; however, as the individual moves into a committed, intimate relationship, family once again becomes central. This occurs as the individual becomes a parent and begins to socialize children into the culture. This serves to renew the bond that the individual has with family ties, as well as with the community and the national, ethnic, or cultural group. It is during this time that a person of mixed heritage may experience difficulties with acceptance in intimate relationships. This can be the case especially in environments in which there might be conflicts in value systems around interracial or intercultural relationships. As an elder, an individual may become a mentor, advisor, or historian during the maturity stage. In this role the individual influences children, adolescents, and sometimes adults to identify with the family, community, cultural, and national groups. As adults often have a strong spiritual orientation later in life, older adults may take on the role of counselor or folk healer.

Difficulties in identity development arise when there is an increase in industrialism and urbanization, as well as economic and political problems. These may cause the extended family to separate as family members look for better opportunities. This separation can negatively impact parents' ability to pass on family and community history, which is vital to the mestizo identity development of children.

Also, generational disparities often develop between parents and children around language, values, worldview, and lifestyle. This causes multicultural or multiracial stress among families, especially when marginalization is a real issue in individuals having to choose between their mestizo identity and that of the dominant culture. In this case identity crises take place as individuals may believe they have to assimilate into the European or dominant culture, thus potentially losing their mestizo connection. An additional factor that is salient in the mestizo culture is the variation in phenotype; it can be common for people within the same family to look very different from one another in terms of features and skin color and hair texture. Some family members who have more European features and a lighter skin tone may enjoy privileges and power that their darker, more indigenous-appearing family members may not.

Chicano/Latino Ethnic Identity Model

A. S. Ruiz (1990) proposed a model of ethnic identity development that addresses the marginality that many Latinas/os face and its impact on their mental health. This model includes five stages that directly address ethnic identity and the thoughts and emotions that accompany the development of this identity. Stages 1–3 focus primarily on ethnic identity conflicts. Stage 4 addresses psychological treatment, and Stage 5 centers on problem resolution.

Stage 1, which A. S. Ruiz (1990) called Causal, is replete with negative attitudes and beliefs about one's own ethnic identity. These negative attitudes may be relayed from parents and family, as well as from the larger culture in which the person develops. Ruiz stated that this stage often lacks positive affirmations of one's ethnic identity. He noted a number of variables that might contribute to ethnic identity confusion, such as rejection from others within one's ethnic identity, lack of familiarity with one's ethnic heritage and culture, lack of exposure to one's ethnic community, and traumatic or humiliating events that center on one's ethnicity. In this stage, a Latina/o might harbor a lack of self-worth based on his or her ethnic identity.

In Stage 2, Cognitive, Latinas/os have come to associate their ethnic identity with prejudice and poverty. They may believe that assimilation is necessary to escape from these conditions and do not take into consideration the ideas of biculturalism or acculturation. Therefore, Latinas/os in this stage might attempt to distance themselves from their cultural, ethnic, and linguistic heritage to obtain success in the dominant culture.

In Stage 3, or Consequence, one rejects various expressions of ethnic identity, including skin color, language, customs, and name. Latinas/os in this stage may perceive their ethnic identity as inferior and feel embarrassed by their accent, neighborhood, ethnic appearance, and so forth. This can result in a fragmentation of ethnic identity that leads to feelings of estrangement from the community, possible denial of one's cultural heritage, and identification with a different ethnic identity.

In Stage 4, which A. S. Ruiz (1990) termed Working Through, Latinas/os experience distress from the internal conflict that arises from the ethnic identity fragmentation. The alien ethnic identity no longer works for them, and they may be more willing to enter into counseling, in which they may be open to exploring their ethnic identity difficulties. It is in this stage that Ruiz suggested that counselors aid Latina/o clients in facing their negative attitudes, self-hatred, and stereotypes. Counseling in this stage helps to facilitate the integration of the Latina/o ethnic identity into the client's whole identity. This process then leads to a healing process of increased ethnic consciousness and the reintegration and reclaiming of the previously rejected ethnic identity.

In Stage 5, Successful Resolution, Latinas/os experience improved self-esteem as they are now accepting of their culture, ethnicity, and self, viewing these aspects as positive rather than negative. Their ethnic identity is now seen as a strength and a resource. Furthermore, Latinas/os in this stage are more likely to engage with others in their ethnic community, finding pride in their ethnic identification.

Multiple Heritage Identity Development Model

Many scholars have begun addressing multiple identities (D'Andrea & Arredondo, 2000), multiple heritages (Henriksen & Paladino, 2009), and biracial and multiracial identities (Wehrly, Kenney, & Kenney, 1999). It has been posited that multiple-heritage individuals experience development and life differently from those who identify with monoracial/cultural majority and ethnic minority groups (Henriksen & Paladino, 2009). Multiple-heritage persons develop on the margins of multiple races or cultures and have difficulty fully fitting into the groups of their many heritages. For example, a young female adolescent growing up in a family with one parent of Guatemalan heritage and another of European heritage might have difficulty with language issues, especially if she is not fluent in Spanish and therefore cannot communicate adequately with her grandmother, who recently moved into the family home. This girl may feel caught between two cultures or heritages and forced to live predominantly within one of her cultural heritages. This lack of fluency in Spanish may also keep her from having full access to the cultural heritage of her Guatemalan background. In addition to feeling as if they are on the margins of their cultural heritage, multiple-heritage individuals may experience issues related to phenotype, looking like neither of their parents. Thus, individuals could consistently be told that they look like neither of their parents or that they have an ambiguous appearance. This can be frustrating for individuals, as they may feel that they always have to explain their cultural heritage to others.

Although people of multiple-heritage backgrounds face many challenges, they also have strengths on which a counselor can help them build. Depending on the degree to which individuals feel comfortable with their race, ethnicity, and culture, these strengths may include the ability to fluidly navigate cultures and environments, communication and social skill sets to negotiate with people from various backgrounds (Henriksen & Paladino, 2009), flexibility, a positive sense of uniqueness, and an ability to be more open and sensitive to others (Wehrly et al., 1999). In fact, the development of a bicultural identity may be a healthy resolution to acculturative conflicts (Miranda & Umhoefer, 1998). Bicultural individuals seem to function more easily in both cultural worlds.

The multiple heritage identity model consists of six stages through which a multiple-heritage person vacillates (Henriksen & Paladino, 2009). Although this model does not speak specifically to the Latina/o population, it can be used to conceptualize the experiences and identity development of Latinas/os from multiple heritages. The six stages or periods are neutrality, acceptance, awareness, experimentation, transition, and recognition. *Neutrality* occurs prior to people becoming aware of or accepting their racial and/or ethnic differences. Individuals in this period may lack awareness of how their race and ethnicity impact their social interactions with people from other backgrounds. It is in the *acceptance* period when family members have the greatest impact, as their statements form the basis for individuals accepting that they have a racial and ethnic heritage. In this period, individuals may realize that they are racially and ethnically different but may not be certain that this is a problem or even know what it means to be different. Individuals may experience negative attitudes from others who are not members of their family regarding their race and ethnicity. For example, a person of Caribbean and Colombian heritage might have family members from one side of the family encourage him or her to deny or reject the other side of his or her heritage.

The *awareness* stage is marked by individuals beginning to understand the meaning of being racially and ethnically different from others. Individuals in this period often experience interactions with others that result in their feeling isolated because of not identifying wholly with a reference group. Among Latinas/os, this might manifest in being denied entrance into a community group because of being viewed as not Mexican enough, not Cuban enough, and so on. Situational factors lead individuals into the *experimentation* period. In this stage, individuals attempt to fit into one part of their racial/ethnic identity to feel a connection with others. Furthermore, not only are individuals attempting to fit in during this period, but they are also actively trying to determine their own racial/ethnic group identity, along with other identities, such as their sexual identity, religious or spiritual identity, and so forth. It is in this stage that individuals may connect with the racial/ethnic groups that hold more similar interests.

During the *transition* period, people begin to recognize that they cannot identify with any one particular racial/ethnic group to the exclusion of their other heritages. This comes from the inner conflict they may feel and from a search for racial/ethnic identity. Individuals may move toward a new recognition of self that includes all of their multiple heritages. In the final period, *recognition*, individuals may come to decide and embrace who they are racially, ethnically, sexually, and in other ways and assume their family heritages. It is in this stage that individuals no longer feel that they have to choose between their identities and instead feel proud of their multiple heritages. They may begin to self-identify as biracial/bicultural or multiracial/multicultural.

Case Scenario Analysis

Let's return to Julia's case for a moment. A counselor might be inclined to address merely the A dimensions of personal identity (P. Arredondo & Glauner, 1992) that Julia mentions in the session. However, more assessment might be needed to better understand the greater context in which Julia is engaging. For example, how does she view her Catholic identity? What values and beliefs accompany this identity? How does she make sense of the intersection of her Catholic identity and her Latina and lesbian identities? Julia clearly speaks about her mother's fears, her partner's lack of understanding, and of her own experience. However, what about the greater context in which she lives? What other forces may be impacting her self-esteem, as well as her sense of rejection and isolation? How might this impact her sense of self? As mentioned in Chapter 2, Latina lesbians often exist on the margins of the family (Anzaldúa, 1987). How might this play out in Julia's family life? How does she understand this as a real possibility that she may not be able to resolve, and how would it affect her? Furthermore, how does acculturation play a role in Julia's life circumstances and identity development?

In this case, the counselor began by validating Julia's struggles, noting the complexity of identity issues that played a role in her distress. This aided in Julia feeling as though she was understood and accepted for her whole self, which allowed her to begin to address the internal conflict she still held around her sexual identity and religious beliefs. Julia also noted her role as the eldest child and the family's expectations for her. She was of the belief that these were cultural expectations that came from her Mexican American background. Julia acknowledged identifying as bicultural, as she accepted many feminist attitudes and beliefs that she perceived were not accepted in her Latina culture, though she also valued and respected her Latina culture and felt a sense of pride in her Mexican American identity. The counselor also infused spirituality into treatment, often using spiritual concepts to help Julia reconceptualize and make sense of her own complex identity issues. Julia expressed gratitude that she had a place in which to explore and honor these identity concepts. The counselor also normalized the difficulty with which some families take the news of a child identifying as a sexual minority, providing education about family processes and resources that Julia might access to gain additional support.

Julia began to explore her own assumptions and biases that contributed to her difficulties. Treatment focused on empowering Julia to integrate her identities. Julia located and began interacting with a church community that was affirming of lesbian, gay, bisexual, transgender, and queer individuals, which helped her to start integrating her sexual identity and religious beliefs. As Julia came to accept her own multiple identities and develop a language with which to discuss them, she was able to better communicate with her mother about these issues. This helped to improve the relationship between Julia and her mother, who eventually came to accept that Julia's sexual identity was not a passing phase. Her mother eventually became interested in meeting Julia's partner, who was also beginning to better understand Julia's family difficulties.

Self-Referent Labels and Identities

According to the U.S. Census Bureau (2010c), approximately 50.5 million Hispanics or Latinas/os reside in the United States, totaling about 16% of the population. Of this number, 31.8 million identify as being of Mexican descent, 4.6 million as Puerto Rican, and 1.8 million as Cuban. Approximately 12.3 million Latinas/os in the United States identify as Dominican, Central American, South American, or of another Hispanic or Latina/o origin. Although people use these terms to categorize themselves, these categorizations were determined by the government for the purposes of collecting census data. These categorizations in and of themselves do not speak to the myriad of ways in which Latinas/os self-identify, which vary according to a number of contextual factors, including region; changes in historical, political, and social contexts; as well as whether these individuals consider themselves to be biracial (Comas-Díaz, 2001; Hurtado, 1997; Schutte, 2000). One's choice of label often reflects the honoring of heritage, in the sense of both traditions as well as cultural traits (Malott, 2009).

To add to the complexity of self-identification, Golash-Boza (2006) found that Latina/o Americans who experience discrimination are much less likely to hyphenate their identity, preferring to use panethnic identity labels. She contended that this comes from having the experience that others do not view them as Americans or even as hyphenated Americans. Not only does the experience of discrimination affect how one uses labels to self-identify, but so too do geographic location and generational status (Kiang, Perreira, & Fuligni, 2011). Second-generation adolescents are more likely than first-generation adolescents to use a hyphenated American identity and less likely to identify using panethnic labels. Therefore, it is necessary to have a basic understanding of the various labels Latinas/os use to identify themselves. This use of terminology can provide clues about how Latino clients identify and warrants more assessment to better understand the meaning Latinos make of these identity labels.

The terms *Hispanic* and *Latina/o* are used interchangeably in much of the literature on multiculturalism (Santiago-Rivera, Arredondo, & Gallardo-Cooper, 2002). Approximately 51% of Latinas/os have no preference for one term—*Latino* or

Hispanic—over the other (P. Taylor, Lopez, Martinez, & Velasco, 2012). However, among those who do have a preference, more people prefer the term *Hispanic*. Although these terms are used interchangeably, they have entirely different roots and meanings. *Hispanic* is a generic term that was developed by the U.S. government for census purposes, as a way to classify people based on a common language, namely Spanish (G. Marín & Marín, 1991; Mize & Delgado, 2012; National Coalition of Hispanic Health and Human Services Organizations, 1986). It has been used as a way to classify large groups of people from various backgrounds, including Mexicans, Puerto Ricans, Cubans, Central Americans, South Americans, and Spanish speakers from other backgrounds. However, many people assume that *Hispanic* racial category and that individuals from each of these backgrounds have a similar culture (Santiago-Rivera et al., 2002). Falicov (1998) suggested that use of this term is actually related to internalized colonization, as use of the term is maintained by groups who are politically conservative and hold racially and ethnically biased views of the superiority of European ancestry. Furthermore, the term *Hispanic* may have little meaning, as most individuals prefer to identify themselves with their country of origin (Santiago-Rivera et al., 2002). Thus, a label of *Hispanic* may be offensive or wrong for many Latina/o groups.

The term *Latina/o* is often used to refer to people whose heritage is related to Latin America, which encompasses many nationalities and those with indigenous roots (Comas-Díaz, 2001; Falicov, 1998). This term excludes people of European background, such as Spaniards, from being considered ethnic minorities in the United States. Santiago-Rivera et al. (2002) suggested that the use of the term *Latina/o* among people in the United States is indicative of a growing political consciousness and ethnic pride. Furthermore, it has been proposed that the term *Latina/o* is linguistically more appropriate as it refers to gender, whereas the term *Hispanic* is nongendered, which follows the dominant English language use (Shorris, 1992).

LatiNegra/o or Afro-Latinas/os

Both of these terms refer to those with African American and Latina/o parentage. Often Afro-Latinas/os are perceived as Black because of phenotypic presentation and may not be acknowledged as Latina/o. Comas-Díaz (2001) suggested that these terms of identification "avoid[s] the partial or total negation of the Latinness of African Latinos by the Latino community" (p. 119). Afro-Latinas/os experience discrimination on the basis of their combined racial/ethnic identification from both the dominant culture and the Latina/o community.

Mexicans

As noted earlier, individuals of Mexican roots make up the majority of Latinas/os in the United States (U.S. Census Bureau, 2010c). The majority of Mexican Americans live in the Southwest, including Texas, California, Arizona, New Mexico, and Colorado, though there are also established communities in the Midwest. According to the U.S. Census Bureau (2010c), more than half of the Latina/o population in the United States lives in California, Texas, or Florida. A considerable population of Latinas/os also lives in New York. Labels this ethnic group uses to self-identify include *Mexican American, Chicana/o,* and *Xicana/o. Mexican American* is a term used by many individuals who are U.S. citizens but are of Mexican descent. However, this term could be considered unacceptable for describing those who identify not with their Mexican heritage but with more of a Spanish heritage (Comas-Díaz,

2001). *Chicana/o* was originally a pejorative term but was reclaimed and adopted by activists in the Brown Power movement during the 1960s and 1970s. Some may reject this term, as it still may evoke offensive connotations. *Xicana/o* is a term that affirms one's indigenous link to the Aztecs. As the acculturation process takes place, Mexican youth tend to take on additional labels to identify themselves, especially labels of racial identities, whereas prior to acculturation, these youth identify primarily with their national heritage of origin (Holley et al., 2009). In fact, those who identify as Mexican, Mexican American, or Chicano are more likely to use Spanish when speaking with their friends, to come from backgrounds of lower socioeconomic status, and to have higher educational expectations.

Individuals of Mexican descent often can trace their ancestry to those living in states that were once Mexican territory prior to being annexed by the United States. Much of the immigration from Mexico has been historically and inextricably tied to changes in the economy and political environment in the United States (W. Pérez, 2009; Santiago-Rivera et al., 2002), with approximately 1 out of 7 Mexican workers migrating to the United States (Lockhead, 2006). Many have immigrated to the United States in response to the negative economic environment in Mexico and the need for cheap labor in the United States. However, this has historically led to some discontent among the dominant racial and ethnic groups in the United States. Mize and Delgado (2012) cited a history of scapegoating Mexicans for elevated levels of unemployment in the United States. More recently some states have passed laws to curb the access of unauthorized Mexican immigrants to needed resources, thus creating a hostile environment as a deterrent to coming across the southern border without documentation.

Passel (2006) estimated that there are approximately 12 million unauthorized immigrants in the United States. Various misperceptions exist regarding the contribution of unauthorized immigrants to the U.S. economy. These include the perception that they are exploiting the economy, that they weigh down public social services, and that they are criminals (W. Pérez, 2009). However, the research demonstrates otherwise. In fact, unauthorized immigrants from Mexico pay more in taxes than they cost in the use of social services (Lipman, 2006). Unauthorized immigrants from Mexico often live in Latino communities and are protected by family from discovery and deportation (Santiago-Rivera et al., 2002).

Puerto Ricans

Puerto Ricans constitute the second largest Latina/o group in the United States (U.S. Census Bureau, 2010c). Approximately 53% of Puerto Ricans live in the Northeast, primarily in New York, and another 30% live in the South. Puerto Rico became a U.S. territory in 1898 after the Spanish-American War (Santiago-Rivera et al., 2002). Puerto Ricans are U.S. citizens, so they can be drafted into the military, are eligible for federally sponsored programs such as public assistance, and are included in census data. However, Puerto Ricans do not pay U.S. income taxes and are not allowed to participate in mainland elections if they live in Puerto Rico. This citizenship status allows for circular migration to and from Puerto Rico to the United States, a pattern that differs significantly from that of Mexican migration. It has been posited that this circular migration pattern may have a negative impact on Puerto Ricans by interrupting schooling and longer term job opportunities. It might also lead to Puerto Ricans experiencing economic, cultural, linguistic and psychological difficulties, especially in regard to acculturation.

Puerto Ricans might identify with a number of identity labels, including *Boricua, Nuyorican,* and *Rican* (Comas-Díaz, 2001). *Boricua* is a term associated with the history of Puerto Rico as a colonized island and seems to highlight a political identity linked to a Spanish-speaking identity as opposed to an English-speaking one. It is used today as a term of endearment among Puerto Ricans. *Nuyorican* is a label typically used by U.S.-born Puerto Ricans, especially those born in New York. Comas-Díaz (2001) suggested that "some Nuyoricans are politically radicalized within their experiences as people of color" (p. 118) in U.S. society. The term *Rican* is often used to refer to second- and third-generation Puerto Ricans on the U.S. mainland. Ricans still maintain close contact with Puerto Rican island communities through the circular migration pattern discussed earlier. Ricans tend to embrace a cultural identity that combines their Puerto Rican and U.S. cultural backgrounds.

Cubans

Cubans are the third largest Latino ethnic group in the United States. Cuba has a similar colonization history to Puerto Rico, but its political history has been very different (Santiago-Rivera et al., 2002). The United States acquired Cuba as a result of the Spanish-American War. However, it was a U.S. territory for only about 3 years, when it became an independent nation. Migration from Cuba has occurred in three waves, largely as a result of political tensions and unrest. The first wave of notable migration of Cubans to the United States occurred around the time of the Cuban Revolution (1953–1959) and consisted of upper class, well-educated, light-skinned Cuban migrants. These Cubans had the means to aid their transition to the United States, allowing them to contribute to the economic growth of Florida, especially Miami and Key West (Masud-Piloto, 1988). The second wave occurred in 1962 after the Cuban missile crisis. This group of immigrants benefited substantially from aid provided by the U.S. government and sponsors in the private sector. The third wave occurred in 1980, after an event at the Peruvian Embassy in Havana in which approximately 10,000 Cubans sought political asylum. Unfortunately, partly because of economic difficulties being experienced in the United States and their lower education and socioeconomic status, these refugees were not as well received as the Cuban refugees of the previous two waves had been. Santiago-Rivera et al. (2002) noted that this cultural group as a whole has the most wealth and education of all Latino groups in the United States and has made the most educational and economic gains.

Dominicans

Considered one of the newer groups of Latino immigrants, the 1.4 million Dominicans living in the United States make up approximately 2.8% of the U.S. population (U.S. Census Bureau, 2010c). Almost 53% of Dominicans reside in the Northeast, primarily in New York, with another 18% residing in the South. Dominicans come from the Dominican Republic, which is located on the island of Hispaniola in the Caribbean. This nation has a history of colonization and received an influx of African slaves brought by the Europeans, resulting in a mixed cultural and racial heritage (Santiago-Rivera et al., 2002). Thus, Dominicans display a wide range of phenotypes. An economic downturn in the late 1960s brought a wave of Dominican immigrants to the United States, both documented and undocumented individuals seeking improved educational and economic opportunities.

Central Americans

Central Americans hail from a plethora of countries, including Costa Rica, Belize, El Salvador, Guatemala, Honduras, Nicaragua, and Panama. Central Americans represent a mixture of European, Indian, and African cultures. According to Houben (2012), most Central Americans prefer to identify with their culture and country of origin as opposed to being referred to as Central American. Although these countries were colonized during the Spanish conquest, they each have different cultural histories. Thus, counselors are again encouraged to remember the heterogeneity among Latinas/os. Individuals from Guatemala, El Salvador, and Honduras, for example, may have more indigenous influences than those from Costa Rica and Belize, who have more European heritage. Approximately 4 million Central Americans live in the United States, or about 7.9% of the total Latina/o population in the United States (U.S. Census Bureau, 2010c). In fact, Salvadorans are the fourth largest Latina/o ethnic group in the United States. The majority of Central Americans live primarily in the South and the West, but there is also a large population of Central Americans in the Washington, DC, area. Some Central Americans, especially those from Nicaragua, El Salvador, and Guatemala, emigrated to avoid civil war (Santiago-Rivera et al., 2002). This led to many Central Americans experiencing trauma responses. The Salvadoran population is larger than other Central American populations because Salvadorans were granted refugee status in the mid-1990s.

South Americans

South Americans represent a number of countries, including Chile, Columbia, Argentina, Bolivia, Brazil, Peru, Ecuador, Guyana, Paraguay, Venezuela, Uruguay, and Suriname. At about 2.8 million strong, this multicultural group makes up approximately 5.5% of the Latina/o population in the United States (U.S. Census Bureau, 2010c). South Americans primarily reside in the Northeast and the South. Similar to Central Americans, South Americans prefer to be associated with their country and culture as opposed to being referred to as South American (Houben, 2012). Also, South Americans reflect a combination of European, Indian, and African cultures. Although Spanish is the official language in most South American countries, this is not the case for Brazil, whose primary language is Portuguese.

Immigration patterns between the United States and South America follow a different route with the colonization of Mexico, Puerto Rico, Cuba, the Dominican Republic, and Central America (Santiago-Rivera et al., 2002). Immigration to the United States has often been the result of political, economic, and social unrest in these areas, including military dictatorships and debt crises. Like the first waves of Cuban immigrants, South Americans who have more privileges, in terms of education and socioeconomic status, typically can more readily leave their country of origin when such unrest occurs. Many Latina/o Jews migrated to South America from Spain to escape the Inquisition during the 15th century, and others fled to South America from Europe when Hitler was in power during the 1930s and 1940s.

Racial Identification

Latinas/os are often stereotyped as having a physical appearance characterized by olive or brown skin, dark hair that is straight (Dávila, 2001; Rodríguez, 1997), and an ambiguous body type that falls somewhere between that of Whites and Blacks (Mendible, 2007). In fact, race is a social construct whose meaning changes based on many factors (D. W. Sue & Sue, 2003). Race is typically based around one's phenotype, including skin color, facial features, and hair texture. As a group, Latinas/os are racially mixed (Rodríguez, 2000). About 53% of Latinas/os identify as racially White, 36.7% identify as some other race, 6% as two or more races, 2.5%

as Black or African American, and 1.4% as Native American or Alaska Native. This mixture of racial identification, or *mestizaje*, is a result of the intermingling of people of European, Indian, and African backgrounds (Acosta-Belén & Sjostrom, 1988; Henriksen & Paladino, 2009; Houben, 2012; Santiago-Rivera et al., 2002). Counselors should be aware of the political and sociohistorical aspects of race (Helms & Cook, 1999). This is especially true as Latinas/os may hold attitudes and beliefs that reinforce internalized racism. Thus, counselors need to have knowledge of racial identity development and understand the role of internalized racism in psychological distress among Latinas/os, as well as in conflicts with families and communities. Counselors furthermore ought to understand the impact of racism and stereotypes of Latinas/os on individuals' experiences of discrimination and oppression on the basis of race.

Racial identity is a part of racial categorization and can reveal the schemas people use (Roth, 2012). Roth suggested that understanding people's racial schemas can help to understand how things are connected from the individual level to the institutional level (or macrolevel) and how people are influenced by the culture of race. Immigrants may face racial acculturation in that they may form new racial schemas when interacting with a new culture. The official classification is typically White or Black, yet not all people identify with these classifications. They may have their own meaning of race that is separate from official classification. Roth discussed a continuum model that stresses that race is determined by phenotype and social factors, not ancestry. Social considerations such as gender, socioeconomic status, and so forth also impact racial classification, especially in some Latin American countries. Racial classification is also relational, dependent on interactions and implicit comparisons. For example, among Puerto Ricans and Dominicans, a child may be nicknamed *el negrito* (little Black one) or *la blanquita* (little White one) because of being the darkest or the lightest in the family. Furthermore, racial terms may be used in different contexts, as a form of either respect or disrespect. Thus, a person might use the term *trigueño* (dark-skinned, often mixed race) or *indio* (indigenous, Indian or Native American) to keep from describing someone as *negro* (Black), thus showing deference or respect.

Case Scenario

Roberto was a 55-year-old Latino of Puerto Rican descent. Roberto also identified as Black. He was having conflicts with his wife of 30 years and stated that he was attending counseling to appease her. When describing the marital conflict, Roberto shared his difficulties with employment, stating that he had been laid off from his job as a city employee. He indicated some suspicion about why he was chosen to be laid off, wondering whether his lack of a college education or his race played a role, but in the next breath he expressed some relief over being laid off as for a long time he had wanted to pursue his interest in art. Roberto shared that he had enjoyed making structural art since he was young, and he hoped he would now have the time to create artistic pieces and sell them. He dreamed that his art would be displayed in public spaces. Roberto stated that his wife was very upset that he was not actively looking for work, and he expressed frustration with her lack of understanding that he wanted to strive for his dream. He acknowledged that he had been the breadwinner in the family, which he reported placed a great deal of pressure on him to continue to provide financially. Roberto shared that he was running out of money to be able to pay the bills and wondered whether his wife should work to help make their monthly payments. He stated that she had been a homemaker for the entirety of their relationship, but he believed that she was capable of entering the workforce. He openly wondered whether it was God's will that he had been laid off so that he could pursue a career in art.

Gender and Sexual Identities

There are many influences on gender socialization, including various dimensions of personal identity among Latinas/os. Counselors might assess adherence to the traditional gender roles of *marianismo* (the expectation that Latinas are spiritually and morally superior to men while also accepting of Latino men's authority) and machismo (the bidimensional construct that describes the negative view of hyper-masculinity as well as the positive view of chivalry) to determine their impact on Latinas/os' lives. These gendered identities place pressure on Latinas/os to conform to rigid gender roles that may not allow these individuals to find fulfillment and meaning, especially if they are called to a life that is in direct conflict with socialization experiences.

Chicana feminists attempt to move the discourse of binaries of gender and sexuality into that of more intersectionality (G. F. Arredondo, Hurtado, Klahn, Nájera-Ramírez, & Zavella, 2003). Chicana feminists take a political stance that challenges the patriarchy that attempts to maintain disempowerment and silence through forms of racism, nationality, homophobia, and class inequity. Arreola (2010) contended that *marianismo* and machismo may prescribe sexual scripts. For instance, in response to machismo, Latino men may attempt to prove their manhood through sex, whereas *marianismo* might encourage Latinas to wait for marriage before engaging in sexual activities as well as to defer to Latino men's sexual advances. Thus, these feminist authors would suggest directly confronting these socializations that may serve to do more harm than good. Yet counselors should be cautioned against challenging these strongly held ideals outright without considering the client's culture. It is important to honor and respect cultural values while gently encouraging Latina/o clients to examine their own biases, attitudes, and beliefs.

Asencio and Acosta (2010) used research from Latina/o studies and sexuality to address the marginalization of Latinas/os in regard to their sexuality. They found that Latina/o sexuality has been largely ignored, except in the context of the medical model and prevention research. In the studies that do exist, contextual factors such as ethnicity, race, culture, and nationality have often been made invisible. They also discovered that the populations examined in this research were those Latinas/os who were most at risk, and therefore they often represented the socioeconomically disadvantaged. This disparity, they contended, results in an oversimplified and often misrepresented image of Latina/o culture and sexuality. However, even given this misrepresentation, it should be noted that the majority of Latinas/os in the United States believe that homosexuality should be accepted (P. Taylor, Lopez, et al., 2012), suggesting that sexuality may not be as invisible as one might believe.

Abalos (2002) contended that patriarchal machismo is a response to attempting to finding meaning in a Latino male's life, to feeling fragmented and needing a sense of power and control, and to the wounded "personal, political, historical and sacred faces of the Latino male" (p. 4). "Machismo is Latino men's inherited understanding of being in charge, of taking command, *un hombre muy macho*" (p. 3). He suggested transforming the identity of Latino men into caring and loving men who can see the sacredness in their lives as opposed to focusing merely on the fragmented and wounded self or the negative aspects of machismo. He suggested that Latino men need to engage in the process of choosing between destructive narratives and those that are "creative stories of transformation" (p. 5).

Abalos (2002) further posited that Latino males are brought up in a culture that subjugates the feminine and promotes negative machismo and patriarchy, which wounds both the body and the psyche. This pain comes from not only a patriarchal society but also one that is racist and oppressive. He shared his own personal story of how he came to redefine what it means to be a Latino male by confronting his machismo, deconstructing patriarchy, and exploring his sexuality. A potential barrier to discussing sexuality is the silence that is often maintained by Latina/o culture (B. V. Marín & Gómez, 1997). Thus, counselors might facilitate breaking the silence to allow for this confrontation to occur. Confronting this silence might also allow counselors to discuss healthy and safe decision making around Latino men's sexual behaviors and to address identity concerns. This is especially important given the results of a study that examined the bidimensional construct of machismo with a group of Latino gay men (Estrada, Rigali-Oiler, Arciniega, & Tracey, 2011). This study found that the bidimensional model of machismo was validated with this group of men, suggesting that gay Latinos also hold this view of Latino masculinity. Furthermore, it was discovered that machismo predicted internalized homophobia and riskier sex practices among this population.

Abalos (2002) contended that some Latino men live the life of a "disappointed male." The disappointed Latino male (a) is angry and wounded, (b) has an ego that is threatened by the breakdown of male privilege inherent in patriarchy, (c) attempts to bring back the past and may resort to violence against himself and others, (d) lacks knowledge of how to change his life, (e) may use bargaining or limited forms of independence to maintain his power, (f) attempts to prevent change by using "fragments of the dying tradition, sin, shame, and guilt" (p. 22), and (g) resorts to manipulation rather than transformation (Abalos, 2002). It may be incumbent on counselors to aid Latino clients in developing a new narrative that empowers and heals the wounded Latino male.

Case Scenario Analysis

Let's revisit Roberto's case. It seems that he may be in the process of creating a new narrative. A counselor might consider exploring the concept of the wounded Latino male with Roberto to ascertain how this may or may not reflect his experience. Roberto seems to want to challenge the traditional male gender role, as is evidenced by his interest in pursuing his art and having his wife begin to work outside the home. However, it is unknown to what extent he may recognize this dream as a manifestation of healing his wounded male self. A counselor would need to thoroughly assess with Roberto the impact of traditional male gender role socialization on his lived experience. It is possible that through such exploration, Roberto could begin to be liberated from a definition of masculinity that possibly limits him as well as affects his family dynamics.

Religion/Spirituality

According to P. Taylor, Lopez, et al. (2012), religion is more important in the lives of immigrant Hispanics than U.S.-born Hispanics, with about 69% of immigrant Hispanics endorsing that religion is very important, compared to 49% of U.S.-born Hispanics. The majority of Hispanics who endorse a religious affiliation report that they are Catholic (62%) or Protestant (19%). The Latina/o Protestant population can be further broken down into Evangelical and Mainline Protestant (Pew Hispanic Center, 2007), with approximately 15% of Latinas/os identifying as Evangelical and 5% as Mainline Protestant. Some of these Latina/o Protestants also identify as Pentecostal or Charismatic. Less than 1% of Latinas/os identify as non-Christian, such as

Jewish or Muslim. Another 8% of Latinas/os identify as secular. This group is composed of more men and youth than Latinas/os who identify a religious preference. Mexicans are more likely to identify with Catholicism than Puerto Ricans, who, of all Latina/o groups, most identify with an Evangelical identity. Furthermore, more Cubans than not identify as secular. It is interesting to note that Catholic identities decline over the generations following immigration, yet Protestant identities strengthen (P. Taylor, Lopez, et al., 2012). Latinas/os are more likely than the general population in the United States to attend religious services at least once a week, with Latina/o Protestants and evangelical Protestants more likely than Latina/o Catholics to attend religious services weekly. Approximately 85% of Latinas/os report that religion is somewhat to very important in their lives.

Among Latinas/os, religion, spirituality, and faith are equally important as values and beliefs (Santiago-Rivera et al., 2002), and God is viewed as an active force in their daily lives (Pew Hispanic Center, 2007). Latinas/os might look to these belief systems and to God to make meaning and find purpose in their lived experiences. According to Houben (2012), Latinas/os believe that change is possible if they pray to La Virgen de Guadalupe or to the saints. Many Latinas/os have an acceptance of their circumstances that comes directly from their faith traditions, a phenomenon often seen as fatalism by those who are culturally insensitive.

As we mentioned in the discussion of mestizo identity development, spirituality is important in the search for identity and meaning (M. Ramírez, 1998). Spirituality provides a link between an individual and the cosmos, in which there is a duality of masculine and feminine principles. This spirituality not only links individuals to supernatural forces but also influences the destinies of individuals and groups. Through developing self-control, developing self-knowledge, and gaining the assistance of a person or spirit who can mediate between individual and supernatural forces, the person can understand the supernatural. *Curanderas/os* (folk healers), *espiritistas* (spiritual healers), shamans, and the clergy can all act as intermediaries for the individual. These spiritual brokers help the individual in his or her search for self-knowledge and identity and also help those who may experience adjustment problems. Religion is often viewed as help to reach harmony and as protection against negative or unwanted supernatural forces. Here religion models codes of conduct that assist people in understanding the purpose of life and death as well as acts as a mode of reconciliation through confession. In fact, Latinas/os are more likely to obtain mental health care through their religion or a priest than from a counselor or psychologist.

Case Scenario Analysis

Let's revisit Julia's case again. Her religious identity is important to her, yet she does not know how to integrate her religious identity with her sexual orientation. This internal conflict is directly related not only to the messages she has received from her original religious community but also to her assumptions about the relationship she has with God. By engaging in an exploration of her relationship with the supernatural and locating a religious community that is affirming of her sexual identity, Julia is better able to merge these two identities, thereby minimizing the internal conflict. Not only does she look to her clergy for help with this, but she is able to explore these confusions in therapy as well, making it clear that her whole self need not splinter while in therapy.

Socioeconomic Status and Poverty

In 2011, the median household income for Hispanics in the United States was $38,624, compared with $55,412 among Whites (U.S. Census Bureau, 2012b). Approximately 25.3% of Hispanics in the United States live in poverty, compared to 9.8% of Whites. Among Latino families with only a mother present in the household, this percentage increases considerably to 44%. This means that about 34% of Latinos younger than age 18 live in poverty. Furthermore, about 30.1% of Hispanics in the United States, or 15.8 million people, lack health insurance. M. H. López and Cohn (2011) cited growth in numbers, high birth rates, and a decline in economic fortune as reasons why so many Hispanic children live in poverty. Two thirds of these children are from immigrant families. Furthermore, most Latina/o children living in poverty have parents who have a high school degree or less. And today, Latina/o children living in poverty are more likely to have at least one parent who is unemployed, a fact that could be attributed to the recession in the United States. According to the U.S. Census Bureau (2012a), educational attainment is lowest for foreign-born Hispanics, with only 48% having attained at least a high school diploma or its equivalent. And although native-born Hispanics have an educational attainment higher than that of foreign-born Hispanics, they still have lower educational attainment than all other native-born racial groups.

Families in poverty share many characteristics, including more family members than families not living in poverty, more dependence on kinship, and a more maternal structure (Gladding, 2002). Impoverished families often deal with problems and stressors that families that do not live in poverty do not face, including less access to adequate health care and an increased risk of obesity (Everson, Maty, Lynch, Kaplan, 2002); fewer educational opportunities (Hochschild, 2003); as well as higher rates of teenage pregnancy, school attrition, alcohol and drug abuse, domestic violence, and incarceration. Many Mexican American college students delay or completely discontinue attending college to help their families financially (Pappas & Guajardo, 1997). In an attempt not to burden their families, these students often work full-time jobs to pay for schooling and help their families, but they are less likely than students who do not live in poverty to accrue debt by taking student loans. Constantine, Gloria, and Barón (2006) reported that many Mexican American college students live around or below the poverty line and are financially dependent on their families. Counselors are encouraged to consider availability, access, and affordability of mental health care for those Latinas/os who may not be able to afford such services, and the impact the lack of services can have. When working with Latinas/os of lower socioeconomic statuses, it is of the utmost importance to identify and utilize resources for housing, health care, food, and so forth.

Concluding Thoughts

Latina/o identity is very complex and multidimensional. Various influences (e.g., family; peers; ethnic, racial, and cultural groups; the larger community; sociopolitical and historical factors) all interact to either facilitate or hinder the development of a healthy Latina/o identity. This chapter followed the cases of Julia and Roberto to illustrate the role that identity and the intersection of identities play in their lived experiences and to demonstrate approaches to identity that might be utilized in therapy. Culturally sensitive therapists are aware of their own biases that might impede the healthy development of Latina/o identity as well as potentially stymie the resolution of identity conflicts. Thus, counselors should refrain from making broad generalizations that only serve to reinforce stereotypes and further isolate Latinas/os. Through awareness of different models of Latina/o identity development, as well as different aspects of self-reference, counselors can help clients to explore these issues and can provide education around these concerns when Latina/o clients may lack awareness, especially in instances of internalized racism, homophobia, sexism, and so on.

• • •

Chapter 5

Education

La ambición nunca se llena.

Ambition never has its fill.

(Sellers, Nelson, & Soto, 1994, p. 42)

• • •

Objectives

- To examine the educational pipeline for Latinos from prekindergarten to the professoriate.
- To learn about the worldviews of Latino families with regard to formal education.
- To understand the systemic barriers that Latinos face in the educational system.
- To examine practices that counselors can apply to support Latina/o educational opportunities.

Sabías que/Did you know that . . .

- One in four (24.7%) elementary students is Latino. Of prekindergartners through 12th graders, 23.9% are Latino (Pew Hispanic Research Center, 2012).
- In 2012, Latinos became the largest ethnic minority group on 4-year campuses (Pew Hispanic Research Center, 2012).
- Hispanic-Serving Institutions educate more than 50% of Latino students in the United States (Excelencia in Education, 2011).

• • •

Case Scenario

Ray's assistantship in graduate school was working with an after-school program at a local YMCA. The city had seen a steady and dramatic increase in the Latino population, and his after-school group was all Latino. After the Christmas break, all of his kids were gone. Ray worried about them because they had made so much progress. The move did not make any sense because their parents were also very supportive of education. Why would they leave? Although there was no forwarding information, Ray was able to track down one family to solve the mystery: Apartment leases and specials on apartments ended in December, and if families did not move, their rent would double. Ray was dejected and confided in his supervisor how hopeless he felt. His supervisor encouraged him to be an agent of social change and reach out to the apartment complexes in the area. To Ray's surprise, the apartment complex managers were willing to meet, listen, and offer school-year specials. Ray was bemused by the experience. What did apartment specials have to do with education? Or being an agent of social change? He had never learned this in grad school.

Latinos and Education in the United States

It is widely known that education is an important component of success in the United States. Except for entertainers, professional athletes, and a few fortunate others, education is related to income (see Table 5.1). That is, in general, the more education one attains, the higher one's income. This relationship is especially true when one considers the differences between the average incomes of a high school graduate and a college graduate. The differences in lifetime income can be staggering. Although income is important to all workers, there are other work-related factors to consider: self-determination, productivity, job satisfaction and safety, health and medical insurance, retirement plans, and vocational fit. With increased education comes access and options.

The intersection of Latinos and education is fairly complex and is usually presented solely in terms of deficits and failures of the Latino culture. Negative stereotypes about Latinos include the following: a culture that does not value education, an overestimation of unauthorized immigrants, persistent language issues, gang involvement, a lack of parental involvement, and a lack of intelligence. People rarely examine or consider systemic issues, such as the lack of Latino and/or culturally competent teachers and administrators, repressive and discriminatory policies, staggered immigration and the separation of families, the forced repatriation of parents of U.S. citizen children, and anti-immigrant and anti-bilingual sentiments. The complete picture is one of strengths and weaknesses, barriers and access, significant regional and state differences, individual and systemic issues, and a decidedly mixed prognosis for educational systems increasingly populated by Latino students.

However, in this book we do not subscribe to deficit theories, nor do we support the idea that the Latino culture does not value education. Instead, we focus on the

Table 5.1
Median Weekly Earnings, 2011

Education	Earnings (in Dollars)
High school graduate	638
Associate's degree	768
Bachelor's degree	1,053
Master's degree	1,263
Professional degree	1,665
Doctoral degree	1,551

Source. Bureau of Labor Statistics (2011).

many ways in which counselors may address barriers, both intentional (e.g., laws passed to curtail access to education for unauthorized students) and unintentional (e.g., apartment policies, as seen in the case scenario). It is our belief that Latinos desire education, especially if that education is culturally sensitive, is empowering, and fulfills the family's dreams. Like all immigrant parents, today's Latino immigrants want more for their children, and education is one of those highly desirable goals.

In 1996, the President's Advisory Commission on Educational Excellence under President Bill Clinton issued a report on Latino education titled *Our Nation on the Fault Line.* In the decades since, research has indicated that Latino participation has declined at every stage of the educational pipeline, resulting in a saturation of Latinos in remedial education and a troubling absence of Latino influence at the highest levels of academia. When combined with demographic realities, the struggles that Latinos face in the educational system should cause alarm. The largest ethnic minority population in the country has the worst educational outcomes. If we add in data about high school graduation and dropout rates, then extrapolate the problem out a few decades, the impact of an undereducated workforce will be staggering to the health of the entire country. A large segment of the population will be undereducated and underemployed.

Although dropout rates and the lack of access to higher education remain serious problems for U.S. Latinos, there is some promising news. Data from Fry and Lopez (2012) indicate that Latinos were the largest ethnic minority group in prekindergarten (pre-K) through 12th grade and in 4-year colleges in 2012. Demographic growth alone does not explain these numbers. It seems that the efforts at high school retention and graduation have been increasingly effective. More Latino students are eligible for and in college now than ever before, but there is a significant difference between college enrollment and graduation (Fry, 2011; Fry & Lopez, 2012).

It is necessary to review one additional point before we delve into the issue of Latino education. As has been said many times before, Latinos represent a heterogeneous group of people with distinctly different racial, cultural, and social backgrounds; unique histories with the United States; and differing reasons for immigration. The largest group of Latinos in the United States is Mexican Americans (who are themselves not a monolithic group), and the remaining 30% of Latinos also represent a diverse array of people. As a consequence of this within-group diversity, experiences with the U.S. educational system may vary significantly according to national origin, language ability, regional attitudes, or local history with Latinos. For example, a Cuban American family in Atlanta may experience a radically different educational environment than a Honduran family in Houston. Likewise, a Puerto Rican student in New York City and one in Orlando are likely to face different challenges and enjoy different advantages. These differences are often lost in research when the panethnic term *Latina/o* is used to average out differences among people. Although data can be presented in the aggregate, context is extremely important. On a related note, areas such as California, Florida, New York, and Texas have a long (and mixed) history of addressing Latino educational issues, given the established Latino populations there. However, areas that experience sudden influxes of Latino students may not have the motivation or proactive preparation to address Latino educational issues in a thoughtful manner.

In this chapter, we focus on the many issues that impact Latino education. Rather than progress through a depressing series of disheartening statistics, we focus on the areas in which counselors can make a difference. Delgado-Romero, Matthews, and Paisley (2007) provided a concrete structure for counselors to follow when intervening in kindergarten through Grade 12 (K–12) education. They convened a school counselor conference focused on addressing the issues facing emerging Latinas/os in the schools. The researchers advocated that counselors, especially school counselors, address the following areas: gaining historical and cultural knowledge about Latina/o students, learning culturally appropriate counseling skills, increasing parental engagement, providing information on college admissions, collaborating with community resources, and conducting research on Latino educational issues. Clearly, a general preparation to work with a diverse clientele is not sufficient to work effectively with Latina/o clients.

Teachers and Counselor Educators

Administrators, teachers, counselors, allied professionals, and parents are the adults that compose the U.S. educational system. Any discussion of education and Latinos is incomplete without incorporating the need for culturally sensitive school personnel. Professional counselors are ideal candidates for bringing about systemic change in school systems through increased cultural and linguistic sensitivity practices. For example, in Athens, Georgia, concerned school counselors noticed an influx of immigrant families from rural Mexico. Rather than focusing solely on Mexican immigrant families and students, the counselors recognized a need for school personnel to increase their cultural sensitivity. They organized a trip to rural Mexico for teachers to learn about the social, economic, linguistic, cultural, and educational context of the families they were now teaching. The fact that several teachers made the journey spoke volumes to the Mexican immigrant population, as those teachers and counselors could now serve as culturally competent role models and cultural brokers. The K–12 educational system and its staff are often the front line of immigration and acculturation (Delgado-Romero, Matthews, et al., 2007) and, as such, are first responders. Thus, engaging with students and families using Latino-informed knowledge and practices is essential.

Although multicultural courses are mandatory for teacher education programs, counselor educators can help design and implement experiences that serve to provide real-world learning. For example, service-learning courses with Latino students, practica in Latino-dominant schools, and service to Latino families may serve to better educate and sensitize teachers to work effectively with Latino students. It is important that teachers know the research, such as research on learning differences between Latina/o subgroups from the same geographical areas (e.g., Dominicans and Puerto Ricans; see Maldonado-Torres, 2011), and counselors can help provide access to this type of specific information. In addition, a counselor with a systemic perspective can identify those people in the system who may need additional support or consultation. For example, it is often the case that teachers who teach English as a second language classes and/or who are Spanish speakers have the unofficial (uncompensated) duty to provide services to Latino students and their families. A culturally informed counselor knows where to find the school personnel who are in need of support.

Systemically speaking, it is vital that colleges of education address both the shortage of culturally/linguistically competent teachers as well as the underrepresentation of teachers from Latino backgrounds. In Georgia, less than 1% of teachers are Latina/o compared with 6.2% of students registered in the school system. The lack of role models must be considered in all efforts to effectively address educational issues. Culturally competent Latina/o or bilingual school personnel provide the interface between the school system, Latina/o students, families, and the larger community. Being culturally competent does not necessarily involve speaking Spanish or being Latina/o. A culturally effective counselor can advocate against oppressive policies (e.g., the classification of Latino students as limited English proficient, the unfair evaluation of foreign transcripts) that discriminate against or deny resources to Latino children and can ensure that monolingual Spanish-speaking parents are provided with legitimate professional translators (i.e., not their children).

Zamarripa and Lerma (2013) reviewed the research and literature on the assessment of Latina/o students in schools. Their review included cultural factors of Latinos and how those factors are accounted for in the assessment process. They also reviewed the tests used, basing their review on the most recent data available. Having access to holistic and culturally sensitive information is critical to understanding the systemic (vs. individual) issues that create barriers for Latino students and parents, especially in high-stakes educational testing. Although counselors may not engage directly in educational policy or assessment, having knowledge of these areas, along with connections and implications for clients, is necessary to bring about culturally sensitive empowerment and social change in institutions.

As a result of advanced graduate-level training, counselors have come to understand firsthand the educational system as it exists in the United States. However, many recent immigrants to the United States were educated in educational systems that may differ significantly (e.g., in terms of norms for education and parental involvement, language) from what counselors know (note that this is not true for Puerto Rico, which has an educational system similar to the one in the United States). For example, information available through the United Nations Educational, Scientific and Cultural Organization (UNESCO; www.unesco.org) can inform counselors on the educational systems of Latin America and the Caribbean. Progress has been made in universal primary education, and the current educational focus in Latin America is timely entry into primary school. UNESCO's stated goal is keeping all children in school through the last year of primary education. The challenges for each country or region in Latin America vary, but certain themes emerge: social class and gender disparities, school desertion in rural areas, the damaging effect of armed conflict, the oppression of indigenous populations, and increasing the quality of education. To best serve their clients, counselors must try to understand the differences and similarities between various educational systems and the one used in the United States. Such differences can be as concrete as a Spanish-language transcript or as abstract as cultural attitudes toward teachers. In this sense, counselors can serve as cultural brokers in schools.

In the following sections, we examine the different levels of the U.S. educational system as well as the relevant research at each stage of the educational pipeline for counselor knowledge, higher education planning, and employment outlook.

Preschool

Intelligence begins to develop *in utero* and continues to develop in the home through the physical, emotional, cultural, and social environment. Unfortunately, many Latino mothers tend not to get adequate prenatal care or enroll their children in pre-K programs (Cabrera, Shannon, Rodríguez, & Lubar, 2009). The reasons for this are likely threefold: First, there is a lack of information on the often free school-related resources available to mothers; second, families hesitate to have young children away from the family unit; and third, repressive, anti-immigrant laws serve to discourage Latino families from trusting schools as a safe environment for their children. Thus, counselors in community health centers and schools must endeavor to educate Latino parents about available resources, work to make schools hospitable places, and advocate against repressive laws. For example, the Parent in Quality Education program began more than 20 years ago in San Diego. The goal of the initiative is to prepare parents to be consumers of education knowledge so that they can better advocate for their child's pathway to college. Parents participate in a 10-week program that culminates in a ceremony at which they receive certificates, including one for perfect attendance. It is an empowering program, especially for immigrant parents who may not have completed high school in their home country.

The number of Latina/o mothers or parents and students eligible for preschool educational programs is significantly higher than the number of mothers or parents and children who actually use these services. This underutilization of publically available resources is not only unjust but is especially unfair given evidence suggesting that participation in pre-K benefits Latino children (E. E. García & Scribner, 2009). Research that addresses ways to effectively engage Latino families is not only instructive but much needed in the Latino community. We discuss programs designed to combat poverty, such as Early Head Start and Head Start, in Chapter 7 when we discuss social class.

Elementary School

As stated previously, Latinos are the largest population in elementary schools, representing 1 in every 4 elementary students (Pew Hispanic Research Center, 2012). This demographic shift represents one of the realities of the future of U.S. education. Research indicates that these children are usually born in the United States and tend to acculturate (e.g., speak English) at a much faster rate than their immigrant parents. E. E. García and Scribner (2009) stated that pre-K through Grade 3 education provides a critical foundation for U.S. Latinos. They reviewed data on home language practices (i.e., language spoken in the home) and educational outcomes in elementary school. Latino children who spoke Spanish in the home lagged behind their monolingual peers in English-only environments, but there seemed to be some support for children's ability to transfer their Spanish language skills to the English language. Consequently, many different interventions of varying effectiveness are targeted toward English language learners (e.g., immersion, sheltered English, dual language programs). The use of a particular intervention may also be a political decision (e.g., English-only instruction). E. E. García and Scribner argued that Latino children benefit from a pre-K through Grade 3 education and that key to these benefits are high-quality teachers and effective leaders who may create a bridge between the school and community.

An important task that begins in elementary school is parental engagement. In Latino culture, the concept of family involves a multigenerational extended family, so that all might be involved in child care. This runs counter to the notion of individualism and the nuclear family, which are highly popularized in mainstream White, upper middle-class society; the literature; and even counselor training. Counselors must be aware of the interplay between immigration, acculturation, education, and parental involvement. In the case study that began this chapter, Ray is dealing with, in part, a lack of engagement with parents. New immigrant families face acculturation issues, economic issues, and potential discrimination and/or persecution. Although they are willing to entrust their children to Ray, they have not established the necessary communication with him. Ray and other social change agents must learn to productively engage parents in a culturally sensitive manner to know how they can be of assistance. Counselors must also be aware that expecting Latino parents to attend school-day parent–teacher conferences but not providing day care or transportation is unfair to those parents who cannot afford the necessary time and money.

There is a certain irony to this practice in the schools. Many employers allow their personnel flex time to go to school events with their children. If the Latino parent works in this type of organization, he or she can take time out during the day. Yet many immigrant parents punch a clock at their place of employment or work two jobs. It is sad that accommodations cannot be made for these parents. Rather, at times teachers and administrators criticize the parents as being uninterested. In this day of the flexible workplace, perhaps school administrators need to reevaluate practices that are not inclusive of all parents. This is another opportunity for culturally responsive counselors to step up and be innovative on behalf of their students and their families.

Middle School

In the United States, middle school often marks several important transitions. First, middle school students may have a different teacher for each subject. Second, the students are expected to individuate themselves from parents and teachers by displaying independence and self-direction. Often this transition is a difficult one for those who are new to the U.S. educational system and for those from collectivist cultures that do not emphasize independence. Preliminary research has indicated that compared with White students, Latino students are more sensitive to the school social climate as it relates to their school conduct. That is, Latinos are more likely than their White peers to report increasingly negative perceptions of school social climate and behavioral norms across the middle school transition.

For Latinos, many risk factors begin to manifest in middle school (unfortunately some increasingly begin in elementary school). These risk factors include alcohol, tobacco, and drug use; sexual experimentation; and gang participation. Other health factors that intensify during this time are obesity, bullying, and teen pregnancy.

In middle school, the issue of school discipline begins in earnest. Studies indicate that ethnic minority students are disproportionately punished, suspended, and dismissed from schools (Rocque, 2010). Recently a call went out for a special issue of the *Association of Mexican American Educators Journal* to examine the school-to-prison pipeline for Latino students. The concern is that strict discipline polices that target Latinos often create a pipeline to prison for many Latino youth. This situation undermines the educational system, excludes Latinos from the job market, and reinforces historical discrimination and mistrust. The school-to-prison pipeline issue is an important one for counselors to investigate and intervene with. Those in the U.S. juvenile justice and prison system also face other issues as a result of incarceration, such as violence, substance abuse, and health problems (such as HIV). The issue of Latinos in the judicial system is explored in Chapter 7, but suffice it to say that unfortunately many Latino youth have much more experience with the U.S. justice system than they do with the educational system.

Ojeda, Piña-Watson, et al. (2012) investigated the role of culture and personality on the career decision self-efficacy of Latino public school seventh graders. They examined the role of acculturation, enculturation, ethnic identity, and conscientiousness on career decision self-efficacy. Acculturation, ethnic identity, and conscientiousness significantly predicted career decision self-efficacy for girls, but only ethnic identity and conscientiousness were unique significant predictors for boys. Enculturation did not significantly predict career decision self-efficacy for either boys or girls. Thus, gender differences in career decision self-efficacy must be examined early on (i.e., earlier than high school). Linda Castillo of Texas A&M University has studied acculturation and enculturation (and the effects of those factors on career decisions) across educational levels, such as in middle school (Ojeda, Piña-Watson, et al., 2012), high school (Castillo, López-Arenas, & Saldivar, 2010), and college (Cano & Castillo, 2010).

Parent Involvement

Public perceptions of ethnic minorities are important to both society and Latinos themselves. Longitudinal research (McGill, Hughes, Alicea, & Way, 2012) has investigated the relationship between African American and Latino adolescents' perceptions of public opinion about their racial group (i.e., public regard) and changes in academic outcomes in middle school. Although results for Latinos were not presented separately by national origin group (i.e., Guatemalans, Puerto Ricans), the results revealed a significant decline in academic adjustment from sixth to eighth grade. Specifically, the researchers found that parenting moderated the association between public regard and the trajectory of academic adjustment. For youth who reported high racial/ethnic socialization and low parent academic involvement, lower public regard predicted lower academic adjustment in sixth grade. For youth who reported both low racial/ethnic socialization and low parent academic involvement, lower public regard predicted a steeper decline in academic adjustment over time. Finally, among youth who reported high racial/ethnic socialization and high parent academic involvement, public regard was not related to academic adjustment. The researchers suggested that a combination of high racial/ethnic socialization and high parent academic involvement may protect youths' academic motivation and performance from the negative effects of low public regard. Counselors need to be mindful of the importance of parent academic involvement regardless of the bilingual abilities of the parents.

High School

High school is both the culmination of mandatory education in the United States and the portal to higher education or vocational training. High school coincides with the changes of adolescence. In the United States, attending high school is one of the rites of passage in becoming an adult. Unfortunately, 38% of Latinas/os older than age 25 lack a high school diploma (compared with 14% of the general population), with the two largest Latino groups, Mexicans and Puerto Ricans, being the least likely among Latinos to have a high school diploma (U.S. Census Bureau, 2009). Region of the country is also important to consider when reviewing data on receipt of high school diploma among Latinos. The highest rates of adults with a diploma are in Florida (Fort Lauderdale–Hollywood–Pompano Beach metro region), but there are areas in central California (e.g., Bakersfield) where half of the Latino adults lack a high school diploma (Pew Hispanic Research Center, 2012). Thus, as with most issues with Latinos, looking at the average for all Latinos obscures the real issues; within-group differences matter. Educational issues have to be examined in a variety of contexts. For example, in Chapter 1, we discussed the top metro centers in the United States where Latinos reside. It behooves counselors who work in those settings to become knowledgeable about student success factors as well as barriers to high school graduation.

Although a college-going culture should be established in elementary school, high school is the time when educational and vocational choices are strongly emphasized. High school counselors can help Latinos with these important choices. To gain entry into competitive colleges, students should take a rigorous curriculum; those who do not may find their educational choices limited. In addition, although many resources on college admission are available to parents and students, this information is useless if not delivered in a culturally sensitive manner. Latino students are less likely to use college resources and apply to fewer colleges than their non-Latino peers (Martinez & Cervera, 2012). An example of a culturally sensitive intervention occurred at the University of Georgia, the university of one of the authors (Delgado-Romero). The student group Students for Latino Empowerment recognized that most Latino parents had never set foot on a college campus and that they were unaware of college as an option for their children. The students arranged a parent visitation day when Latino parents of high school children could come to campus to learn about the university, hopefully aiding in the recruitment, retention, and graduation of Latino youth. This is a great example that can be replicated. In another university, a graduate student returned to her high school to speak about her journey to students and their parents. This created a pipeline to the university, because there was evidence that the place was safe and a good place to entrust one's child.

Research supports the importance of public regard (impressions of the extent to which one's ethnic group is valued by others) for Latino middle school students. Rivas-Drake (2010) found that public regard was also a meaningful dimension for Latino adolescents' relationships with adults in high school. Latino adolescents at an urban high school who perceived more positive regard from adults at school were more engaged and achieved more than those who perceived negative public regard.

There is evidence that among Latinos, differences in academic adjustment in high school can be partly explained by gender (B. Sánchez, Colón, & Esparza, 2005). Using a sample of mostly Mexican American and Puerto Rican high school senior Latinos, researchers found that Latinas reported more positive educational outcomes than boys. Sense of belonging in school predicted academic outcomes for the entire Latino sample but was not explained by gender. Thus, the Latino gender achievement gap remains a somewhat unexplained but very real phenomenon. B. Sánchez et al. (2005) proposed examining these issues in more detail among Latino males. They also reviewed research that indicated that Latino males were often seen as having behavior problems and that teachers seem to have low and negative expectations of Latino male youth. At the same time, gender socialization is a salient factor for the sexes. In Chapters 2 and 10 there is contextual discussion about expectations for girls and boys regarding roles, rules, and responsibilities. Differences in upbringing and expectations set forth have a bearing on the gender gap in education.

Dropping out of high school is a particularly salient issue for Latino youth. The limited research indicates that educational professionals can impact the trajectory of career and identity development. E. M. Lopez (2001) examined the efficacy of two models of guidance for Latino high school students in relationship to math achievement and career identity. Downs and colleagues (2008) found evidence that models targeted toward increasing the career and college knowledge of Latino families might be effective for Latinos in general. Arbona and Nora (2007) reported that one's high school curriculum was the greatest predictor of whether that person attended a 4-year college. Specifically, students in an academically rigorous track (vs. the vocational track, often perceived as being for kids who use only their hands to work) were 46% more likely to enroll in a 4-year college. Counselor educators need to ensure that school and guidance counselors are aware of the long-term effects of tracking students into less academically rigorous programs. Although academic rigor is important, the role of expectations is critical, as Latinos with higher academic expectations are more likely to enroll in college.

Counselors may help design programs that raise the academic expectations of Latino students and their families early in high school and may share the anticipated outcomes for later in life for a person with a high school versus a college degree.

Latinos are drawn to enroll in the U.S. military after high school for a variety of reasons. Some may join the military as a hoped-for path to citizenship. Others may join for economic reasons and on-the-job training. However, it seems that the lure of the GI Bill has had the most direct effect on Latinos joining the military. Educational benefits (money for college for the enlistee or his or her family members) have resulted in a doubling of the Latino presence in the military from 1994 to 2007 (Ure, 2009). The history of Latinos in the U.S. military has often been overlooked. As part of its educational efforts, the Smithsonian Latino Center (2012; www.latino.si.edu) has published *Latino Patriots in American Military History*, a bilingual resource that traces the involvement of Latinos in the military from the Revolutionary War to the Vietnam War (see also Chapter 1).

General Education Development (GED)

As part of the Deferred Action for Childhood Arrivals program, described in Chapter 2, unauthorized immigrants who came to the United States before age 16 and who were younger than age 31 as of June 15, 2012, can apply for a waiver of deportation. Such a waiver may allow them to get a driver's license and work permit for 2 years. To receive such a deferral, candidates must

> [be] currently in school, have graduated or obtained a certificate of completion from high school, have obtained a general education development (G.E.D.) certificate, or [be] an honorably discharged veteran of the Coast Guard or Armed Forces of the United States. (U.S. Citizenship and Immigration Services, 2012)

This requirement revived interest in the GED for Latinos. For those who had dropped out of school, attaining a GED became especially important. The amount of paperwork and effort required to apply for the Deferred Action program has made that task imposing as well. Not all states and counties chose to implement Deferred Action, and the deferment was only for a 2-year window, with no promise of renewal or citizenship. Quite an imposing gauntlet for unauthorized Latinos to face! Counselors may assist with this or future citizenship efforts by helping to organize relevant professionals and lending support to an uncertain process. One particular counseling graduate student organization aided the cause by providing additional space for suddenly large GED classes. Finally, counselors might want to become involved politically on the national and local levels to advocate for issues that matter to Latino education as well as to work toward permanent paths to citizenship for unauthorized Latinas/os (e.g., the Development, Relief, and Education for Alien Minors [DREAM] Act). It should also be remembered that the DREAM Act and the Deferred Action legislation apply to non-Latinos as well.

College

The path to a college degree is not always clear for first-generation Latinos or for Latinos who have not had family members go to college. Not only is the college admissions process confusing, but financial aid issues can be daunting. The cost of tuition is rising at the same time state support for universities is drying up. It is the perfect storm, just as more Latinos are seeking college admission in greater numbers. Personal income is down for Latino families, and although they continue to work through the economic recovery, their average salaries are lower than those of other groups: Only 4% of Latino families earn more than $50,000 a year (Motel, 2012). Therefore, the issue of attending college can be a source of stress for Latino families.

Latinos who are unauthorized may face additional barriers that originate on the state political level. Some states have passed laws that either charge unauthorized students out-of-state rates, deny financial aid (Diaz-Strong, Gómez, Luna-Duarte, & Meiners, 2011), or prohibit unauthorized students from attending certain colleges altogether. In addition, some states, such as Arizona, have curtailed cultural empowerment programs such as Latino studies, programs that claim to increase college attendance rates. Clearly the zeitgeist in some states and counties involves denying access to higher education to unauthorized young adults. Denying access to a higher education (even at out-of-state rates) seems shortsighted when one is dealing with the fastest growing as well as youngest population in the United States. If we extrapolate the issue out a decade or two, what will become of the vast number of unauthorized youth who are denied education in an increasingly technological society? This seems to be a practical, economic, and moral issue. Some educators have also argued that an unprepared workforce is a national security risk.

For many students, starting on the path to college may mean enrolling in community (2-year) or technical colleges that are often located in Latino areas and are less expensive than 4-year institutions. Arbona and Nora (2007) noted that many precollege factors, such as taking care of family members, may influence a Latino student's decision to go to a community college or drop out altogether. Although some strong community colleges may indeed provide a path for students to obtain 4-year degrees, others become a dead end, and their students rarely move on to 4-year institutions. Counselors have to be aware of the placement and graduation rates of community college graduates as well as be sensitive to the daunting nature of the transfer to 4-year institutions. For example, liaisons should be put in place to facilitate transfers from 2-year institutions to local 4-year institutions. There is a need for education, research, support, and a critical evaluation of the role of 2-year colleges. Beyond the qualities of a given institution, certain behaviors correlate with not graduating from college: working, earning power over the lifetime, having dependents, and being a part-time student. Arbona and Nora emphasized that attending college full time (along with attending college continuously) is one of the most important predictors of obtaining a degree.

The college system in the United States is a complex one, with an entire industry devoted to college choice. Alumni children and children of college graduates often have many advantages in the admissions process. First-generation students often feel lost in the process of choosing a college and applying for admission, and this may be because they have not been involved in a college-going culture at their high school. Choosing a college begins early in high school when students select a rigorous curriculum and/or take advanced courses. Arbona and Nora (2007) demonstrated empirically that the following factors were important in Latino high school students' decision to attend a 4-year college: expecting to get a degree, attending college right after graduation, completing a rigorous curriculum in high school, and having peers who also planned to go to a 4-year college. First-generation Latino students face the challenge of navigating the U.S. educational system at the same time they are dealing with acculturative stress. Often this can be a lonely process, with parents being supportive of educational attainment (Maldonado & Farmer, 2007) but lacking the information and resources to provide guidance to their children.

Research has indicated that important student factors correlate with persistence and, eventually, graduation (Arbona & Nora, 2007). Some of those experiences are commitment to achieving a degree, engagement with academic activities on and off campus, and first-year grade point average (GPA). Nora and Cabrera (1996) noted that first-year GPA was much more important to Latinos' educational persistence than that of their White peers. Why would that be the case? GPA is a tangible number that may confirm or disconfirm factors such as stereotype threat and the imposter syndrome (the feeling that one doesn't belong in or is unprepared for his or her academic pursuits). In addition, GPA can make the difference between keeping a scholarship and being on probation.

The U.S. college and university experience is not confined to the classroom. It involves several important adjunctive educational experiences, such as residence life, varsity and intramural sports, and student groups. Involvement in student groups may be an ideal way for Latinos, who are traditionally from a collectivist culture, to complement their academic experience in college. Participation in mainstream and Latino-focused student groups may be important to Latino college students (Delgado-Romero & Hernandez, 2002; Delgado-Romero, Hernandez, & Montero, 2004). Delgado-Romero and colleagues (2004) offered a typology of Latino-focused student groups, including professional groups (e.g., medical, engineering, or law groups), social-cultural heritage groups (either general Hispanic/Latino groups or specific national groups), Greek fraternities and sororities (Muñoz & Guardia, 2009), and social action groups (e.g., Movimiento Estudiantil Chican@ de Aztlán). Latino-focused student groups may be ideal vehicles for cultural pride, support and mentoring, and community education and/or service. The growth of Latino student groups may be met with resistance by administrators and fellow students (Delgado-Romero et al., 2004), yet these groups are a natural and necessary part of the college experience and are key to retaining students who are invested in their ethnic identity and heritage as Latinos.

Like their high school completion rates, Latinos' college completion rates are best understood when examined in context. Once again, South Florida has the highest college completion rates (25%) and central California the lowest (5%; Pew Hispanic Research Center, 2012). One important contextual factor for educational outcomes is generational and immigrant status (vs. being U.S. born). Although the Latino population is often portrayed as a population of immigrants, the number of second-generation (U.S.-born) Latinos eclipsed that of first-generation (foreign-born) Latinos in 2010 (Migration Policy Institute, 2012). Preliminary reports have indicated that educational outcomes may vary significantly by generation in the United States, with second-generation Latinos (especially Latinas) enrolling in and graduating from college at significantly higher rates than first-generation immigrants. Unfortunately, the opposite is true for postsecondary technical training: For these highly skilled, high-wage opportunities, completion of technical programs declines after the first generation (Maldonado & Farmer, 2007). There is also evidence that prevention efforts work more effectively for U.S.-born Latinos than foreign-born Latinos (Cordova, Huang, Pantin, & Prado, 2012). Thus, the two groups may differ significantly in many areas, a fact worth noting for counselors.

Maldonado and Farmer (2007) pointed out that few Latinos graduate from postsecondary technical programs, although graduates of these programs are hired for high-skill, high-wage work. Part of the reason for this seemingly illogical situation is an overemphasis on attaining a bachelor's degree and a lack of understanding by teachers, counselors, and parents of the economic opportunities afforded by technical programs. Internalized racism, prejudice, and an educational system that does not promote excellence for an entire group of people (i.e., Latinos) prevent progress. Gándara (2006) emphasized that the modern workplace is composed of an increasingly technological workforce that requires higher education and technical training. As computer technology has become commonplace in the U.S. workforce, knowledge of and facility with technology have become prerequisites for many occupations. Latinos who have limited experience with technology because of cultural reasons (*personalismo*, or the valuing of personal relationships and personal interactions), poverty, or a lack of access may find themselves increasingly left out of the modern workplace.

Hispanic-Serving Institutions (HSIs)

Half of Latino undergraduates can be found at those institutions known collectively as Hispanic-Serving Institutions (HSIs). An institution is designated an HSI when Latinos make up 25% or more of the student body; the majority of HSIs are public community colleges located in states with majority representations of Latinos (i.e., California, Texas, and Florida). There are 293 HSIs in the country, and this number is only growing (Excelencia in Education, 2011). Because of population growth and an increase in the number of college applications, many universities are on the verge of becoming HSIs. Torres and Zerquera (2012) found that potential HSIs can be classified as unaware, aware, or committed institutions according to their preparedness for becoming an HSI. Far more Latino faculty, staff, and administrators are found in HSIs than in non-HSIs.

Very little is known about the transition from HSI to graduate school, for example the role that HSIs play in education in terms of psychology, the most popular undergraduate major for Latinos (Brown & Delgado, 2010).

The role of context is extremely important in understanding how Latino college students deal with individual and environmental oppression (Soto et al., 2012). Issues facing Latino students at predominantly White institutions as both undergraduates (Gloria & Castellanos, 2003) and graduate students (Herrera, 2003) also deserve attention. Latinos in higher education may often feel isolated or tokenized when few other Latinos are present in the institution, particularly if none of their professors are Latino. Rivas-Drake and Mooney (2009) examined the relationship between three minority status orientations (assimilation, accommodation, and resistance) and academic adjustment in Latino college students at highly selective as well as predominantly White colleges and universities. They found that those who used a resistance strategy (e.g., questioned the openness of the institution to ethnic minorities) reported similar grades than those who used the other strategies. Rivas-Drake and Mooney also pointed out that the conventional wisdom is that resisters would be oppositional and disengaged. The opposite was found to be true, as resisters became progressively involved in campus activities. This research offers some interesting insights into how Latinos might successfully navigate college in a variety of ways.

In Latino culture, family plays an important role in college students' success or lack thereof. Llamas and Morgan Consoli (2012) examined the deleterious role that intragroup marginalization (i.e., perceived interpersonal distancing by family members when an individual exhibits cultural characteristics of the dominant group) had on thriving for Latino college students. Intragroup marginalization predicted college adjustment, resilience, and thriving, and family support was found to mediate the relationship between thriving and intragroup marginalization. Thus, the stress of not being accepted by one's family compounded the stress of attending college and made it difficult for Latinos to focus in college. Again, context is important; for Latinos who wish to remain tied to their heritage culture, the context of family support or lack thereof seems to be a key factor.

A key issue in secondary and postsecondary education is the decline in participation by the Latino male. Saenz and Ponjuan (2009) examined a variety of reasons for this decline, including sociocultural factors, peer dynamics, labor force demands, and the lure of the military. They argued that the Latino male is "vanishing" from higher education, a statement also made of Black men. Concurrently, the unique issues faced by Latinas in higher education (i.e., familial involvement and connections with family, peers, and university personnel as a means of coping; Gloria & Castellanos, 2012) and filial responsibility for parental care (Rudolph, Chavez, Quintana, & Salinas, 2011) also deserve more attention in research and policy (Orozco, 2003). For example, Ojeda, Navarro, Rosales Meza, and Arbona (2012) examined the relationship between demographics and ethnicity-related stressors (i.e., perceived discrimination, stereotype confirmation concern, and own-group conformity pressure) and the life satisfaction of Latino college students. Results indicated that younger students, women, and students who reported higher stereotype confirmation concern and own-group conformity pressure reported less life satisfaction than their demographic counterparts.

Latino youth are key to President Barack Obama's college graduation goals for 2020, and he expects that these youth will be major contributors toward meeting these goals. According to Excelencia in Education (2011), Latino students will need to earn 5.5 million certificates or degrees to meet the President's goals. Although Latino students were the largest ethnic minority group enrolling on college campuses in 2011, their graduation rates lag behind those of their non-Hispanic peers. More often than not, they take 6 years to graduate. But an even more disappointing fact is that many of the students are not earning workforce-ready degrees or degrees with high earning potential. This important fact is one that college advisors and parents must not overlook. As it is, far too many Latinas/os are currently in occupations that pay poorly or have limited opportunity for upward mobility (Motel, 2012).

Graduate School

A constricted pipeline results in very few Latino students enrolling in doctoral programs and even fewer (just more than half) finishing a doctorate in 10 years (Council of Graduate Schools, 2008). Latinos are underrepresented in many fields, especially science and technology. However, bachelor's and doctoral degrees in psychology are the most popular degrees among Latinos. In addition to master's degrees in psychology, master's degrees in education, such as those in community, mental health, and school counseling, are popular with Latinos. Clearly Latinos are drawn to helping professions in which they may give back to their communities by helping others.

Although Latinos are drawn to helping professions such as counseling and psychology, this does not mean that they or their non-Latino peers are prepared to work effectively with Latino students and families. With the exception of those who either attended an HSI or those who live in areas with established Latino populations, most counselors have not received the necessary training in the Spanish language or Latino/cultural skills to work effectively with Latinos. Fortunately, the body of research available regarding Latino issues has grown in size and sophistication. Several journals, such as the *Hispanic Journal of Behavioral Sciences, Journal of Hispanic Higher Education,* and *Journal of Latina/o Psychology,* may contain relevant research. Reading (and generating) culturally relevant research may have an empowering effect on Latino graduate students and on graduate students seeking to work with Latinos. For example, Zamarripa, Lane, Lerma, and Holin (2011) detailed the positive impact that taking a course in Mexican American counseling and mental health had on Mexican American graduate students.

Why don't Latinos attend graduate school and get degrees? Possible reasons could include a lack of academic preparation; an overreliance on culturally biased admissions tests; a lack of value on recruiting and retaining Latinos on the part of graduate programs; a lack of Latino role models; overt or covert discrimination; stereotype threat; and the fact that many graduate training programs are located in rural areas, such as Athens, Georgia, or Lincoln, Nebraska. Another salient reason could be that Latinos do not receive adequate mentoring, academic advisement, or career advice as undergraduates. Almost 3% of all full-time faculty and administrators on college campuses are Latina/o, which creates limited opportunities for all Latina/o student populations to connect with potential Latina/o mentors (Castellanos & Jones, 2003). Moreover, these potential mentors often face discrimination or barriers themselves. When Latinos do receive advice, this advice may be partly based on stereotypes that might preclude them from pursuing more academic (vs. applied) majors (Delgado-Romero, Manlove, Manlove, & Hernandez, 2007). For example, Latinos are often directed to health service provider subfields of psychology (clinical, counseling, and school; Leong, Kohout, Smith, & Wicherski, 2003) rather than more academic subfields (e.g., social, neuroscience, developmental, and biological).

Case Scenario

Felix graduated from New Mexico State University, not far from his family in El Paso. This gave him the opportunity to drive home on weekends to keep up with family events and also to help out at his parents' business. Because of his exceptional talent in math, Felix was being recruited by a professor at one of the California research universities. Initially he was flattered and excited. The professor's research was exactly what Felix wanted to pursue. He was also going to receive a fellowship, easing the financial burden. When Felix shared the great news with his parents, they smiled and told him they were proud of him. Then they said, "Why do you have to go all the way to California? The university in El Paso is very good. Besides, we thought you were going to be a math teacher. Why do you have to study some more?"

Issues of race, class, and gender compound the struggles of Latino doctoral students as they adjust to the independent and competitive culture of doctoral programs, wrestle with self-doubt, and try to deal with physical and psychological distance from their families and culture (Figueroa et al., 2001; Herrera, 2003; Solórzano & Yosso, 2001). Doctoral students who have a strong commitment to researching Latino issues may find that they are discouraged from pursuing such personal topics. Conversely, some Latino graduate students become so involved with Latino and diversity issues on campus that their work and progress toward the degree suffers. Consequently, counselors and counselor educators must work to ensure that graduate programs actively promote and support diversity among their graduate students. Coordinating efforts with university institutions (e.g., Office of Institutional Diversity, Graduate School, and International Life) is the key to recruiting and retaining students of color and ensuring that they graduate.

Latinas are much more likely than their male counterparts to pursue a doctoral degree, and they represent the majority of the growth in Latina/o academics. Gender issues seem salient at every level of the educational pipeline, and graduate school is no exception. Fortunately, Castellanos, Gloria, and Kamimura (2006) offer many perspectives in *The Latina/o Pathway to the Ph.D.: Abriendo Caminos*. This volume addresses Latinas/os' pursuit of the doctorate as well as gender issues formally (Hurtado & Sinha, 2006) and through the personal narratives of successful Latina/o doctoral graduates. We recommend the book for all Latina/o doctoral students, their professors, and perhaps even their family members.

Latino Faculty

Castellanos and Jones's (2003) book *The Majority in the Minority: Expanding the Representation of Latina/o Faculty, Administrators, and Students in Higher Education* examines the challenges and successes of Latina/o faculty and administrators in higher education. They found that many Latina/o faculty and administrators face barriers to entering the world of academia, especially at flagship institutions that tend to report the least diversity (but the most prestige). Ibarra (2003) pointed out that Latina/o faculty are largely non-tenure track instructors and lecturers and that the majority of Latina/o instructors in the United States are Mexican American. For individuals of Mexican heritage, the largest Latino group in the United States and the one with the longest history in this country, such a finding is troubling, especially because this kind of analysis that goes beyond panethnic labels is rare. In New York City and New Jersey one can typically find Puerto Rican faculty and individuals from other Latin American countries.

Ibarra (2003) went on to propose ways in which to initiate a culture shift in academia that might make it more welcoming of Latina/o academics. Similarly, Verdugo (2003) examined how discrimination impacts Latina/o faculty, and Delgado-Romero, Flores, Gloria, Arredondo, and Castellanos (2003) examined developmental issues for Latino faculty. Although Latinas have actually made inroads into academia, their struggles deserve special attention as well (P. Arredondo & Castellanos, 2003). Recently an edited volume titled *Presumed Incompetent: The Intersections of Race and Class for Women in Academia* (Gutiérrez y Muhs, Flores-Niemann, González, & Harris, 2012) examined the narratives of 40 women academics of color, many of whom were Latinas.

In terms of Latino administrators, many senior academic positions are filled from the ranks of full professors with tenure. Given the low numbers of tenured Latino faculty and the even lower numbers of Latino faculty who have been promoted to full professor, this means the pool of Latina/o candidates is alarmingly small. Haro and Lara (2003) examined the politics and barriers facing Latinos advancing to senior academic positions, such as vice president, provost, and president of the university. They found many barriers and very little impetus for change within academia and suggested that groups such as the Hispanic Association of Colleges and Universities and the American Association of Hispanics in Higher Education might alter the landscape of academia through Latino-focused academic leadership programs. At the same time, the Association of Public Land-Grant Universities and the American Council on Education, traditional higher education professional associations, can also do more to prepare eligible Latinas/os for the most senior positions (P. Arredondo & Castillo, 2011). As with faculty in general, there are specific experiences and challenges for Latina administrators (P. Arredondo & Castellanos, 2003; Canul, 2003). Very few Latina/o university presidents, provosts, and deans are typically found at HSIs, smaller public institutions, and community colleges. As of this writing, there is no Latina/o president at a Research I university.

Community Educational Engagement and Social Change

In the case that began this chapter, the counselor, Ray, is hesitant to engage community businesses and resources. He is primarily conceptualizing the problem as an individual or family issue and does not see the role that the community plays in education. Luckily, his faculty advisor encourages Ray to engage with the community. Often in the community one can find several potential partners that either want to profit from Latino business or want to help serve the Latino community.

For example, Latinos often gravitate to the Catholic Church as a resource, although research indicates that Protestant churches have made significant inroads in Latino membership. The point is that religious organizations may serve formally or informally as providers of educational and social services. Many counselors are trained in secular programs, and interfacing with religious organizations may present unexpected challenges and barriers—and often rewards. Counselors must commit to developing their consultation skills and learn how to focus relevant resources in service of the Latino population. Counselors must be attuned to the fact that cooperation with the community is likely to increase investment in the educational system and that such investment benefits *all* members of society, not just Latinos.

Concluding Thoughts

The power of bias and prejudice in the education of Latinos cannot be underestimated. Education professionals can intentionally or unintentionally steer their students toward or away from certain professions or opportunities. The ethical problem arises when the guidance given to students is based on covert or overt prejudice and stereotypical and/or inaccurate perceptions of the career interests and aspirations of Latino people. For example, academic psychologists have challenged the perception that Latinos are not interested in academic (vs. practice-oriented) careers (see Delgado-Romero et al., 2003), and research has dispelled the myth that Latinos are not interested in certain careers such as agriculture (see Mullinix, Garcia, Lewis-Lorentz, & Qazi, 2006). Counselors and counselor educators may play an important role in addressing prejudice and bias in the U.S. educational system and assist in ensuring a better future for all U.S. citizens through their work with Latina/o education and competency development.

As the United States transitions into an economy and workforce based increasingly on technology, the role of educational preparation is paramount. Latinos have strong beliefs about the importance of education for upward mobility (Hill & Torres, 2010). The educational system in the United States is increasingly emphasizing advanced technology in virtually all fields of work. Computers, laptops, and the Internet are used in elementary schools, and proficiency with technology is quickly becoming a prerequisite for most careers. This prerequisite presents a barrier for Latinos, as they have been shown to use the Internet at half the rate of Whites, which may be due to economic issues (e.g., a lack of personal or school access to technology) or cultural issues (e.g., the fact that technology tends to be impersonal). In addition, when states pass laws that restrict access to higher education the educational pipeline constricts again. In California, one of the most populous Latino states, there are now waiting lists for the comprehensive universities and community colleges. It is a sad irony now that more Latinos are moving toward a college education. Thus, one of the main engines of social and economic mobility may actually be working against Latinos.

• • •

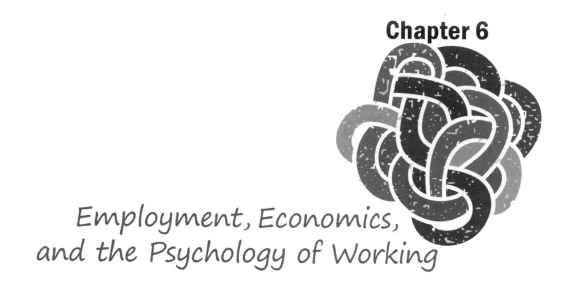

Employment, Economics, and the Psychology of Working

Palabras sin obras, guitarras sin cuerdas.

Words without deeds are like guitars without strings.

(Rovira, 1984, p. 103)

• • •

Objectives

- To review the employment status of Latinas/os older than age 16 according to different criteria.
- To examine earnings and their correlations with social class, poverty status, and family living conditions.
- To highlight the contributions over the decades of agricultural workers and other Latino-heritage workers to the U.S. economy.
- To discuss worker programs and other legislation that have affected Latina/o immigrant workers and others perceived to be unauthorized immigrants.

Sabías que/Did you know that . . .

- After the 2007–2009 recessions, immigrants had a faster rate of job recovery than native-born Latino workers (American Enterprise Institute, 2011).
- Latinas/os are underrepresented in management, professional administration, and related occupations.
- Approximately 47.1% of Latino families earned less than $20,000 a year in 2010 (Motel, 2012).
- The need for self-determination is a psychological driver for Latinas/os in the workforce.
- In 2012, Latinos expressed confidence in their personal finances and the direction of the country (Pew Hispanic Research Center, 2012).

• • •

Case Scenario

Jaime was 15 years old, in 10th grade, and a well-liked student. But in a matter of 2 weeks, he seemed to have changed. He became short-tempered with friends, slammed his locker door, and seemed listless in class. Concerned, Ms. Lorenzo, his math teacher, invited him in for a conversation. Jaime was sullen but said everything was okay. Not sure what to do, Ms. Lorenzo went to the school counselor, Mr. Peña. Mr. Peña knew Jaime and his parents very well, as their families had all grown up together and attended St. Teresa's Church. Jaime's parents, Maria and Victor, had enrolled their two children in Catholic schools since prekindergarten. As first-generation college graduates themselves, they had high expectations for their children. Flor and Jaime were attending St. Teresa's high school in downtown Denver where Mr. Peña was the counselor. The school had become a destination for many Latino families because of the quality education, and thanks to the Latino parents, the school, once targeted to close, was thriving. In the fall, Maria had been informed about a layoff at the advertising company where she worked. They were going to eliminate administrative positions like hers, thereby reducing the payroll by cutting higher earning professionals. Just a year ago, she had been promoted and started receiving a six-figure salary that allowed them to buy a new home in an upscale neighborhood. Victor was the district manager for a Denver-based bank; his salary was good but less than $100,000 and certainly not enough to manage the family budget. Victor had confided in Mr. Peña one day after Sunday Mass. He felt distressed but was trying to put on a brave front for the family. Maria, in contrast, was very calm, behaving as though everything were normal. Knowing what he knew about Jaime's behavior and the family situation, Mr. Peña considered the course of action he should follow. The most logical thing to do was to call Jaime into his office and have a discussion about his changed behavior. Should he bring up the family situation if it was not mentioned? Should he call Victor? He did not want to violate personal and professional boundaries, but he wanted to help the family.

How often do counselors confront such dilemmas? Although there is not yet any research on this topic, it is not uncommon for Latinos to work in communities where they grew up or to become known in Latino communities because of their outreach and involvement in different sectors of life. Moreover, are counselors aware of how the downturn in the economy has affected students and their families in their respective schools? What about the counselors themselves? Dishonest mortgage lenders overvalued property and perpetuated harm on many innocent people. Mr. Peña may not have been one of these innocent people, but perhaps he had family members who were affected.

The American Dream

The American Dream is the belief that anyone can succeed in the United States through determination, hard work, and courage (Hill & Torres, 2010). Success is attributed to individual effort and hard work. The American Dream implies that contextual factors such as immigrant status, race, gender, and socioeconomic status are not factors in the achievement of success and the attainment of wealth. The American Dream is often known as the Horatio Alger myth or the rags-to-riches story. Key to the preservation of inequality is the endorsement of meritocracy, which is the belief that merit is assigned solely on the basis of competence and ability (Wiley, Deaux, & Hagelskamp, 2012). That is, people get what they work hard to get. Both people in the United States and new immigrants to the country are aware of this myth—and so too are Latinos. The American Dream, however, may serve to perpetuate and legitimize inequality between Whites and racial and ethnic minorities, often referred to as *non-Whites.*

One requisite of the American Dream is that there are always examples of people who have made it and who have pulled themselves up by their bootstraps. For the myth to endure both positive and negative examples must be widely known. In the case of ethnic minority groups, this involves identifying model minorities and those who fail to live up to the dream. Research has indicated that second-generation Latinos endorse the myth of meritocracy less than those in the first generation. Meritocracy was negatively linked to ethnic identity and, through it, support for collective action among the second generation. Among the first generation, meritocracy was not related to ethnic identity and was positively related to support for collective action (Wiley et al., 2012). Latinos are aware of the myth of meritocracy because several Latino subgroups have been identified as either being model minorities or failing to achieve the American Dream. For example, Shorris (1992) examined the historical, socioeconomic, and immigration contexts of different Latino subgroups. Although he focused on many different groups, much of the attention rightfully belongs to members of the three largest Latino-heritage groups: Mexicans, Cubans, and Puerto Ricans. Each group has had different historic entry points into the U.S. workforce with implications for differential earning power, employment and career opportunities, and socioeconomic advancement.

Social class, classism, and *social capital* are relevant terms in a discussion of Latino economics and employment. Although classism occurs in the United States, it is highly enacted and in place in Latin American countries. Social class status is signified by color, heritage, education, and income. Social class and classism are legacies of conquest, with land ownership assumed by the Europeans, who immediately became wealthy. If counselors watch the *telenovelas* (soap operas) on Spanish-language networks, they will come in contact with classic classism. The *telenovelas* generally feature White, wealthy, troubled families served by indigenous servants. The latter are often stereotyped in their appearances, but they are consistently darker phenotypically and visibly different from the homeowners. The indigenous and mestizo servants were relegated to work the land and homes of the landowners for decades.

Often, a major culture shock for Americans moving to Latin America is *classism*—prejudice or discrimination based on social class. However, classism is beginning to play out in some Latino communities in the United States as well. In a story first published in 2007, reporter Kate Pielemeier of the *Pittsburgh Post-Gazette* reported on rifts between authorized and unauthorized immigrants from Central and South America. The former were primarily professionals with formal education, and the latter were in low-paying jobs. Accordingly, stratification between the groups reflecting the socioeconomic inequality prevalent in Latin America was becoming evident. A spokesperson for the Community Justice Project stated that the Latino professionals "who have achieved the American dream don't want to be confused with *los 'Mexicanitos'*" (Pielemeier, 2007). Another example of classism had to do with social separation at Mass. Apparently the more well-to-do Latinos sit in the front of the church and the lower class in the back. In some churches in the Milwaukee and Boston areas, one of the authors (Arredondo) has seen a similar practice. The Latino congregants, primarily immigrants, attend Mass in the church basement, complete with their own choir and visiting priest. The fact that this is allowed suggests collusion by the church leaders with discriminatory practices.

In the sections that follow, we provide a brief accounting of the work history of the three largest Latino groups and also describe some within-group differences that portray Cuban Americans as the model minority. This is followed by specific work-force data on the industries and occupations in which the majority of Latinos are employed, occupational health and safety concerns, earnings, *remesas* (remittances), poverty indicators, and Latinos as consumers and entrepreneurs. The final section discusses the psychology of work and indicators with particular relevance to a Latino worldview and the effects of organizational climate on Latino performance.

A Historical Perspective

Country of origin, immigration status, region of the country, and historical era have largely dictated the nature of work available and the preparedness of newcomers to assume particular employment needs. In the industrial and preindustrial eras, immigrants readily found employment in the frontier of the expanding United States. Although Irish immigrants overcame prejudice such as "Irish need not apply" signs in Boston and on the East Coast in the late 19th century, xenophobia continues to be a factor in attitudes toward Latina/o workers. So it is that in the 19th, 20th, and 21st centuries, individuals of primarily Mexican and Puerto Rican origins have been associated first with the agricultural industry and second with the manufacturing industries. In effect, these work histories and patterns also coincide with the employment needs and opportunities and the economies of different regions of the country. In the 20th century, the service and construction industries grew, attracting more Latina/o immigrant workers. With changing education and employment needs, there are shifts as well in opportunities for the young and growing Latina/o workforce. However, insomuch as we are trying to promote a comprehensive understanding of Latina/o individuals and different heritage groups, it seems appropriate to provide a historical context for the Mexican American and Puerto Rican workforces and their past and current contributions to the U.S. infrastructure and economy.

Mexican-Origin Families and the Agricultural Industry

Mexicans and more recently immigrants from Central America have historically been overrepresented in the agricultural industry. Seasonal farm workers and their *familias* (families) followed the crops, arriving in Washington State for apple-picking season and heading down to Florida to pick oranges and other food crops. The majority of agricultural workers have always been and continue to be of Mexican heritage. They arrived through different channels, such as guest worker programs for migrants and seasonal farm workers. For many decades, others arrived through porous borders long before their presence as illegals became criminalized. Still other families, such as that of civil rights leader César Chávez, tilled the soil on their family lands, which were lost to self-appropriating Americans as a result of the Treaty of Guadalupe Hidalgo in 1848.

The National Agricultural Workers Survey, published by the U.S. Department of Labor (2003), documents data on the workforce from the previous 10 years. The survey classifies workers as crop workers and international and domestic immigrants. The findings revealed the following:

- 75% of the workers were born in Mexico.
- 53% of all respondents were not authorized to work in the United States.
- Foreign-born newcomers made up 16% of the hired crop labor force.
- On average, foreign-born crop workers had entered the United States 10 years before being interviewed (2001–2002), but the majority of these workers (29%) reported that they had been in the United States for 15 or more years.
- Agricultural workers are employed in almost all 50 states. (p. 1)

Employment Eligibility

Employment eligibility varies for foreign-born workers and crop workers as well. The term *migrant* has often been associated with agricultural and seasonal farm workers, but some distinctions in types of migrants can be made. These distinctions also have implications for eligibility for particular services funded by the federal government. According to the National Agricultural Workers Survey, *migrants* are defined as "persons who travel at least 75 miles during a 12-month period to obtain a farm job" (U.S. Department of Labor, 2003, p. 2). In 2001–2002, migrants made up 42% of crop workers, down from 47% in 1993–1994.

Even further delineation can be provided. Those migrants who leave their home base and travel the 75 miles within the United States to work in one location are referred to as *shuttle migrants*. Individuals who travel to various locations throughout the year are called *follow-the-crop migrants*.

Foreign-born newcomers, undocumented and increasingly from southern Mexican states and Central America, present with different types of circumstances, sadly reminiscent of the conditions faced by the farm workers César Chávez championed in the 1960s and 1970s. Involuntary servitude was chronicled in *Nobodies* (Bowe, 2007), a harsh reminder of the ongoing abuses of contemporary foreign-born migrant workers, who are often unauthorized. Bowe (2007) described labor camps or slavery rings in South Florida that exploited the humanity of the workers. Often these individuals were constantly threatened with death; received low pay to no pay; and lived in abominable, unhealthy conditions. Because 40% of the farm laborers in Florida each year are newcomers, they are subject to abuse and manipulation. In talking with workers, Bowe learned that many had worked the land in their home countries; they had experienced hard work but not the kind of mistreatment they encountered in the United States. Not knowing the law and being isolated in remote Florida areas made them easy targets for abuses, Bowe and the Coalition of Immokalee Workers discovered. A constant threat for undocumented workers are the U.S. Immigration and Customs Enforcement patrols that arrest employees who have no legal papers and those who imprison them to work.

Although agricultural workers continue to be a part of the U.S. workforce, they are not afforded the same rights as other workers. Agribusiness was historically allowed to ignore labor rules, which only penalized the workers. According to Bowe (2007), in 1938, at the time of the New Deal when minimum-wage laws were enacted, farm workers were excluded thanks to the strength of the agriculture lobby. This remained in force through 1968, the time of the Farm Workers movement. Even today, however, many laborers, unlike other hourly workers, do not receive overtime pay, medical insurance, or sick leave and are often denied federal protection by exploitive employers. In 2011, the Wage and Hour Division announced new protocols and has since begun certifying nonimmigrant visa applications for those immigrants who are victims of crimes and are willing to cooperate with law enforcement in the investigation and prosecution of those crimes. Far too often, however, immigrants will remain silent for fear of being deported.

Puerto Rican Migration

Puerto Ricans (self-referred to as *Boricuas*) are the second largest Latino-origin population in the country. Their arrival to the mainland began at an important historical moment, the beginning of World War I, a time when foreigners, particularly those from Europe, were not allowed into the country. With the passage of the Jones Act in 1917, Puerto Ricans became U.S. citizens. Almost immediately, many Puerto Rican men were drafted into World War I, and others were hired to construct ships and armaments in industrial complexes primarily on the East

Coast and in the Midwest. Seen as cheap labor, Puerto Ricans were recruited by employers to work, particularly in the New York city area, beginning in the 1930s. Migration steadily increased. By 1953 an estimated 75,000 people had left the island, and by 1964 the Puerto Rican community made up 9.3% of the population of New York City, living primarily in East Harlem and Brooklyn (Latino/a Education Network Service, n.d.).

To meet workforce needs, Puerto Ricans settled in other urban areas across the country, including Boston, Jersey City, Chicago, Philadelphia, and Hartford. During the 1950s and 1960s, more than 20,000 were hired as contract farm laborers. They toiled in the agriculture industries along the Connecticut River Valley and southwestern New Jersey, often exploited because they did not speak English and had little formal education. Dishonest employers often did not comply with the law regarding work contracts and put Puerto Rican workers at a severe disadvantage. For example, often workers had to pay for transportation on installment plans, and these costs were subtracted from their wages. Medical coverage was rare, and because they lived in rural areas, these workers had to buy at the company store. Living conditions in the North were harsh for these islanders, who were accustomed to humidity and hot weather.

Puerto Rico's proximity to the mainland has brought more Puerto Ricans to central Florida in the past 20 years. These citizens have increasingly been displacing the dominant Cuban population of the last 50–60 years. In fact, in the 2012 Presidential election, the Puerto Rican and Central American vote was underestimated. With more than 800,000 residing in and around Kissimmee and Orlando, this populous, largely Democratic, voted overwhelmingly for President Barack Obama. In contrast to the conservative Cubans in South Florida, the political rise of this Central Florida Latino group seemed to catch the country by surprise.

Cuban Refugee Migration to the United States
In the 1950s and 1960s the United States was embroiled in a war against communism on several fronts. Fidel Castro and his army overthrew U.S. interests in Cuba during the Cuban Revolution and a mass exodus of Cubans began. These refugees had their property taken by Castro's regime; they fled communism and made their way to the capitalist United States with just a suitcase and the clothes on their back. Given the reality of the Cold War and their refugee status, Cubans were greeted in the United States with formal relocation programs (with $1.3 billion dollars of aid in 1966) and given several privileges (government assistance, English courses, and low-cost education and business loans). The first bilingual school in the country was established in Coral Gables, Florida, in the late 1960s, a deliberate strategy to fast-track the Cuban refugees into the mainstream. The new Cuban immigrants, of course, were most appreciative of this newfound acceptance. The rapid acculturation and success of Cuban Americans meant that they were held up as a model minority. As the third largest Latino group in the United States (only slightly larger than Salvadorans), Cuban Americans lead other Latino groups in most markers of success (and unfortunately they also lead in negative markers, such as high divorce rates; see Delgado-Romero, Rojas, & Shelton, 2007). They have held political office, primarily in Florida, as state senators and representatives or Congresspersons, and many have gone on to higher education and professional careers. Cubans are a capitalist success story, and even subsequent waves of Afro-Cubans in the 1980s were able to benefit from that reputation (after initial vilification).

Yet the reality is that in addition to having strength and a commitment to succeed, Cuban Americans received benefits and advantages that are unheard of among modern-day immigrants. This point was brought out in previous discussions regarding immigrants' acculturation to the United States. Political climate matters, as do the relations between an immigrant's home country and the United States. Clearly, the U.S. government had an investment in demonstrating that life in its democracy was superior to life in communist Cuba. Thus, Cuban refugees to the United States experienced social and financial advantages and often attributed their success to their individual efforts in working hard in a capitalist society.

Contrast this example to the experiences of Mexican Americans. Mexicans occupied much of the Southwest before it was the United States and have experienced waves of immigration and repatriation tied to economic conditions in the United States and Mexico. Mexican Americans both have the longest tenure in the United States and are among the most continuous as well as most recent immigrants. Mexican Americans have faced historical and contemporary discrimination and what Shorris (1992) termed *racismo* (racism) from other Latino populations who sought to distance themselves from Mexican Americans. A history of exploitation and historical discrimination in the United States is often ignored when stereotypes are perpetuated about Mexican Americans. Mexican Americans are often blamed for their lack of economic success and are stereotyped as lazy and criminal. Mexican Americans are often the scapegoats in harsh economic times and invisible in the good times (see the movie *A Day Without a Mexican*; Artenstein & Arau, 2004). Consequently, both Whites and Latinos themselves unjustly stereotype Mexican Americans as the Latino group that has failed to realize the American Dream.

The myth of the American Dream reaches beyond Mexican Americans, Puerto Ricans, and Cuban Americans and impacts all Latinos as they try to advance in all facets of life in the United States. This book is being written in a historical time for the country, a time when more Latinos than ever before are voting in the Presidential election. The fact that Latinos were a swing vote for President Obama in 2012 is indicative of the effect this increasing populous has on the economy, politics, and employment.

Latinos as Chief Executive Officers and in Senior Government Positions

In 2012, there were six Latino chief executive officers of Fortune 500 companies, accounting for 1.2% of all Fortune 500 chief executive officers: Antonio Perez (Eastman Kodak), George Paz (Express Scripts), Paul Raines (GameStop), Enrique Salem (Symantec), Josue Robles (United Services Automobile Association), and Cristóbal I. Conde (SunGard). Latino governors are primarily located in the Southwest, with two governors of New Mexico being of Mexican American heritage: Former Ambassador to the United Nations Bill Richardson, a Democrat, was followed by Susanna Martinez, a Republican. Antonio Villaraigosa was the first Mexican American mayor of Los Angeles. This has a certain irony, as Los Angeles is the largest metropolitan area in the country with a breadth of Latino-heritage residents. San Antonio, a city densely populated by persons of Mexican heritage, has had several Mexican American mayors. Perhaps the most recognized is Henry Cisneros, who later went on to become Secretary of Housing and Urban Development in the Bill Clinton Administration. Another mayor, Julian Castro, spoke at the 2012 Democratic Convention. Characteristic of many of these visible leaders is their family stories. The majority are immigrants or children of immigrants.

In 2010, President Obama appointed Sonia Sotomayor to the U.S. Supreme Court, a source of enormous pride for Puerto Ricans and all Latinos. He also appointed Hilda Solís to serve as Secretary of Labor.

Latinos and the Labor Movement

Through the leadership of César Chávez, Dolores Huerta, and other civil rights leaders in the 1960s, the United Farm Workers Union was formed and the grape growers were challenged. Workers went on strike and a grape boycott took place nationally, all to improve the working and living conditions of workers and their families. Workers lived in unsanitary conditions, had their paychecks withheld, and were forced to work exhaustive hours. One of the many concessions made by the landowners was the elimination of the short hoe that contributed to literally back-breaking labor. Although the days of widespread abuse of agricultural workers seem to be a thing of the past, abuses continue, as in the example of labor camps in Central Florida.

The move to organize agricultural workers in the 1970s led to the formation of representative unions not unlike César Chávez's United Farm Workers Union in the Southwest. These sought to negotiate more equitable contracts that improved working conditions. Other groups emerged, committed to reform for Puerto Rican farm workers. In Connecticut, these included the Comité de Apoyo al Migrante Puertorriqueño (Puerto Rican Migrant Support Committee), Asociación de Trabajadores Agrícolas (Agricultural Workers Association), and the religious group Ministerio Ecuménico de Trabajadores Agrícolas (Ecumenical Ministry Farmworkers). Many seasonal migrants did not return to Puerto Rico after the termination of their contractual obligations but instead moved to surrounding urban regions. A "conservative estimate" places the number of contract workers who opted to stay on the mainland at 10% (Sanchez Korrol, n.d.). Under such circumstances, it was not unusual for seasonal laborers to make initial inroads into specific geographic regions, establishing enclaves for future migrants. Entire communities soon sprouted that traced their origins to specific towns and cities in Puerto Rico. Today, there are few Puerto Rican laborers in the agricultural industry. Because they are U.S. citizens, children of those early workers have had the opportunity to pursue formal education and other career tracks.

The Latino Workforce

The Latino workforce aged 16 and older is the fastest growing sector of the labor force today. In 2011, 15% of the U.S. labor force was Hispanic or Latino. The majority of Hispanics in the labor force were Mexican (63%). Others were Central and South American (25%), Puerto Rican (8%), and Cuban (4%). Whites made up the majority of the labor force in 2011 (81%) and Blacks and Asians an additional 12% and 5%, respectively. Native Americans and Alaska natives composed about 1% of the labor force, as did persons of two or more races. Native Hawaiians and other Pacific Islanders made up less than 1% (Bureau of Labor Statistics, 2012a).

Consider these data on Latinas/os in 2011:

- The nearly 23 million Latinas/os in the workforce represented 15% of the U.S. labor force.
- Of Latinos aged 16 and older, 58.9% were employed, and approximately 1 in 5 was working part time.
- Women made up 41% of all Latinos in the labor force compared to 46% of Whites in the labor force. Latinas represent a smaller share of the labor force because of both the high labor force participation of Latino men and the lower labor force participation of Latina women compared to White women.
- A total of 5.8% of Latinos were self-employed.
- By 2018, Hispanics are expected to make up 18% of the labor force (U.S. Department of Labor, 2012).

Occupational Categories and Industries

Several sources (e.g., the American Community Survey, Bureau of Labor Statistics, U.S. Census Bureau, and Pew Hispanic Center) provide data about the Latina/o workforce based on gender, industry, occupation, and detailed occupation. These data are also compared to data on other groups based on ethnicity and race. Because age 16 and older is the baseline for this reporting, the data are not further detailed by age across the different groups. Comparisons among Latino, Asian, Black, and White groups will always reveal totals and percentages that are greater for the White population. This is not surprising, because White people make up the majority (70%) of the contemporary workforce (Blacks, 10.8%; Asians, 4.9%; and Latinos, 15%).

- At 15% of the total workforce, Latinos are overrepresented by a substantial amount in several industries and occupational categories. They account for 50% of miscellaneous agricultural workers; 18% of service workers (cleaning and maintenance); 46% of hand packers and packagers; 29% of construction workers; 41% of painters; 43% of carpet, floor, and tile installers; 38% of butchers; and 40% of food processing workers (Motel, 2012). These occupations require minimal to no formal education and training. The breakdown is different for other racial/ethnic groups:

  - Blacks make up 11% of all employed workers but account for 33% of nursing, psychiatric, and home health aides; 27% of security guards; and 27% of taxi drivers.
  - Asians make up 5% of all employed workers but account for 55% of miscellaneous personal appearance workers (makeup artists, manicurists and pedicurists, shampooers, and skin care specialists), 27% of software developers, and 16% of physicians and surgeons.
  - Whites make up 82% of all employed persons but account for 96% of farmers, ranchers, and other agricultural managers; 95% of firefighters; and 94% of construction managers.

Industry Sectors

- A total of 18% of employed Hispanic men worked in construction in 2011, a larger share than White (12%), Black (7%), or Asian (3%) men.
- A total of 12% of employed Black men work in transportation and utilities compared with 7% each of Hispanic and White men and 36% of Asian men. About 17% of employed Asian men work in professional and business services, more than their White (13%), Latino (12%), and Black (11%) counterparts.
- A large share of women in all racial and ethnicity groups worked in education and health services in 2011: Blacks (42%), Whites (36%), Asians (31%), and Hispanics (30%; Bureau of Labor Statistics, 2012a).

Case Scenario

Señor Pablo Torres was 75 years old when his daughter Miriam brought him to the community health center because of his persistent migraines. Miriam's father had suffered from migraines all of his life, but not this bad. Miriam recalled her father requiring bed rest in a dark room when he came home from his job as a bartender in a local restaurant. Originally from Ponce, Puerto Rico, Mr. Torres had arrived to Hartford, Connecticut, with his parents in the early 1950s to work on a farm. When the work ended, he moved with his family to Chicago, where family members, also from Ponce, resided. Manufacturing work was plentiful in the 1970s. After a few years, Mr. Torres moved on to restaurant work, eventually becoming a bartender. Recently, Señor Torres returned from a visit with his son in Hartford; the headaches returned with great intensity.

A counselor, Alicia, a woman in her mid-30s, was assigned the case. She too was Puerto Rican and spoke Spanish; however, Alicia felt uncomfortable because Señor Torres was her grandfather's age. As she assessed the situation, it occurred to her that perhaps she could use her relationship experiences with her *abuelo* (grandfather) when speaking with Señor Torres. Her *abuelo* was a storyteller, and rather than focus on the headaches, Alicia decided to invite her new client to tell his story. Señor Torres gave Alicia an accounting of his early years, eventually recalling an incident that contributed to his first migraine.

Hardships for Workers

Immigrants often face many barriers in the struggle to establish themselves economically in the United States. For example, educational and credentialing systems in Latin America are often not recognized in the United States, which prevents some immigrants from pursing their occupations. In many Latin American countries the graduate education system differs from the one used in the United States, and thus professionals are not able to obtain credentials or employment commensurate with their education. For those who are able to get credentialed, language issues, racism, and discrimination may then present as barriers.

As we have discussed, Latino immigrants who are unauthorized and who are not well educated are ripe for exploitation by employers and others. The prevailing wisdom is that such Latinos will do jobs that other people will not do, and they are often subjected to unsafe working conditions, economic exploitation, and the threat of deportation. For example, Latinos working in agricultural settings might be exposed to toxins, workplace injuries, and even economic exploitation. Immigrants have related stories about how the U.S. Immigration and Naturalization Service would conduct raids before payday. Undocumented and uneducated Latinos in such situations have almost no legal rights.

Occupational Health and Safety

With Latino men largely employed in the construction industry and other occupations that demand physical labor, it may not be surprising that incidences of accidents and deaths among Latino men are higher than among other ethnic and racial groups. According to preliminary estimates from the Bureau of Labor Statistics, in 2010 Latino workers experienced a high rate of work-related fatal injuries: 3.7 incidents per 100,000 full-time equivalent workers, compared to 3.6 for Whites and 2.8 for African Americans. However, there were 4.3% fewer work-related fatal injuries in 2010 compared to 2009 (Byler, 2013).

According to Singley (2012):

- In 2011, 729 Hispanic workers died from an occupational injury, compared to 707 workers in 2010. Although the number of Latino fatalities increased in 2011, the Latino fatality rate was unchanged from 2010, at 3.9 deaths per 100,000 workers. The national fatality rate was 3.5.
- In 2011, the foreign-born share of fatally injured Latinos was the highest in 5 years. Approximately 69% of Latino workers killed on the job in 2011 were born outside of the United States. Although immigrant workers have typi-

cally accounted for the majority of Latino occupational fatality victims, 2011 was the first year since 2005 that immigrant workers accounted for 69% or more of Latino fatalities.

- A rise in fatalities in landscaping services likely contributed to the increase in Latino fatalities. In 2011, 167 workers in landscaping services were killed on the job, up from 133 workers in 2010. Latinos represent 43.7% of landscaping workers but 14.5% of the total employed workforce. Tree trimmers and pruners experienced the largest increase in fatalities. Falls, slips, and trips were the leading causes of death in landscaping work, followed by contact with objects and equipment.

A report from the National Council of La Raza (2011) includes stories of many immigrants and their work-related injuries, many that were life threatening and put an end to their employment status. For example, *We Needed the Work: Latino Worker Voices in the New Economy* discusses Reynaldo's back injury and his employer's abusive behavior. Rather than filing a worker's compensation claim, the employer fired Reynaldo and his brothers, leaving them indebted with medical bills. Because they have informal arrangements with employers, many immigrants do not have the paperwork to substantiate claims in court, and the employers know this.

Earnings, Poverty, and Health Insurance

A Pew Hispanic Center report (Motel, 2012) with data from the 2010 American Community Survey provides stark information about earnings and poverty levels for Latinos in the United States. In 2010, 47.1% of Latinos earned less than $20,000 a year, 38.9% earned $20,000 to $49,999, and 4.1% earned $50,000 or more. Among year-round employees, 53% earned less than $20,000. Only Blacks, 54.2% of whom earned less than $20,000, earned less. Moreover, 24.6% of Latino households nationally earned less than $20,000 in 2010. Finally, 32.4% of those living in poverty were younger than age 18, 20.9% were between the ages of 18 and 64, and 18.7% were 65 or older. With respect to health insurance, 14.2% younger than age 18 did not have health insurance, as did 43.1% of those aged 18–64 and 5.3% of those older than 65.

More recent data point to discrepancies in earnings and employment based on occupation, race, ethnicity, and sex for 2010 (Bureau of Labor Statistics, 2011). A few facts point to Latino earning power:

- Half of Latinos working full time earned at least $549 per week in 2011. This median weekly wage was only 71% of that earned by Whites (U.S. Department of Labor, 2012).
- In this analysis, the highest paying major occupation groups, inclusive of full-time jobs in management, professional, and related occupations, were analyzed. Among those employed in management, professional, and related occupations, the earnings ratios of White, Hispanic, and Black men to Asian men were 92%, 72%, and 68%, respectively. In contrast, the earnings of White men employed full time in production, transportation, and material-moving occupations were higher ($667) than the earnings of Black, Asian, and Hispanic men ($595, $584, and $525, respectively; Bureau of Labor Statistics, 2012a).
- In 2011, foreign-born Hispanics or Latinos who were full-time wage and salary workers earned 77% as much as their native-born counterparts. Among Whites, Blacks or African Americans, and Asians, foreign-born and native-born workers had similar median weekly earnings (Bureau of Labor Statistics, 2012b).

- Findings revealed the weekly earnings shown in Table 6.1. A factor in these findings is the actual percentages of workers by race and ethnicity found in this highest paying occupation group (see Table 6.2). Percentage-wise, very few Latinas/os are in the highest paying major occupational category of management, professional, and related occupations. In 2011, 47% of employed Asians worked in this occupational group, compared with 38% of employed Whites, 29% of employed Blacks, and 20% of employed Hispanics (Bureau of Labor Statistics, 2012a).

The Demographics of Job Recovery

It is impossible to discuss workforce data since the 2010 Census without commenting on the greatest recession since the Great Depression, which began in October 1929 with the stock market crash. It took nearly 10 years for economic recovery to begin, because even then the country was involved with international imports and exports. A discussion of economic recovery relies on two types of changes: changes in employment levels (e.g., employment rank, position, and status) and changes in employment rates (e.g., the percentage of the population that is employed; Kochhar, 2012). These changes have affected Latinas/os differently. For example, unemployment data need to be considered.

In *The Demographics of the Jobs Recovery*, Kochhar (2012) cited trends for different U.S. ethnic groups. The period for the modern recession is defined as the fourth quarter of 2007 to the fourth quarter of 2009. For example, in 2009 Latinos and Asians had higher employment levels than before the recession commenced in December 2007, and Latino and Asian immigrants were also experiencing a faster rate of growth than native workers. The explanation may have to do with new workforce entrants aged 16 and older for these two ethnic groups, which is higher than for other ethnic groups in the U.S. Unemployment varied among the foreign- and native-born Hispanic labor force in 2011. Among those who had not graduated from high school, the unemployment rate for the native born (17.4%) was much higher than the rate for the foreign born (10.8%). In contrast, native-born Hispanics with a bachelor's degree or more had a lower unemployment rate (5.0%) than their foreign-born counterparts (6.7%). The unemployment rate for those with some college experience but not a bachelor's degree was about the same for native- and foreign-born Latinos (Bureau of Labor Statistics, 2012b).

A surprising finding in these data is that women overall did not keep up with men in terms of job gains. The reasons for this result remain unclear. Several factors could have contributed to the smaller decline in unemployment among Latina women. One potential factor is their disproportionate participation in industries that have continued to experience job losses, such as state and local government. For example, 55% of Latino government workers in 2011 were women (Bureau of Labor Statistics, 2012b).

Table 6.1
Weekly Earnings, 2010

Ethnicity	Wages (Dollars)	
	Men	Women
Asian	1,414	1,122
Black	965	825
Latino	1,019	818
White	1,294	948

Source. Bureau of Labor Statistics (2012a).

Table 6.2
Percentage of Workers in the Highest
Paying Major Occupational Category
of Management, Professional, and
Related Occupations, 2011

	Percentage	
Ethnicity	*Men*	*Women*
Asian	49	44
Black	24	34
Latino	16	25
White	35	42

Source. Bureau of Labor Statistics (2012a).

With the recovery under way in 2011 and 2012, employment has increased more for Latinos and Whites than for Blacks and Asians. In fact, employment of Latinos increased from 19.5 million in the fourth quarter of 2009 to 20.7 million in the fourth quarter of 2011, an increase of 6.5% (Kochhar, 2012).

Remesas

Despite their low wages, immigrants continue to send cash transfers, or *remesas* (remittances), to support their families in their home countries. All told, the world's 215 million international migrants transferred about $372 billion to developing countries in 2011 compared with $332 billion in 2010 (World Bank, 2011). Ranking first and second in terms of remittances received were families in India (receiving $64 billion) and China (receiving $62 billion); families in Mexico ranked third. Mexican families were the recipients of $24 billion of such aid in 2011. There was also an increase in remittances to families in El Salvador and Guatemala. The World Bank projects that remittances will reach $467 billion by 2014 (World Bank, 2011).

The Inter-American Dialogue, a Washington-based think tank, predicted "a 7% or 8% increase in remittances to Latin America and the Caribbean" in 2012 (Jordan, 2012, p. A16). This would mean an increase to $69 billion, up from $64 billion in 2010. An official with the Inter-American Dialogue discussed the reasons for these continuing and increasing remittances. With the increase in the number of seasonal work visas issued by the United States, more workers are sending money back home. In addition, Mexican working women, some of whom are college graduates or have some higher education, "send more money than anybody" (p. A16). About one third of Mexican women working in the United States have a college degree or some higher education, and their ranks have been growing.

Entrepreneurship and Business Ownership

The spirit of entrepreneurship, creativity, and innovation is not new to Latinas/os, nor is the common expression that people have to pull themselves up by their bootstraps. A visitor to any Spanish-speaking country will readily see a preponderance of vendors in marketplaces, with kiosks or small trucks or carts and other open-air setups designed to sell something and earn a living. That same behavior is evident in many U.S. cities and communities with a critical mass of Latinas/os, particularly immigrants. According to the U.S. Census Bureau (2010b), the number of businesses owned by Hispanics more than doubled from 2000 to 2010.

The rate of entrepreneurial activity among Latinos decreased from 0.56% in 2010 to 0.52% in 2011 but remained at a high level relative to previous years and in comparison to other cultural groups. The rate of entrepreneurial activity among Asians also decreased in 2011 (from 0.37% to 0.32%). Although 2011 saw a decline in the rate, Latinos began to experience a sharp upward trend in entrepreneurship in 2006 (Fairlie, 2012).

The report *America's New Immigrant Entrepreneurs: Then and Now* (Ewing Marion Kauffman Foundation, 2013) showed that 24.3% of engineering and technology startup companies have at least one immigrant founder serving in a key role. Furthermore, another study showed that immigrants founded one quarter of U.S. technology startup companies (Minority Business Development Agency, n.d.).

Hispanic-owned businesses make up another segment of economic growth in the community at large and in the United States. A report from the Minority Business Development Agency (n.d.) cited several indicators of growth:

- "Hispanic-owned firms generated $351 billion in economic output to the U.S. economy and created 1.9 million jobs" (p. 1).
- In 2009, buying power was $978.4 billion for Latinos and $2.46 trillion for all minorities. This purchasing power was deemed greater than that of countries such as Indonesia, Australia, The Netherlands, and 14 other countries across the world.
- In this same period, Latino firms were most concentrated in the following industries: construction (15%); administrative, support, and waste management and remediation services (14%); and health care and social assistance (10%).
- From 2002 to 2007, Latino-owned firms grew faster than the national average in 27 states and Washington, DC. The highest rates of growth were reported for Arkansas (160%), North Carolina (136%), Georgia (78%), and Alabama (76%). The latter two states have been particularly harsh with anti-immigration legislation targeted at unauthorized immigrants, the majority being of Latino heritage.
- From 2002 to 2007, Latino-owned firms were concentrated in states with large representations of Latinos, such as California, Florida, Texas, and New York. It is also noteworthy that both California and Texas are now considered majority-minority states, with Latinos making up the majority of the population in these states.
- From 2002 to 2007, Latino businesses engaged in more export activity (5.1%) than other ethnic minority firms (4.7%).
- From 1992 to 2009, the top three countries for ethnic minority firm exports were Mexico, Brazil, and the Dominican Republic.

Latinos as Consumers

The notion that Hispanics in the United States make up a distinct, culturally contained population with its own tastes, language, and needs has long been embraced by corporations eager to get their share of Latino buying power, which is projected to rise from $1 trillion today to $1.5 trillion by 2017 (G. Garcia, 2012).

Most Americans spend the largest share of their annual income on housing, which includes mortgage payments, property taxes, and insurance. Latinos spent 37% of their average annual income on housing in 2010. African Americans' share was 39%, higher than Whites (34%) and Asians (35%). Latinos had lower median earnings than other racial and ethnic groups. They spent a higher portion of their income on food (16%), which is often explained by the fact that they have larger families and eat at home more than outside of the home. Finally, 5% of Hispanics' annual income was spent on apparel, more than the shares of income spent by Whites (3%) and Blacks or African Americans (4%). Again, larger families are an explanation for this spending (Bureau of Labor Statistics, 2012b).

Case Scenario

Melinda was thrilled to have a position as a school counselor outside of Washington, DC. She had grown up in northern Virginia, where her parents had settled after escaping the civil wars in El Salvador. Melinda was very appreciative of her parents' sacrifices and often talked about this during lunch breaks with her colleagues. She also felt lucky to be in a school that served a critical mass of children of Latino immigrants and was always willing to get involved with parents outside of the school setting. One day she was approached by the head counselor with a concern. It appeared as though other counselors considered her engagement with Latino parents as an ethics violation, specifically a boundary issue referred to as *dual relationship.* Melinda was dumbfounded. At school she was the go-to person to translate for parents regardless of the situation. Outside of school, she ran into children and their parents at one of two Catholic churches, at the grocery store that catered to Latino families, and at community cultural events. Socializing with them seemed natural, and there were few other Latinas at work, so Melinda felt a part of the local Latino community. Melinda was confused about the feedback and decided to consult the office of ethics of the American Counseling Association.

Latinos and Taxes

Despite popular myths, all workers, including immigrant workers, pay taxes in America as a result of their hard work. A recent study by Citizens for Tax Justice revealed that the lowest income workers—who average about $13,000 in annual earnings—paid a total of 17% (or $2,262) of their income on state, local, and federal taxes. And according to the Social Security Chief Actuary, undocumented workers paid $12 billion in payroll taxes to Social Security in 2007, though they are ineligible to receive benefits (National Council of La Raza, 2012).

Physical and Mental Health Stressors

To recognize and appreciate the types of mental health stressors encountered by Latinas/os in the workplace, one must consider models and concepts from vocational psychology, multicultural counseling, and Latino psychology. Individuals work in settings ingrained with their own cultures and worldviews. At times, these are at variance with the worldviews and cultural backgrounds of the employee. More specific to Latinos (who are overrepresented in the service and agricultural industries and who are often mistreated, with low salaries, no benefits, and no health insurance), emotional, physical, and spiritual stressors are often masked by the desire to work hard and be accountable. In counseling settings, educational institutions, and different workplaces, counselors have to broaden the lens they use to facilitate the well-being of their Latina/o clients and employees. The next section on the psychology of working links theoretical principles to prevalent Latino values and research-based examples of how these are enacted.

The Psychology of Working

The psychology of working, work identity, and factors such as racism and sexism affecting employment well-being have been discussed by vocational psychologists (Blustein, 2006; R. T. Carter & Cook, 1992; Fouad & Byars-Winston, 2004). These psychologists are giving voice to the role of work as a dimension of one's total lived experiences and how, over time, thinking about the role of work as a vocation has evolved from and built on Frank Parsons's (1909) original framework. Indeed, Parsons focused on the working poor and immigrants and the types of interventions that could benefit their well-being and sense of self-efficacy.

Blustein (2006, 2008) discussed the psychology of working and the psychology of careers as two different constructs, with the latter more about "an optimal match in the world of work" (2008, p. 233). Of particular relevance in this discussion of the Latino workforce are three human needs that, according to Blustein, working can fulfill: the need for survival, the need for relatedness, and the need for self-determination. In their study of Latino immigrants in the Midwest, L. Y. Flores and her colleagues (2011) mentioned barriers and access to work as additional factors that affect one's work experience and psychological well-being.

Considering the preponderance of Latinos primarily in nonprofessional roles and in low-paying, low-skill industries, counselors need to understand and appreciate these three human needs in order to support individuals in context. Thus, a counselor might question why adults are willing to work 12–14 hours in the fields or why they take on two jobs while their children have to fend for themselves. The worldview of a graduate student regarding work and the need for survival is not the same as the worldview of an immigrant with less than a high school education and the obligation to support a family in the United States and in his or her homeland. For these two people, work has different meaning and value that must be appreciated without judgment. In an article on immigration precipitating an identity crisis it was stated that immigrant workers struggle with inferiority over their competence, embarrassment and humiliation, and feelings of being overwhelmed, but they know they must persist and survive for the collective good of their families (P. Arredondo, 1986).

The Need for Survival and Power

Immigrants have historically arrived to the United States with one primary goal—to improve the living conditions and well-being of their families and themselves. Latino immigrants have been at the forefront of the U.S. labor force for nearly 150 years, eking out an existence in dangerous, hazardous, and abusive work conditions. Contemporary Latino immigrants, like the European newcomers chronicled by Handlin (1951) in *The Uprooted*, make enormous sacrifices to survive and follow through on their objectives to come to the United States. In *We Needed the Work: Latino Worker Voices in the New Economy* (National Council of La Raza, 2011), immigrant workers describe persistence in the midst of adversity, including work-related injuries that required hospitalization. For example, Reynaldo suffered a back injury when he fell from the roof of a house on which he was putting shingles. He was uninsured, and his employer insisted that he was not going to provide coverage with the company's insurance. Reynaldo lamented, "I have this belt to support my back and I am in a lot of pain. I don't know feel well and I don't know if I'm going to be able to work well again" (p. 2). In spite of multiple obstacles, he was not giving up but was concerned about his ability to work as he once had. This is a statement of survival and power.

L. Y. Flores and colleagues (2011) found further rationale for the drive to survive along the lines of Maslow's (1950) hierarchy of basic needs. Working for basic necessities was essential because this affected one's well-being and that of the family. Interviewees had the following mantra: "You want something? You have to work. You want shoes? You have to work" (p. 528). Immigrants expressed a desire to improve circumstances for their families in the United States and in their home counties. *Remesas* were included in immigrants' spending plans. Interviewees also spoke about education for their children and provided them with clothes, books, and a home they owned.

Immigrants also want to get ahead. In one study, those who experienced the 2008–2010 economic downturn, left home countries with fragile economies where they depended on seasonal employment, recognized the tenuousness of employment. Thus, they prepared themselves by enhancing skills and getting new training, improving their English speaking and writing skills, and networking in their communities. All but one participant talked about desires for advancement and promotion (L. Y. Flores et al., 2011) and becoming supervisors and being trainers. The employees knew their work so well and recognized that they could lead others and that their bilingual capabilities were assets to supervising and training other immigrants.

The Need for Social Relatedness

The need for social relatedness is particularly relevant for Latinos in the workforce. The collectivist culture and the values of *personalismo* (valuing/building interpersonal relationships) and *simpatia* (accord, agreement, and harmony in relationships) point to how the work setting can enhance a sense of connection and well-being. Immigrants may work in settings where they can relate by speaking Spanish or be understood by a supervisor who is bilingual. In work settings with a sense of positive relatedness, individuals may have a greater sense of connection to the social fabric of the external community (Blustein, 2008). L. Y. Flores and colleagues (2011) learned how their study participants perceived social connections at work as forms of social relations and supports with both coworkers and supervisors. Network development with family, friends, and coworkers was mentioned because it gave the individual a means to manage difficulties at work. Sometimes these difficulties related to a relationship with a supervisor. By speaking with coworkers, particularly other Latinas/os with a longer work history in the factory, the newcomer learned how to address a problem situation. Of course, this does not mean that there are harmonious relations among all Latino coworkers and supervisors. Sometimes the Latino supervisor played favorites, as occurs in other workplaces, causing disgruntlement and frustration.

For Latina/o college graduates in professional settings, the need for relatedness versus isolation is critical (P. Arredondo, 2010; L. Y. Flores et al., 2011). The only-lonely phenomenon is often experienced by many Latinos who may be the only one in their department or at a particular level of the institutional hierarchy. Many variables may affect an individual's sense of well-being as the visible or invisible Latina/o. These include phenotype, English language fluency, university affiliation, region of the country, supervisor, mentor or sponsor, size of the organization, and so forth. In *The Tale of "O"* (Kanter, 1979), the stress and demands on underrepresented individuals in the professional work environment are discussed. These individuals, often labeled *tokens* in the social psychology literature, are expected to give voice to the opinion of all Latinas/os, be spokespersons with community groups on behalf of the university or company, appear at cultural events, and sit on committees to represent the Latina/o viewpoint. When this occurs, the need for relatedness is not enhanced; rather, it is likely that performance anxiety and extra demands contribute to emotional stressors as well as a sense of isolation and confusion about who one really is in this environment (P. Arredondo, 1986).

The Need for Self-Determination
The need for self-determination is evident in the historical accounts of the persistence of Latino immigrants and families in the face of myriad barriers to employment, unhealthy working conditions, and other indignities to their personhood. In *We Needed the Work: Latino Worker Voices in the New Economy* (National Council of La Raza, 2011) individuals share their stories of motivation, self-determination, mutual support, and honesty. Here is "Rosa's Demand for Respect," a snapshot of why she lobbies to unionize other hotel workers:

> More than anything, it is the stress that turns you into knots. They give us a raise of $.15 cents a year; nobody makes more than $10.50. All of the hotels in this area pay $14 an hour. If we leave this fight, everything will stay the same and they will continue exploiting more people. (p. 18)

A strong work ethic was discussed by Latino immigrants in the Midwest (L. Y. Flores et al., 2011). This meant putting the company's interests ahead of their own, even if it meant staying longer at work. One participant in this study reported that she would do whatever was requested, even if it was something extra, and another immigrant spoke with pride about her collectivist motivation to work hard. Her sentiment was that it was "important to show employers that immigrants can succeed" (p. 530). Immigrants are aware of the discriminatory perceptions and low expectations of Latino workers and want to demonstrate their can-do attitude.

Specific to the psychology-of-work perspective, Blustein (2008) pointed to motivational psychology to further understand why individuals continue in work situations even when "job satisfaction and the expression of intrinsic interests are not readily available" (p. 234). This statement suggests the worldview of privilege often projected by vocational psychologists that job satisfaction is optimal and that working is driven by intrinsic interests versus external demands. To be culturally responsive, counselors need to appreciate that many Latinas/os do not have a choice to be in occupations that they (the counselors) would consider as not providing satisfaction or fulfilling intrinsic needs. Although not specific to Latinas/os, research indicates that it is possible to experience self-determination even in jobs that are not intrinsically motivating if other conditions are present that foster a sense of autonomy, competence, and relatedness (Deci & Ryan, 1985, 2000).

This was also discussed by P. Arredondo (1986) as she described the virtues or ego strengths of immigrants as they work through Erikson's (1964) life-cycle tasks. The ego strengths of hope, will, purpose, and competence serve immigrants as they participate in the world of work and other changing life situations. *Orgullo* (pride) and *dignidad* (dignity) are motivating cultural values for Latinas/os. Although the work of a hotel maid or a worker in a chicken processing plant may not seem desirable to a counselor, pride and dignity are core to one's work identity and mental well-being; these cannot be minimized as individuals exercise their need for self-determination, regardless of the occupation. It is fair to conjecture that these ego strengths are also assets, examples of resilience for contemporary Latina/o professionals who find themselves navigating unfamiliar workplace cultures and being the other. Earning tenure in a department in which one is the only Latina junior professor, or making it up the corporate ladder in a financial investment company in which one is the first Latino hire, requires that individuals appreciate their competence and have a support network that validates them as well.

Latino Values for Accountability
Another construct for understanding the three fundamental human needs proposed by Blustein comes from a four-factor model of worldview introduced by

Derald Wing Sue (1978). The model describes the role of privilege and oppression as factors that differentially and negatively affect ethnic minorities. In this discussion, the focus is on work and careers.

The four factors are IC/IR, EC/ER, EC/IR, and IC/ER. IC/IR individuals believe that they have internal control and internal responsibility for driving their careers and choices in other life situations. The opposite worldview is EC/ER: Individuals externalize control and externalize responsibility, generally because they believe they have no power or ability to effect change in their lives and thus do not take action to change their situation. The EC/IR factor reflects individuals who view the limitations to their control—for example, they cannot change laws that give lower wages to immigrants, especially those who are unauthorized—but still work because they must assert responsibility. The IC/ER perspective characterizes individuals who have the credentials or skills to pursue employment but choose to wait for the right job to come along. They have privilege but do not exercise it and externalize their responsibility. Our contention is that Latinos, particularly low income wage earners and the underemployed, hold an EC/IR worldview. The data indicate that overall Latinos older than age 16 participate in the workforce at a rate of 19.5% (U.S. Census Bureau, 2010a). A report from the National Council of La Raza (2011) amplifies this point through the voices of Latinas/os.

Workplace Barriers

Affirmative action policies were introduced into the workplace more than 50 years ago. Designed to provide equity to underrepresented groups such as women and ethnic minorities, the policies have had varying levels of effectiveness and have also brought about the negative effects of stigmatization. That is, being viewed as an affirmative action hire introduces another form of stress for Latinas/os entering the academy. If the home department has a positive view of affirmative action, provides a sense of community, and engages in relevant mentorship of their new hires, it is likely that Latino faculty will report more job satisfaction and less self-doubt (Niemann & Dovidio, 2005). Complicating self-doubt are feelings related to stereotype threat (Steele, 1997); the only-one phenomenon; and performance anxiety related to meeting expectations for teaching, research, and public service.

The borderlands experience is a metaphor one can apply when working with Latina professionals—yet it could apply to men as well. The concept suggests that Latinas, in particular those in professional roles, bear psychic stress due to expectations of family and self-expectations, role conflicts, doubts about competence, and double standards that play out in the workplace (P. Arredondo, 2011). Because they are underrepresented, they often encounter what is called the "chilly" climate (Sandler & Hall, 1986), a workplace fraught with exclusion and microaggressions. Furthermore, because most workplaces are primarily White, the only person noticed is the visible racial ethnic group (Helms, 1990), in other words Latinas. Phenotype is visible, and although Latinos span the color kaleidoscope, distinguishing physical attributes and sometimes an accent bring undesirable attention. A person knows that she stands out and others notice too. "Niceness," reported Alemán (2009), can be a liability for Latinas. Because most are typically socialized to be polite, to respect authority, and to defer to men, they engage in behavior that may come across as noncommittal or engaging. Latinas' consideration of others through niceness, respect, and decorum may mean that they do not express dissatisfaction and appear too appeasing and agreeable (P. Arredondo, 2011). Unfortunately, if this behavior is reinforced by their supervisor, the Latinas will be disadvantaged.

In Chapter 3, acculturation and acculturative stress were discussed among a number of factors that may affect the mental and physical well-being of Latinos in transition. In that context, unemployment and underemployment were cited as stressors in the acculturation process. However, as reports about the recent recession indicate, the negative effects of the recession have been greater for Blacks and Latinas/os (Goldsmith & Diette, 2012), especially as they relate to long-term unemployment. In Chapter 7 we focus specifically on the myriad stressors affecting Latinos, and counselors will gain an increased appreciation of contextual, interpersonal, and intrapersonal factors that affect Latinos, often over the lifetime. Because people cannot change their phenotype and leave many dimensions of their immutable identities at the office door, because of subtle and overt reminders of difference, they have to be prepared to manage these uninvited stressors. Counselors can make a difference through culturally informed and responsive interventions.

Case Scenario Analysis

Let's return to Mr. Peña's situation for a moment. The dilemma confronting Mr. Peña is one faced by many counselors as they work with children of families who are encountering economic hardship. The downturn of the economy has affected people of many ethnicities, including counselors themselves. If you were Mr. Peña, would you feel protective of the parents or the child who is acting out? Counselors are empathic; does this mean they allow inappropriate behavior because they know the student is going through a hard time? Two Latino-specific competencies state the following: "Culturally-skilled counselors can incorporate knowledge about specific social, economic, and familial characteristics in a cultural context and informed framework that leads to effective helping of families" and "Culturally competent counselors can advocate for a family in need of services" (Santiago-Rivera, Arredondo, & Gallardo-Cooper, 2002, p. 55). Mr. Peña has to put aside his personal feelings and take charge so that both the child and the parents are supported.

Another observation has to do with counselors who themselves may have been affected by the economic conditions that began in 2008. Depersonalizing is not easy, yet ethical standards remind counselors to be nonjudgmental, be respectful of diversity, and otherwise act in the best interest of the client. Counselors cannot bring their biases and feelings into situations like that facing Mr. Peña. It is easy to get caught up in anti-Latino immigrant sentiments and blame the victim. When counselors begin to have such feelings and or overidentify with the plight of their Latino clients, supervision is in order.

Concluding Thoughts

Although it is possible to consider the employment and economic situations facing Latinos as challenging and even oppressive, their optimism and striving for self-determination comes through in the different accounts throughout this chapter. A report by the Pew Hispanic Research Center (2012) revealed Latinos' growing confidence in their personal finances and the direction of the nation. One third (33%) of the respondents in the study reported that their finances are in good or excellent shape, up from 24% in a 2011 study. Another positive indicator is that the poverty rate among Latinos fell to 25.3% in 2011 from 26.5% in 2010. Finally, with respect to unemployment, the rate for Latinos at the end of the third quarter of 2012 was 9.9%, down from 11.2% in 2011 (DeNavas, Proctor, & Smith, 2012). Perhaps Latino accountability reflects their optimism and their willingness to persist in the midst of economic adversity.

Counselors would be interested to learn that in the same study Latinos expressed greater satisfaction with the direction of the country than any other Americans. For example, 51% reported satisfaction in contrast to only 31% of others. Only 43% of Latinos said that they were dissatisfied; for others it was 64%. The same study indicated that foreign-born Latinos expressed greater satisfaction than native-born Latinos (Pew Hispanic Research Center, 2012).

What are the new or additional knowledge points for professional counselors? How might the data, scenarios, and other historical information about Latinas/os as workers in particular industries and occupations, as entrepreneurs, as consumers, and as taxpayers broaden counselors' understanding of the complexity of the Latina/o population in the United States? We hope that the following facts might be put in a counselor's toolbox, irrespective of work setting. Keep in mind the following:

- College students may have family members still working in the agricultural industry, and this can be a source of both pride and embarrassment.
- Although data indicate that Latinos spend more on food and clothing, this likely means that they are spending on children or even extended family members who are staying with them. Generational differences, family size, immigrant status, geographic location, and so forth should be taken into account.
- Immigrants or foreign-born workers are still seen as low-wage earners, and employers continue to exploit them.
- Not all Latinas/os have family histories in the agricultural and manufacturing industries.

Knowledge is power, so review the facts introduced in this chapter and the following Latino-specific competencies. Culturally skilled counselors are able to do the following:

- Describe Latino-specific values that serve as reference points to understand individuals' attitudes about work and dignity.
- Recognize their own biases about certain types of employment held by Latino workers.
- Learn more about the work history of Latino groups in the city or local community.
- Learn more about legislation that affects Latinos and other marginalized groups in their state and nation.
- Identify opportunities to engage in social action on behalf of Latinos who are marginalized based on class and other immutable identity factors.

• • •

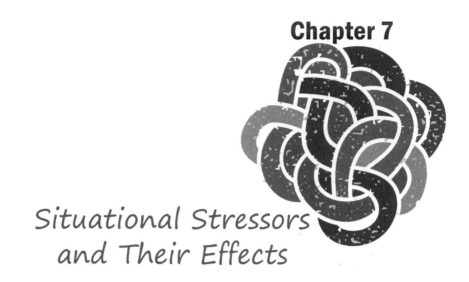

Chapter 7

Situational Stressors and Their Effects

También de dolor se canta cuando llorar no se puede.

Sorrow also sings, when it runs too deep to cry.

(Sellers, Nelson, & Soto, 1994, p. 32)

• • •

Objectives

- To understand how Latino interactions with the educational, health, political, and correctional systems in the United States can be stressors.
- To examine the role of racism and colorism as stressors and factors in Latino social and economic mobility.

Sabías que/Did you know that . . .

- External racism and discrimination and internalized racism are salient negative stressors in Latinos' day-to-day experiences.
- The threat of deportation for oneself or for family members weighs on one's psyche.
- Stereotype threat has a psychological effect on performance in different contexts.

• • •

Case Scenario

Surrounded by buildings that were hundreds of years old, Susanna wondered what she had ever done to earn the privilege of attending this private college. As she watched her wealthy classmates walk across campus, she thought about life in her inner city hometown. She remembered the concrete buildings, metal detectors, and dangerous walks to school. Her family scraped to get by, and Susanna knew her parents often went hungry to feed her and her siblings. In college there was an abundance of food, security, and safety. Most of her classmates had never known anything else but this life.

Susanna had made good friends, but there were few Latinos and other students of color on campus. Furthermore, she did look like the other blue-eyed, White students who went shopping in New York City on the weekend. Susanna often felt that she was a token or an imposter, but her friends dismissed the thought. She was very bright and had worked hard to get here. She had been granted early admission and had also gotten the highest score possible on several Advanced Placement exams, testing out of certain general education requirements. But Susanna still had an uncomfortable feeling as she looked at the world beyond the campus gates. How could both of these worlds exist? And where would she find herself once she graduated? And finally, what about her brothers and sisters? Were they ever going to have this opportunity? Here there was a wonderful health center; if she sneezed, she could stop in for a quick checkup. Meanwhile, her parents and siblings had no health insurance. Her parents worked jobs that did not provide the benefits. What about her cousin Lalo, who was in jail? Would he ever get to see this campus?

Susanna felt pressure to graduate to help get her family out of their home and into a better life. She felt selfish for being at this lovely university while her family needed financial help. Susanna had offered to quit and come home to work, but her parents would not hear of it. Everyone had sacrificed so much to get Susanna into college. The silent and unrelenting pressure Susanna felt often gave her headaches. Who could possibly understand what she was feeling and thinking? Perhaps she was living a lie.

Overview

Throughout the text, there are intersecting themes and examples of life situations for individual Latinos and *familias* (families). Although this highly heterogeneous, polycultural group has been present for centuries on what is considered U.S. territory, there have been continuous experiences of oppression in different contexts and in different forms—covert, overt, and internalized. *Xenophobia,* or fear of foreigners, is a shadow over most Latinos today, regardless of their family's long-term history in the United States (10 generations or more) or their own third- or fourth-generation status. For Latino immigrants the circumstances are even more stressful.

In this chapter, we introduce different types of stressors reported in the literature as well as by Latino individuals in this country. Because this is a book about counseling, it is fair to say that all of the stressors have a psychological impact that is both immediate and chronic. However, this would be too simplistic. Rather, we want to convey the interaction of stressors on daily and future well-being and their effects not only on individuals but also on their families, their communities, and the country as a whole. Perhaps the most well-known social ecological model used to illustrate the interaction of individuals and systems is Bronfenbrenner's (1979) ecological systems theory, discussed in Chapter 4. Environmental or external stressors affect the individual, as well as the layers in between. Thus, individuals are affected by all levels—macro-, exo-, meso-, and microsystems. In short, stressors, be they legislative actions that limit access to health care, hate crimes, or another type of external action, affect an individual and his or her family's sense of well-being. Counselors must understand what triggers stress because, as argued by Kurt Lewin (1935), behavior is the result of a person's interaction with the environment. In this chapter, we also provide examples of Latino cultural assets that contribute to resilience. Latinos must persist to transcend adversities, and the fact that they continue to thrive as individuals and as an evolving, contributing demographic group in this country can be a lesson to counseling professionals. Thus, as you read this chapter, please do role-taking and begin to think about how you will be able to use this information in your role as a counselor.

Racism and Colorism

Contrary to popular belief, Latinos are not a distinct racial group, as we have discussed. Instead, Latinos have a mixed heritage representing Europe, the United States, Latin America, and the Caribbean. In many Latin American countries the issue of race is conceptualized along a continuum of racial descriptors (Duany & Silver, 2010), and the panethnic term *Latino* has no significant meaning. However, keep in mind that rather than a scientific construct, race is a social construct. Race is used in U.S. society as a pliable construct that conveys power relationships between groups; in the United States these groups are Whites and non-Whites (e.g., Blacks). Consider this tangible example of a way in which the majority culture seeks to dissect and redefine Latinos: The 2010 Census officially broached the notion that in the United States Hispanic was an ethnicity, and Hispanics/Latinos had to then also choose a race. The dominant White/Black binary conceptualization of race was forced onto Latinos, and, as was reported in Chapter 1, more Latinos chose to self-identify as White versus Black Hispanic. Vasconcelos's (1925) characterization of Latinos as members of a cosmic race because of intersecting cultural identities or the polycultural attributions proposed by M. Ramírez (1998) have been subjected to a standard of racial classification that truly does not fit.

Latinos do not universally embrace this concept of Hispanic ethnicity, and there are several ways in which Latinos resist being labeled as *Black* or *White* (Diaz McConnell & Delgado-Romero, 2004). On entering the United States, Latinos encounter a new system for classifying race and ethnicity, and this new system for self-identification and ascription can be confusing. For example, a person from Bogota, Colombia, may find herself classified as Latino alongside people from countries with different traditions, foods, and customs. Although they all might speak Spanish, the language has different accents, words, and rhythms. Phenotype is another variable. Latinos are often referred to as "brown" people, and although a majority may be darker than persons from northern Europe, they vary in their placement across the color spectrum. Latinos may have blond hair and green eyes, reflecting European heritage; may look Asian in facial appearance, a tribute to indigenous ancestry; or may be visibly Black, evidence of African heritage. The label *Latina/o* or *Hispanic* glosses over significant differences between national groups and even within those national groups. Consequently, Latinos in this country are potentially faced with an identity crisis and attributions about who they are that do not fit their self-perception (see Chapter 4).

One of the authors (Arredondo) participated in a workshop called Modelos para Jovenes, a role model program for middle school students in a bilingual classroom. One of the students, a young woman of Dominican descent, asked, "Did you always like being Mexican?" The student was visibly Black, spoke English with a minimal accent, and looked like some of the other Latino children in the room but not like others. Her question was indicative of an issue we ourselves have faced, one that is pervasive in U.S. society, which has predominantly White role models in visible positions (except perhaps for professional sports and entertainment, areas in which Latinos still continue to be unrecognized).

New immigrants to the United States are quickly socialized into the country's racial classification system, which divides society into the classifications of White versus non-White. Evidence indicates that this racially dichotomous system impacts immigrants, who then begin to adopt the system themselves (i.e., they begin to think of themselves as either White or not White). For many Latinos, feeling White is a marker of success and inclusion. Tafoya (2004) stated, "Whiteness is clearly associated with the immigrant experience. Thus, the U.S.-born children of immigrants are more likely to declare themselves White than their foreign-born parents, and the share of Whiteness is higher still among the grandchildren of immigrants" (p. 1). Tafoya also found that among immigrants from the same country, those who became U.S. citizens were more likely to identify themselves as White than those who did not become citizens.

Choosing White or Some Other Race

Tafoya (2004) and Logan (2003) analyzed census data to create a portrait of Latinos according to their chosen racial classification. Tafoya examined the differential portrait of White Hispanics versus Some Other Race (SOR) Hispanics. She found that SOR Hispanics were less educated, were less likely to be U.S. citizens, were poorer, were less likely to be monolingual English speakers, and had lower rates of intermarriage with non-Hispanic Whites. Tafoya reported that White Hispanics occupied the middle ground between (non-Hispanic) Whites and SOR Hispanics in terms of status and outcomes. Tafoya stated a concern that SOR Hispanics were feeling excluded from the U.S. mainstream. Similarly, Logan analyzed census data by race and found three groups of Hispanics: White Hispanics, Black Hispanics, and Hispanic Hispanics (i.e., those who chose Hispanic as their race). White Hispanics had the highest levels of success and education and Black Hispanics the lowest. Hispanic Hispanics occupied the middle ground and were the most rapidly growing group. As Latinos continue to develop their sense of identity, new ideas of race will challenge U.S. thinking about race. It is important to note that Latinos differ in how they feel about their racial or cultural identity (e.g., cultural pride vs. shame) depending on the circumstances that brought them to the United States, the area of the country where they choose to live, attitudes toward other racial groups, and the extent to which they can retain the Spanish language and/or Latina/o culture. In our opinion, cultural pride and shame may be two sides of the same coin.

Although self-identification is important, Latinos must also live within the U.S. racial system, which means that others might try to ascribe racial characteristics to them. Some Latinos might be treated as if they were White or Black/African American, and this imposed racial categorization may have both positive (privilege) and negative (discrimination) consequences. Thus, the issues of external racism and discrimination and internalized racism are salient ones for Latinos. A. S. Ruiz (1990) posited that part of a healthy Latino identity involves developing an identity free from internalized racism and stereotypes.

Colorism, Racism, and Classism

Colorism, racism, and classism coexist. Throughout history many different ethnic groups have immigrated to the United States, but European Whites have been the dominant group politically, socially, economically, and numerically. Although there has been considerable discrimination against certain groups of Whites (e.g., the Irish, Mormons), eventually most Euro-Americans have been accepted as part of the dominant group. However, ethnic minority groups may be assigned value and worth based on the interaction of their race and class. Often ethnic minority groups are thought of as being of a lower social class and less intelligent than Whites, and unequal educational, judicial, and financial systems create and perpetuate this belief. The cycle of poverty then ensures that marginalized groups remain marginalized.

Comas-Díaz (1996, 2012) has examined how internalized racism plays a role in Latino societies. She tied colorism and racism to the legacy of the colonial mentality. Spanish conquistadors colonized much of Latin America and brought with them racial schemas based on their own mixed racial history (see Nieto-Phillips, 2008). The Spaniards, and later the Americans, enforced a colonial system of educational, racial, economic, and political control. This control involved the valuation of White heritage and the devaluation of African and Indigenous heritage. Comas-Díaz (2012) proposed a postcolonial mentality for Latinos that included embracing the reality of African and Indigenous heritage and resisting attempts to "Whiten" Latinos through denial or marriage to Whites. For example, she noted the increasingly popular use of the self-designation *LatiNegra* by Latinas of African descent. She proposed that a postcolonial psychology would be liberating and would create a new *raza* (collective multicultural identity) of Latinos focused on a new future of pride and self-determination.

Stressors

Classism and Poverty as Stressors

Classism for Latinos varies along many variables: perceived race, English fluency, circumstances of immigration, national origin, and the region of the country where one lives. Attitudes, economic conditions, and the sociopolitical climate surrounding immigration influence the economic situation for Latino people in the United States. Although it is clear that Latinos as a group struggle with the reality of poverty, there are many factors to consider when examining the issue of economics and class. Race, language, and culture are often intertwined, as one of the tenets of assimilation is the surrendering of racial, linguistic, and cultural distinctiveness. That is, to move up the economic and social ladder in the United States immigrants and ethnic minority populations are expected to take on the preferences and social conceptualizations of the dominant White majority. As we have stated previously, the less Latinos are associated with being White, the worse their educational, health, and vocational outcomes. Conversely, those who choose to identify as White Latinos have better outcomes (Logan, 2003). Because race is a social construction, it seems logical to infer that improving social class in the United States is tied to assimilation to White norms rather than actual ability, hard work, or innate characteristics. As has been discussed, the educational, correctional, and health systems of the United States consistently fail to treat non-White Latinos fairly, obstructing pathways to improving socioeconomic well-being and social class. Thus, many Latinos are caught in the cycle of poverty—or worse, resigned to a marginalized existence in which the threat of deportation, economic struggles, or incarceration looms large.

To address issues of classism and poverty counselors must understand how to bring necessary resources, information, and technological training to the Latino population. They must also conceptualize the issue as having both psychological (e.g., internalized racism) and environmental (e.g., unsafe schools, environmental racism) components. Finally, counselors must understand that poverty is also related to worse health outcomes (e.g., obesity, heart disease); mental and physical health disparities; lack of insurance and preventive care; and injuries resulting from working low-paying, dangerous jobs. Workplace protections that are available to U.S. citizens are usually not available to unauthorized workers, thus making them even more vulnerable to injury and exploitation.

The cycle of poverty is insidious and pervasive. Social inequality is perpetuated and maintained by societal classism and internalized classism. As discussed in Chapter 5, poverty is not equally distributed among the Latino population. That is, certain groups in certain areas of the country (e.g., Mexican Americans in central California) seem to be particularly vulnerable. Thus, once again the importance of context must be emphasized. Cuban Americans tend to have the highest educational and economic attainment of all Latino subgroups, but even this success is below the average mean for Whites in the United States. This situation calls to mind the image of a glass ceiling.

Lack of Health Care Access as a Stressor

Health insurance is often a benefit of work in the United States. Estimates indicate that around 32% of Latinas/os younger than age 65 are uninsured, whereas the percentage of uninsured Whites and Blacks is half that number (U.S. Census Bureau, 2009). When a person lacks insurance, the only medical care available is in the emergency room. This means that preventive factors would have limited effects because access to health care insurance is the barrier to having a primary care physician. This leads to a vicious cycle in which only the most ill receive medical care. Seriously ill Latinos cannot work to afford health care, and because they do not have insurance, they cannot get well. The cycle leads to chronic illness, unemployment, and poverty. Remember how in the case scenario at the beginning of this chapter Susanna reflected on the wonderful health center on campus and the plight of her family, who lacked health insurance despite being employed.

The following *dicho* (proverb) is expressed by many Latinos, particularly immigrants and older adults: *No hay mal que dure cien años, ni un cuerpo que lo resista* (There is no evil that lasts a hundred years, nor any body who could resist it). It speaks to the mindset of many Latinos, or *fatalismo* (the acceptance that one cannot control everything in life), with respect to health and mental health problems and conveys an acceptance of life circumstances but also a belief that one's body can withstand life's challenges.

When people do not have health insurance they lack access to mental health care. Latinos in general tend to use mental health care at much lower rates than Whites, and within the broad Latino category, the utilization rates for Puerto Ricans are twice those for Mexican Americans (Alegria et al., 2007; Alexandre, Martins, & Richard, 2009). Issues of lack of insurance and access to services are even more pronounced for Latino immigrants (U.S. Department of Health and Human Services, 2001). Nonfluency in English is often the primary barrier to obtaining health care for Latina/o clients (Preciado & Henry, 1997), especially in the monolingual United States.

An unexamined barrier to culturally competent care is the lack of an adequately trained bicultural and bilingual health workforce. There are few Latino medical doctors (3%), psychologists (1%), social workers (4.3%), and registered nurses (1.7%; Chapa & Acosta, 2010). The lack of sensitivity to Latino physical and mental health issues leads to culturally insensitive or ineffective treatments (Tucker et al., 2007) and the exclusion of Latinos as participants in psychological research (Delgado-Romero, Galván, Maschino, & Rowland, 2005; Shelton, Delgado-Romero, & Wells, 2009). Structural issues like these can lead to Latino clients reporting low levels of satisfaction with care, noncompliance with treatment, and poor outcomes (Chapa & Acosta, 2010).

Language and a lack of insurance are not the only barriers to obtaining health care. Access (or the lack thereof) is a significant issue for Latinos. Access issues include a lack of physical access to services (i.e., a lack of reliable transportation), affordability, a lack of awareness of treatment options, and a lack of bicultural and bilingual health care providers and support staff. Some researchers have found that innovative treatment delivery, such as telemedicine, can prove effective with Latinos and can serve to overcome barriers to treatment (Baker-Ericzén et al., 2012).

Legislative Impediments as Stressors

Stressors come in many forms; some are more tangible than others, creating cycles or mazes that prevent Latinos from getting ahead. For example, to ensure that services are provided to legal residents only, several states require a government identification to access any government service. Multiple issues emerged in the 2012 Presidential elections, with many more Latinos registering to vote for the first time. Anecdotes about deliberately being told that absentee ballots had to be dropped off in the wrong location or being told incorrect information about necessary documents have been reported.

In most instances, to qualify for public services, one is registered with a driver's license. Obtaining a driver's license usually involves taking a written test and demonstrating one's driving skill. Some states have proposed that English be the only language in which to take the written test. Although most people with a driver's license have a certain level of income, income has little to do with whether a person can afford an automobile and insurance. And access to a driver's license is even more important than income, because getting a license requires having documentation of one's citizenship status. However, driving is also necessary for individuals to get to work. This is particularly the case in cities with poor public transportation systems, such as Los Angeles. For Latinos who work two jobs a day, driving is a necessity.

The implementation of such laws requiring government identification also serves to suppress voter turnout, and the requirement to show a government ID before voting proved to be controversial in the 2012 Presidential elections. One of the authors of this book (Delgado-Romero) recently had to provide a driver's license to renew his license as a psychologist! Thus, legislation affects all citizens and creates more work for state government. It may also feed the underground market for counterfeit licenses.

Laws that single out undocumented Latinos often end up impacting the social, legal, and educational environment for all Latinos, including those who are citizens. For example, even in the most draconian of anti-immigrant legislation, there is usually a provision that exempts access to emergency health services such as ambulances, emergency rooms, and police intervention. However, that provision is not always known or observed. One author (Delgado-Romero) knew of a Latina professor, a U.S. citizen, who was denied emergency medical transportation until she could provide proof of citizenship. Luckily her situation was not life threatening. In other words, ID laws can also cause unintentional inconvenience to citizens, who must also now produce documentation. In addition, some anti-immigrant efforts, such as roadblocks to check for undocumented immigrants, violate the civil rights of all people.

Negative Societal Portrayals of Latinos

In addition to the stressors identified previously, Latinos face barriers to employment and day-to-day life. These result from implicit and covert racism; monolingual bias; institutional racism; racial profiling; hate crimes; microaggressions; stereotype threat; and a lack of Latinos in the higher levels of education, business, and government. Concurrent with the economic downturn, anti-immigrant and anti-Latino sentiment has grown in the United States, and racial profiling and hate crimes against Latinos are on the upswing (Southern Poverty Law Center [SPLC], 2011).

Politicians are emboldened to blame Latinos for economic troubles and espouse draconian immigration reform such as Arizona HB1070 and laws in Nebraska and Alabama that make it a crime to rent to unauthorized immigrants. For example, Arizona HB1070 was written to ensure that individuals who were considered "illegals" would be removed from the state. Police officers were given permission to stop individuals they suspected were illegal. In short, the legislation sanctioned racial profiling, among other hardships, of Latinos and others suspected of being in the country illegally. In the political rhetoric Latinos are commonly stereotyped as recent immigrants (usually illegal), criminal, violent, unskilled, and guilty of taking jobs away from Americans. It is not uncommon to read or hear in the news that an unauthorized immigrant has been involved in an accident or a crime. Although these incidents are not at an epidemic level, the newscasters readily indicate that the person is an illegal alien or an undocumented immigrant (seemingly more politically correct). These portrayals were not born in Arizona in the past decade; rather, these stereotypes have existed and been used against Latino populations for decades. For example, the second wave of Cuban immigrants in the 1980s, the *marielitos,* who were not of an upper social class and who were also visibly Black, were stereotyped in this manner.

The tide of negativity is slowly changing since the 2012 Presidential election as more myths about Latinos are being debunked. Voting from all groups and from regions of the country that have grown in Latino population (Central Florida) is indicative of self-determination and awareness about U.S. politics. There is generally an underestimation of Latino interest in sociopolitical issues. However, in most Spanish-speaking countries, political engagement across socioeconomic groups is commonplace. It is understandable that that interest would persist for newcomers and second- and third-generation individuals.

Hate Crimes

A headline in SPLC's *Intelligence Report* read "Anti-Latino Hate Crimes Spike in California"—by almost 50% ("Anti-Latino Hate Crimes Spike," 2011). The time in question was 2009–2010, which saw an increase in reported hate crimes from 81 to 119. This finding took some people by surprise because there had been a drop from 2008 to 2009. However, Latinos, considered by some outspoken nativists to all be illegal, saw a spike in hate crimes from 2003 to 2007. The increase was attributed to negative media rhetoric propagated by media figures such as then–CNN host Lou Dobbs, Rush Limbaugh, and then-Congressman Tom Tancredo (R-CO).

The SPLC is the most active national organization fighting hate crimes on behalf of targeted groups, from Latinos to Muslims to lesbian, gay, bisexual, and transgender individuals. This organization takes on cases that private lawyers will not accept and has a track record of winning against big businesses and other non-law-abiding entities. For example, on October 30, 2012, it was announced that the SPLC had won a judgment of $11.8 million on behalf of guest workers against Eller and Sons Trees, Inc., based in Georgia. The initial lawsuit was filed in 2005, with the SPLC arguing that the company had cheated more than 4,000 guest workers from Mexico out of wages (SPLC, 2012). The court found that the company had violated the Fair Labor Standards Act and the Migrant and Seasonal Agricultural Worker Protection Act multiple times.

The SPLC has also interceded in school districts in Alabama and Louisiana that are engaged in discriminatory practices against Latino families. Another hate crime, this time involving two police officers in Georgia and a Latino, was brought to court in 2010 and settled. By their own admission, the officers had stopped the man riding his bicycle because of the color of his skin. Not only did they request his identification, but the officers beat the man, resulting in a broken nose and damage to his eye socket (SPLC, 2011). Sadly, there are many incidents such as these against law-abiding, hard-working Latinos. The Immigrant Justice page on the SPLC website (http://www.splcenter.org/what-we-do/immigrant-justice) provides additional examples of cases they have taken on. In 2011, the SPLC counted 1,018 active hate groups in the United States. These groups promote beliefs and practices against an entire group or class of people largely because of their immutable characteristics. As in the examples provided here, activities can involve unlawful behavior (like that of the tree company) or, more often, hate crimes against individuals. Counselors may want to refer to the Latino dimensions of personal identity model discussed in Chapter 4. Counselors cannot urge Latinos to change the dimensions of their identity, because these are part of their birthright.

Psychological Stressors

Stereotype threat is a recently examined phenomenon (Steele & Aronson, 1995) with implications for the academic performance, career decision making, and employment progression of Latinos. Stereotype threat is an internal belief that one's group (in terms of race/gender/ethnicity) does not perform well at a given task because of one's group membership. The anxiety that this threat produces serves to suppress performance on the task. One example for Latinos involves the pursuit of an academic science career. Researchers have found that when Latino science students are exposed to chronic stereotype threat, this leads to dis-identification with science and eventually to a decline in pursuing an academic science career (Woodcock, Hernandez, Estrada, & Schultz, 2012). Thus, the stereotype that Latinos are not good at science ironically leads to the confirmation of the stereotype, even among otherwise qualified students.

Guyll, Madon, Prieto, and Scherr (2010) pointed out that stereotype threat, self-fulfilling prophecies, and stigma consciousness are psychological factors that negatively impact educational and vocational outcomes and that these factors are relatively underexamined. Furthermore, the dynamics of bias toward Latinos seem to be distinct from traditional White–Black intergroup relations, and White bias toward Latinos needs to be understood as a separate phenomenon (Dovidio, Gluszek, John, Ditlmann, & Lagunes, 2010). As we have noted many times throughout the book, Latinos cannot simply be forced into existing categories; their experiences and the experiences of other groups are unique.

Workplace Stressors

Discrimination and oppression that are rooted in history and economic conditions are formidable barriers to economic advancement. These barriers may be manifested overtly (through outright prejudice and discrimination), covertly (through behaviors and policies that serve to discriminate against Latinos, often known as *aversive racism*), or internally (through internalized racism and prejudice; i.e., Latinos come to believe and amplify stereotypes out of self-hatred). This context of discrimination interacts with racial/ethnic identity and has direct implications for career development (e.g., Torres & Delgado-Romero, 2008). Researchers have begun to examine the role that the perception of barriers and motivators plays in Latino career development and what counselors might do to ameliorate barriers and facilitate career motivators (Gushue, Clarke, Pantzer, & Scanlan, 2006; Shinnar, 2007). The perception of barriers and discrimination may prove motivating to one individual and demoralizing to another. In general, the more mental energy that Latinos spend thinking about barriers such as microaggressions, the less energy is available to dedicate to other matters. For example, in the opening scenario, Susanna is not free to live a carefree life and enjoy the privileges of being a college student. She worries about her family and is sensitive to social inequity. She may feel like an impostor or a sellout. Susanna could use a culturally sensitive individual or group counselor to help her process and normalize her cognitive and emotional dissonance and to engage in some reframing. Perhaps a counselor can also give her some career or vocational guidance and help Susanna conceptualize her career in terms of her relationship with her family rather than just individually. Thinking differently about the situation can lead to stress reduction and decreased feelings of guilt.

Several researchers have tested specific career theories and models to examine the vocational issues facing specific populations of Latinos. For example, Lisa Flores at the University of Missouri has conducted a line of research that focuses on the career issues of Mexican Americans (e.g., L. Y. Flores & O'Brien, 2002; L. Y. Flores, Ojeda, Huang, Gee, & Lee, 2006; L. Y. Flores, Robitschek, Celebi, Andersen, & Hoang, 2010; Navarro, Flores, & Worthington, 2007), including applications to assessment (L. Y. Flores, Spanierman, Armstrong, & Velez, 2006) and immigrants (L. Y. Flores, Ramos, & Kanagui, 2010). The work of Flores and her colleagues is specific to Latino subgroups, contextual, and rigorous. Counselors should become familiar with the growing vocational literature on Latino people and look for trends in advancement as well as persistent barriers. This knowledge as well as counselors' self-examination of biases regarding work and careers is necessary for culturally responsive counseling.

Acculturative Stress

In other chapters, we have discussed acculturative stress and how this affects even those born in the United States because of their "differentness." For immigrant adults, first-generation college students, and college graduates who step into a workforce where they are distinctive, there will be experiences of acculturative stress. Because of their multiple heritages and historically bicultural experiences, Latinos have learned the *movidas* (steps) for adaptation. However, entering a new environment that is considered mainstream will reintroduce the need to be an observer first, role-take, engage in bicognitive thinking, and evaluate when it is safe to participate in certain contexts.

Managing multiple responsibilities, immigrant adults also have to adjust socially at work, as they shop or buy gas, and as they engage with their children's teachers. It is a new game in another language with an educational system different from those in Latin America. Acculturative stress is both practical and psychological, as individuals' sense of identity, competence, and self-efficacy is challenged (P. Arredondo, 1986). College students like Susanna also have their struggles with acculturation. Susanna's scenario depicts the self-doubts that can emerge and likely some guilt about what she has and what her parents and siblings must continue to endure. Yes, Susanna is privileged in some ways, but privilege and social capital are relative and cannot be compared to what one's peers may know and have. Susanna is adjusting to a new lifestyle beyond the college experience, which makes her feel uncomfortable and out of place. Note that Susanna begins to exhibit somatic symptoms first (headaches). Because many Latinas/os do not speak about stressors, their anxieties may manifest in physical symptoms. Only after experiencing these physical symptoms do they seek help. Culturally sensitive relationships with medical doctors and other health care professionals may be helpful in making appropriate referrals for counseling.

The Justice System and Latinos

The myth of meritocracy has two sides. One is that you get what you earn. The flip side is that those who do not work hard also get what they deserve. In the United States this usually means that those who fail to live up to the mythical American Dream often end up dealing with the justice system. Education and physical and mental health care are important factors in economics and class in the United States. However, perhaps no other institution is doing more to oppress Latinos than the justice system. The United States has the highest incarceration rate in the developed world (Bureau of Justice, 2009; Freudenberg, Daniels, Crum, Perkins, & Richie, 2005). Justice is not blind—far from it. Racial and ethnic minorities are overrepresented in the U.S. prison population, with Latinas/os, African Americans, and Native Americans fueling the growth of the prison industry. Morin (2008) pointed out that factors such as the racialization of crime, criminal justice policy based on fear, the war on drugs, the operation of the court system, and stereotypes perpetuated by the media negatively impact Latinos in the justice system. Morin pointed out that Latino immigrants have been stereotypically (and falsely) associated with criminality. Taken together, these factors contribute to the overrepresentation and growing number of Latinos in U.S. prisons.

In *Lost Opportunities: The Reality of Latinos in the U.S. Criminal Justice System* (Walker, Senger, Villarruel, & Arboleda, 2004), the National Council of La Raza criticized the U.S. criminal justice system at all levels for its treatment of Latinos. They found that Latinos (compared to non-Hispanic Whites) were more likely to be arrested, more likely to experience racial profiling, more likely to be charged with more severe crimes, more likely to be detained before trial, more likely to serve longer sentences *even if* the crimes were similar, more likely to be incarcerated in prisons and jails as youths, and more likely to be portrayed by the media as criminals. They also noted that Latinos were no more likely than non-Hispanic Whites to use illegal drugs (and were less likely to use alcohol) but more likely to be arrested and charged with drug offenses.

The overrepresentation of Latinos in the criminal justice system is troubling on many fronts. First, these facts are illustrative of discrimination and oppression. Second, the sum total effect on society is that many young people are denied education and work opportunities while in jail. Consequently, prisoners enter a cycle of mass incarceration in which the door to prison is a revolving one. Garland, Spohn, and Wodahl (2008) stated that the disproportionally high risk of incarceration faced by African Americans and Latinos is the most serious issue facing policy makers. They based this assertion on the negative impact that incarceration has on individuals and communities and the subsequent lack of integration of Latinos into the larger social, economic, and political landscape of the United States. The National Council of La Raza report concluded with a call for increasing the number of culturally competent Latino and bilingual professionals in the prison system and as attorneys, public defenders, and advocates (Walker et al., 2004). That call should sound familiar to counselor educators.

A 2011 report from the Department of Justice indicated that Latino men and Latinas make up the second largest group of inmates in state or federal prisons behind African Americans (Carson & Sabol, 2011). The most common types of crimes committed by Latino inmates are violent crimes (54%; e.g., murder), drug crimes (20%), and property crimes (16%; e.g., burglary). M. H. López and Light (2009) reported on the relationship between immigration enforcement and the changing profile of federal prisoners. They noted that from 1991 to 2007 the percentage of federal convictions for immigration offenses increased from 7% to 24%, with most (80%) of that population being Latina/o.

Noncitizen Latinas/os (which represent 75% of immigration sentences) tend to be convicted of unlawful entry into the United States, whereas citizen Latinas/os (19%) tend to be convicted of smuggling, transporting, or harboring an unlawful alien and of unlawful entry. Because of sentencing guidelines, Latinos in federal custody tend to receive shorter sentences than individuals of other ethnicities. However, rather than being subjected to immediate deportation, noncitizen Latinos are deported after serving their sentences, which costs taxpayers unnecessarily.

The population of incarcerated Latinas is unfortunately growing. Latinas are twice as likely as White women to be incarcerated and tend to receive harsher sentences than Whites (e.g., more lifetime sentences; Sentencing Project, 2003). Relative to their numbers in the total population, Latinos are twice as likely to be in state prisons and almost 5 times as likely to be in federal prison. Latinas are also disproportionately sentenced for drug offenses. Galvan (2012) reported that the intersection of drug offenses, prison terms, and a lack of documentation means that many incarcerated Latinas are separated from their children and have no information on where the children are. Galvan, a federal corrections psychologist, implemented a culturally adapted (see Bernal & Domenech Rodríguez, 2012), empirically supported parenting group for incarcerated Latina mothers and found that the adapted intervention was more successful than one not designed for Latinas.

M. H. Lopez and Livingston (2009) examined the criminal justice system from a different lens. They examined the confidence that Latinos have interacting with police, courts, and prisons. Their results indicated that Latinos have low confidence in but high exposure to law enforcement, and their low levels of confidence are closer to those of African Americans than Whites.

The International Association of Addictions and Offender Counselors (IAAOC), a member division of the American Counseling Association, works with juvenile and adult offenders. Counselor educators and practitioners specializing in addictions and the justice system have an opportunity to play a more active and responsive role with Latinas/os. Furthermore, through their frameworks for prevention, intervention, and cultural competence, they can prepare prison staff and others in the criminal justice systems to better understand the harm of separating children from mothers. In the field of culturally adaptive evidence-based practices, IAAOC counselors have a new call to action that promotes social justice and benefits Latina/o families and children.

Models of Resilience

Given the multiple stressors and grim statistics discussed, counselors could have a pessimistic view of the state and future of Latinos in the United States. However, that type of thinking focuses solely on pathology, and in their training counselors are called on to examine variables such as resilience and cultural strengths.

Consider the following: Latinos have considerable strengths that manifest themselves in health outcomes that are puzzling (the so-called Latino paradox). For example, in the first calculation of Latino life expectancy the Centers for Disease Control and Prevention found that Latinos outlive Whites by an average of 2 years and Blacks by an average of 7 years (Arias, 2010). Researchers have struggled to explain this paradox. Some propose that immigrants have superior diets (e.g., they avoid fast food), exercise more (e.g., by walking), support one another in the family, and do not indulge in tobacco or alcohol as a general rule. Sadly, these protective factors tend to decline the longer immigrants live in the United States, as they take on the dietary, health, and substance abuse habits of the majority. It is important for counselors to examine resilience and strengths so that these factors may intentionally be used or supported for the benefit of the Latina/o population.

Researchers are starting to understand the value of examining resilience, adaptation, and optimal functioning. Berkel et al. (2010) examined the role of cultural values as a mitigating factor against the negative impact of discrimination in Mexican American adolescents. Specifically, they examined how Mexican American values (e.g., familism, respect, and religiosity) may serve as either a moderator (protective factor) or mediator (risk reducer). They found a role for Mexican American values as a risk reducer; that is, adolescents who experienced more ethnic socialization from their parents also reported more pride in their ethnic group and greater endorsement of Mexican American values. Concurrent with these values was a reduced risk of negative mental health symptoms and better grades. The researchers suggested that such culturally grounded values and ethnic pride may promote and reinforce greater connections to family and the community.

Szalacha and colleagues (2003) examined the relationship between perceived racial and ethnic discrimination and anxiety, self-esteem, and depression in a sample of Puerto Rican youth. They found that younger children tended not to perceive discrimination, whereas half of the adolescent sample perceived discrimination. Lower self-esteem and higher levels of depression and stress were associated with perceiving and worrying about discrimination. The study was not a longitudinal one, but the authors did speculate on how the perception of and anxiety related to discrimination—but not the discrimination itself—may lead to negative outcomes. Thus, counselors might help design programs to address anxiety and provide an empowering framework (bolstering ethnic pride) to aid Puerto Rican youth in dealing with discrimination. It should be noted that Szalacha and colleagues pointed out that overall the sample was very healthy.

Positive psychology is a branch of psychology that promotes the roles of strengths, resilience, and optimal human functioning. However, these components of positive psychology are not universally held across cultural groups, indicating that positive psychologists must examine the role of culture in the expression of strengths and virtues (Sandage, Hill, & Vang, 2003). Capielo, Mann, Nevels, and Delgado-Romero (in press) suggested that to understand cultural conceptions of strengths, virtues, and optimal functioning, researchers and practitioners need to attend to the value orientations of different cultures, including relational, time, spirituality, and activity orientations. For example, Capielo and colleagues pointed out that among Latinas/os, a relational orientation may be expressed through cultural values such as *personalismo* (the valuing of relationships) and *familismo* (family-centeredness and the valuing of family as primary to all other relations). For Latinas, a relational orientation may include self-sacrificing and submissiveness attitudes (P. Arredondo, 2002b). Positive coping needs to be discussed and appreciated in the framework of the Latino worldview. If being self-sacrificing to preserve the family accommodates the collectivist Latino culture, the individual will enact this behavior. The challenge for counselors is to see various culture-based behaviors as adaptive, positive, and culturally congruent, even if they do not agree with them personally.

Concluding Thoughts

Life in the United States can be difficult for both immigrants and ethnic minority Americans. They are at once faced with pervasive prejudice and discrimination, yet the myth of the American Dream indicates that they should simply work harder. In a true meritocracy, individual variables such as culture, socioeconomic status, ethnicity, race, and gender should not impact the ability to succeed. However, in reality, educational, economic, and social successes in the United States are intertwined with race, ethnicity, and social class. That is, there is a wide divide between the outcomes for Whites and those for individuals considered non-White. As we have seen, the educational, correctional, and health care systems in the United States perpetuate and exacerbate these disparities.

Latinos both are victims of prejudice and discrimination and can perpetuate discrimination both within themselves and toward other ethnic minority groups (e.g., African Americans). Internalized racism can lead to a preference for intermarriage with Whites and the belief that giving up visible, audible, and other cultural aspects of the Latino identity is necessary for success in the United States. Internalized racism can lead to foreclosing vocational options or accepting stereotypical notions about one's Latino identity and potential. The role of race in the United States and a denial of the reality of one's indigenous and African heritage can result in U.S.-born and immigrant Latinos having a major complex about race and color.

Susanna is the future generation of Latinas/os who must be understood by her professors and university support services personnel as a positive statistic. In her young life thus far, she has had to weather adversity. And her buffers? Her parents, her family, and her ability to navigate two worlds (her bicultural expertise). Susanna is an example of the need to identify and augment cultural strengths and resilience. Susanna might remember her mother telling her that she has to *tener ganas* (have the will) so that she can succeed. Maybe Susanna becomes the client of a culturally informed counselor who helps her identify and claim her cultural capital as a strength that can help her persevere and eventually graduate.

Similar to clients, counselors must also focus on their strengths and resilience when doing emotionally exhausting work. It is easy to focus on the negative factors and outcomes that affect their clients. However, counselors must also search for inspiration and resolve in working with oppressed populations. One inspirational example comes from faculty in the state of Georgia. Arizona-style immigration reform resulted in a legislative ban on unauthorized students from the Top 4 higher educational institutions in the state. Thus, a group of concerned faculty founded Freedom University (http://www.freedomuniversitygeorgia.com). Freedom University is a group of faculty who meet in secret with undocumented students to provide them with an education that is the equivalent of the instruction found at the top institutions in the state. This type of positive, nonviolent, and socially relevant resistance is an example of how concerned educators can help to combat unjust legislation, ensure social justice, and model resilience. Note that the students and faculty at Freedom University are not just Latino but represent a mix of backgrounds. The collective faculty leaders who make Freedom University possible are excellent examples of social justice advocates who focus on students' possibilities.

In closing, we suggest a few Latino-specific competencies. Culturally skilled counselors

- Attend to potential internal and external stressors for Latino youth
- Recognize that a first-generation college student arrives on campus with cultural strengths in a culturally different environment
- Become more cognizant of the roles of colorism and racism in the interpersonal interactions Latinos experience across the developmental spectrum and in different settings
- Attend to their own biases and prejudices about Latino clients, peers, and supervisors
- Become familiar with legislation that may affect Latino clients and students
- Do not buy in to the myths about Latinos.

• • •

Chapter 8

La Familia Latina:
Strengths and Transformations

Honra a tus mayores y aprecia a tus menores.
Honor your elders and appreciate your young.

• • •

Objectives

- To assess perceptions about Latino families.
- To gain knowledge about factors and events that affect Latino family transformation.
- To learn about Latino life-cycle models across the life span.

Sabías que/Did you know that . . .

- *Familismo* attitudes persist across generations, but *familismo* behaviors change over time.
- Latinos as an ethnic minority group have the highest incidence of mixed unions.
- Distrust toward new governments, public policies, and financial advantages historically prompted civil unions in Latin American countries.

• • •

Case Scenario

Francisco and his family were referred for therapy because of Francisco's resistance to attending middle school. He had missed 8 months of school because of anxiety attacks that included gastrointestinal problems that flared up whenever he went to school. He was afraid of having an accident at school and preferred to stay home. He was a good student, was registered in home schooling, and was meeting grade-level expectations. He had neighborhood friends, participated with his family in weekly Christian services, and was a member of a youth group. Francisco and his family had relocated from Chile when he was 3 years old. Spanish was the preferred language in the family. Francisco's sister was a high school honor student who was not close with their mother. His mother stayed home and was very close to Francisco. His father worked long hours and was described as disengaged from the family. Francisco's mother also reported that she was isolated and rarely left the home because she did not know English and could not drive. She was suffering from multiple medical conditions and had to take many medications. She had lost two significant family members in the past 9 months and was very distraught because ongoing immigration procedures would not allow her to leave the United States to visit relatives. Because the family had neither medical insurance nor extra savings, a local nonprofit children's organization arranged for a bilingual mental health professional to provide services on a pro bono arrangement. For 6 months and on a weekly basis, the professional provided in-home individual counseling with Francisco. He was eager to meet with his counselor every week but had not attended school since treatment had begun.

Framing the Context

With the increase in the population of Latinos in the United States since the 1970s and the sizable flow of immigrants into the country, Latino family values have been interwoven into the fabric of U.S. society (Landale & Oropesa, 2007). Social scientists agree that *la familia* (the family) is a central unifying force that mediates the well-being of many Latinos across the life span (Landale & Oropesa, 2007; Pew Hispanic Center, 2009; Suro, 2007; Szapocznik & Kurtines, 1993; Zambrana, 1995). Immigrant families can have a substantial impact on family patterns in terms of a tendency toward larger families (Phinney, Ong, & Madden, 2000), an increase in the number of second-generation Latinas/os, and a rise in fertility rates (Suro & Passel, 2003). The growth in the number of Latino marriages, the fertility rate, and the number of intact families raising children (Landale & Oropesa, 2007) undoubtedly reflects increasing trends in systemic stability in the United States (Suro, 2007).

However, Landale and Oropesa (2007) warned that individuals cannot assume that all Latino immigrant families maintain the traditional family mold. Family patterns are also changing in immigrants' countries of origin because of social, economic, and political changes. Transformations are inevitable and constantly affect within-group and between-group differences, such as family changes from generation to generation (Fernández, 2001). Lifestyle characteristics also impact newly arrived Latino families. Immigrant parents from agrarian societies may hold a different perspective on child development that contrasts with that of industrialized nations. According to Inclán (1990), parents from agrarian communities perceive fewer developmental stages before reaching adulthood (i.e., infancy, childhood, adulthood), whereas in industrialized societies children are perceived as undergoing multiple developmental stages (i.e., infancy, toddlerhood, preschool age, childhood, preadolescence, adolescence, adulthood). These different developmental perspectives influence parenting and family dynamics.

In the United States, *la familia* is also transformed by experiences of acculturation (Chung & Akutsu, 2002; Santisteban & Mitrani, 2002) and other sociocultural and economic factors and conditions. Based on demographic data, some scholars have posited a decline in family structures based on the rise in the number of out-of-wedlock births, teenage pregnancies, divorces, and incidences of cohabitation among native-born Latinos (Landale & Oropesa, 2007; Suro, 2007). The effects of acculturation on Latino families have been extensively studied but findings are inconsistent, in part because of variance in Latino subgroup sampling and contextual variables (Chung & Akutsu, 2002; Gonzalez, Fabrett, & Knight, 2009). Studies have indicated that high levels of acculturation are detrimental to systemic functioning in terms of increased family disengagement (Brooks, Stuewig, & Lecroy, 1998; A. G. Gil & Vega, 1996; Phinney et al., 2000), intergenerational conflict (Parke et al., 2004; Phinney et al., 2000; Szapocznik, Kurtines, Santisteban, & Rio, 1990), high levels of stress (Vega & Amaro, 1998), familial separations, and poor bonding (Hwang & Wood, 2009; McQueen, Getz, & Bray, 2003; Santisteban & Mitrani, 2002).

In contrast, other researchers have identified positive effects of acculturation, as evidenced by an increase in extended family help (Suro, 2007), an increase in social network support (Landale & Oropesa, 2007; Luna et al., 1996), improvements in parenting skills (Cabrera, Shannon, West, & Brooks-Gunn, 2006; Parke et al., 2004), improvements in children's adaptive skills (Calzada, Brotman, Huang, Bat-Chava, & Kingston, 2009; Moreno, 1991), and better mother–child relations (Loukas, Suizzo, & Prelow, 2007). Marín (as cited in G. Marín & Gamba, 2002) offered an explanation for these conflicting empirical findings. He identified two dimensions of *familismo* (family obligation, solidarity, loyalty): attitudinal and behavioral. Based on his extensive study of acculturation, Marín argued that *familismo* attitudes persist across generations but that *familismo* behaviors change over time. This is an important point to remember when working with families and individuals, as cultural conflicts could stem from attitudes of *familismo* that are not actualized with *familismo*-congruent behaviors. Parents may resent their adult children for not visiting often or demonstrating a more attentive and caring behavior. Likewise, adults may struggle to adapt to new lifestyle changes (e.g., a new job in another state) that are in conflict with core values of *familismo* associated with living in closer proximity to their families.

In addition, acculturation is an uneven process (Montalvo & Gutierrez, 1989; Szapocznik & Kurtines, 1993) that needs to be understood as a multidimensional and complex phenomenon that impacts family members differently (Harwood, Leyendecker, Carlson, Asencio, & Miller, 2002). Adaptation to different types of stress is necessary—stresses associated with language, family expectations that clash with the host culture, immigration, economics, peers, school and academics, work, the neighborhood, and so forth (R. C. Cervantes & Cordova, 2011). The turbulence of immigration places parents and children, at different ages, at risk. Constructive parenting that yields success with immigrant children may counteract the multiple stressors that immigrant parents may experience (Parra-Cardona, Córdova, Holtrop, Villarruel, & Wieling, 2008) and provide an opportunity for parental empowerment and family cohesion. Therefore, clinicians who follow a research-practitioner approach need to consider the compatibility of the Latino samples used in research studies and their own clients and their ability to understand the complexity of families' differential acculturation processes as discussed in Chapters 3 and 10.

Lastly, family transformations also occur with the merging of ethnicities, races, classes, religions, and generations. Of all ethnic minority groups in the United States, Latinos have the highest incidence of mixed unions. The U.S. Census Bureau (2010c) identified two major groups of mixed unions among married and unmarried Latinos: (a) White non-Hispanic with Hispanic of any Hispanic ethnicity and (b) Hispanic with non-Hispanic (excluding White non-Hispanics). Among both married and unmarried couples, the incidence of Latino cross-cultural and biracial unions was considerably higher than in other non-Hispanic groups (e.g., 37.6% and 7.3% of the U.S. population for married unions and 42.4% and 7.9% of the U.S. population for unmarried unions). A similar trend of cross-cultural and biracial same-sex unions was also evident for the same classifications that exceeded the rates among other ethnic and racial groups (Passel, Wang, & Taylor, 2010). These figures confirm that the increasing visibility of Latino intermarriage leads to new systemic configurations that require additional knowledge and skills. Latino intermarriage has led to biracial or multiple-heritage families (couples and/or children of different races), cross-cultural families (parents and/or children of different ethnicities or from different countries of origin), and bicultural families (parents and children with different levels of acculturation; Santiago-Rivera, Arredondo, & Gallardo-Cooper, 2002).

The merging of Latino couples from different socioeconomic backgrounds or the mixed-class family is another form of intermarriage not captured by Census data. Latino artists, writers, poets, and musicians have brought attention to the pain caused by class and racial differences through their music and writings, and these can be valuable resources for helping professionals. Even today, the plots of popular Spanish television *telenovelas* (soap operas) revolve around the conflict between classes, and individuals characterized as "the other" are generally visibly *mulato* or mestizo. That is, the servants are generally darker in phenotype than their employers. The mix of classes may seem to dissipate when Latinos immigrate to the United States, but frequently covert conflicts between extended family and in-laws occur because of class prejudice and histories of power differential. McGoldrick and Preto (1984) posited that intermarriage tends to accentuate differences during periods of stress, become personalized, and create havoc in family functioning. Falicov (1998) indicated that the more different the cultural characteristics between partners, the greater the potential for conflict.

One approach to addressing these differences is to discard old labels and create new definitions. A. Padilla (2006) acknowledged that the mixing of differences is creating new identities. Two new labels exemplify the merging of multiple identities. The South Florida Jewish community of Cuban heritage defines itself as "Jewbans." In addition, Generation ñ is a concept created by Bill Teck, a Miami resident with Jewish and Cuban roots who felt that individuals of Latino heritage did not fit the Generation X of the 1990s (Zeitlin, 2008). At the core of the label is the premise that a vibrant generation exists that integrates bicultural and bilingual characteristics with unique developmental experiences. A new identity niche was established that responds to the realities of the growing young Latino generation without conflicts of cultural loyalty. Individuals can choose to identify with Latino culture, American culture, or both cultures simultaneously. The concept addresses the special lifestyle and pop culture interests of Latinas/os who reside in Los Angeles, New York City, and Miami. Initially, Teck addressed Generation ñ by publishing a magazine, and later he established an online network. Although Spanglish (i.e., communication that mixes Spanish and English) is often used, Generation ñ appeals to bicultural Latinas/os who do not speak Spanish and also responds to culturally relevant reviews, marketing ventures, videos, documentaries, links, and entertainment productions ("Generation ñ," n.d.; Zeitlin, 2008). As witnesses of globalization and multicultural realities, Latino-centered professionals need more empirically based knowledge and strategies to respond to the mental health needs of the increasingly mixed Latina *familia* and the psychocultural characteristics that facilitate developmental and positive functioning.

Family Values and Cultural Orientations

The characteristics of the traditional Latino family have been extensively reviewed in the professional literature and in Chapter 2. Learning these characteristics is a sensible point of departure in clinical practice that has to be approached cautiously given the substantial variability among Latinos. As counselors assess a family's cultural characteristics they simultaneously dismantle and reconstruct the family's process based on nationality, socioeconomic status, history, geographic location, level of acculturation (Harwood et al., 2002), English/Spanish dominance (Gallardo-Cooper & Zapata, 2013), idiosyncratic personal beliefs and aptitudes (Zayas & Rojas-Flores, 2002), and contextual variables. The frequency of contact with the country of origin and the involvement of extended family also need to be considered to determine allegiance to cultural values.

As we explained in Chapter 2, the motor of *la familia Latina* is energized by the values of *familismo* (family obligation, solidarity, loyalty), *respeto* (respect, obedience, deference), *cariño* (caring, affection, physical demonstrations), and *simpatía* (warmth, positive disposition, avoidance of conflict). Multiple studies have endorsed these values as protective factors that alleviate family stress (Germán, Gonzales, & Dumka, 2009; Szapocznik et al., 1990; Vega, Gil, Warheit, Zimmerman, & Apospori, 1993). The sociocentric or allocentric worldview seems to be a commonality among all Latino parents, driven by the emphasis on *familismo* and *respeto* (Cauce & Domenech-Rodríguez, 2002; Harwood et al., 2002). Families may endorse cultural values differently depending on the nature of the problem. For instance, second-generation Latino parents may continue caring for their elders at home but may not expect their children to do the same for them *"cuando nos llegue nuestra hora"* (when their time arrives to be cared for by others). Therefore, clinicians working with families and couples cannot assume that Latino values are linear and consistent. As discussed in the previous section, fluidity is a common characteristic of bicultural and polycultural individuals like Latinos.

Another important factor that needs to be taken into consideration is that *la familia* is often guided by a hierarchical or vertical organizational structure, with parents and elders holding roles of maximum authority in the system. Again, as children acculturate and new generations develop, the system may become more democratic or horizontal and somewhat similar to that of mainstream families. Yet families may follow both vertical and horizontal organizational orientations depending on contextual variables. Parents may expect their children to follow a hierarchical orientation in problem solving with grandparents but may be more democratic when making decisions with their own adolescents. Similarly, immigrant parents may expect their children to blindly respect the authority of teachers and other adults but may be more flexible with their authority at home when dealing with specific family issues. One of the authors (Arredondo) remembers her mother admonishing her and her siblings about always being on their best behavior in school even if they were mischievous (little *diablitos* [little devils]) at home.

In addition, Latino families typically have well-defined gender role expectations that tend to change with acculturation. A system based on a hierarchical organization will tend to have clearer gender role expectations for solving problems and assigning household chores. Girls, for instance, are often given clear instructions to assume household responsibilities and care for family members. Boys are expected to have more worldly experiences, to run errands outside the house, and to engage in more independent tasks. Working-class families, however, may rely on an older son to care for younger children to ensure their overall functioning based on the son's hierarchical status and his level of maturity. Espín's (1998) work with young Latina immigrants in particular brings to light the psychological burden placed on adolescent girls and young women as couriers of native country values at a time when they want to adapt to the host culture. Research and clinical practice support Espín's (1998) work, as young Latinas face more family conflicts when they pursue college (Gloria, 1997) or a more egalitarian gender role (McGoldrick, 1992). Other immigrant families may be very open about *la vida moderna* (the modern life), and parents do not frown on their daughters being independent, living with boyfriends, or pursuing male-dominated careers. Nonetheless, a new family life-cycle event (e.g., a divorce, an unplanned birth for a college-going son) may cause the family to revert to a more traditional position. For example, when grandchildren arrive, grandparents, the spouse, or the in-laws may expect the mother to relinquish an established career to become the primary caregiver for the children. Proximity matters, and the closer the new parents live to the grandparents, the more likely there will be a little more intrusive behavior and cultural transfusions.

The role of the Latino father has suffered from stereotypical misconceptions (Cabrera & García Coll, as cited in Cabrera, Aldoney, & Tamis-LeMonda, 2013) and has not received much attention in longitudinal studies (Cabrera & Bradley, 2012). In particular, the study of the Latino single father needs further empirical exploration (Eitle, 2005). According to Hofferth (2003), Latino fathers tend to be less involved than mothers in supervising their children and more likely than Euro-American and African American fathers to be permissive. However, we believe that there is wide variability among Latino fathers that may be mediated by age, acculturation, education, country of origin, place of residence, modeling of their own father, and personal characteristics.

A recent review of empirical findings supports the positive impact of Latino fathers on child development (Cabrera et al., 2013). There is also a need to consider multiple sociocultural factors and to use causative research designs to further understand the specific variables that impact Latino fathers' parenting (Cabrera & Bradley, 2012). For instance, Latino fathers in rural communities may adhere to more traditional gender role socialization practices. Although many Latino fathers rely on their spouses to make family decisions and manage family affairs, many are supportive and involved in parenting, as are fathers of other ethnic backgrounds. In a recent study, researchers found that Mexican American fathers share coparenting responsibilities (Sotomayor-Peterson, Figueredo, Christensen, & Taylor, 2012) and are affectionate and nurturing with their children (Coltrane, Parke, & Adams, 2004).

Contextual factors such as the quality of the relationship between the mother and father as well as other socioeconomic realities also influence parental roles. Cabrera, Ryan, Mitchell, Shannon, and Tamis-LeMonda (2008) reported that nonresidential Latino fathers are able to maintain more active parenting involvement with their toddlers when the relationship with the child's Latina mother is stable. This trend may be attributed to the couple upholding a romantic or more intimate relationship despite residential separation. In instances where Euro-American single mothers are prone to having new male partner relationships, there is less involvement of the child's biological father. Other factors may contribute to Latino father parenting and intrafamilial expectations of children.

Latino Family Life Cycles

The family life cycle is a developmental framework that describes naturally occurring events across the life span that require appraisal and reorganization to reach individual family homeostasis. As a triggering event, change produces unsettling reactions. At times of stress, people tend to automatically revert to their deeply held core beliefs and behaviors, what they have learned from their families through osmosis or have been taught directly. Dormant psychocultural beliefs and expectations tend to reactivate as they interpret new emotional situations. The fusion of different worldviews and values shapes family members' attitudes and behavior when faced with a new life-cycle stage. However, stage-based developmental models designed for the mainstream culture fail to reflect the cultural course of Latinos' life-cycle tasks (Santiago-Rivera et al., 2002). Typically, low and high acculturation are positioned on ends of a continuum of adaptation and change for immigrants; however, there is considerable gray area in between. For example, monolingual Spanish speakers may be categorized as having low acculturation; however, if they listen to rock-and-roll and enjoy Chinese food, this would be considered evidence of high acculturation. Low and high acculturation are generally measured by behavior. Speaking Spanish, having Latino friends, preferring Latino food and music, and maintaining traditional celebrations associated with Latino heritage signal low acculturation. Being bilingual, having non-Latino friends, and so forth signals high acculturation.

Young Latinas/os low in acculturation (see Chapter 3) may address the launching (leaving home) stage of development later in life and under different motives. Young Latinas may attempt to reach more autonomy through early marriage or may mask their independence by attending college away from home. A reciprocal reaction may also play out when Latino fathers want to hold on to their protective role with their daughters at this stage (McGoldrick, 1992). At the midlife stage, Latino adults may have to assume responsibility for the long-term home care of elderly parents, a pattern that has been observed and supported empirically (H. F. S. Kao & Travis, 2005).

Family therapy scholars have made monumental contributions to clinical work with ethnically diverse families as well as put forth several family life-cycle developmental models (B. Carter & McGoldrick, 2005a; Falicov, 1998, 2008; McGoldrick, Giordano, & Garcia-Preto, 2005a; McGoldrick & Hardy, 2008). B. Carter and McGoldrick's (2005a) text on family life cycles covers models for specific life events and populations (e.g., marriage, divorce, siblings). Life cycles represent a specific family map of life events or "the family, as a system moving through time". A life-cycle approach does not provide a normative standard for what a "normal" family should be. In addition, it focuses not on specific ages but on processes during specific life events. The transition from stage to stage is natural and depends on the family's situation and the contextual factors it encounters. This approach to therapy allows for an in-depth understanding of specific issues with Latino families.

Several family life-cycle models deserve discussion because of their applicability to Latino families. These include the (a) Latino life cycle (Falicov, 1998, 2008), (b) life-cycle migration (M. Hernandez & McGoldrick, 2005), (c) immigration family cycle (Gallardo-Cooper & Zapata, 2013), (d) ethnic family (McGoldrick, 1992), and (e) Latino parent–child developmental cycle (Gallardo-Cooper, as cited in Santiago-Rivera et al., 2002) models. Table 8.1 compares the first three models, and Table 8.2 provides examples from the Latino parent–child developmental tasks. Therapists are encouraged to study these frameworks and borrow from different models, as clients may be experiencing critical stages in their family life trajectory simultaneously (e.g., immigration and the death of a child). M. Hernandez and McGoldrick's (2005) model focuses on when the migrant or immigrant family arrives in the host country. Falicov's (1998, 2008) framework delineates the specific stages that surround cultural socialization, acculturation, rituals, and other events commonly experienced by Latinos. These examples of family transitions with specific tasks alert the clinician to the types of questions to ask, areas to explore, and therapeutic strategies to use.

McGoldrick's (1992) ethnic family model includes eight stages, two of which are optional: intermarriage and immigration. Given the exceptional demands

Table 8.1
Comparison of Family Life-Cycle Models

Latino Life-Cycle Model[a]	*Life-Cycle Migration Model*[b]	*Stages of Family Immigration*[c]

Families with young children
  New parents
  Values: relatedness or
    autonomy
  External, not internal
    transitions
Families with school-age children
  Institutional contact
  Separations and reunions
  Boundary negotiations
Adolescence
  Parent–child clash of cultures
  Sexual practices
  Teenage pregnancy
  Rituals (*quinceañeras*)
  Dating
Young adulthood
  Staying home and gaining
    autonomy
  Courtship: sanctioned
    distancing from parents
Marriage: separating or
  returning to the fold?
Middle age: a full nest
Old age: losses but a shared life
  Hard reality, unknown
    environment
  Multiple jeopardy
  Networking
  Retirement
  Nursing home
  Death and grief
	Migration experience
	  Change in social networks
	  Change in socioeconomic
	    status
	  Change in culture
	Time of migration
	Young adults
	  Identity consolidation away
	    from family and away
	    from familiar social
	    contexts
	New couple
	  Adaptation fluctuates
	    between partners and
	    creates conflict
	  Parallel processes of
	    adaptation to multiple
	    stressors
	  Lack of social support
	    makes couple more
	    interdependent at expense
	    of social isolation
	Families with children
	  Strength of family may be
	    diluted by acculturation,
	    reversed hierarchies
	  Differences in the family are
	    accentuated because of
	    different levels of
	    acculturation
	  Children are pressured to
	    acculturate by peers
	  Children: culture brokers
	  Parents feel rejected by
	    children's lack of support
	    of parents' culture
	  Isolation of family and
	    higher interdependence
	    if social supports are not
	    available
	  Parent–child conflicts
	    increase because of cultural
	    differences
	  Children begin to shape their
	    own ethnic identity
	Families in later life
	  Older individuals have more
	    adjustment difficulties
	  Fear of being a burden
	    with old age, adjustment
	    to retirement, availability
	    of resources
	  More generational conflicts
	  Status as elder may not be
	    respected or endorsed
		Arrival stage
		  Vulnerable period
		  High level of distress: language,
		    employment, skills, learning
		    new policies and rules
		  Full or partial family separation
		  Mode of entry stress
		  Community receptiveness
		  Availability of support network
		  Family faces new institutions:
		    schools, health services
		  Loss and trauma
		  If applicable: deportation fear,
		    family separation
		Awakening stage
		  More established, knows
		    community and rules
		  Examines: cost of immigration
		  Mixed emotions
		  Yearnings for native country
		  Awareness of discrimination,
		    exploitation, barriers faced,
		    dreams shattered, racism,
		    sacrifices made
		  Cultural polarization begins:
		    children acculturate faster,
		    parents pull toward encultura-
		    tion, conflicts arise over
		    different levels of acculturation,
		    gender role changes
		  Children: language and cultural
		    brokers
		  If applicable: deportation fear,
		    family separation
		Accommodation stage
		  Intersection between cultural
		    accommodations and life cycle
		  Acculturation differences are
		    more distinct and more
		    conflictual
		  Integration of cultures begins
		  Children: loss of native
		    language and raised in a
		    cultural vacuum ecology
		  Parents may pressure
		    children, especially girls,
		    to conform to values of the
		    native culture
		  Vocational options may
		    diminish with a lack of
		    English skills
		  Visits country of origin, if able
		  If applicable: deportation
		    fear, family separation
		  Resignation, *fatalismo*

[a]Falicov (2008). [b]M. Hernandez & McGoldrick (2005). [c]Gallardo-Cooper & Zapata (2013).

Table 8.2
Latino Parent–Child Developmental Tasks

Stage	Child	Parent	Family
Infancy	Attachments; meet developmental milestones	Provide safety and affection; define parental roles and support network; extend infancy; developmental milestones not generally seen as internally driven	Assign *padrino* and *madrina* (godparent) roles; grandparents and extended family seen as resources of support and care for the infant; birth of child solidifies marriage
Preschool age	Languages and socialization; expected to develop affective and social skills; *cariño, respeto*, developmental tasks reflected by external events (e.g., birth of sibling, starting day care)	Focus is to teach social graces and bonding; developmental milestones seen as dependent on child's readiness and not norms; reinforces interpersonal connections versus independent/autonomy	Children incorporated into all adult social activities; home care preferred over day care; grandparents or extended family may be involved in child care; family history used to confirm developmental milestones
School age	Adjustment to school; exposure to new system; challenges with language and academic demands; peers; may be language broker for family and window to American culture	Encourages *respeto* (respect) to other authority figures; discourages activities outside the family; education level determines degree of school involvement and perception of schools	Older child may be given responsibility to oversee younger siblings or relatives at school; older child given duties to care for sibling at home; encourages familial peers and socialization
Adolescence	Gender-defined family responsibilities; sexual interests and identity development; may prefer dominant culture; gender role conflicts with parents	Provides strict supervision, especially with daughters; holds to native culture standards and strategies of discipline; cultural values threatened	Culture and intergenerational conflicts; concerns with social problems (drugs, teenage pregnancy, gangs); gender expectations differ
Young adulthood	May or may not be leaving home; college; marriage; career development; incorporation of spouse's family; parenthood; seeks parental guidance and support	Continues to support adult children (financial shelter, etc.); may share household with married children; loss of adult children not as drastic a transition because of continuity of togetherness (vs. empty nest syndrome)	Encourages togetherness, family rituals, and frequent contact; grandparents assume supportive role; marriage or college are acceptable reasons to leave home; marriage seen as permanent long-lasting decision; couple expected to have children
Middle age	Growth of family; illness or death of parent; care of elders; daughters seen as primary caregivers of elders while sons provide financial help; retirement less conflictual transition because of the focus on family	Sought for guidance and help; extension of parental duties with adult children redefines own marriage and older adult developmental tasks; may long for old ties and return to native country	Duty to maintain cultural values; recycle life-span developmental tasks; a *buen hijo* or *hija* (good son or daughter) never abandons the family or parents; nursing home may be seen as abandonment
Older age	Assumes responsibility in the family; role defined through familial tasks or duties; reinvestment in old ties and cultural connections; practice of traditional religious, medical, and cultural rituals	Adult children and grandchildren seek elders' support, guidance; value their input (*respeto*); rituals/practices during terminal illness and after death	Family contributes to providing care for elders; religious and cultural rituals allow for the expression of grief and sorrow (catharsis) and reconnection to the past

Source. Gallardo-Cooper (2001b). Reprinted with permission.

on adaptation necessary with these two events she defined them as specific stages. Problems of intermarriage are accentuated when the survival of the group is threatened, especially when many cultural differences exist between the couple. Immigration, she argued, is a chaotic stage that involves multiple levels of individual conflict and family restructuring demands that can seriously compromise family functioning. The dissonance in the immigration stage may have many causes—poor adaptation to the host culture because there is a yearning or a plan to return to the native country—or multiple stressors such as low-paying employment for the parents and bullying experiences for the children.

Gallardo-Cooper (as cited in Santiago-Rivera et al., 2002) created a Latino-centered model based on child–parent–family life cycles across the life span (see Table 8.2) that provides a blueprint of expected life stages and tasks. Critical issues in this life-cycle stage model are parental endorsement of ethnic pride as a young child, parental support for ethnic identity during adolescence, and parental responsibility for guiding children between two cultures with a complementary and enriching perspective. Another stage addresses school-age tasks that may be stressful for both children and parents, especially immigrant parents who do not know the American educational system or the language. An area of conflict revolves around conflicting expectations between parents and teachers. Hill and Torres (2010) described how Latino parents may base their expectations for schools on their own personal experiences in their home country, which often contrast with the collaborative parent–school approach of American education. In many countries in Latin America, teachers hold a highly regarded and esteemed role. Therefore, it may feel incongruent to Latino parents when American teachers involve them in the educational decision-making process.

In this parent–child model, the stage of adulthood is reached in a fluid, non-age-bound process in which the relational element with family members defines the individual's competency as an adult. That is, young adults may continue living at home and under the financial support of parents and, once working, may also opt to live with parents. Parents become less intrusive and more respectful of privacy boundaries but might still expect their son or daughter to join them for dinner. This prolonged process soothes the launching stage and the transition into the empty nest for parents.

From a developmental perspective across the life span, Rajaram and Rashidi (1998) offered a culturally mediated belief system model that can facilitate understanding of stressful life events or stages with Latinas/os. They described the construct of culturally explanatory models (CEMs) as a mechanism of evaluation mediated by sociocultural beliefs that help individuals find meaning during difficult situations. In particular, CEMs have been applied to understanding how ethnic minority individuals cope with illnesses. CEMs include cultural, personal, popular, and biomedical beliefs that motivate behaviors. Life-cycle events also rely on CEMs, as families undergo a new transition that requires appraisal and readjustment. Some of these stages may be more difficult for Latinas/os than others. For instance, when adult children leave home (McGoldrick & Preto, 1984), attending to CEMs can help individuals "find personal and social meaning" (Borrayo, Goldwaser, Vacha-Haase, & Hepburn, 2007, p. 488). Given that transitions from one stage to the next may create discomfort, some degree of systemic friction may be expected. Exploring with family members' CEMs is a cognitive intervention that may increase understanding of divergent views and support family cohesion, resulting in adaptive homeostasis for all. The combination of a focus on stage-based life-cycle events and the application of CEMs can provide a framework of intervention that is based not on pathology but on an expected period of reorganization of cultural beliefs, personal attitudes, and behaviors to reach adaptation.

Borrayo and associates (2007) utilized CEMs to study Latina/o caregivers of family elders. They reported that Latinos have higher rates of elder home care responsibility than the mainstream population and that typically Latinas take on the primary caregiving role. They studied the CEMs of a heterogeneous sample of Latina/o caregivers who had provided an average of 3.5 years of home care to family elders who had Alzheimer's disease and other related dementias. Borrayo and her group found that caregivers' coping beliefs relied on value-centered cognitions of *familismo* and *marianismo* (devotion to the Virgin Mary, a concept that communicates to women an expectation of living up to the example of the Virgin Mary as long-suffering, caring, self-sacrificing, loving, etc.). Latina caregivers were ruled by the "self-sacrificing and nurturing" (p. 494) value of *marianismo,* and the family justified the caregiving process as a means of teaching the new generation about family obligation (*familismo*). CEMs provided caregivers a sense of meaning for their sacrifices. *Fatalismo* (i.e., accepting the inevitable) and cognitive and behavioral changes were described as strategies used to reduce stress, and a strong dose of spiritualism helped caregivers pull on their personal strengths. In analyzing the participants' narratives the researchers discovered that there is no Spanish translation for the word *caregiver.* This supported participants' explanations that *caregiver* translates to family care because the elder—regardless of his or her condition—continues to be a member of the family. Caregivers also had difficulties eliciting assistance from social supports, occasionally felt isolated without extended family support, and lacked necessary information about the course of the care recipients' diseases.

When consulting with laypersons in these demanding caregiving situations, counselors, who themselves may have a strong sense of obligation and duty, may need to suspend judgment. One might say, "Why doesn't she get other family members involved? She is being overinvolved." As we have mentioned, the caregiver is there for the family; this is an implicit cultural expectation. Moreover, well-intended home care professionals may create undo distress on Latino caregivers who refuse to send their sick elder to a nursing home. The pressure to comply with decisions that go against core cultural values can be overwhelming, leading many caregivers to terminate much-needed home care services. The clinician working from a culture-based family life-cycle orientation anticipates these life crises and can prepare strategically without imposing mainstream expectations.

Changes in Family Structures

Latino families tend to stay together longer than non-Latino families (Landale & Oropesa, 2007; Suro, 2007). The norm is to support marriage, even if at a very young age, although this has changed in the United States because of higher education, changes in families' socioeconomic situations, and adaptation to U.S. practices. Especially among foreign-born Latinos, divorce is avoided and is seen as a significant stressor that runs counter to cultural expectations (Contreras, 2004). However, the numbers of out-of-wedlock births and teenage pregnancies (Suro, 2007), which had been increasing for a few years, have now declined (Martin et al., 2012), and within-group variation exists. One study found that compared to other groups in the United States, unwed Latino teenage mothers and fathers were more accepting and less conflicted with their pregnancies (Landale & Oropesa, 2007).

There is a consensus in the psychological literature that single parenting inevitably causes problems for children, adolescents, and families (Pan & Farrell, 2006). Latina single mothers may experience economic pressures, lack of parenting support, and depressive symptoms. A divorced father with a child with a disability may not assume his parental responsibilities (Correa, Bonilla, & Reyes-MacPherson, 2011). Despite these difficulties, Latino single mothers have demonstrated that the quality of their relationship with their preadolescent and high behavioral monitoring does not diminish because of the practice of *familismo* (Zeiders, Roosa, & Tein, 2011). As with all families led by a single parent, multiple social issues may occur, and clinicians must identify various contributing factors when applying an ecological perspective. Keep Bronfenbrenner and Morris's (1998) model of intersecting ecological levels in mind as changes in Latino family structures are discussed (see Chapter 4).

Latino single parenting has been associated with children's lower academic achievement (Battle, 1997), acting-out behaviors (Zeiders et al., 2011), and substance abuse (Eitle, 2005). Mexican American adolescents living with single parents had a higher incidence of substance abuse, received less parental supervision, and engaged in less parent–child communication (Wagner et al., 2010). The risk factor of Latino single parenting has also been associated with a higher incidence of marijuana abuse among adolescent boys and delinquency among adolescent girls (Eitle, 2005). However, a strong supportive relationship with the Latina mother reduced drug use and delinquency (Pan & Farrell, 2006). Therefore, providing support for Latino single parents with an emphasis on improving parenting skills and communication may be a beneficial counseling intervention (Wagner et al., 2010). One of the authors (Arredondo) participated in a seminar for teenage girls and their mothers, both single and married. The focus on difficult discussions (e.g., the use of contraceptives) illuminated the desire on the part of mothers and daughters for more open and regular communication on tough, age-appropriate topics.

Coparenting (i.e., the sharing of parenting responsibilities), when available, positively impacts intact Mexican American families (Sotomayor-Peterson et al., 2012) as well as improves the parenting skills of unwed teenage Puerto Rican mothers who share child responsibilities with their partners (Contreras, Mangelsdorf, Rhodes, Diener, & Brunson, 1999). Sotomayor-Peterson and associates (2012) found that when separated parents share similar cultural values such as *familismo* and *simpatía*, there is more effective shared parenting and a positive family climate. In particular, they recommended that clinicians identify, if evident, the value of *simpatía* as a cultural strength, given that some parents may restrain from sharing divergent views to avoid confrontations. Thus, affirming cultural congruence among divorced or separated Latino parents who seek therapy may promote positive outcomes.

As in the general population, cohabitation among Latinos is increasing. Compared to White and African American groups, however, Latinos have the highest number of stable cohabiting unions with children, thus implying that these unions appear to be culturally endorsed (Landale & Oropesa, 2007). Considering the common practice of civil unions in some Latin American countries, many immigrant couples with these unions marry after their arrival in the United States. Consensual unions are perceived differently in Latino and non-Latino industrialized countries and regions and in Latin American countries that are more traditional. In industrialized countries these unions are founded on gender equality, couple's rights, and women's sense of gender emancipation. Despite their frequency, Latino civil unions in traditional regions of Latin American do not share the same legal protections and equalitarian gender roles as those in industrialized countries and large urban communities.

In Latin America and the Caribbean, these unions stem from historical, political, and economic reasons and sometimes from different classes (Vignoli, 2005). *Uniones civiles* or *uniones de hecho* (civil unions and common-law unions) have been entered into for centuries in Latin America and are often evident among populations of low socioeconomic status (Castro Martín, Martín García, & Puga González,

2008; Landale & Oropesa, 2007). Many families in Latin America and the Caribbean were established from civil unions between slaves or indigenous individuals and their European colonizers. Distrust toward new governments, public policies, and financial advantages prompted these civil unions.

Latino Families With Children With Disabilities

When a family member has a disability, the entire family is affected. The effects on the family functioning correlate with the severity of the condition (Risdal & Singer, 2004) and can often result in parental separation and family discord (Risdal & Singer, 2004; X. Wei & Yu, 2012). Parents or parent figures may experience deep emotional pain, a sense of loss, a fear of the future, and at times fear of not being able to care for a child whose fragile health depends solely on them. For many families the impairment caused by the disability encompasses a lifelong commitment with prolonged distress. Nevertheless, families can adapt when they resolve troubling emotions as well as when they accept and adjust to the disability with realistic expectations (Hughes, Valle-Riestra, & Arguelles, 2008).

Case Scenario

Pedro and Migdalia Ortiz were an upper middle-class couple with successful careers in architecture. Both were first-generation immigrants. Pedro had come from Cuba at age 5 and Migdalia was from Puerto Rico. Migdalia had been raised in Puerto Rico and had relocated to Florida to attend college. Pedro's parents were divorced, and his brother lived in California. Both Pedro and Migdalia were fluent in Spanish and English, but Pedro preferred to communicate in English. Migdalia's extended family resided in Puerto Rico, whereas Pedro had a few extended family members within a 2-hour drive.

Their 5-year-old son Miguel had been recently diagnosed with autistic spectrum disorder (ASD). Miguel attended a special education preschool program, and after-school supervision was provided in a private child care facility. His parents were referred for supportive therapy to help them deal with the recent diagnosis of ASD. Migdalia, who was very verbal, related during the first meeting that she had been worried about Miguelito since he was 2 years old because "he was so different from our friends' children" and "he used to talk a lot and then stopped talking at the age of 2." Pedro stated that Miguel's behaviors related to his uniqueness. He said that he had never questioned that his son was different, but he felt that at times he was too demanding and would get easily upset over minor changes.

Migdalia was very distraught about the diagnosis of autism and felt overwhelmed. Since the diagnosis had been made she had been crying almost on a daily basis and spent considerable time on the phone with her family in Puerto Rico. Although she received support from her parents, aunts, and sisters, none of them could come immediately for any extended period of time. Migdalia's mother proposed a long stay in Puerto Rico so that relatives and friends in the medical and educational fields could reevaluate Miguelito and provide more help. Although Pedro was not opposed to visits to Puerto Rico, he felt that it was not necessary and added, *"Todo está bajo control, mi esposa sólo tiene que simplemente tranquilizarse"* ("Everything is under control, my wife just needs to calm down").

Migdalia disagreed several times with Pedro during the visit and was more confrontational. Although Pedro did not argue with his wife, there was a clear polarization of their positions. For instance, Pedro had researched ASD and felt that his son had been misdiagnosed because he was "not that severe of a case," and Migdalia responded that she had also sought out information on ASD and concurred with the diagnosis. She said to her husband in Spanish, "I know it is hard for us to accept, but we have to accept it: We have a child with special needs." When asked what she wanted to obtain from therapy she answered, "We need help to accept Miguelito's condition, my husband still does not believe it and his family supports him. . . . I know in my heart that my Miguelito is different, I just wish my mother could be close." Pedro felt as though the purpose of therapy was to work together as a couple with his wife for "Miguel's behavior problem." Miguel needed better discipline because he was too overindulged as an only child. "We need help on how to control him. . . . Maybe we are not expecting enough from him."

When asked how they coped, Migdalia answered, "We are both nonpracticing Catholics. Both my mother and my mother-in-law are very religious, so I pray to God that my Miguelito will be okay." She added, "My mother tells me to pray, but she does not know what it is like to have a special needs child." In response to the same question, Pedro laughed and said, "I just watch sports."

In this case scenario, the therapist is confronted with a family's disability issues that will define a treatment plan: (a) initial stage of acceptance and emotional turmoil surrounding disability diagnosis, (b) different acculturation levels between parents, (c) family support issues, (d) health and economic resources, (e) nature of problem and prognosis, (f) healing and coping skills, (g) father's availability for treatment, (h) child's behavioral history, (i) cognitive explanatory mechanisms, (j) marital discord risk, (k) language factors, (l) divergent coping styles, and (m) different parental treatment goals reported.

This case scenario reflects how the emotional and adaptational demands a family faces when raising a child with a disability are compounded by parallel psychosocial stressors. For many parents the stressors of language barriers, acculturation, legal status, poverty, and discrimination further compromise an already fragile system in crisis. Latina mothers with children with disabilities have reported on the compounded effects of discrimination not only for their ethnicity, race, or language but also because they have a child with a disability (Alvarez McHatton, 2007). A single mother with a child with a disability may miss days of work because of medical appointments and school meetings. An immigrant mother may not have access to adequate care, may not have the language skills needed to advocate for treatment, and may not be compensated for missed work.

Coping Strategies

Latino families with a child with a disability differ from Euro-American families in that they are more prone to coreside with their child for a lifetime (Borrayo et al., 2007; Magaña & Smith, 2006). These families use an array of coping strategies that include cultural beliefs, positive attributions, and spiritual healing. Borrayo and colleagues (2007) studied Latina mothers of adults with disabilities and discovered that they were driven by a strong sense of *familismo* (Magaña, 1999; Magaña & Smith, 2006). Mothers, in the role of primary caregiver, reported narratives associated with *marianismo* and *fatalismo* that served as explanatory cognitions supporting their sense of responsibility (Borrayo et al., 2007; Magaña, Seltzer, Krauss, Rubert, & Szapocznik, 2002; Magaña & Smith, 2006; Magilvy, Congdon, Martinez, Davis, & Averill, 2000).

Positive attributions have also been identified as a mediator of effective coping. Latinas tend to see the problematic behaviors of their children with disabilities as a reflection of their condition and not as intentional acting out. By relying on these attributions, mothers experience less distress, resulting in a more positive parent–child interaction when faced with challenging behaviors (Chavira, López,

Blacher, & Shapiro, 2000). Magaña and Smith (2006) studied Latina and non-Latina White mothers of children with ASD across several variables. Latina mothers were identified as having a more positive outlook and more positive cognitive explanatory models than mainstream mothers. These characteristics modulated higher levels of perceived well-being and reduced distress. Magaña and Smith suggested that because these Latinas did not report the child's behavior as problematic and stressed the importance of the maternal role, the value of *marianismo* impacted on their positive outlook and satisfaction with their parental role.

Latino families rely on spiritual beliefs when facing crises (Comas-Díaz, 2006b; Mogro-Wilson, 2011; Skinner, Correa, Skinner, & Bailey, 2001). Skinner and associates (2001) discovered that faith or personal religion, more than church attendance, significantly predicted internal strength among Mexican American and Puerto Rican parents (married and single) of children with intellectual disabilities. They contended that the actual experience of having a child with a disability might drive parents to seek out spiritual explanations and more positive attributions. Some Latino parents who initially report guilt and responsibility over a child's disability in counseling become more accepting with time, and the guilt fades away. A sense of reconciliation and existential meaning is reached through the use of cognitive explanatory models based on spiritual beliefs. These attributions transform the painful impact through positive interpretations of the disability. Some positive interpretations and healing messages we have witnessed include *Dios me mandó un angelito* (God sent me a little angel) or *Tengo fé que Dios no nos abandona* (I have faith that God will not abandon us).

The power of fatalism also facilitates healing. A Puerto Rican mother, distressed over her baby's recent diagnosis with cerebral palsy, reported that the most powerful healing she experienced came from one of her maternal aunts. Her aunt said, "Do not pray to God for the baby's full recovery; pray that He gives you *fortaleza* [internal strength], because you do not know what plan He has for you." This mother experienced a sense of relief with a shift in perspective. She changed from a more individualist perspective ("I can change the present and future if I work hard at it") to a fatalistic yet empowering perspective ("I accept the inevitable and focus on the only thing I can truly control or change: my internal strength").

An extended network of support is often available to assist Latino families in distress. According to Correa et al. (2011), Puerto Rican single mothers with a child with a disability have "blurred and indistinct boundaries" (p. 72) between nuclear and extended family systems that contradict ecological support models applied to mainstream populations. Even among those living in the United States, the support system extends to those living on the island. The system of support often relies on relatives from the maternal side of the family, such as *abuelas* (grandmothers) and *tías* (aunts), as well as the kinship system of *madrinas* (godmothers) and non–blood relatives. In their study, many single mothers chose being a mother over being a wife when husbands made excessive demands on them. This disclosure is often encountered in counseling with Latina women (Santiago-Rivera et al., 2002).

The interdependence fostered in *familismo* includes the contribution of siblings. B. Kao, Romero-Bosch, Plante, and Lobato (2012) reported that in Latino families, siblings contribute by becoming actively involved in the care and supervision of the child with a disability. Parents in these families communicate openly with their children about the nature of the disability as a means for siblings to take care of the child with the disability and reinforce the value of *familismo*. Updegraff, McHale, Whiteman, Thayer, and Delgado (2005) also reported high levels of sibling helpful involvement with other common family problems.

Despite these adaptive findings, Latina mothers struggle when their children have chronic disabilities. Magaña, Seltzer, and Krauss (2004) reported that Latina mothers of adult children with intellectual disabilities were more prone to depression. Self-perceptions of parental competence also impacted on behaviors that were detrimental to the family. Devine, Holbein, Psihogios, Amaro, and Holmbeck (2012) found a negative relationship between maternal sense of competence and perceptions of child vulnerability among Latina mothers of children with spina bifida. Mothers with low levels of competence engaged in more overprotection, supervision, and levels of care, which resulted in parental burnout and family stress.

Attention should be given to the *pobrecito* syndrome ("I feel sorry for you" syndrome). Although caring, empathy, and encouragement are always positive attitudes toward children with disabilities, a *pobrecito* perspective may hinder developmental progression, as the child's abilities are underestimated and opportunities to learn new skills diminished. Parents with this perspective also may not set the necessary limits to manage problematic behaviors.

Despite these challenges, Latina mothers with children with disabilities want to be involved with interventions at home, at school, in hospitals, and in other avenues of treatment. In school, they may expect professionals to provide detailed reports about their children's skills (e.g., using a fork, going to the bathroom), as some may feel worried and helpless (Hughes et al., 2008). Clinicians need to explore these issues in therapy to confirm whether system issues are at stake or whether mothers may be experiencing realistic fears or distrust of institutions.

Finally, Latino parents are not typically guided by the mainstream culture's value of independence and tend to do more tasks for their children than non-Latino parents may do. This tendency, as well as cultural biases in popular instruments (e.g., goes outside to play in the neighborhood by himself/herself; many Latino parents do not allow their elementary school-age children to play outside without supervision, even in their own neighborhoods), can lead to lower scores on assessments of adaptive functioning. Therefore, caution should be exercised in expecting independent behaviors or a push for independent living among children and adults with disabilities. Clinicians need to utilize the cultural gauge and explore with Latino parents their expectations for their child with a disability and integrate these perceptions into a culturally and developmentally relevant collaborative intervention plan.

Perspectives on Latino Parenting

Latino researchers have sparked interest in the study of Latino normative development with an emphasis on context, resiliency, and cultural characteristics that correlate with mental health (Contreras, Narang, Ikhlas, & Teichman, 2002; Fuller & García Coll, 2010; García Coll & Pachter, 2002; Grau, Azmitia, & Quattlebaum, 2009; Harwood et al., 2002) through two shifts in perspectives. First, *human development* is currently defined as the interaction between internal factors and context (Fuller & García Coll, 2010). Correa-Chavez and Rogoff (as cited in Fuller & García Coll, 2010) articulated this position well when they explained that thinking results from an interaction with context and not from neurological activity alone. Second, there is an interest in learning how diverse parental expectations affect learning and shape children's social cognition (Fuller & García Coll, 2010). For example, empirical data support the fact that Latino parents socialize children differently than parents in other U.S. ethnic and racial groups (Grau et al., 2009; Harwood et al., 2002) and that within-Latino-group variance exists (Domenech Rodríguez, Donovick, & Crowley, 2009; Grau et al., 2009). These changes in perspectives about human development provide culture-specific counterpoints to the overfocus on the social and psychological ills of Latino children and their families that has dominated the professional literature for decades (Harwood et al., 2002).

In their review of the literature, Grau and associates (2009) classified two types of Latino parenting behaviors: (a) culture general and (b) culture specific. The first represents the similarities among mothers in child-centered sensitivity and child responsiveness across all Latino ethnicities (Contreras et al., 1999). These behaviors could be considered universal maternal characteristics that persist across generations despite acculturation. The second involves Latino-specific values that may differ by psychocultural variant.

Because family is a driving force across the life span for most Latinas/os, understanding Latino parenting processes is crucial in therapy. For instance, clinicians must explore the cultural relevance of a parent's complaint when they initiate therapy, as these concerns may be culturally grounded. A *falta de respeto* (failure to respect; e.g., talking back, not obeying) may be a serious transgression for Latino parents but may be interpreted differently by highly acculturated Latino or Euro-American parents. Therefore, the cultural beliefs of childrearing, parental expectations, parents' past experiences as children (i.e., how they were parented, country-of-origin practices, and acculturation status), and what is perceived as deviant and optimum behavior should be explored in parent–child therapy. For example, when one of the authors (Arredondo) was growing up, her mother considered a friendship with a 17-year-old girlfriend who had a 21-year-old boyfriend to be unacceptable. The mom had been born in the United States but had seen teenage pregnancies in the community and did not want her daughter to be "tempted."

In this section, we discuss several areas that are pertinent to understanding family functioning: (a) parental expectations, (b) gender role socialization, (c) parenting styles, and (d) family structures and extended networks of support.

Parental Expectations

One of the primary goals of Latino parents is to help develop children with social relatedness, both with adults and peers. In their review of the literature Harwood and associates (2002) found that regardless of socioeconomic status, Latina mothers consistently ranked proper demeanor and obedience to authority high on the list of preferred childhood objectives and focused less on independent and creative skills. Puerto Rican (González-Ramos, Zayas, & Cohen, 1998) and Mexican American (Azmitia & Brown, 2002) mothers share cultural congruency in their preferred attributes in children. The highest ratings in these two samples were for the values of *familismo* and *respeto*. Thus, cultural socialization matters.

These objectives are what Latinas/os refer to as *un niño/una niña bien educado/a*, or a boy or girl raised well, with proper social and moral education (Fuller & García Coll, 2010; Grau et al., 2009; Hill & Torres, 2010; Santiago-Rivera et al., 2002). *Educación* is not defined as schooling or academic education but the learning of solid moral values, proper demeanor, socioemotional maturity, and interpersonal skills (Hill, Bush, & Roosa, 2003; Hill & Torres, 2010; Santiago-Rivera et al., 2002). The opposite of *educación* is *malcriado* (poorly raised), which denotes socioemotional immaturity, self-centeredness, disrespectfulness, and inappropriate behavior. Note that both of these terms, *bien educada/o* and *malcriada/o*, not only reflect child characteristics but also imply competent parenting. As seen by this example, collectivism goes both ways, as the child represents the collective competence for either positive or negative parental behaviors.

To meet the standard of *bien educada/o*, parents rely on the triad values of *respeto, personalismo*, and *familismo*. Children are expected to be courteous, obedient, friendly, attentive to others' needs, and family oriented as well as to engage in self-control, self-regulation, and demonstrative behaviors (e.g., hugs). Because the value of *familismo* persists despite acculturation (Harwood et al., 2002; G. Marín & Gamba, 2002), we propose that a parental emphasis on *familismo* socialization leads children to develop internalized *familismo*. This internalized process may explain what Peña and associates (2011) confirmed empirically as a mental health protective factor for children and adolescents. When children have a sense of family obligation, bonding, and loyalty they are less prone to engage in acting-out and risky behaviors.

Others endorse the values of *familismo, respeto,* and *educación* as the three primary cultural socialization markers that establish the standard of behavior and motivate child-rearing practices (Cauce & Domenech-Rodríguez, 2002; Grau et al., 2009). Higher levels of acculturation shift parental socialization guidelines toward a mainstream value system. High-acculturated Puerto Rican mothers endorsed more Euro-American values (e.g., independence, self-maximization) than low-acculturated mothers as preferred traits in their children (González-Ramos et al., 1998). Furthermore, Varela and Hensley-Maloney (2009) explained that the collectivist values of *personalismo* and *simpatía* interfere with Latino children's ability to engage in self-advocacy when facing adversity in U.S. society because of a tendency for self-control, conformity, and avoidance of conflict. Driven by allocentric values, these children adapt to stressors at the expense of their own preferences (Anderson & Mayes, 2007). Varela and Hensley-Maloney therefore recommended that parents attend to the emotions of their children or adolescents, as exerting more discipline for self-regulation may mask important troubling emotions that may be suppressed. Furthermore, children also need to learn how to release emotions appropriately inside and outside of home settings.

Given that Latinos tend to have extended social networks, children learn to adapt and to respond to multiple generations, family friends, and different social settings (Zambrana, 1995). Large families, extended family, and kinship networks are some examples of social circles in which Latino children learn to adapt. This is a psychosocial strength that allows Latinos to engage in novel social situations as well as a prosocial skill that facilitates interpersonal skills.

For instance, Latino parents typically take their children and adolescents to adult social encounters (Santiago-Rivera et al., 2002) and expect them to behave properly for several hours at a time. In these gatherings children play together while adults socialize, but parents expect that their children will greet adults, politely ask for what they need, obey all rules, and always respond with social graces. Often Latino parents, typically the mother, cue their children on these behavioral expectations prior to these social events. Some examples include the following: *Toca con los ojos* or *Toca con los ojos y mira con las manos* (Touch with your eyes and look with your hands, or Do not touch anything in the house you are visiting), *No te olvides de saludar a . . .* (Don't forget to greet . . .), and *Espera y no interrupas* (Wait and don't interrupt). Behavioral cues can also reflect a family orientation (*Te encargo a tu hermanito* [I am giving you the responsibility to care for your little brother]) and place responsibility on the children to avoid bringing shame to the family (*No me hagas quedar mal* [Do not make me look bad]). In other words, if a child misbehaves or becomes *malcriado,* his or her actions become a direct reflection on the parents.

Gender Role Socialization

Latino parents utilize different child-rearing practices in gender role socialization (Cauce & Domenech-Rodríguez, 2002; Domenech Rodríguez et al., 2009). Early socialization with girls emphasizes *cariño* and *marianismo*. Girls are encouraged to express affection and to be emotionally demonstrative (Vazquez-Nuttall, Romero-

García, & de León, 1987) as well as to be more engaged in taking care of others. Driven by the value of machismo, boys are expected to be independent, to suppress emotional reactions, to be protective of the family, and to endorse masculine traits. However, Latino boys who struggle with multiple psychosocial stressors might engage in somatization or aggressive behaviors, as these behavioral manifestations do not compete with machismo values (Anderson & Mayes, 2007). Expressing emotional distress may be seen as a personal weakness for Latino boys, as is the case for boys and men in general. Adolescent girls of Mexican American heritage may experience more internalized symptoms (e.g., anxiety, depression) when they endorse low levels of affiliation with the Latino culture (McDonald et al., 2005). Umaña-Taylor and Updegraff (2007) posited that for some Latino boys, affiliation with the machismo construct may be psychologically detrimental, whereas Latina adolescents' endorsement of cultural values may be a protective factor.

As first-generation children acculturate, differential gender role attitudes may result in parent–child friction. In family therapy, Latina adolescents communicate the need for more autonomy and resent the traditional expectations of parents, especially when brothers have parental consent to engage in more freedom and autonomy. Latina girls and adolescents may interpret this differential parenting approach as rejection or parental preference toward the brothers in the family (Santisteban & Mitrani, 2002), an issue that can be detrimental to family equilibrium.

Parenting Styles

A Latino style of parenting has emerged from clinical observations and empirical findings as reflecting high levels of supervision and monitoring of child behavior (Harwood et al., 2002; Pokhrel, Unger, Wagner, Ritt-Olson, & Sussman, 2008; Santiago-Rivera et al., 2002) as well as being more directive, structured, and demanding (Ispa et al., 2004). High levels of parental supervision have been identified empirically as a protective factor that prevents substance abuse (J. R. Ramírez et al., 2004) and disruptive disorders (Pokhrel et al., 2008). In addition, Latino parents have been identified as more comfortable with intrusive tactics than mainstream parents (Ispa et al., 2004). Family boundaries tend to be looser with Latina/o parents when supervision and discipline are involved. For instance, a Euro-American mother may protect the privacy of her children in part because of an egalitarian and democratic value system, but a Latina mother may exert her authority to explore her son's belongings based on the hierarchical structure of the family.

Latino parenting places more demands on the child, involves stricter behavioral standards, and involves more environmental structure (Grau et al., 2009). Compared to their White counterparts, Latino parents expect to establish skills in interdependence (i.e., helping the family) at an early age and personal independence at a later age (Harwood et al., 2002). Latino parents generally have more rules than Euro-American families and have stricter expectations when it comes to outside activities (Halgunseth, Ispa, & Rudy, 2006). Mexican American and Puerto Rican mothers tend to exert more parenting control and place more behavioral expectations on their children than other mothers in the United States (Grau et al., 2009). Harsh parenting practices may not be perceived negatively among Mexican American immigrant families because children are seen as being accountable to help with family adjustment (Parke et al., 2004).

The term *hostile parenting* has been used in the literature to describe a negative parenting approach associated with highly controlling disciplinary practices. Contrary to findings with Euro-American mothers, a controlling parenting style among Latinos has not been correlated with negative child outcomes (Pokhrel et al., 2008).

Actually, the common practice of close monitoring and supervision has been linked to a lower incidence of substance abuse and acting out (Eamon & Mulder, 2005). The benefits of this controlling approach may be due to the fact that Latina mothers also utilize warmth (Gorman-Smith, Tolan, Henry, & Florsheim, 2000; Vega & Amaro, 1998) and acceptance (Hill et al., 2003) as well as sensitivity and responsiveness (Carlson & Harwood, 2003). Dominican and Puerto Rican mothers, for instance, build close relationships with their children through a combination of a responsive and loving approach and firm discipline (Guilamo-Ramos et al., 2007).

Acculturation also impacts on parenting style (Contreras, 2004; García Coll & Pachter, 2002; Hill et al., 2003). Low-acculturated Latina mothers tend to be more strict and controlling than high-acculturated Latina mothers and tend to adhere more to Latino cultural values. Higher levels of acculturation tend to change these practices, as mothers become more egalitarian and implement less monitoring, similar to the parenting practices of the host culture (Halgunseth et al., 2006; Parke et al., 2004). Adapting to the host culture also involves different rates of acculturation among family members. This imbalance may create familial dissonance as well as acculturative stress, outcomes that may further compromise the effectiveness of parenting (García Coll & Pachter, 2002; Parke et al., 2004).

Informal supervision is another parenting strategy used to monitor adolescents. Cultural traditions such as *chaperonas* (parents or relatives who provide supervision for adolescents) seem to be diminishing with time, family separation, acculturation, and other socioecological factors (e.g., parents holding multiple jobs). However, Latino parents continue to enlist a network of close friends or young relatives to provide informal supervision. Girls in particular are highly chaperoned to prevent sexual behaviors and their perceived vulnerability when faced with unwanted male advances.

Good parenting may be the single most important contributor to mental health. Findings from research on Latino parenting can have profound implications for practice, as data can guide effective and culturally relevant parent training, an intervention that is cost effective, is attractive to Latinos, and can reach more families. Many parenting programs adapted to specific Latino populations have been carefully researched (for a review, see Zayas, Borrego, & Domenech Rodríguez, 2009). The interest in research on Latino-centered parenting is fundamental given that earlier research relied on theoretical models developed for middle-class Euro-American parenting. Since the 1960s parenting research has been based on four parenting paradigms developed by Baumrind (1966): authoritative, authoritarian, permissive, and neglectful. Of the four styles, authoritarian has received the most support because of its positive outcomes. Based on cultural values and its high levels of supervision, high levels of warmth, and hierarchical structure, Latino parenting has been associated with an authoritative style based on Baumrind's three domains: warmth, parental control, and autonomy granting (Santiago-Rivera et al., 2002).

The work of Domenech Rodríguez et al. (2009) has made significant strides in increasing experts' understanding of the Latino-specific parenting style. They studied the parent–child interactions of 51 dyads of low socioeconomic status parents and their children (ages 4–9) from a rural community in the western region of the country. Most parents were of Mexican American heritage. The research was driven by the inconsistency in study findings on Latino parenting styles based on Baumrind's (1966) paradigm. Through an extensive process of observations, Domenech-Rodriguez and associates (2009) discovered a new culturally relevant parenting style, a protective style in first-generation Latino parents that did not fit the four styles hypothesized by Baumrind. They also identified variations on autonomy granting and types of demands between boys and girls. That is, their findings suggested that Latino parents might expect different behaviors from daughters and sons across the life span. Young girls may be expected to mature earlier (demandingness), but as boys grow older they are expected to assume more responsibilities, such as getting a job to help the family (autonomy granting). These findings further support the combination of consistent child monitoring and positive relational methods Latino parents utilize and the differential gender role socialization discussed previously.

Family Support: *Abuelos,* Extended Family, and *Compadrazco*

Latino families receive support from *abuelos* (grandparents), extended family members, and *una red de apoyo* (a social network of support) linked to *compadrazco* (kinship) relationships (*madrinas, padrinos* [godparents]) and close friends. Latino families tend to be larger in size (Suro, 2007), live in close proximity to the extended family, and may include several generations living in a household (Fields, 2003). However, this is changing, as newly arrived individuals and families move into their own space or away from where they originally settled with parents or other extended family members. In 2011, the average Latino family consisted of 3.14 persons (U.S. Census Bureau, 2010c), and family proximity in certain parts of the country may persist, but it is not generalizable to all Latinos today. Grau et al. (2009) posited that these family preferences involve both stressors and protective strategies. Large families may struggle financially but are available to provide different forms of support.

Compared to other ethnic groups, Latino single and couple working parents rely more on grandparents and family members for child care than on babysitters and child care centers (Contreras, 2004; Santiago-Rivera et al., 2002). Extended family support may also be experienced through aunts, third-generation aunts, and kinship networks (Correa et al., 2011). Latino grandparents not only assist with parenting but are also available to support with crises due to mental illness, substance abuse, economic woes, or child disability (Correa et al., 2011; Fuller-Thompson & Minkler, 2007). Help is provided in many forms, either with household chores, direct child care, homework assignments, transportation, emergency appointments, or financial aid. Grandparents become agents of cultural transmission, native language development, traditions, and parenting consultation (Silverstein & Chen, 1999). Many Latino grandparents who are 45 years or older may share residency and coparenting duties with their adult children (Fuller-Thompson & Minkler, 2007). Grandparents with visas or who are citizens may visit from their country of origin to provide family support for extended periods of time. Often grandparents with economic resources care for grandchildren during summers and vacations, providing the children with opportunities to learn the culture and language as well as experiences to build relationships with the rest of the extended family.

In many Latino families, grandparents are highly valued, as they provide guidance, teach values, and provide support. Latina mothers, regardless of their nationality, are more receptive to extended family support and child-rearing *consejos* (advice) than other groups in the United States (Contreras, 2004). Often young families relocate to live closer to grandparents and extended family when children arrive. Adult parents typically continue to exert *respeto* to the elders and do not compete with them. This generational boundary may support the involvement of *abuelas* and *abuelos* in disciplinary actions with their grandchildren without parental conflict. If grandparents are available, the grandmother typically cares for the children and the grandfather provides transportation and other types of support. Among Central American grandparents, however, grandfathers tend to be more frequently available as a source of support than grandmothers (Fuller-Thompson & Minkler, 2007). This is often because work-related injuries and disabilities grandfathers suffer in construction or in the field force them to stay home. In contrast, Central American grandmothers continue in the workforce for a longer period of time because their work (e.g., child care or housecleaning) often poses less risk of work-related injury. However, this is not necessarily generalizable.

Cross-cultural couples with Latino and Euro-American partners may, however, experience more conflicts, as Euro-Americans may be more sensitive to the intrusiveness and spontaneous coaching (*consejos*) of a Latino grandparent. Likewise, some mainstream working grandparents may feel burdened caring for another generation, given that the retirement years are highly valued as a time of adult enjoyment and relaxation. When Latina grandmothers coreside and coparent, they are key members of the family and need to be included in family therapy. Sometimes differences in opinion on how to handle specific situations with the children are best addressed in family therapy, as Latino parents may not confront their own parents directly.

Despite their valuable contribution, grandparents and extended family are often overlooked, as they too suffer from poverty, unemployment, severe stress, and language barriers that interfere with their access to health care and other services (Bullock, 2005; Cox, Brooks, & Valcarcel, 2000). In particular, Fuller-Thompson and Minkler (2007) reported that Central American grandparents (Salvadoran, Guatemalan, and Hondurans constitute the largest population) experience more psychosocial stressors associated with legal status, lack of health coverage, low-paying jobs, low social assistance, and financial limitations. Many also present with the highest risk for work-related disabilities. Given their young age, Central American grandparents may parent two generations simultaneously: their young children and their grandchildren (Fuller-Thompson & Minkler, 2007).

Contreras's research on the role of the Latino grandparent deserves further discussion given its implications for therapy. In one study, the level of acculturation of teenage Puerto Rican mothers determined level of parenting stress and overall psychological adjustment when a grandmother provided parenting support. Fewer acculturation-related conflicts were reported with the grandmother when the teenager had low levels of acculturation, given that both generations endorsed similar values. Low levels of adolescent acculturation were also associated with better adjustment and less parenting stress. High social support of the partner was associated with psychological adjustment but more parenting distress. The degree of perceived partner support moderated these findings (Contreras et al., 1999).

Another study was also conducted with adolescent Puerto Rican unwed mothers who either resided with or did not reside with the grandmother. Contreras (2004) found that coresidence with the grandmother was related to perceived maternal positive social support. However, excessive grandmother assistance with child care with coresidence was associated with poorer parenting skills and lower levels of positive behaviors among the mothers. If the grandmother provided additional social support for the adolescent mother to work or attend school, an important developmental task prior to adulthood, the mother's ability to connect and teach her child was reduced and her positive behaviors diminished. However, the provision of child care support by nonresident grandmothers was linked to a lack of perceived social support but better maternal parenting skills and more positive behaviors. In general, involvement of partner support with either coresidence or nonresidence resulted in positive maternal behaviors. Based on these two studies, clinicians need to enlist the participation of grandmothers and partners of Latina adolescent mothers to ensure maternal parenting competence and mental health as well as to enhance positive relationships and developmental maturity. Contreras's studies also raise several clinical questions: How much help is necessary before it compromises parent–child bonding, parenting skills, and adolescent development? How does the level of acculturation between the mother and grandmother impact on family relationships and functioning? How do perceptions of support need to be negotiated to produce positive outcomes?

Immigrant grandparents at times assume full legal responsibility for their grandchildren in cases of neglect and substance abuse and/or when the grandchild has a disability. One of the authors (Gallardo-Cooper) worked with grandparents from Costa Rica who had assumed full responsibility for their young grandchild, who had a rare congenital disorder. The daughter-in-law had abandoned the child and returned to her native country in Central America, and the father, the clients' son, was a war veteran with disabilities and a history of problems retaining odd jobs. The dedication of these grandparents was admirable given that they were caring for two generations. Problems were evident in family therapy, given the lack of maturity of the father to be able to assume full parental responsibility and the deteriorating health of the grandparents. Family therapy focused on increasing the grandparents' trust in community resources, connecting the grandparents and father to Spanish-language services, and engaging a public assistance case manager to oversee the child and the family.

Latino Family–Centered Therapeutic Strategies

In this section, we focus on several strategies that, according to empirical findings and clinical observations, are useful to consider when working with Latino families. These strategies focus on culturally grounded assessment, planning, and engagement approaches.

Identify the Presenting Problem

Mental health professionals who work with Latino parents may be asked whether the problematic behavior is a phase, whether the child requires stricter supervision, or whether there is a need to send the child or adolescent to live with another relative or out of the country. At times, Latino parents have undertaken drastic measures to protect their children, such as uprooting the family to another town to prevent adolescent daughters from relating with boys of whom they disapprove. Before a clinician can answer these questions, he or she needs to assess the psychological, developmental, contextual, and psychocultural variants of the presenting complaint. Responses to questions such as "What would be the worse thing your child could do to your family, to his or her sister or brother, to you as his parents, or at school?" and "What do you fear the most?" can provide information about the level of parental tolerance and the cultural values held in greatest esteem by the family. Equally important is to engage the parents with strengths-based inquiries, such as "What does your child do that makes you proud?" and "When is your child *bien educadito* or *bien educada?*" These empowering questions also provide valuable therapeutic information that can be utilized as a protective factor.

Assess *La Familia*

Given the tendency for Latinos to include grandparents, extended family, and kinship relationships (e.g., coparenting and coresidence) among sources of family support, it is important for the clinician to determine the relevant family members involved with childrearing. Which members constitute the family system is an important question to include in assessment and to consider in intervention. In addition, grandparents themselves may be at risk for either acute or chronic problems and may be without resources despite their best intentions to support their children and grandchildren. These predicaments also need to be explored and evaluated in terms of how they impinge on caregivers' capabilities and risk factors and interfere with parent–child bonding issues. Marked discrepancies and conflicts between parents and grandparents can also compromise family functioning and child-rearing practices. If a family member has power in the family system but lives far away, explore whether it would be clinically sound to incorporate his or her involvement in therapy through a telephone or Skype connection during the session.

Assess the family's strengths. Latino parents utilize cultural frameworks, extended family, spirituality, and personal problem-solving skills to successfully cope with stressors (Lee & Liu, 2001; Perreira, Chapman, & Stein, 2006). Throughout this chapter we have discussed strengths of Latino families that should be considered in therapy and the importance of attending to processes that reinforce the Latino family unit. First identify cultural and systemic strengths and build the intervention from these strengths. A strong emphasis on the collective or *familismo* value not only creates systemic cohesion but also endures as a personal protective factor through internalized *familismo*. Some examples are included in this section. Parents and extended family contribute to the ethnic socialization and cultural adaptation of children (Umaña-Taylor & Guimond, 2012) as well as kinship networks (Correa et al., 2011). Latino grandparent support has been identified as practical (financial aid, child care, cooking meals, etc.) and personal (listening and supporting, giving advice, being present during times of crisis), a highly valuable resource to the family (Correa et al., 2011). The sibling relationship (Alfaro & Umaña-Taylor, 2010) and parental encouragement (Hill & Torres, 2010) have also been associated with academic motivation and outcome, respectively. Both children with disabilities and their siblings have benefited from sibling care (B. Kao et al., 2012). It is a win–win situation when all family members are actively involved in the solution to a problem. Parents have the opportunity to communicate to children about real-life problems, and children learn how to cope and become empowered with their family contribution. High levels of child behavior monitoring and parents' practice of giving *consejos* to their children (Halgunseth et al., 2006) should be affirmed as a strength, as should parental teachings of *respeto, personalismo, simpatía*, and *educación*, important socialization skills.

Understand Immigrant Families

Clinicians need to be cognizant of the fact that immigrant families tend to have their own set of challenges that differ from those of many other Latino families. These realities impact on overall family functioning (Harwood et al., 2002; McGoldrick, 1992). Many immigrant parents struggle to adapt to a new culture and language, and many have the compounded exacerbation of stressors linked to an unauthorized status, as discussed in Chapter 7. Perreira and associates (2006) found that continuous honest and open dialogue about cultural adaptation was the most beneficial strategy for ensuring communication, bonding, and resilience in immigrant families. Santiago-Rivera and colleagues (2002) stressed the therapeutic value of discussing the trajectory of immigration with all family members. The sacrifices parents made for a better life can be a motivating force for children and adolescents.

Examine Acculturation Processes

Acculturation is a complex, multidimensional, dynamic process that needs to be attended to throughout the course of therapy, not only at the initial assessment stage. This silent phenomenon plays into family dynamics and parenting (Hill et al., 2003). Scholars have stressed that acknowledging the differential effects of acculturation among family members is an essential element in the efficaciousness of interventions given that most Latino parent–child conflicts are rooted in different levels of acculturation (Chung & Akutsu, 2002; Hwang, 2006; G. Marín & Gamba, 2002; Santisteban & Mitrani, 2002; Szapocznik, Hervis, & Schwartz, 2003). Acculturation dissonance is particularly threatening to immigrant families (Perreira et al., 2006; Szapocznik & Williams, 2000). Mothers and fathers may share the same generation status and country of origin but may have different levels of acculturation that exacerbate disparities in marital and parental dynamics. Parent–child and husband–wife conflicts rooted in acculturation are masked as personal conflicts (Szapocznik et al., 1990). These personalized conflicts need to be reframed as cultural events (Szapocznik, Kurtines, Foote, Perez-Vidal, & Hervis, 1986; Szapocznik et al., 1990; Szapocznik, Santisteban, Kurtines, Perez-Vidal, & Hervis, 1984). The clinician needs to set the pace for openly discussing cultural adaptation with the family as well as educating the family about cultural transmission, native and host culture processes, and divergent acculturation perspectives (Santisteban & Mitrani, 2002). Also, the counselor should consider empirically supported and clinically useful treatment programs designed to address these conflicts, such as bicultural effectiveness training (Acevedo-Polakovich & Gering, 2009; Szapocznik et al., 1997; Szapocznik et al., 1984). Bicultural effectiveness training was designed as a structured psychoeducational 12-lesson intervention program for Latino families who face acculturation stress and related intergenerational conflicts. Interventions address cultural values, behavioral expectations, and coping strategies.

Explore the Power Differential

Immigrant mothers feel that schools with a mainstream value structure do not support important cultural values (e.g., *respeto*) and that the rapid acculturation of their children place them as the parent at a disadvantage (Leidy, Guerra, & Toro, 2012). Leidy et al.'s (2012) study underscores that these two perceptions negatively impact parent–child power dynamics. When children become language brokers and are more knowledgeable than their parents about American institutions, mothers feel disempowered. Language brokering is also a source of stress for Latino adolescents (R. C. Cervantes & Cordova, 2011). Therefore, the practice of language and cultural brokering with Latino children is discouraged (G. Flores, 2005; Leidy et al., 2012; Santiago-Rivera et al., 2002). Furthermore, when children threaten to report their parents to authorities for harsh discipline, parental roles become compromised. As a result of parental authority being undermined, children may engage in serious defiance and acting out. Helping parents to develop positive discipline skills and educating them about child laws and institutions is one way to address these problems and empower the entire family. This is a social justice responsibility of the counselor. In contrast, acculturation and an extended period of residence since arrival in the host country increase the risks for single-family households, lower fertility rates, and higher divorce rates (Landale & Oropesa, 2007; Suro, 2007). Landale and Oropesa (2007) proposed that cultural values, assimilation levels, and social-structural frameworks be considered and discussed. However, regardless of generational status, both foreign-born and native-born

Latinos still have higher rates of intact families than non-Latino Whites and African Americans.

Promote Ethnic Socialization, Ethnic Pride, and Ethnic Identity

Learning from an early age about one's own cultural heritage, values, traditions, and practices can be an empowering experience that becomes a protective factor for children and youth (A. Padilla, 2006; Umaña-Taylor & Guimond, 2012). Ethnic identity has been linked to better academic outcomes (Fuligni, Witkow, & Garcia, 2005), lower rates of depression and problems with low self-esteem (Umaña-Taylor, Gonzales-Backen, & Guimond, 2009), and positive development (Schwartz, Mason, Pantín, & Szapocznik, 2009). Therapy needs to reinforce family values such as *familismo, respeto,* and *cariño* as well as respect the preferred problem-solving style of the family (i.e., a vertical or horizontal orientation). Family loyalty and solidarity (*familismo*) creates a sense of belonging and acceptance among children that has been identified as a protective factor against acting-out behaviors (Hill et al., 2003). Clinicians need to incorporate family values into interventions and recognize how inflexibility in the adherence to cultural values can interfere with coping.

Reinforce Native Language Development

It is important that first- and second-generation families who speak a native language continue to reinforce their language. The maintenance of a native language enhances bilingual development, cognitive development, ethnic identity, and family communication and cohesion (Bialystok, 2011; Calzada et al., 2009; Gallardo-Cooper & Zapata, 2013; E. E. García & Nañez, 2011; Santiago-Rivera et al., 2002). Parents concerned with their children's mastery of English need to be assured that children have the capacity to learn two languages, and the stronger the first language, the easier it will be for them to learn the second. Bilingual individuals easily translate from one language to another. Furthermore, Hwang and Wood (2009) argued that changes as a result of acculturation can erode first language development among immigrant children, resulting in emotional distance between children and their parents. They claimed that the loss of the family's preferred language jeopardizes the developmental necessity for children and adolescents to maintain an emotionally close relationship with their parents because of lack of a common language. Extended family relationships, such as those with grandparents, are also compromised (Santiago-Rivera et al., 2002) at a developmental stage when children and adolescents need attention, *consejos,* and a trustworthy person with whom to share problems and concerns. When communication diminishes between family members, so does emotional intimacy.

Support Biculturalism

Becoming bicultural is an important adaptive and cognitive strength that allows children and adults to maneuver successfully two cultures, or be bicultural. Whenever generational or acculturation conflicts arise in therapy, it is important to integrate the strengths of both cultures so that they can complement each other. Findings support biculturalism as a key determinant in reducing depression (M. Wei et al., 2010), increasing prosocial behaviors (Schwartz, Zamboanga, & Hernandez Jarvis, 2007), increasing adaptive skills (Calzada et al., 2009), and developing objectivity during development (A. Padilla, 2006; Szapocznik & Kurtines, 1993).

Calzada and associates (2009) researched the effects of Latino bicultural parents of preschool children in a public school in New York City. They found that high levels of parental biculturalism were associated with higher levels of adaptive functioning and lower levels of internalizing problems (i.e., anxiety, sadness, withdrawal). In contrast, Latino parents who endorsed U.S. culture had higher rates of children with acting-out behaviors. The researchers explained these unexpected findings by referring to protective factors inherited from the Latino culture, which includes high levels of behavioral monitoring and supervision of children.

Address Discrimination and Racism

Discrimination is rampant in U.S. society. Studies of adolescents have revealed that experiences of discrimination damage self-esteem, academic achievement, and relationships. Race, ethnicity, and language are some of the things bullies target with ethnic minority youth (see Chapter 9). Parents, therefore, need to discuss prejudice, discrimination, and oppression openly with their children to teach them about coping strategies and to allow children to disclose troubling experiences. However, parents may not want or may not know how to discuss these topics with their children. Sometimes parents themselves have unfinished issues with their own experiences of discrimination and prefer not to talk about them to protect their children. Therefore, the counselor should lead the discussion of discrimination in therapy to be more psychoculturally responsive and effective.

Consider Language Preference in Therapy

Working with different levels of acculturation and language proficiency within a family therapy session can be an arduous and challenging task for the therapist. In addition to bilingual competencies, several scholars provide guidelines for bilingual therapy (Altarriba & Santiago-Rivera, 1994; Santiago-Rivera & Altarriba, 2002; Santiago-Rivera et al., 2002) that should be implemented. Gallardo-Cooper and Zapata (2013) address bilingual language dynamics in family therapy that could be helpful to the family therapist. For instance, language preference should be openly discussed early in bilingual family therapy. English language preference may be associated with diminished Spanish language skills, ethnic identity conflicts, or acting-out behaviors.

Facilitate Home–School Collaboration

Immigrant parents should be educated about the U.S. school system and its cultural values and objectives. Preparing parents for school meetings is a valuable intervention that can enhance parent participation in schools and facilitate relationships with educators. Leidy and colleagues (2012) also recommended collaboration and advocacy by school administrators to improve the cultural competence of immigrant families and to provide additional support with the loss of extended family networks.

Concluding Thoughts

In this chapter, we have addressed characteristics and trends of the Latino family. Transformations in family structure are constant, but core Latino cultural values persist across generations. Family strengths include *familismo, colectivismo* (togetherness), *respeto, cariño,* extended family support, and a parenting style that is protective and that relies on high levels of supervision. We endorse a life-cycle developmental model grounded in Latino culture as a framework for addressing the presenting problems of families and individuals. Likewise, an understanding of relevant elements of Latino family functioning is necessary for culturally responsive and ethical practice. Lastly, we have included throughout the chapter clinical examples to elucidate salient family therapy issues that need attention. The following Latino-centered guidelines are proposed for the important work counselors will undertake with *familias*.

Culturally skilled counselors

- Recognize the role of changes introduced by acculturation on the life of a family
- Assess their biases about normal family functioning
- Appreciate the interdependence of many families, particularly the involvement of *abuelos* and *abuelas*.

We have included throughout the chapter clinical examples to point to salient family therapy issues that need attention. Lastly, we have offered guidelines for culturally skilled counselors. Some of these guidelines include recognizing the role of changes introduced by acculturation on the life of the family, assessing counselor biases about "normal" family functioning, and appreciating the interdependence of many families.

• • •

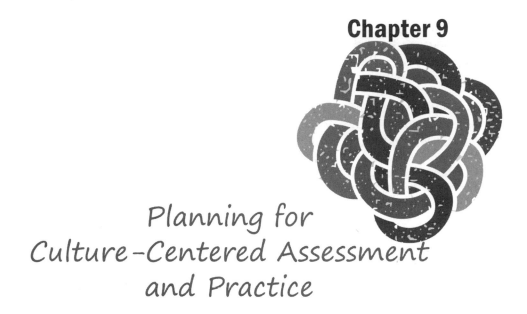

Chapter 9

Planning for Culture-Centered Assessment and Practice

Lo que bien empieza bien acaba.

A good start has a good ending.

• • •

Objectives

- To become knowledgeable about protocols for culturally sensitive assessment procedures.
- To become familiar with the interface between culture and clinical assessments as well as with the cultural syndromes most applicable to Latino groups.
- To examine biases about relationship-building practices that are more culturally congruent for Latinos.
- To explore accommodations to clinical practice that facilitate the development of the therapeutic alliance and adherence to treatment goals.

Sabías que/Did you know that . . .

- Interpreters are not free of bias, even if they are Latinos.
- Diagnoses are generally culture bound.
- Relationship building is essential to culturally effective counseling with Latinos.

• • •

Case Scenario

Dr. Jones had recently obtained her doctorate and was working toward her state license, supervised by Dr. Krauss, in a child psychiatric outpatient clinic. Dr. Jones, who described herself as proficient in English and Spanish, was hired as a bilingual clinician to respond to the growing immigrant Latino population. She indicated that her maternal grandfather was from Argentina and that she had studied Spanish in college. The clinic director was pleased because Dr. Jones was the only bilingual professional on staff, and there was a need to respond to the Latino population. This was the first time Dr. Jones indicated to her supervisor that she was working in Spanish.

During the course of supervision Dr. Jones noted that all of her child therapy sessions were conducted in English. She explained that she always started in Spanish, but her clients would shift to English immediately. Dr. Jones also spoke of concerns about the level of resistance of the parents of her child clients, stating that they tended to attend only one or two of the scheduled sessions. She reported that when she met with parents, they presented as inhibited, with limited verbal output. Dr. Krauss, her supervisor, responded that many Latino families are unauthorized and illiterate, which is a possible reason they speak so little. Dr. Krauss explained to Dr. Jones that these families are poor and probably ignore the process of therapy. She also added that these families might be resistant to therapy because they do not have papers or might be unable to participate because they hold multiple jobs. This perspective did not correspond with Dr. Jones's impressions, but then again, she had never worked with this population. With two unqualified professionals working with Latino clients, it is unlikely that therapy will be effective. Moreover, from the information presented here, it is clear that both the clinician and supervisor are practicing outside their area of competence and thus engaging in unethical practice.

Assessment

Among diverse populations, particularly Latinas/os, several factors may compromise the process of gathering relevant information while responding to the cultural interpersonal protocol required in building therapeutic relationships. The first encounter with the Latina/o client should focus on gathering information that will facilitate the clinician's understanding of the presenting problem and the identification of risk factors in need of immediate clinical attention. When one has a diverse clientele, taking time to acquire additional clinical and cultural information in subsequent sessions is generally recommended to respond to cultural expectations and engagement early in treatment (Paniagua, 2005; Takushi & Uomoto, 2001). Furthermore, the use of well-developed counseling microskills allows Latina/o clients to openly disclose their concerns in a safe setting where they can feel heard, understood, and culturally affirmed.

Today, competent Latino-centered clinicians are cognizant that best practices in assessment integrate cultural and clinical domains. Before clinicians can implement Latino-centered assessment, it is necessary to consider some critical dilemmas. First, clinical and cultural processes in mental health assessment (e.g., interviews, intakes, structured or semistructured interviews, crisis evaluations, rating scales) are prone to bias. Meticulously constructed diagnostic procedures (Alegría et al., 2009; Canino & Alegría, 2008; Kirmayer, 2001; Minsky, Vega, Miskimen, Gara, & Escobar, 2003) are imperfect as well, as objective, rigorously developed psychometric instruments have variance and probabilities of error.

Furthermore, assessment forms, historical intakes, and rating scales translated from English to Spanish may have errors due to literal translations that lack cultural meaning (Rogler, 1999) or vocabulary choices that imply different behaviors. There are also many ways to describe the same behaviors in Spanish. One of the authors (Gallardo-Cooper) translated a child behavior rating scale from English to Spanish with a colleague from Spain. The first drafts were done independently. When both drafts were examined there was a marked discrepancy in how behaviors were translated into Spanish. Most items had cultural relevance across the two cultures of the translators (Puerto Rican and Spanish), but some items differed because of regional variations in the Spanish language. There is ample variability in the Spanish language; even within the same country language varies between regions. The stakes can be high when an assessment is unclear, culturally insensitive, misinterpreted, unreliable, or biased.

A similar dilemma is encountered with the assessment of Latino children. Because children's assessments require observations by significant adults, biases may be further compounded. L. M. Chavez, Shrout, Alegría, Lapatin, and Canino (2010) studied perceptions of the severity of children's problems among clinicians and parents of Latino and Euro-American heritage. Parents and providers (of both Latino and Euro-American heritage) were presented with vignettes that were identical except for the use of Latino and Anglo names. Both parents and providers rated children in the Latino vignettes as having more severe psychopathology, even when their problems were mild. However, the children in the Anglo vignettes were rated as in need of more mental health services, even though their problems were rated as less severe than those in the same vignettes using Latino names. Thus, children with Latino names were perceived as having greater psychological impairment but were rated as being in less need of psychological treatment. The results suggest that Latino parents may have biases about the effectiveness of mental health services that negatively affect their willingness to seek treatment. Similarly, providers' biases may relate to their perception that Latino children's problems (even mild ones) are more severe because Latino parents seek treatment for their children when they perceive problems are too serious or severe.

Second, ethnocultural mental health assessments are generally intricate, with no set gold standard format (Adeponle, Thombs, Groleau, Jarvis, & Kirmayer, 2012). Fortuna, Porche, and Alegría (2009) found that clinicians were confused about how to introduce culture in the interview process and how much weight to give cultural factors compared to clinical information. Ambivalence in the interpretation of cultural and clinical factors has been explained as a problem of a lack of skill and training (Vega, 2005). Furthermore, lack of knowledge about culturally grounded behaviors may distort clinicians' observations. In their investigation of clinical services, Minsky and associates (2003) discovered that the behavioral presentation of immigrants characterized by high compliance to authority, passivity, and limited assertiveness led clinicians to mistake these observations for helplessness and hopelessness because of a lack of consideration of culture in the assessment process. If culture-based explanations had been explored, the mental health provider may have considered alternative interpretations, such as (a) the effects of a novel clinical experience, (b) a previous negative history with a provider, (c) a power differential (i.e., interaction with a clinician who is perceived as an authority figure), and/or (d) stigma related to mental health services stemming from a belief that services are rendered to crazy people. Other culture-based rationales to explore may be related to Latinos' deference to authority through listening and not disagreeing (i.e., *respeto* [respect, obedience, deference to authority figures, and boundaries in relationships] guides the interpersonal encounter) and their history of oppression and exploitation.

Third, knowledge, practice, and supervision are required to implement flexible yet pertinent assessment tools. An assessment tool is germane when it includes cultural and clinical domains that facilitate understanding of the client. Assessments of Latinos need to explore the client's bilingual skills, acculturation level, bicultural skills, immigration history (reasons for immigration; preimmigration, immigration, and postimmigration accounts), ethnicity and values, psychocultural stressors, ethnic self-identification, family kinships and structure, religious orientation and healing beliefs, idioms of distress, help-seeking style, and so forth. Clinical domains reflect the presenting problem, precipitating events and length of symptoms, emotional and cognitive functioning, work or school functioning, interpersonal relationships, differential diagnosis, and culture-bound syndromes, to name a few. In particular, strengths and resources at the personal, cultural, and systemic levels need to be identified early on in treatment.

The use of flexible tools enhances the flow of the assessment discourse without being rigid and insensitive. Given Latinas/os' preference for a personable approach (*personalismo*), conducting an interview based on a list of questions without responding to the tone, emotions, and needs of the client would have disastrous results. Body language and other nonverbal behavior are essential to take into account but need attention and clarification. For example, a Latina client appeared anxious, stroking her hand through her hair and watching the clock. When these observations were explored, the client reported concerns about the length of the session and her ability to pick up her children from school on time. However, she felt as though she could not interrupt the dialogue with the clinician or end the session abruptly because this would have been disrespectful. Flexibility also involves revisiting previously disclosed information that has changed, is unclear, or is openly revealed again at a later time during the course of therapy. After all, therapy is an ongoing process of multiple assessments.

Fourth, synchronicity of language proficiency between Latina/o clients and their clinicians is necessary during assessments. Language barriers continue to be the variable that interferes most directly with diagnostic outcomes (Bauer & Alegría, 2010; Bauer, Chen, & Alegría, 2010; Díaz et al., 2009; Minsky et al., 2003; Santiago-Rivera & Altarriba, 2002; D. W. Sue & Sue, 2003). For Spanish-dominant clients, working with a clinician who is not fluent in Spanish is a poor match. Not only might these clinicians be unable to relate to clients on an emotional level, but they may be unable to understand the intricate messages in spontaneous oral communication.

Both research and clinical findings show that when Latinas/os are evaluated in their nondominant language, misdiagnoses occur (Bauer & Alegría, 2010; Díaz et al., 2009; Marcos, 1973; Marcos & Urcuyo, 1979). Several studies have identified differences in diagnostic conclusions when Latina/o clients are interviewed in English and Spanish. Price and Cuellar (1981) found that when Latino patients with schizophrenia were interviewed in Spanish, more psychopathology was disclosed because of their level of comfort communicating in their dominant language. Minsky and colleagues (2003) discovered that compared to Euro-American and African American groups, Latino immigrants were overdiagnosed with major depression, although a significant number of psychotic symptoms were overlooked. In addition, Latina/o clients may be misdiagnosed when their primary language is not Spanish. For instance, Mayan languages are very different from Spanish in terms of structure and syntax. Nonfluent Spanish-speaking clinicians may erroneously perceive the client's Spanish as reflecting a language disorder, cognitive deficit, or emotional instability.

Scholars have also underscored the relevance of language as an instrument that regulates cognitive processes (e.g., attitudes, attributions, explanatory cognitions, thought disorders), perceptual experiences (e.g., hallucinations, spiritual experiences, trances), emotions (idioms of distress, emotional expressive style), and physiological symptoms (Bauer & Alegría, 2010; Comas-Díaz, 2012; Santiago-

Rivera & Altarriba, 2002; Santiago-Rivera, Arredondo, & Gallardo-Cooper, 2002). Distress and pain tend to be expressed in the primary language (J. M. Cervantes & Lechuga, 2004; Santiago-Rivera et al., 2002) because emotions are learned at a very young age. Among clients who are learning English as a second language, emotional expression is facilitated in their native language, as they can access a complete description of their emotions and can emphasize their feelings in detail (Marcos, 1973; Marcos & Urcuyo, 1979; Santiago-Rivera & Altarriba, 2002).

In addition, clinicians who work with immigrants need to be knowledgeable about processes of second language acquisition. Proficiency in a second language develops over two stages and may take up to 10 years to achieve (Alvarado, 2011; E. E. García & Náñez, 2011). Cummins is a leader in second language acquisition learning. According to his theory, during the first 1–3 years oral proficiency, or basic interpersonal communication skills, is acquired. English learners demonstrate social and interpersonal communication skills in this stage. Achieving complex academic language proficiency requires advanced language development and cognitively demanding skills (Cummins, 1984; E. E. García & Náñez, 2011). This stage is characterized by the development of skills that are associated with academic learning (e.g., reading and writing) and may be achieved from 5 to 10 years of age with ongoing English instruction. Alvarado (2011) further explained that when a second language is introduced and is heavily supported in schools and in the community, there is a natural process of diminishing skills in the first language (native language loss phenomena; Schmid & Kopke, as cited in Alvarado, 2011). If the native language is not supported at home or in other systematic, enriching activities, Latina/o youths may gradually lose the family's preferred communication language.

One of the authors (Gallardo-Cooper) recalls a Mexican preschooler whose teachers and monolingual language therapist considered him to have either selective mutism or some traits of mild autism. When evaluated in Spanish by an unfamiliar, bilingual professional, the child could not stop talking. He maintained eye contact throughout the interview and demonstrated mature interpersonal skills. Yet in the classroom he avoided making eye contact and refused to speak when the teacher talked to him in English.

Bilingual professionals continue to be in the minority in the mental health field (Bauer & Alegría, 2010; D. W. Sue & Sue, 2003), and even professional bilingual proficiency standards have not been established with any specificity (Bauer & Alegría, 2010; Gallardo-Cooper, 2008). In work with a Spanish-dominant client or a recently arrived immigrant, the complexity of therapeutic discourse may require Spanish-language skills that go beyond the clinician's Spanish heritage language (i.e., the first language learned at home).

Fifth, because there are insufficient numbers of bilingual clinicians (Vega et al., 2007), interpreters must be used. However, the use of interpreters in the mental health field and in health services has not received overwhelming endorsement, and many consider the use of interpreters as a last resort (G. Flores, 2005, 2006). Problems identified with their use include a lack of training, a lack of knowledge about the therapeutic processes, translation mistakes, and behaviors that interfere with the client–provider relationship (Bamford, 1991; Bradford & Muñoz, 1993; G. Flores, 2005, 2006). Unfortunately, when agencies lack bilingual licensed clinicians they rely on bilingual paraprofessionals to deliver direct services to Latina/o clients, compromising the quality of services. Of course, this occurs in school settings as well, as we discussed in Chapter 5. Far too often, monolingual English counselors and school psychologists rely on teachers or unqualified personnel (e.g., custodians, school volunteers, and teachers who speak Spanish) to serve as interpreters.

One of the authors (Gallardo-Cooper) had an experience with a recently arrived Filipino calculus teacher who served as an interpreter to a recently arrived Filipino student during a psychological evaluation. The clinician provided some basic training about the function of the language facilitator and asked that the translator translate verbatim only what the clinician and student expressed. However, the teacher's translations were very long and were accompanied by an intense tone, gross hand movements, and a frowning face. When asked about what she had said, the teacher responded, "I told him what you said, and I also told him that his demeanor was inappropriate, he was not sitting straight, he was not giving the respectful answers expected of Filipino students, and I was going to contact his father."

A response to these dilemmas, albeit not a perfect one, involves focusing at the microlevel in the assessment session. Nonfluent bilingual professionals may need to spend more time with Spanish-dominant clients to ensure understanding and to optimize their interviewing and counseling microskills. Clinicians may also complement information gathering with multiple assessment procedures, such as family interviewing, the use of parallel rating forms available in Spanish and English, and consultation with other bilingual professionals. Non-Spanish-speaking clinicians and their interpreters may need to be trained together on the proper format for translation in therapy (i.e., sitting arrangements, nonverbal communication; Bradford & Muñoz, 1993; Paniagua, 2005), clinical and cultural vocabulary, confidentiality standards, and boundaries in service delivery. For a review on how best to utilize language facilitators or interpreters, see Bradford and Muñoz (1993) and Paniagua (2005).

Sixth, mental health assessments need to produce the information necessary to develop a solid treatment plan to meet clients' needs. The assessment tools used by a guidance counselor will differ in content and focus from those used by a therapist who works with battered women. However, the assessment protocol of an elementary school guidance counselor will overlap with the interview protocol of a private practitioner in child and adolescent therapy. Clinicians also have to use work-generated assessment protocols. Unfortunately, some agencies' predeveloped intake forms are not sensitive to cultural factors. In these circumstances therapists will have to supplement agency forms with additional psychocultural assessments as well as advocate in their agencies for a more adequate revision of the form that includes ethnocultural variables. These recommendations are supported by hospital and community mental health agencies that are monitored by licensing boards, such as the Joint Commission of Accreditation, that require the inclusion of both clinical and cultural data in mental health assessments.

Despite the discussion of these dilemmas, assessment continues to be a challenging task in work with Latina/o clients. For a review of instruments and methods for use with Latinas/os, see Fontes (2008), Paniagua (2005), Pérez Foster (1998), Rhodes, Ochoa, and Ortíz (2005), and Suzuki, Ponterotto, and Meller (2001). In an effort to organize information that could be useful to most clinicians who work with Latinas/os, we discuss relevant areas in mental health assessment here: diagnostic guidelines, interviews, acculturation, language, and family functioning. However, a review of rating scales and other norm-referenced instruments used with Latina/o clients is beyond the scope of this chapter.

Diagnostic Guidelines

Most therapists have to be trained on diagnostic criteria, specifically the American Psychiatric Association's *Diagnostic and Statistical Manual of Mental Disorders* (*DSM*). (Note that at the time of this writing the fifth edition of this manual [the

DSM-5] was still in press, so our discussion here is based on the *Diagnostic and Statistical Manual of Mental Disorders, Fourth Edition, Text Revision [DSM-IV-TR]*; American Psychiatric Association, 2000.) Another common diagnostic classification system, the World Health Organization's International Classification of Diseases–10, is not discussed here because in the United States the *DSM* is the standard (or *summa auctoritate*, "highest authority") in the classification of mental disorders. The two systems of classifications attempt to correspond, but different words used in their guidelines have led to disagreements about diagnoses (Canino & Alegría, 2008).

Alarcón (2009a, 2009b) claimed that although the fourth edition of the *DSM* made advances by introducing cultural factors into diagnostic processes, the changes have been insufficient to motivate professionals to implement and improve diagnostic procedures. In addition, research has been undertaken since the publication of the latest edition to incorporate new cultural elements that will enhance psychiatric diagnoses (Alarcón et al., 2002), but many diagnostic criteria fail to provide clear cultural guidelines and examples (Paniagua, 2005). Advances in the *DSM-IV-TR* include (a) the incorporation of acculturation and acculturative stress as one of several stressors in the Axis IV configuration, (b) several references to cultural factors in specific diagnostic criteria, (c) the inclusion of culture-bound syndromes, and (d) the provision of a Cultural Formulation model to consider in the diagnosis process (Appendix I).

When required to use the *DSM-IV-TR* system for diagnostic purposes, culturally competent clinicians can capitalize on opportunities to address cultural factors. For instance, they complete the Axis formulation, follow the cultural formulation guidelines, and examine V codes (Axis IV Psychosocial or Environmental Problems). Three V codes address cultural factors that may be a focus of clinical attention: religious or spiritual, acculturation, and noncompliance with treatment. Also, cultural impact may be explored with other V codes, such as the effects of culture on partner relations, parent–child relational problems, and identity-related issues (e.g., Latino ethnic identity conflict). Although the Identity Problem V code does not specify ethnic identity (Paniagua, 2005), clinicians need to explore the role of cultural variables in identity-related issues for individual Latinas/os and their families. Culturally competent clinicians also ensure that acculturation problems are documented. Acculturation can be perceived as the white elephant in the therapy room and can be easily overlooked. Stress associated with language barriers, legal status, discrimination and exploitation, adjustment, and socioeconomic problems also needs to be specified under Axis IV (D. W. Sue & Sue, 2003).

Culture-Bound Syndromes

Culture-bound syndromes are a set of symptoms of distress found in different cultures. Much research has been conducted on culture-bound syndromes, in particular *ataque de nervios* (Guarnaccia & Rogler, 1999; Lewis-Fernández et al., 2010). The literal translation of *ataque de nervios* is "attack of nerves"; however, an *ataque* may manifest on a continuum from an anxiety attack to a nervous breakdown. Individuals typically collapse, faint or lose consciousness, sometimes thrash around, and scream hysterically. Although culture-bound syndromes are a worldwide psychological phenomenon and specific cultural groups sanction symptomatic manifestations, some question whether similarities exist between actual *DSM* criteria and culture-bound syndromes (Alarcón, 2009b). Lewis-Fernández and associates (2010) found a relationship between Latino idioms of distress and specific histories of trauma that may or may not concur with specific diagnostic criteria but that are clinically relevant for intervention. For instance, high correlations were found between *ataque de nervios* and interpersonal trauma as well as between *nervios* (nerves-related condition), a condition that may precede an *ataque de nervios* and may be related to a persistent history of trauma. Yet, posttraumatic stress disorder is a diagnosis that has a strong cultural load and may not be consistent among different populations (Alegria et al., 2007). Nevertheless, all scholars recommend assessing idioms of distress with Latina/o clients; in particular, they recommend exploring childhood and adult trauma, dissociative features, and suicide risk regardless of the existence of a full *DSM* clinical diagnosis (Guarnaccia & Rogler, 1999; Lewis-Fernández et al., 2010).

Guarnaccia and Rogler (1999), in their systematic review of the empirical literature on culture-bound syndromes, contended that instead of fitting culture-bound syndromes into *DSM* criteria it is more important to explore comorbidity. Manifestations of *ataque de nervios* tend to coexist with anxiety and affective disorders. Different features or subtypes of *ataque de nervios* may explain associated features of specific psychiatric disorders. Marked physiological reactions, such as an inability to breathe and chest pains, may be related to a coexisting panic disorder. Aggressive outbursts, in contrast, may be linked to depression. Similarly, an incident of *ataque* without other symptoms may reflect the potential to develop comorbidity with a psychiatric diagnosis. Recent studies support the psychiatric vulnerability of comorbidity among individuals who suffer from *ataques de nervios* (Guarnaccia et al., 2010). Guarnaccia and Rogler further argued the importance of attending closely to specific descriptions of symptoms (e.g., loss of consciousness, screaming, transitory amnesia, seizure-like behaviors, and suicidal gestures) and their frequency of occurrence to understand the severity of symptoms.

Referred to as the "Puerto Rican syndrome," *ataque de nervios* is also commonly found among Caribbean, Central American, and South American groups (Guarnaccia & Rogler, 1999; Keller, 2006) and tends to occur in Latina women older than 45 without a high school education. More important, Guarnaccia and Rogler (1999) found consistent support that *ataque de nervios* are usually precipitated by a painful unexpected loss in the family or by threats to the social well-being of the family. The event, they claimed, communicates deep suffering and a "plea for help (*socorro*)" (p. 1325). Rivera-Arzola and Ramos-Grenier (1997) identified suppressed anger and cultural gender pressures as underlying dynamics for *ataque de nervios* in Puerto Rican women that may be precipitated by a multitude of stressors, including loss, witnessing trauma, family conflicts, and socioeconomic problems.

Symptoms of Distress

The *DSM-IV-TR* list of Latino culture-bound syndromes is incomplete. Comas-Díaz (2012) added several common idioms of distress recognized in several regions of Latin America. Among these are *patatús* (dizzy spell), *salazón* (physical state of dehydration), *corriente de aire* (health risk due to a stream of air), *cuerpo cortado* (malaise, flu symptoms), *musarañas* (daydreaming, lack of focus), *telele* (an *ataque* due to unfinished work), and *fiaca* (laziness). As idioms of distress, Latino culture-bound syndromes are also linked to Spanish metaphors and descriptors that communicate emotional states or negative emotional reactions (see Table 9.1). Although they are not classified as culture-bound syndromes in the *DSM*, these examples add to the compilation of idioms of distress reported by Comas-Díaz (2012) and should be taken seriously, as they may describe important mental health problems that require further exploration during assessment and therapy.

We have discussed here just a sample of the many idioms of distress manifested throughout Latino countries; other idiosyncratic labels are used to describe stressful responses and emotional states. It is important to listen for these

Table 9.1

Examples of Latino Emotional and Behavioral Idioms of Distress

Idiom	Literal Translation	Symptoms
Aflojó el estómago	Loose stomach	Gastrointestinal reaction to stress
Apagado	Without light, muted, off	Disorientation, limited ability to problem solve, depression, low energy level
Desencajado	Disjointed, fragmented, unglued	Lack of energy, limited focus, poor disposition to pursue an action
Echo un basilisco	Becoming a basilisk	Extreme anger, out-of-control state, inability to reason
Lelo or lela	*Lelo* or *lela*	Immobilization, inertia, shock
Nervios a flor de piel	Exposed nerves	Intense anxiety
Nervios de punta	Nerves on edge	Anxiety, tension, nervousness
Soponcio	*Soponcio*	Physiological reaction to stress (dizziness, fainting, heat flare, gastrointestinal distress, etc.)

Note. Meanings may vary by region and country.

descriptors, as some Latino clients express their discomfort with common words that should not be taken lightly. For instance, Latino men may use the word *nervios* (nerves, anxiety) to describe depression because the word *deprimido* (depressed) reflects a more serious sign of mental illness that may not be congruent with a strong emotional stance associated with machismo. *Crisis nerviosa* (nervous crisis, or crisis of nerves) has an even stronger connotation of severity. However, these terms do not have the stigma associated with mental disorders. We recommend that to connect with Latinos clinicians communicate with the same idioms the clients use in discourse. For example, if a Latino man uses *nervios* or *estoy nervioso* (I am nervous/feeling anxious) to describe his emotional state, generate questions around the idiom by referring to behavioral and cognitive manifestations, such as "When you have the *nervios*, what thoughts run through your mind?" or "If you brought me a picture of yourself when you have the *nervios*, what would I see?"

Because bilingual clients tend to express emotions in their primary language (Pérez Foster, 1998; Santiago-Rivera & Altarriba, 2002), the clinician needs to be careful not to take their translations at face value. In English *nervios* translates as "nerves," but it may not have the same implications when it is used in Spanish. Comas-Díaz (2012) postulated that idioms of distress might represent messages of "cultural disconnection" (p. 215) among immigrants from different countries. Therefore, do not assume that *nervios* automatically translates to a diagnosis of anxiety. Sometimes *nervios* can represent more severe symptoms and other times a transitory reaction. Comas-Díaz (2012) also offered a culturally sensitive approach to working with clients who perceive their distress as illness through the use of interview questions that revolve around sickness (e.g., "How do you explain your illness?" "What does this illness mean to you?").

Cultural Formulation Model

Another cultural contribution to the *DSM-IV-TR* is the Cultural Formulation model. The Cultural Formulation model assists the clinician with differential diagnosis by incorporating cultural factors. Lewis-Fernández and Díaz (2002) described an excellent step-by-step application of the model with a Latina client and demonstrated the clinical utility of following a process of systematic cultural assessment to reach diagnostic conclusions. Although the Cultural Formulation model has not been tested, Alarcón and others claim that it is a valuable assessment supplement during the initial visit because it accesses the patient's own perception of his or her condition (Alarcón, 2009b; Alarcón et al., 2002; Fortuna et al., 2009; Lewis-Fernández & Díaz, 2002). The Cultural Formulation model includes five domains: (a) the cultural identity of the individual (e.g., ethnic identity, acculturation level), (b) cultural explanations of the individual's illness, (c) cultural factors related to the psychosocial environment and levels of functioning (e.g., environmental variables, family, social networks, work relations), (d) cultural elements of the relationship between the individual and the clinician, and (e) overall cultural assessment for diagnosis and care (American Psychiatric Association, 2000).

Empirical results of the effectiveness of the Cultural Formulation model have been mixed. However, the clinical utility of the model has been supported with Latino clients with a differential diagnosis of posttraumatic stress disorder (Fortuna et al., 2009). Because severe mental disorders (psychotic disorders) were misdiagnosed in a sample of patients of diverse ethnicities, some researchers have concluded that misdiagnoses among ethnic minority populations are common based on clinicians' tendencies to either overdiagnose or underdiagnose (Adeponle et al., 2012). Without a solid accumulation of empirical data, as well as data to support the fidelity with which the Cultural Formulation model is implemented in practice, it is too early to make any conclusions about its efficacy.

Cultural Competence and DSM Use

Culturally competent therapists, therefore, integrate culture, context, and clinical knowledge to reach a diagnostic conclusion. The *DSM-5* is expected to reflect advances in psychiatric knowledge based on extensive research accumulated since the publication of the *DSM-V-TR*. The integration of culture into the *DSM-5*, including additional cultural training for psychiatrists, has received increasing scholarly support, and the *DSM-5* will include clearer guidelines for addressing individuals not of Euro-American heritage (Alarcón et al., 2002; Lewis-Fernández & Díaz, 2002; Lewis-Fernández et al., 2011; Rounsaville et al., 2002; Stein et al., 2010). Therapists also have to be aware of symptoms of distress and syndromes that have been identified empirically in Latino subgroups. For instance, Latino children tend to exhibit more somatic complaints than their non-Latino cohorts (Canino, 2004), Latina mothers with multiple stressors are at risk for depression (Magaña, Seltzer, & Krauss, 2004; Magaña & Smith, 2006), and agoraphobia has been identified as a common complaint among immigrants (Alegría et al., 2008).

Instead of focusing on diagnostic impressions, Canino and Alegría (2008) recommended first exploring the contexts in which symptoms occur. In particular, children's distress may be associated with a negative environment (Canino, 2004; Canino & Alegría, 2008). Similarly, undocumented immigrants who exhibit agoraphobia may need to be understood as individuals who experience a hostile environment and the risk of detention and deportation as well as have limited resources (in terms of English skills, lack of transportation, unemployment). Preferring to stay in the safety of the home or experiencing anxiety when leaving home may not be pathological but may be a natural coping response to a real problem. Similarly, poverty and a lack of support may negatively impact the mental health of single Latina mothers. Identifying these contexts and realities will enhance the clinician's cultural competencies with diagnostic procedures (Kirmayer, 2001).

Finally, gains made with the inclusion of cultural variables in the *DSM-5* must be considered in light of the fact that private, state, and national health insurances may not cover culture-bound syndromes (Paniagua, 2005). Even though scholars agree that Latinas/os who experience culture-bound syndromes have real psychological pain that requires therapeutic attention, public and private policies work against mental health utilization among at-risk populations. This issue as well as the lack of coverage for V codes requires social justice advocacy at the national and state levels to ensure that mental health services are provided to all who need them, regardless of the etiology or severity of their condition.

Interviews

Interviews may be informal and open, structured, or semistructured. Informal interview formats may be preferred by experienced clinicians, but using this approach, they run the risk of missing essential information. In addition, some do not recommend using open interviewing methods to avoid biases with putative symptoms, as Latinos tend to be perceived as having high levels of somatization and nonassertiveness (Minsky et al., 2003). Many providers prefer semistructured interview formats, in which they and the client can engage in a spontaneous dialogue, for their ease of implementation (Alarcón, 2009b; Alarcón et al., 2002; Santiago-Rivera et al., 2002; Zayas, Torres, & Cabassa, 2009). Semistructured interviews are popular as information-gathering tools in therapy because of their easy utility and economic value and, more important, because their use does not interfere with the important task of initiating a therapeutic relationship with the client.

Structured interviews are often used in research studies and can be long and draining. The benefits in terms of thoroughness are diminished by the extensive time required to complete them, and their use can create frustration and the risk that Latina/o clients will not return to therapy. Gallardo-Cooper (as cited in Santiago-Rivera et al., 2002) provided a sample semistructured interview that has been useful in mental health settings. The Culture-Centered Clinical Interview taps relevant cultural and clinical domains valuable in treatment planning, risk management, and diagnosis (see Appendix A).

With Latinos in particular, a lack of *personalismo* and *respeto* may be perceived if the clinician places more attention on completing paperwork than getting to know the client through *la charla* or *la plática* (small talk; Paniagua, 2005; Santiago-Rivera et al., 2002). In addition, the fact that Latino clients have decided to seek therapy suggests that they have a need to explore, express, and seek help. Not allowing them, because of extensive use of a seemingly impersonal interview, could hinder their satisfaction with the initial visit.

Several interview models can be integrated to fit the style of the mental health provider. Guarnaccia and Rodríguez (1996) offered the Social and Cultural Assessment of Hispanic Immigrants in an interview format that is very useful for both new and seasoned professionals who want to develop culture-centered clinical interviewing skills. The authors provided examples of inquiries for each domain. They noted that it is critical to assess the following during the first visit: (a) language proficiency, literacy, and language preferences; (b) social connections (family structure and social supports); (c) migration experiences; (d) religious beliefs and practices; and (e) health care preferences and utilization patterns (healing practices, health utilization experiences, help-seeking tendencies).

Takushi and Uomoto (2001) proposed another model for use with diverse clients that is applicable to Latina/o clients. They recommended that the clinical interview focus on the following objectives: (a) initiating the therapeutic alliance, (b) defining clearly the presenting problem or clinical question, (c) identifying the client's strengths, (d) gathering historical information, and (e) developing a tentative diagnosis. The time restrictions on initial interviews and the pressure to reach a diagnosis in the first visit are work-related stressors that few mental health professionals resolve easily. The objectives proposed by Takushi and Uomoto are nevertheless sensible given that engagement with the client is essential and that the assessment process can be extended to future visits. Furthermore, an interview that can be extended allows the Latina/o clients ample time to express their concerns without the interview being redirected.

Acculturation Considerations

The assessment of acculturation with Latina/o clients is essential because for more than 2 decades the process of cultural adaptation has been empirically supported as an explanatory variable in the mental health status of immigrants (Zane & Mak, 2003). In addition, consideration of cultural adaptation can support *DSM-IV-TR* V code diagnoses (Paniagua, 2005); assists in the selection of therapeutic strategies (Cardemil & Sarmiento, 2009); and provides critical information about cultural transmission, change, and adaptation. Many acculturation scales were initially developed for research purposes, and many were designed for specific Latino ethnic groups. The three domains typically associated with acculturation—language (e.g., preference, retention of native language, and level of proficiency), generational status, and social affiliation preferences—are included in many of these instruments.

Zane and Mak (2003) and Paniagua (2005) provided thorough reviews of acculturation scales that can be used with Latinas/os. For example, the Brief Acculturation Scale (Burnam, Telles, Karno, Hough, & Escobar, 1987) has been recommended as a simple and useful tool for use in clinical practice (Comas-Díaz, 2012; Paniagua, 2005). This scale has only three questions reflecting three domains: generational status, language preference, and social affiliation (i.e., the preference to socialize with the same ethnic group, other groups, etc.). A 5-point Likert scale is used to generate a total score that reflects three levels of acculturation: mild, medium, and high.

However, of the currently available rating scales, none measure the multidimensional quality of the acculturation construct (Zane & Mak, 2003), all lack depth in measuring other critical cognitive and socioemotional variables, and all are weak psychometric tools (Marín, as cited in Sciarra, 2001; also see Chapters 3 and 4). Acculturation is not a dichotomous construct that can be represented visually with two extreme points on a line. This simplistic view suggests that as individuals increasingly adapt to the host culture, they lose their native culture, or vise versa. In reality, research has indicated that acculturation is complex and is best explained by cognitive variables (attitudes, cognitions, values, worldviews, attributions, etc.) and behavioral variables (actions that support affiliation with cultural values; Marín, as cited in Sciarra, 2001). That is, an individual can adapt more to the host culture but also retain and grow in his or her affiliation with his or her native culture. A Latina may be very aligned with her native culture (i.e., she may have frequent contact with her native country, peers, and family; maintain her language; affiliate with Latino friends; etc.), but depending on the situation she may make decisions based on Euro-American values.

For these reasons, culture-centered clinical interviews are optimized by the knowledge base of clinicians who have a deep understanding of the complexity of acculturation. By exploring the presenting problem, the clinician can obtain more information regarding acculturation-related issues. For example, acculturation conflicts can underlie generational discord with elders or children, conflicts in cross-cultural couples, psychocultural stressors associated with language barriers and poor adaptation, or nostalgia over the loss of customs or the native country.

For clinicians who prefer to use a quantitative measure, the combination of both a rating scale and good interviewing skills can provide the most thorough approach to the assessment of acculturation.

Considerations of Language Use

Retaining one's language enables one to retain the culture embedded in the language. That is, language preference, fluency, and literacy provide information about a Latina/o's level of acculturation. Similarly, maintaining two languages reflects bicultural skills, an ability to maneuver two cultures. The two languages typically assessed among Latinas/os are Spanish and English, but other languages may also be spoken. However, not all Latinas/os have a corresponding level of language proficiency in two languages, and it is necessary to explore in what context the languages are used. A Latino may communicate about work-related issues in English because this is the language he uses at work, but he may communicate with his wife about family matters in Spanish.

The clinician needs to examine the client's preferred language for therapy in two main areas. First, the client should be asked about the development of his or her native and second language to identify the therapeutic language needs of the client. Second, the provider has to respond to ethical questions. The clinician must consider the following questions: In terms of his or her language history, how will this client receive the highest quality of care? Do I have the language skills necessary to address the client? Who is the best clinician to respond to these language needs? The initial historical paperwork and the interview should ask for the following information:

- What was the first language spoken?
- At what age was the second language introduced?
- Was formal education provided in Spanish, in English, or in both languages?
- Did client attend schools in their home country?
- What is the literacy level in Spanish, in English, and in any other language?
- What is the generational status of the client (e.g., immigrant or first generation, second generation, third generation)?
- At what age did the client immigrate to the United States?
- What language or languages are spoken at home (i.e., with the nuclear and extended family) and with friends?
- What language is spoken at work?
- Does the client visit the country of origin on a regular basis?
- What language is used during self-talk, prayer, endearment, anger?

Even if this preliminary information is acquired during a phone intake, the clinician is responsible for quickly assessing whether he or she has the language skills necessary to respond to the client's needs or whether a referral needs to be made. There is no need to conduct a full battery of standardized tests to identify language and second language proficiency. Nevertheless, clinicians must assess the developmental sequelae of language acquisition.

Targeting emotional content with emotional language allows for the release of more affect, whereas disclosing emotional content in the acquired second language may inhibit affect or produce a "detachment effect" (Marcos, as cited in Altarriba, 2002, p. 6; see also Marcos & Urcuyo, 1979). If emotions were learned in Spanish, there is a higher probability that in therapy emotional content may be manifested in Spanish. Memory processes include retention of the language used in past experiences (Altarriba, 2002; Santiago-Rivera, & Altarriba, 2002). However, children's exposure to English early in life may result in the generation of emotional disclosures in both languages. In the case of a bilingual Latino man married to a monolingual English non-Latina woman, chances are that both English and Spanish may be used in couples therapy, as the clinician may need to explore whether the Latino man may be minimizing emotion at home. Even among highly acculturated Latinas/os who report a preference for English-language therapy, phrases and sentences are often spontaneously expressed in Spanish. In these circumstances, the clinician should encourage the client to express emotional content freely and later translate the affective experience.

Bilingual counseling is a specialty practice receiving increasing attention in academic training and clinical supervision (Gallardo-Cooper, 2008). In addition to bilingual competence to conduct assessments and facilitate the therapeutic relationship, bilingual clinicians need to be knowledgeable about psycholinguistic factors that impact the therapeutic process and how these processes can be used strategically. Some examples include language choice, code switching (i.e. switching languages while communicating), memory, meaning, and contextual variables (Altarriba, 2002; Marcos, 1994; Marcos & Urcuyo, 1979; Santiago-Rivera & Altarriba, 2002). These processes provide opportunities for valuable strategic therapeutic interventions. For instance, bilingual therapists may utilize shifts in language either to control emotional reactions (second language) or to expand emotional content (native language) with their clients.

Family Functioning

Because Latinas/os are often seen in mental health settings as a family or with some members of the family present, we discuss here some useful recommendations for systemic assessment. Assessing the family yields rich cultural and contextual information. Gallardo-Cooper and Zapata (2013) identified important family processes to assess in family therapy. They recommend identifying (a) the members of the family (e.g., extended family members, kinship, close friends who are considered family), (b) the worldview or value priorities of family members, (c) the family's problem-solving style, (d) the style of emotional expression and communication in the family, and (e) the structure the family endorses (vertical/hierarchical or horizontal/democratic). Also valuable is identifying family rules, the roles of family members, and rituals (traditional and idiosyncratic; Anderson, Anderson, & Hovestadt, as cited in Santiago-Rivera et al., 2002). When families do not bring all of the pertinent participants in the family system to the session, chances are the clinician will not have an accurate impression of the presenting problem and treatment outcomes may be compromised. The case scenario that follows exemplifies how Latino values are unveiled in the assessment of the family and how important it is to include the entire family system in the therapeutic arena.

Case Scenario

Ricardo was a college-educated Colombian father, 22 years older than his Peruvian wife, Consuelo. Ricardo had been a naturalized U.S. citizen for 20 years, spoke English fluently with a slight accent, and owned an accounting practice, whereas Consuelo had had 2 years of college in Peru. She lacked proficiency in English and did not drive. She communicated with her children in Spanish, and her friends were all Latinas/os. Consuelo was a homemaker who was very caring toward her in-laws, who lived in the same neighborhood. Ricardo and Consuelo had two children, Esteban and Cristina.

On the recommendation of the school principal, Ricardo called for an appointment for his 8-year-old son, who was having difficulties at school. Esteban cried often and complained that his classmates made fun of him. The initial appointment was made, at which time his parents would come alone to provide more detailed information. Ricardo came by himself and reported that his wife could not come. During this visit Ricardo explained that his son did not exhibit any difficulties at home; he was loving and playful and got along very well with his sister and parents. Ricardo reported that his problems manifested at school and that maybe Esteban had a learning problem. Two appointments were then scheduled, one for the parents and one for Esteban.

During his first appointment, Esteban presented as an immature child who seemed to enjoy the individual session. He expressed being stressed at school and at home and often feeling lonely. The clinician stressed the need for Consuelo to come to the next session with Ricardo. When they were seen together, Consuelo described many concerns about her son, such as some irritability and aggressiveness toward his younger sister when she touched his toys. Yet Esteban was an affectionate boy who was obedient to parents and enjoyed family activities. When the therapist asked Ricardo about his wife's concerns, he reported that he was constantly at work and usually came home late, when the children were typically doing their homework or getting ready for bed. He had witnessed those behaviors but they were not frequently manifested and not a serious concern. Consuelo reiterated that they had a stable family life and that Ricardo was a thoughtful, caring, and dedicated husband and father. He was sometimes "too protective" and often chose to handle all family issues on his own "so that I do not have to worry."

In this case example the father's role in the family is congruent with Latino cultural values and not necessarily representative of systemic pathology. Assuming responsibility of the family outside the parameters of the home was Ricardo's gender role expectation. In addition, issues associated with transportation logistics and work stressors were at play.

Family Therapy Tools

Scholars of family therapy have developed powerful assessment tools that can be used in the early stages of therapy with families, couples, and individuals (Garcia-Preto, 1996; Hardy & Laszloffy, 1995; McGoldrick, Gerson, & Shellenberger, 1999; McGoldrick & Hardy, 2008). Bowen introduced the genogram as a tool for exploring family-of-origin histories and dynamics that impact on current family functioning (Guerin, 1976). The genogram is a diagram or visual summary of the family across generations and is constructed with the client(s). The picture that results is very valuable not only from a systemic perspective but also as an instrument for exploring psychocultural factors such as immigration, ethnic identity, gender roles, acculturation, and social networks. Modifications to the genogram have been made with different foci, such as the eco-genogram (Hartman, 1995) and the cultural genogram (Hardy & Laszloffy, 1995). With the former, the clinician is able to learn the ecology of the family or the individual in terms of the neighborhood, school, work, church, or community and the interplay of social networks and conflicts experienced. The cultural genogram in particular has gained popularity as a valuable tool for cultural assessment. Hardy and Laszloffy (1995) adapted the cultural genogram to include key domains in multicultural assessment. McGoldrick, Giordano, and Garcia-Preto (2005b) included a guide on the questions to ask as the cultural genogram is being constructed. Basic inquiries relate to family functioning, such as demographic information, history of the problem, life-cycle stage of family members, family structures (nuclear and extended), work, school, hypotheses of problem resolution, and other relational history. Cultural inquiries revolve around language skills, acculturation levels, spirituality and healing beliefs, cultural heritage (race and ethnicity), stressors, migration history, and stressful events since the immigrant's arrival to the United States. The completion of a cultural genogram can take several sessions, as this tool generates rich psychocultural information, encourages disclosure, triggers intense emotional content, and provides a comprehensive method of psychocultural assessment and intervention planning.

Another culturally relevant systemic interview tool is the Multicultural/Multiracial Experience Inventory (M. Ramírez, 1998), as previously discussed in Chapter 3. Similar to the cultural genogram, this tool involves the collection of considerable information about an individual's family history (i.e., parents and grandparents alike). It is also highly contextual, with inquiries about school, the neighborhood, and friendships.

Relationship-Building Factors

The therapist is an agent of change in the therapeutic encounter regardless of theoretical orientation. Attitudes, communication style, interpretations, and behaviors affect the client's readiness to engage, trust, and develop a therapeutic alliance. A well-established dogma in the counseling field involves the application of Rogerian constructs—empathy, unconditional regard, and genuineness—as the basic foundation of a meaningful therapeutic connection with the client. With a diverse client population, however, developing a therapeutic alliance is complicated by the need to apply cultural connectivity and consciousness, given that all relational processes are culture bound (Comas-Díaz, 2006a; Vasquez, 2007). Latinas/os in particular are highly skilled in assessing a therapist's demeanor and interpersonal style (Comas-Díaz, 2006b). Some have argued that a lack of cultural fit may lead to confusion and ambivalence about the therapeutic process (Bernal, Jiménez-Chafey, & Domenech Rodríguez, 2009), a sense of disconnection with the therapist (Comas-Díaz, 2006a), dismissal of culturally relevant content (Comas-Díaz, 2012), or unintentional microaggressions (P. Arredondo, Tovar-Blank, & Parham, 2008; D. W. Sue et al., 2007).

Because successful outcomes rely on the synchronization of Latino culture and people skills (Bernal & Sáez-Santiago, 2006; Bernal, Sáez-Santiago, & Galloza-Carrero, 2009; Vasquez, 2007), we make several recommendations to facilitate the therapeutic relationship:

- Focus on similarities shared with clients. Falicov (1998) recommended emphasizing similarities with clients instead of differences to increase your connection with the client.
- Develop cultural empathy. Comas-Díaz (2012) described the importance of developing a vicarious experience that includes affect and cognitions revolving around the client's cultural being.
- Unveil internalized personal and cultural biases. Attending to your internalized personal and cultural biases is critical in relationship building (Comas-Díaz, 2012; D. W. Sue, Arredondo, & McDavis, 1992).
- Disclose and ask about differences and similarities. Delgado-Romero (2001) recommended disclosing some personal and professional information in the first meeting to explore the client's comfort level and preferences.

- Attend to and explore psychocultural stressors. Being responsive to relevant psychocultural features in treatment enhances the therapeutic relationship and outcomes as critical issues are addressed (Mendez & Westerberg, 2012).
- Seek to communicate in the same language as the client to facilitate the quality of care, discussion about barriers to treatment, and the therapeutic relationship (Bauer & Alegría, 2010; Bauer et al., 2010; Santiago-Rivera & Altarriba, 2002; Santiago-Rivera et al., 2002; Vega et al., 2007).
- Be congruent with the level of formality or informality of the client or the family. Initially some Latina/o clients may present as more formal, or the father in the family may lead the initial meeting (Añez, Silva, Paris, & Bedregal, 2008; Paniagua, 2005).
- Check and verify with Latina/o clients directly that you are responding to their needs.
- Be responsive to communication style and language to facilitate engagement.

Latino Values in Relationship Building

Because Latino values support the dignity of familial and community networks through social relatedness, clinicians need to be cognizant of variables that enhance and interfere with the relationship. Achieving cultural attunement starts with reviewing the impact of cultural values on communication and engagement.

La Plática, La Charla, *and Self-Disclosure*

Driven by the value of *personalismo*, generation status, and unfamiliarity with the norms of counseling, many Latinas/os may initiate the relationship by engaging in small talk and asking direct personal questions of the therapist. Some Latinas/os may need to perceive providers as an extension of their family system to develop a therapeutic alliance. This requires more familiarity through increased knowledge about the clinician's background or personal life (Comas-Díaz, 2006b, 2012; Falicov, 1998; Gallardo, 2009; Paniagua, 2005; Santiago-Rivera et al., 2002). Nevertheless, there are exceptions. For example, a client with a mandated order for therapy might not engage in small talk in the same way a self-referred client who is more motivated might. Thus, Latino-centered mental health providers must be aware of the apparently intrusive approach many Latinas/os may take during therapy. In addition, therapists should not be offended by personal questions or become preoccupied by ethical concerns of self-disclosure. Of course, appropriate judgment must be used. Not answering a question directly and redirecting it to the client (e.g., "How will learning about my country of origin help you during therapy?") could trigger an undesirable reaction. It is best to approach these questions directly and without surprise.

Conversely, *plática* may be a useful tool for gaining a general impression of a client when the clinician does not have a priori information. Language preference, nationality, and other characteristics may be unveiled in a short 5-minute informal conversation. If the client asks the therapist for personal information (e.g., nationality, time living in the United States, family composition, religion), the therapist can hypothesize that the value of *personalismo* is very important to developing a trusting relationship and that the questions asked reflect important domains that may impact counseling. Other clients who may be more reserved initially and may not ask much out of a sense of *respeto*, but the relationship may still be driven by *personalismo*.

At least in the initial stages, a rule of thumb for transitioning from *plática* to therapy discourse is arriving in the office. Delgado-Romero (2001) described a valuable *plática* or introduction to therapy approach that includes some personal and professional self-disclosure. He prepares prior to an initial session with a Latino client and engages in self-exploration about the similarities and differences of his future client. More important, his introduction to therapy places cultural differences and issues at the forefront, opening the door for cultural discourse.

Formalismo

Another important value to consider in the early stages of counseling is *formalismo* (formalism; Añez et al., 2008; Paniagua, 2005). Latina/o clients typically perceive the therapist as an expert. Too much informality at the beginning of the first encounter may prove detrimental. However, informality is the preferred approach after rapport develops. Men, parents, and elders may respond best to an initially formal approach. Elders also require use of the titles *Doña* or *Don* to communicate respect for the hierarchical structure of the family. Introducing yourself with your title may be an example of using *formalismo,* as might be using formal Spanish when appropriate (e.g., the *Usted* form of address rather than *Tú*). Some clinicians effectively mix *formalismo* with *personalismo;* for example, they use an informal personal approach with formal Spanish (Cardemil & Sarmiento, 2009). The underlying premise is that a clinician competent in counseling Latinas/os needs to mold himself or herself to the characteristics and needs of the client, adapting to the client's preferred communication style.

Personalismo *and* Familismo

Personalismo directs communication in that the *persona* (person) is more important than any administrative task. It also implies that the therapist has an underlying level of acceptance of the client's psychocultural history and attributes. The allocentric quality of Latino values requires a more intimate interaction to consider the therapist as a family member (*familismo*). Therefore, clients may invite the therapist to family celebrations such as a graduation or a *quinceañero* (the celebration of a girl's 15th birthday, a coming-of-age celebration with cultural and religious significance). These invitations should be considered a sign that a therapeutic alliance has been established and that the clinician is now considered part of the extended family. In addition, it is important to discuss use of the word *familia* among many Latino ethnicities. Close friends are referred to as *familia.* Even among professional organizations, mental health providers communicate with *familia*-like greetings. Relevant also is the fact that Latino professionals may disclose more intimate personal reactions in homogeneous Latino organizational meetings than in mixed Latino and non-Latino meetings.

Simpatía *and* Respeto

Many Latinas/os guide their interactions with *simpatía* (i.e., personable presentation of one's self in a positive light that parallels the "looking good" variable) and *aguantarse* (self-control) to maintain harmony. These values, as well as the vertical or hierarchical relational style Latinos endorse (Comas-Díaz, 2006b; Falicov, 1998; Santiago-Rivera et al., 2002), may lead clients to avoid expressing dissatisfaction directly with the therapist (Santiago-Rivera et al., 2002). When a level of discomfort is experienced during the session, subtle *indirectas* (nondirective communications) may be used (Añez et al., 2008; Comas-Díaz, 2006b; Falicov, 1998) and smiles may be observed with little relevant disclosure. Unsatisfied clients may also communicate discomfort with treatment by discontinuing therapy with an evasive excuse or by not responding at all to follow-up attempts (Santiago-Rivera et al., 2002).

Polo, Alegría, and Sirkin (2012) found many reasons for Latinas/os' poor health management behaviors and low levels of collaborative participation with their providers. In addition to cultural values that interfere with questioning the authority of the provider (*respeto*), they found that other interpersonal and structural barriers are very relevant indeed, such as differential power dynamics, limited service options, lack of resources, and mental health issues. Therefore, they recommended against assuming that Latinas/os have difficulties asking questions and that deferring health decisions is culturally grounded and instead advised considering multiple explanations (e.g., power dynamics, logistical problems) when Latino clients do not participate as expected during collaborative provider–patient interactions. Agencies and providers must do their part to be more culturally responsive and design programs and approaches that are more relevant to Latinas/os.

Confianza, Profundizar, *and* Intimidad

The value of *personalismo* provides the relational tools to reach *confianza* (i.e., a level of trust that leads to deeper disclosure) through *profundizar* (i.e., the opportunity to discuss an issue at length). *Intimidad* (i.e., personal comfort to address difficult themes) evolves into a higher degree of *confianza*. Without the prospect of reaching these relational levels, the therapeutic alliance and treatment outcome may be compromised.

Relevant to efficacious counseling outcomes are Latino relational preferences. Mulvaney-Day, Earl, Díaz-Linhart, and Alegría (2011) identified group differences in relational preferences among African American, Latina/o, and White clients in therapy. Latinos preferred to develop a strong relationship with the clinician to *profundizar* or achieve a deeper understanding of their own affective state. Similar to African Americans, Latinos preferred the development of a therapeutic relationship facilitated by emotional disclosure early in treatment. Latinas/os also expected the therapist to keep careful attention on the client without distractions (e.g., writing notes) and disliked indefinite remarks ("Yeah . . . Hmmmm"). An effective clinician was described as an expert with authoritative status but not a judgmental approach, as well as direct and willing to give advice. However, if a state of *confianza* was attained in the relationship, the clinician could become more direct and confrontational over time. When trust is built, the conversations between a counselor and client can be more candid. At the same time, counselors must abide by the *ACA Code of Ethics* (American Counseling Association, 2005) in terms of boundary limitations and respect in the counseling relationship. The introduction of Section B states, "Counselors recognize that trust is a cornerstone of the counseling relationship. Counselors aspire to earn the trust of clients by creating an ongoing partnership, establishing and upholding appropriate boundaries, and maintaining confidentiality" (p. 7).

Agradecimiento

Latinas/os typically express gratitude by giving gifts, sharing personal experiences (e.g., invitations to family events), and bringing family members or friends to meet the clinician. Not accepting these symbols of *agradecimiento* (gratefulness) can be detrimental to the relationship. Clinicians and students in training need to be equipped with the skills to address these issues. An act of *agradecimiento* may be a therapeutic opportunity to explore the meaning of gift giving with clients. Latino-centered therapists should be graceful in acknowledging the gift or invitation. Often these acts of *agradecimiento* are metaphors for a positive therapeutic relationship. Invitations to graduations and weddings, for example, can be addressed by attending the ceremony and not the social celebration (G. M. Arciniega, personal communication, March 25, 2007). Many Latino-sensitive clinicians accept gifts as long as they are of negligible monetary value and represent a personal act of *agradecimiento* (e.g., pastries, children's artwork, a handmade item). Discussion with the client about the meaning of gift giving and *agradecimiento* is always recommended to deepen awareness, validate cultural practices, identify the client's motives, and avoid offending the gift giver.

One of the authors (Gallardo-Cooper) experienced an unusual demonstration of *agradecimiento*. In the middle of a session, her Latino client, who owned a design and construction company, asked how many bathrooms she had in her house. When she responded, "How will that information help you with your child?" the client responded, "I am so grateful for all that you have done for my family that I would like to redo your bathrooms at no cost. I got a lot of extra granite in my shop I can use." The therapist declined the offer with *respeto*, briefly explained ethical standards, and underscored that the client's expression of satisfaction with the counseling experience was valuable feedback. Obviously there are limits to the gifts a provider can accept, no matter how culturally sensitive he or she is.

Time

Many Latinas/os have a fluid concept of time. Latinas/os also tend to have a present time orientation that influences communication, the format of the session, and the focus of treatment. For instance, the clinician may initiate a session with a here-and-now question: "How can I be of help to you today?" to address the present orientation of the client. Latinos unfamiliar with counseling may seek assistance to resolve specific problems. Thus, the here-and-now question introduces a problem-solving approach. Scheduling problems may also arise. Occasionally clients may come to the appointment considerably late. This may be a cultural issue that reflects old traditions, as in some Latino countries patients have to wait long periods of time—sometimes the entire day—to be seen. Therefore, educate clients about the parameters of the services provided at your agency and institution. If transportation is an issue, address this concern in the first session and plan with the client accordingly.

Time is also a tricky concept for Latina/o clinicians. Some Latino providers feel uncomfortable setting limits when concluding the session. Careful attention and cultural sensitivity is needed not to err by *falta de respeto* (failure to respect). Because many Latina/o providers are socialized by *personalismo*, they may find it disrespectful to interrupt the client's disclosure. If the clinician interrupts with, "I'm sorry but our time is up. Let's keep talking about this important issue in our next session," there is a high probability that a Latina/o client with low acculturation and no previous experience in therapy may feel disrespected, which then compromises the therapeutic alliance and the attractiveness of therapy. As Mulvaney-Day and colleagues (2011) observed, some Latino clients expect to spend more time in session to discuss more issues and *profundizar* (engage in deep discussion) on emotional content. At the same time, it is the counselor's responsibility to be clear about the time limits and perhaps mention "We have only 10 minutes left" or state at the beginning of the session how long the session will last and the agency's limitations on hourly appointments. A clock in the room helps.

Saludos, Despedidas, *and Physical Proximity*

Most Latinas/os engage in greetings and farewells with a hug. This is a cultural ritual that has no sexual or romantic connotation. Touching the client on the forearm may be a nonverbal way to accentuate an important issue. Latinos tend to be more comfortable than other ethnic groups being in closer physical proximity and touching. Issues of gender and age of clients and providers must also be considered with matters of physical proximity and touch.

Latino-Centered Accommodations to Practice

In addition to relational factors, other variables influence counseling engagement and treatment progress with Latinas/os, such as readiness for psychosocial and psychocultural therapy and active participation in therapy. Because the therapeutic process is the result of multiple interactive and nonexclusive variables, we consider here Latino-specific accommodations to practice that facilitate involvement in and adherence to treatment.

Acculturation

Level of acculturation is an invisible variable that impacts the therapeutic alliance and the effectiveness of interventions (Hwang, 2006; Santisteban & Mitrani, 2002). Research supports the fact that level of acculturation should be considered when selecting therapeutic methods (Cardemil & Sarmiento, 2009; G. Marín & Gamba, 2002). Low-acculturation Latinas/os may respond best to more culturally based strategies, whereas highly acculturated Latinas/os may respond best to mainstream approaches (Cardemil & Sarmiento, 2009). Matching the client's acculturation level with strategies selected also impacts the client's motivation to engage in treatment.

Acculturation is also a dynamic construct with a wide range of variability. A congruent match between the client and the therapist in terms of age, bilingual ability, ethnicity, gender, and number of years of residence in the United States may be compromised if the clinician trained in the United States in English with a mainstream counseling approach. That is, the counselor's level of professional socialization may contrast with the application of a culturally relevant therapeutic process.

Another important variable associated with acculturation relates to Latina/o clients' beliefs concerning the benefits of treatment offered. Mendez and Westerberg (2012) examined the implementation of a culturally adapted program for Latino parents of preschool-age children. They found that the perceived benefit of treatment was an important factor for parental participation. Parents with high levels of native cultural congruence and affinity had fewer barriers to treatment than parents with low levels of native cultural competence. The researchers explained that preparing parents who had limited experience with the U.S. culture appeared to have beneficial effects in terms of readiness for and engagement in treatment.

Language

Language and cultural congruence with Latina/o clients facilitates treatment outcomes (Eamranond, Davis, Phillips, & Wee, 2009; Mendez &Westerberg, 2012), the counseling relationship, and the effectiveness of treatment (Bauer & Alegría, 2010; Paniagua, 2005; Santiago-Rivera & Altarriba, 2002; Santiago-Rivera et al., 2011). Bilingual clients may use two languages in conversation (language switching). Matching the language chosen by the client during the course of the session also enhances the therapeutic alliance (Gallardo-Cooper, 2008; Santiago-Rivera & Altarriba, 2002). Some clinicians have indicated that with bilingual clients in family therapy, the language a family member chooses can reflect important dynamics, and thus language itself can be used as a therapeutic tool (Gallardo-Cooper & Zapata, 2013). English dominant bilingual clinicians may invite clients for whom Spanish is their first language to say what they would like in Spanish first and then translate for the counselor in English. Not only does this empower the client but it allows the individual to think through and provide greater clarity.

This type of affective translation should allow first for full emotional catharsis in the native tongue because expression of emotional content in a second language is often suppressed or less intense (Marcos & Trujillo, 1981; Marcos & Urcuyo, 1979). When a nonverbal expression signals to the counselor that the client has more to say, the counselor can invite the client to share the emotion in Spanish (Gallardo-Cooper, 2008; Santiago-Rivera et al., 2002). There is ample research to suggest that one's primary language is the language of emotions (Santiago-Rivera & Altarriba, 2002), and the counseling setting is a safe place in which to be emotionally expressive.

Researchers and clinicians alike recommend therapists with bicultural experiences and bilingual skills as the most suitable for engaging in exemplary practices with Latinas/os (Cardemil & Sarmiento, 2009; Domenech Rodríguez, Baumann, & Schwartz, 2011; Gallardo, 2009; Gallardo-Cooper, 2008; Santiago-Rivera & Altarriba, 2002; Santiago-Rivera et al., 2002). Given that there are no current standards for bilingual proficiency in the counseling profession (Gallardo-Cooper, 2008), Polo and associates (2012) recommended that providers monitor their language exchanges in Spanish and recognize their limitations with the Spanish language to avoid misunderstandings. Asking for clarification is also a core communication strategy in bilingual counseling. Having clarity and understanding in the therapeutic discourse builds confidence and trust in the client–therapist relationship.

Another important language-based intervention that facilitates cultural meaning is the use of *dichos* (proverbs) and metaphoric language. *Dichos* promote cultural congruence and cognitive permanence, as Latinas/os hold on to popular wisdom to resolve conflicts, recall admonishments or lessons from their grandparents and parents (Zúñiga, 1992), and act as an indirect mode of confrontation when they are faced with interpersonal conflict (Añez et al., 2008). One *dicho* that can be used when accountability or responsibility are under discussion is *Guitarras sin cuerdas, obras sin manos* (You cannot play a guitar that does not have strings, nor can you accomplish tasks without doing the work).

Logistics

Research on health disparities identifies a lack of basic resources as a major barrier in the utilization of mental health services among Latinas/os. Poverty is often the underlying barrier and is reflected in a lack of transportation, unemployment, parental distress, a lack of child care support, rigid work schedules, and unauthorized status (Alegría et al., 2002; Mapp, 2003; Mendez, Carpenter, LaForett, & Cohen, 2009). Therefore, a client's lack of engagement in therapy may be due to these contextual variables and not to psychogenic reasons or resistance to receiving help. Refer to Chapters 1 and 6 for additional information about earnings, poverty, and employment among Latinas/os.

Consejos

Many Latinas/os prefer therapists to provide advice in each session (Paniagua, 2005; Santiago-Rivera et al., 2002). This is similar to indigenous healing systems that provide *remedios* (prescriptions) in each session or when a family member or *madrina* or *padrino* (godparent) is consulted to solve a problem. There is also a preference for concrete and specific *consejos* (advice) and a therapist who is more active than passive and more verbal than nonverbal. However, counselors should not misconstrue this as passivity or laziness on the part of clients. Rather, when Latino clients are in counseling for the first time and their only experience with health practitioners has been with physicians who prescribe medications, it is understandable that they will also be looking for advice or a script from the counselor.

Therapist Skills and Comfort Level

The therapist needs to learn Latino-centered competencies (Santiago-Rivera et al., 2002) to develop the awareness, knowledge, and skills needed to address sensitive topics in therapy, such as race, age, gender, spirituality, sexual orientation, disability, and others. They also need to self-evaluate their level of comfort with clients' characteristics. For example, a young Latina provider might have difficulties working with an elderly Latina who could be her *abuelita* (grandmother). Likewise, the elderly Latina may have similar difficulties or may not disclose important issues because of age differences. Therefore, therapists need to address very early in treatment divergent characteristics with their clients and how clients feel about working with them.

Latino–Sensitive Counseling Competencies

Since the creation of the Multicultural Counseling Competencies 2 decades ago (P. Arredondo et al., 1996; S. Sue, Zane, Nagayama Hall, & Berger, 2009), ethnic-specific counseling guidelines have been developed to assist practitioners and students alike. Although Latino counseling recommendations are abundant in the literature, we discuss here several guidelines and models that can be helpful (Bean, Perry, & Bedell, 2001; Gallardo, 2009; Garcia-Preto, 2005; Houben, 2012; Paniagua, 2005; Santiago-Rivera et al., 2002; D. W. Sue & Sue, 2003; B. A. Taylor, Gambourg, Rivera, & Laureano, 2006). Table 9.2 summarizes recommendations for practice made by several scholars.

Bean et al. (2001) reviewed several Latino publications and identified 11 factors to consider in Latino family therapy. Their recommendations have been seen as restrictive given their limited consideration of specific clients' characteristics, needs, and contextual variability (Falicov, 1998; B. A. Taylor et al., 2006). Many of the recommendations noted by Bean and associates can be adapted to other immigrant non-Latino populations. We agree with B. A. Taylor and associates (2006) that a how-to approach can blind clinicians inside of a concrete, nonprocess interface with overgeneralizations. Guidelines, however, as the word indicates, can be helpful when a prudent and dynamic exploration examines multiple variables in need of confirmation, modification, or exclusion.

Another model is represented by the results of a qualitative study conducted by B. A. Taylor and associates (2006). Through extensive interviews with nine mental health providers who worked with Latinos, primarily those of Mexican American heritage in California, they identified five areas of Latino cultural competence. The authors support a social constructive interactional perspective of Latino cultural competence as one that evolves from a meaningful cultural narrative that is solidified by the quality of the client–therapist relationship. These qualitative findings contribute to clinicians' insights and their perception of areas that are relevant when working with Latinas/os.

The Latina/o Skills Identification Stage Model represents an adaptation for Latinos of the Skills Identification Stage Model (Parham, 2002) originally developed for use with African Americans but with universal utility (Gallardo, Parham, Trimble, & Yeh, 2012). The purpose of the model is to build clinical skills and confidence in effective assessment and intervention. Gallardo (2009) adapted the Skills Identification Stage Model domains for use with Latino clients, creating the

Table 9.2
Guidelines and Recommendations for Efficacious Counseling With Latinas/os

Author	Source	Suggested Factors to Consider
Bean et al. (2001)	Eleven factors to consider in Latino family therapy from a literature review	1. Consider family therapy as the preferred treatment mode 2. Incorporate folk healing beliefs and practices 3. Advocate in the community 4. Assess immigration history 5. Consider levels of acculturation 6. Seek bilingual clinicians 7. Assert the father's role in the hierarchical structure of the family 8. Provide separate interviews for extended family subsystems 9. Reinforce family relationships 10. Generate concrete and simple-to-carry-out recommendations 11. Apply the interpersonal style of *personalismo* to engage initially with the family
B. A. Taylor et al. (2006)	Results from a qualitative study with Latina/o mental health professionals who identified the most relevant factors in therapy	1. Importance of language 2. Impact of social class, gender, and power on the therapeutic relationship 3. Immigration and culture 4. Definition of the family 5. Unique constructions of cultural competence based on clinician's own self-awareness
Cardemil & Sarmiento (2009)	Commonalities relevant to clinical work and research from a literature review	1. Increase cultural knowledge and make adaptations in therapy 2. Increase awareness of psychocultural stressors 3. Incorporate spirituality and healing practices 4. Provide a broad range of services (e.g., transportation) 5. Incorporate the family in treatment 6. Consider clients' use of alternative medicine 7. Provide bilingual services and if possible bicultural providers
Gallardo (2009)	Latina/o Skills Identification Stage Model adaptation of Parham and Parham's (2002) Skills Identification Stage Model	1. Connect with clients 2. Utilize culturally congruent assessments 3. Facilitate awareness 4. Set goals 5. Instigate change 6. Provide feedback and accountability
Gallardo-Cooper et al. (2006)	Latino-centered counseling competencies approach based on the Multicultural Counseling Competencies for Latino-specific individual and family counseling	1. Developmental sequelae 2. Ethnic identity 3. Acculturation 4. Language 5. Family factors 6. Stressors 7. Protective factors

Latina/o Skills Identification Stage Model. This model incorporates cultural domains, such as spirituality, class, gender, and sexual orientation, that work with culture at the "core or deep" level (Cardemil & Sarmiento, 2009, p. 333). The model is applicable to different modalities of therapy and provides a well-developed list of the skills and tasks necessary for successful therapy with Latinas/os (Acevedo-Polakovich & Gering, 2009; Gallardo, 2009; Ortiz Salgado, 2009), as well as a guide for multicultural counseling training.

Evidence-Based Treatment Models

After reviewing findings regarding cultural adaptations to evidence-based treatments with adult Latinos, Cardemil and Sarmiento (2009) identified seven commonalities relevant to clinical work and research. Because their conclusions were based on empirical findings, Cardemil and Sarmiento gave substantial weight to Latino-centered guidelines and clinical observations. Despite their strong foundation, application of these guidelines can be problematic because of the scarcity of evidence-based data on adult Latinos (Comas-Díaz, 2006a, 2006b), limited usability among practitioners (Cardemil & Sarmiento, 2009), low practicality due to the extensive amount of time it takes to make specific cultural adaptations to evidence-based treatments (Domenech Rodríguez & Baumann, 2010), and the need to always fit the intervention to the Latino subgroup in question (Alegria et al., 2007). Cardemil and Sarmiento concluded that Latino-centered competencies "offer the most promise for the long term in helping develop novel theoretical approaches to conceptualizing and [treating] distress that explicitly incorporate culture" (p. 340) as well as provide a comprehensive map that is easy to apply to regular practice. Supporting this position, a Latino-centered counseling competencies approach is another resource that can guide both seasoned and new professionals in the field.

Santiago-Rivera and colleagues (2002) were the first to address Latino-specific counseling competencies. These were incorporated throughout their book to raise awareness of the relevant knowledge and skills necessary in Latino counseling practice. A few years later, under the leadership of Dr. Patricia Arredondo, then the president of the American Counseling Association, the competencies model was expanded. In 2005 a task force was established to develop Latino-specific counseling competencies. Based on clinical and empirical findings, the task force focused on the implementation of exemplary practices through the comprehensive incorporation of Latino-sensitive cultural dimensions and related psychological processes. The counseling professionals developed an iconic model (see Figure 9.1) that guides assessment and intervention through the interaction of the three constructs of the Multicultural Counseling Competencies (i.e., awareness, knowledge, and skills) and seven elements applicable to assessment and intervention (Gallardo-Cooper et al., 2006). These are the Latino-centered counseling competencies domains: (a) developmental sequelae of the family and family members (e.g., family life-cycle stage, bicultural development, gender role socialization), (b) identity (e.g., Latino ethnic identity stages and model, ethnic pride, multiple identities), (c) acculturation (e.g., levels of acculturation, assimilation, encapsulation, generational conflicts, cross-cultural and bicultural conflicts; acculturation-driven interventions), (d) language (e.g., bilingual and monolingual communication, bilingual development, use of metaphors and proverbs [*dichos*], second language issues, language style and use), (e) family factors (e.g., definition of family; extended networks and *compadrazco* [kinship network]; communication style; problem-solving preferences; hierarchical structure; values; rituals; rules; roles; parenting styles; grandparents' roles; history of moves and separations; and the cross-cultural, multiethnic, and multiracial characteristics of the family), (f) stressors (e.g., socioeconomic stressors, trauma, work-related injury, unemployment, lack of health resources, history of immigration, racism, exploitation, oppression, language barriers, historical-political events, institutional discrimination or oppression, legal

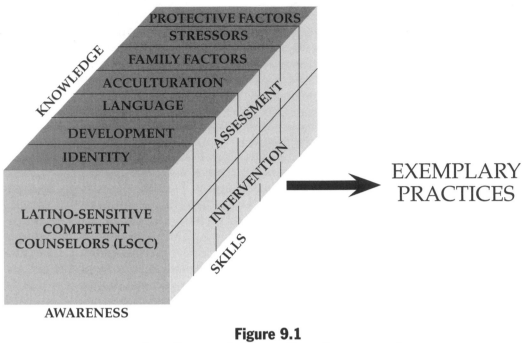

Figure 9.1
Latino-Centered Counseling Competencies

Source. Gallardo-Cooper et al. (2006).

status, and social justice issues), and (g) protective factors (i.e., cultural values, spirituality, healing practices, help-seeking preferences, culture-based strengths, personal assets, and systemic-based strengths). The components of each of these elements provide a comprehensive blueprint of relevant areas for the clinician to examine throughout the course of individual and family therapy.

Because the Latino-centered counseling competencies approach is based on the Multicultural Counseling Competencies, the model guides the clinician to continuously practice self-evaluation, to expand his or her knowledge of Latino processes, and to increase his or her Latino-centered clinical skills. An interpersonal, culturally based etiquette is recommended, as are adaptations to the family's preferred communication and problem-solving style. That is, the client is reached at his or her unique cultural level, and the clinician has well-established comfort addressing differences in language, developmental stages, discrimination, racism, immigration, family dynamics, social justice advocacy, and healing practices. The Latino-centered counseling competencies iconic model was recently adapted for use in Latino-centered clinical supervision (Gallardo-Cooper, Arciniega, Santana-Pellicer, Tovar-Blank, & Estrada, 2012).

Concluding Thoughts

In this chapter, we delineated Latino mental health assessment processes and discussed recommended accommodations to practice and several models that can guide Latino-centered treatment planning. Although clinicians have a bounty of methods and resources available, we emphasize the need to integrate culture, relational factors, communication synchronization, and practice accommodations with Latina/o clients. Culture colors the lenses through which Latino individuals interpret situations, express emotions, relate to others, solve problems, heal, and seek help. Tools for assessment, relationship building, and practice formats provide an array of clinical and cultural strategies that help clinicians understand, engage with, and improve the mental health of Latina/o clients. Culture is an integral element in clinical assessment regardless of whether diagnostic, interview, or systemic methods are used. The tools discussed here also include pragmatic ways to plan and deliver Latino mental health services to encourage the development of the therapeutic alliance and to sustain motivation throughout treatment. For the past few decades different fields have united to advance the assessments of Latinos and improve the delivery and utilization of services among Latinos. Still much needs to be done, as statistics continue to reflect the presence of health and mental health disparities among Latinas/os. As the *dicho* says, *Paso a paso se llega a lejos* (Step by step you get further along). As clinicians, we can contribute to reducing mental health disparities nationwide by providing culture-centered assessment and accommodations for each Latina/o client we touch.

• • •

Chapter 10

Latinas/os in Counseling

Con virtud y bondad se adquiere autoridad.

With virtue and kindness authority is acquired.

• • •

Objectives

- To learn about Latino-centered counseling frameworks.
- To learn how Latino-specific worldviews can be integrated with universal psychological models and practices.
- To become knowledgeable about the integration of spirituality and healing practices into counseling applications.
- To learn about how social justice and liberation theories can inform counseling practices.

Sabías que/Did you know that . . .

- Cultural adaptations of mainstream evidence-based practices require multi-dimensional cultural knowledge and clinical skills.
- Cultural capital involves ethnic pride, biculturalism, traditions, spirituality, and collectivist worldviews.
- Language proficiency requires 6 to 7 years to develop.
- Engagement in spiritual healing activities can lead to positive physical and mental health outcomes.

• • •

Case Scenario

José was a 34-year-old first-generation Colombian immigrant. A college-educated engineer, he was experiencing multiple stressors related to his work, his marital relationship, and his mother's health. His preoccupation with suicidal ideation and his inability to work and sleep had led him to seek emergency outpatient services. This was José's first therapy experience.

Dr. Rivera met with José for the initial appointment. On the way to the office José asked Dr. Rivera about his nationality, his religion, and how long he had resided in the United States. Dr. Rivera shared that he was a second-generation Catholic Latino of Puerto Rican parents.

The interview was conducted in Spanish and in English, as José used both languages. José provided details about his life story. When he was an adolescent, his parents had sought political asylum in the United States after left-wing militia had threatened the family. Soon after his arrival in the United States, José's father, a successful businessman in Colombia, died unexpectedly. José was troubled with thoughts of dying specifically because his mother had been diagnosed with cancer and needed him now more than ever. Suicide was against his Catholic beliefs, and he was troubled by his reoccurring thoughts of death. His wife was a non-Latina White woman of German heritage who threatened to divorce him because of all the time José spent caring for his sick mother. Close to the end of the session, José asked Dr. Rivera to place his hands on his head and pray for him; he also asked him to recite the Lord's Prayer. Dr. Rivera complied but explained that he knew the Our Father only in English. José then asked Dr. Rivera to keep his hands over his head while he recited the prayer in Spanish. A suicide risk assessment revealed no need for hospitalization, and José agreed to come and see Dr. Rivera twice a week.

At the end of the day Dr. Rivera met with his supervisor to discuss emergency cases. He shared with his supervisor that he was confused about how to handle José's request for prayer during the session, as he had never experienced that before. He added that his gut feeling was that he needed to comply with the request as a means to affirm José's cultural and spiritual needs given José's inquiry about religion early in the session. On learning this, the supervisor reprimanded Dr. Rivera: "You are not a priest. That is not your role, and you need to take charge of your sessions. Let your client go to a priest for that."

The Latina/o client brings to the counseling arena a wealth of cultural traditions and beliefs, formative experiences in different contexts, and a history of adaptation to multiple cultural worlds. Providers are challenged to utilize Latino-centered methods judiciously and expeditiously to respond to the demands of practice but may have limited time to explore in-depth psychocultural factors. Some mental health professionals may have to assist Latinos in brief single-session formats, such as a school meeting, a hospital family intervention, a single counseling session, or a crisis. Others may face restrictions on the number of sessions allotted due to institutional or third-party payment guidelines. Therefore, to ensure exemplary Latino counseling competency regardless of practice demands, providers need discernment based on a strong foundation of Latino-sensitive counseling frameworks, knowledge of common problems and stressors Latinas/os experience, and a sensible repertoire of Latino-specific therapeutic strategies.

Latino-Sensitive Counseling Frameworks

The growth in the Latino population in U.S. society has encouraged scholars to place at the forefront of research and clinical practice the best ways to tailor counseling with Latinas/os. Several factors contribute to a Latino-centered counseling approach: (a) the utilization of dynamic multidimensional perspectives, (b) the integration of culture and therapeutic structures, (c) the application of strengths-based models, (d) the consideration of situational and contextual interpretations, (e) the inclusion of spirituality and healing practices, and (f) the implementation of social justice directives.

The Utilization of Dynamic Multidimensional Perspectives

A core premise of multicultural counseling is the interaction of multiple dimensions, such as culture, race, economics, history, sociopolitical factors, and personal characteristics on human behavior. Two models rooted in multicultural theory are helpful with case conceptualization, assessment, and intervention (P. Arredondo & Glauner, 1992; Falicov, 1998). The first is Santiago-Rivera, Arredondo, and Gallardo-Cooper's (2002) comprehensive Latino dimensions of personal identity model, which has been applied successfully to interviewing formats and family therapy (see Chapter 4). The second is Falicov's (1998) multidimensional ecosystemic comparative approach. Developed with a Latino family therapy orientation, the multidimensional ecosystemic comparative approach incorporates multidimensional domains, the client's cultural history and current contexts, and the comparative evaluation between the therapist and the client. Falicov (1998) recommended managing the concept of culture as a changing construct to avoid errors of cultural generalization. The clinician's ongoing self-evaluation is a necessary ingredient for positive outcomes. Both of these models have utility and applicability to all populations.

The use of a multifaceted perspective also facilitates an understanding of the client as unique given the comprehensive orientation of multiple domains that interplay with personal characteristics (P. Arredondo & Glauner, 1992; Falicov, 1998; Withrow, 2008). Uniqueness is defined by the degree manifested in each domain and contextual variability. Level of acculturation, for instance, has been identified as a critical determinant of treatment selection. As we discussed in Chapter 3, levels of acculturation vary for individuals and within families for a myriad of reasons (e.g., language, age, and educational attainment). Acculturation assessments tend to yield findings that categorize individuals on a continuum from low to high acculturation. Latinas/os with low levels of acculturation tend to respond best to culture-specific modalities, such as the use of traditional healing practices, herbs, or visits to a *curandera* (healer) or priest, whereas individuals with high levels of acculturation may respond to more Western or mainstream therapeutic methods (Cardemil & Sarmiento, 2009). The diversity within Latinas/os may be overlooked when clients identify by nationality, distracting the clinician from other critical domains such as differences in social class (Withrow, 2008). Race is another domain that needs to be carefully explored. Latinos do not use the polarized American labels of *Black* or *White* but instead use many words to describe shades of skin color (i.e., *huero* for white and *trigueño* for dark-skinned). Similarly, different levels of linguistic fluency (e.g., English and Spanish proficiency levels), legal status (e.g., citizenship, resident, unauthorized status), discrimination, immigration history (e.g., preimmigration, immigration, and postimmigration events), and educational level interface with the individual and his or her family constellation. Thus, the use of a multifaceted assessment generates a more realistic understanding of the risks and strengths Latinas/os face as an ethnic minority group in U.S. society.

The Integration of Culture and Therapeutic Structures

Three basic levels of cultural integration are necessary in Latina/o counseling: (a) culturally grounded integration with universal psychological practices, (b) the integration of therapeutic structures and culture, and (c) cultural adaptations to evidence-based methods.

Culturally Grounded Integration With Universal Psychological Practices

Scholars who endorse this position propose the integration of Latino culture as the core foundation of clinical methods (Comas-Díaz, 2003, 2006a; Falicov, 1998,

2009; Ho, 1987; McGoldrick, Giordano, & Garcia-Preto, 2005b; Pedersen, 1997a). This orientation borrows from universal psychological healing perspectives and has been referred to as a bottom-up approach (Gallardo-Cooper & Zapata, 2013). Liberation psychology can be classified as a bottom-up cultural approach, as it was designed specifically to address the oppression of marginalized populations in Latin America (Aron & Corne, 1996).

Rogler (2000) posited that established mainstream clinical tools are unsuitable for use with the Latino population. In his research, a translated Spanish version of a well-established family test identified Puerto Rican parents as highly dysfunctional. This was because of the tool's reliance on the democratic problem-solving preference endorsed by the mainstream culture. Latinos, Rogler (2000) explained, are prone to a hierarchical approach to problem solving with specific gender role assignments. Rogler was, therefore, an early proponent of a bottom-up culture-specific foundation in psychological methodology and together with colleagues developed the TEMAS assessment tool (i.e., the Tell Me A Story projective personality test), *cuento* (story) therapy (Costantino, Malgady, & Rogler, 1986, 1988; Malgady, Costantino, & Rogler, 1984; Malgady, Rogler, & Costantino, 1987, 1990), and two additional Latino-specific clinical adaptations. *Cuento* therapy relies on the use of stories about Latino heroes and heroines that convey treatment goals for children, such as standards of behaviors and coping skills. Scientific investigations have also supported the use of culturally grounded designs as a viable approach to understanding best Latino characteristics and dynamics. For instance, Domenech Rodríguez, Donovick, and Crowley (2009) identified a Latino-specific parenting style that is not reflected in mainstream postulates of parenting styles (see Chapter 8 for more information).

Many other scholars have utilized cultural paradigms to inform therapeutic applications (e.g., assessment, therapy). Clinical and empirical support has been documented for the inclusion of spiritual and healing practices in counseling (Bracero, 1998; J. Cervantes, 2010; Comas-Díaz, 1981, 2006b, 2012; Guinn & Vincent, 2002), the use of social justice community interventions to address prejudice and oppression (P. Hernández, 2002; P. Hernández, Almeida, & Dolan-Del Vecchio, 2005), the use of bicultural effectiveness training to address acculturation-related issues (Szapocznik, Santisteban, Kurtines, Perez-Vidal, & Hervis, 1984), and the use of *dichos* (sayings or proverbs) in therapy (Aviera, 1996; Zúñiga, 1991, 1992). Culturally driven methods have been praised as being responsive to the realities of Latinos, ensuring congruence with worldviews, psychocultural stressors, and healing beliefs. The familiarity of a culturally congruent orientation increases the attractiveness of engaging Latinos in counseling (Santiago-Rivera, 2002) and the motivation to remain in treatment (Antshel, 2002).

Cardemil and Sarmiento (2009) noted in their thorough analysis of the use of evidence-based treatments with Latino adults that the cultural approach is responsive to Latina/o-specific stressors, utilizes preferred contextual approaches to problem resolution, and uses a developmental and protective factors perspective instead of a disease model. However, they warned that culture-based methods are not widely available in mental health organizations and continue to be minimally accepted by mental health institutions and insurance providers. Based on their analysis, Cardemil and Sarmiento (2009) also concluded that there is little guidance on how to effectively utilize the culture-based approach when presenting problems that are not culturally driven or when the clients are highly acculturated. Moreover, more training is needed on how to incorporate culturally grounded interventions into counseling (J. Cervantes, 2010). Given that 53% of U.S. immigrants are from Latin America, we propose that there is also a need to explore nonmainstream methods that are successfully implemented in Latin America. For instance, in Guatemala mental health providers have incorporated cultural healing practices into community activities, such as when women gather together on a regular basis with community leaders to work with textiles (A. A. C. C. de Coma, personal communication, March 26, 2011).

Integration of Therapeutic Structures and Culture

This orientation is based on a clinician's documentation of the effectiveness of mainstream traditional therapeutic methods integrated with cultural accommodations. This position relies on the vast body of clinical and empirical findings that support the fusion of diverse orientations and methods of practice (Beutler, Consoli, & Lane, 2005; Comas-Díaz, 1994). Multiculturally oriented clinicians in particular require a strong foundation in ecological and family therapy frameworks (Gallardo-Cooper & Zapata, 2013; McGoldrick, Giordano, & Garcia-Preto, 2005a; P. Hernández, Siegel, & Almeida, 2009; Santiago-Rivera et al., 2002).

According to Beutler and colleagues (2005), providers cannot dismiss the depth of knowledge accumulated over the past decades in therapeutic methods. Beutler et al. developed a carefully planned prescriptive and integrative selective treatment method called systemic treatment selection. Using systematic selection procedures the therapist adopts the best treatment orientation and specific methods to meet the client's need. In other words, no single counseling approach can respond to all of a client's needs. This method parallels the Aptitude × Treatment interaction paradigm used in research (Santisteban & Mitrani, 2002), to which we add the variable of culture: Aptitude × Treatment × Culture. Guided by this equation, the Latina/o-competent clinician discerns the what, when, and how of the methodology that will best meet the client's psychocultural needs during the course of therapy.

The clinical expertise of practitioners has contributed to this type of cultural integrative approach. How to best select an approach is founded on several considerations. First, there should be congruence between cultural values and the mode of treatment. Family therapy (Bean, Perry, & Bedell, 2001; Gallardo-Cooper & Zapata, 2013; McGoldrick et al., 2005b), multifamily group therapy (P. Hernández et al., 2009), group therapy (Rosselló, Bernal, & Rivera-Medina, 2012; Stacciarini, O'Keeffe, & Mathews, 2007; Torres-Rivera, Wilbur, Roberts-Wilbur, & Phan, 1999), and filial therapy (Garza & Watts, 2010) reinforce the collectivist worldview of Latinos and strengthen the central value of *la familia* (the family).

Second, a culturally congruent therapeutic method is selected that responds to the presenting problems. For instance, a feminist therapy orientation empowers clients who are oppressed by power differential dynamics (Comas-Díaz, 1987, 1988, 2012; Espín, 1998), or a social justice approach can be used with marginalized populations (P. Hernández, 2002; P. Hérnandez et al., 2009). A Latina client who perceives the presenting problem as an illness may require further exploration to identify motivating factors that contribute to this belief and may benefit from an approach that integrates the spirit, mind, and body.

Third, a selection is made from a variety of therapeutic orientations based on the therapist's skills in anchoring cultural adaptations to fit the client's needs. Some examples include cognitive behavior therapy and reality therapy (P. Arredondo, 2006), psychodynamic therapy (Hoogasian & Lijtmaer, 2010; Marcos & Urcuyo, 1979), behavior therapy (Matos, Torres, Santiago, Jurado, & Rodríguez, 2006; Santiago-Rivera et al., 2011), assertiveness training (Comas-Díaz, 1981), structural family therapy (Garcia-Preto, 2005), strategic family therapy (Szapocznik, Hervis, & Schwartz, 2003), postmodern narratives (P. Arredondo, Tovar-Blank, & Parham, 2008; Dass-Brailsford, 2012; Santiago-Rivera et al., 2002), solution-focused brief therapy (Corcoran & Pillai,

2009; Santiago-Rivera et al., 2002), relational-cultural therapy (E. Ruiz, 2012), motivational interviewing (Añez, Silva, Paris, & Bedregal, 2008), mixed interpersonal and feminist therapy methods (Ortiz Salgado, 2009), and life enhancement psychoeducation for older adults (Weisman, 2005). These examples reflect both cultural fit and clinical fit between client characteristics and the methods selected. Cultural fit is accomplished with a comprehensive assessment of the client's values, traditions, and preferred communication and relational style.

Cultural Adaptations to Evidence-Based Methods

The evidence-based movement has driven the current empirical approach to cultural integration. This orientation stems from the American Psychological Association guideline that practice is founded on the "integration of the best research with clinical expertise" that will best fit the client's needs (American Psychological Association Presidential Task Force on Evidence-Based Practice, 2006, p. 273). Researchers and practitioners have joined forces to seek quantitative validity of mainstream counseling methods with Latinas/os (Bernal, 2006; Bernal & Domenech Rodríguez, 2009; Bernal, Jiménez-Chafey, & Domenech Rodríguez, 2009; Bernal & Scharró-del-Río, 2001; Domenech Rodríguez, Baumann, & Schwartz, 2011; Gallardo, Johnson, Parham, & Carter, 2009). Proven interventions are considered as long as multiple psychocultural factors are explored to ensure suitability. Cultural characteristics and language are examined, as are help-seeking preferences, situational and contextual variables, and the client's specific needs (Bernal, Sáez-Santiago, & Galloza-Carrero, 2009). An example of a cultural adaptation designed to assist a group of Latina mothers with youths who are acting out may include the specific and personal needs of the children and their mothers as well as maternal preferences to rely on the extended family to solve problems, the characteristics of the community and neighborhood, work schedules, protective institutions, the child care support system, legal status, financial resources, and the partner's role in the family. An evidence-based approach to therapy also utilizes treatment protocols recommended by professional and mental health organizations, which endorse specific treatment protocols for specific diagnostic criteria (Whaley & Davis, 2007) and prevention programs (D'Angelo et al., 2009).

Although G. Bernal is a contemporary leader of the evidence-based movement with Latinos, early work in Miami and in New York City forged the road for Latino-specific research (Costantino et al., 1986, 1988; Rogler, Malgady, Costantino, & Blumenthal, 1998; Szapocznik & Kurtines, 1993; Szapocznik et al., 1984). Latino cultural adaptations of evidence-based approaches developed for the mainstream culture have been empirically supported with parenting programs (Corcoran, 2000; D'Angelo et al., 2009; Domenech Rodríguez et al., 2009; Matos et al., 2006; Parra Cardona et al., 2009, 2012), cognitive behavior therapy (Piedra & Byoun, 2012; Rosselló & Bernal, 1999; Shea et al., 2012), interpersonal therapy for depression (Rosselló & Bernal, 1999; Rosselló, Bernal, & Rivera-Medina, 2008), behavior therapy (Field, Korell-Chavez, & Rodríguez, 2010; Santiago-Rivera et al., 2008), guided imagery (La Roche, D'Angelo, Gualdron, & Leavell, 2006), child-centered play therapy (Garza & Bratton, 2005), and strategic family therapy (Muir, Schwartz, & Szapocznik, 2004; Santisteban, Suarez-Morales, Robbins, & Szapocznik, 2006; Szapocznik et al., 2003).

Also, researchers have delineated steps undertaken to adapt evidence-based interventions for use with Latinos. According to Cardemil and Sarmiento (2009), adaptations can be classified as either superficial (e.g., translation from English to Spanish, the use of bilingual staff) or deep rooted (e.g., the integration of cultural values, worldviews, psychocultural stressors, protective factors, or contextual variables). They reported that evidence-based adaptations receive support when "deep structural" rather than "surface" adaptations are used (p. 333). Two examples of successful Latino culture adaptations include systemic and spiritual values. Weisman (2005) demonstrated the effectiveness of a culturally adapted treatment for patients with schizophrenia by incorporating spirituality and reinforcing Latino beliefs. Weisman's research with Latino families with a family member with schizophrenia revealed the relevance of religion and spirituality as coping attributions and stress-reducing tactics that enhance family cohesion, minimize expressed emotionality, and minimize blaming the patient for his or her symptoms (Weisman, Gomes, & López, 2003). These two latter factors moderate the successful integration of the adult with schizophrenia into the family system. Latinos, she reported, tend to understand and accept schizophrenia as a devastating physiologically based illness and tend to tolerate symptoms with minimal to no levels of criticism. This is due in part to the strong value Latinos place on maintaining family cohesiveness and unity. Similarly, Kopelowicz and associates included the Latino family in social skills training with patients with schizophrenia (Cardemil & Sarmiento, 2009; Kopelowicz, Zárate, Smith, Mintz, & Liberman, 2003). Family members were used as coaches to facilitate the generalization of positive changes. They received detailed social skills training on how to best coach and maintain learned skills at home. Positive outcomes resulted from the training of both family members and the patient.

Domenech Rodríguez et al. (2011) provided the most explicit and detailed descriptions of the stages that need to be undertaken to implement evidence-based cultural adaptations. The process follows four principles that emerged from a literature review of Griner and Smith (2006): (a) incorporation of cultural values as it relates to the context of the intervention, (b) availability of professionals who are congruent with clients in terms of language, race, and ethnicity to increase clients' understanding of the counseling process and treatment adherence, (c) accessibility of services that are adapted to the realities of clients, and (d) collaboration with community resources that is congruent with clients' characteristics as well as the inclusion of spiritual traditions and the family network. Involvement with key community leaders and consumers is a critical necessity when one is developing community-based interventions. Focus groups are conducted during the process of program development to ensure that the program has Latino-specific ecological validity with the targeted population (Domenech Rodríguez et al., 2011; Uttal, 2006). These cultural adaptations go beyond in-session methods, as they consider organizational and logistical (e.g., transportation) factors (Cardemil & Sarmiento, 2009; Griner & Smith, 2006). Nevertheless, the process as described is complex and exhaustive, taking many months or years to accomplish (Domenech Rodríguez et al., 2011). These examples indicate that investing one's time and making a commitment to make adaptations are not short-term undertakings.

When culture is an active dimension in clinical work regardless of the counseling approach selected, there is greater probability that Latina/o clients will more readily comply with treatment (Alegría, Atkins, Farmer, Slaton, & Stelk, 2010; Cardemil & Sarmiento, 2009). Nevertheless, Comas-Díaz (2012) cautioned about the need to use evidence-based methods judiciously with ethnic minority individuals to avoid overlooking critical historical and sociopolitical variables that may impact the therapeutic process. Although limited data support the fact that cultural adaptations are superior to the original mainstream evidence-based interventions (Cardemil & Sarmiento, 2009; Lakes, López, & Garro, 2006), new meta-analytic research demonstrates that cultural adaptations are indeed superior to traditional, unmodified treatments (Domenech Rodríguez et al., 2011).

The Application of Strengths-Based Models

Advocating for positive psychological processes is not new. For instance, personality theorists have postulated about personal strength for more than 50 years (W. B. Walsh, 2003), and strengths-based models have been established for some time (Comas-Díaz, 1987; Day & Rottinghaus, 2008; De Shazer, 1985; Espín, 1994; M. Ramírez, 1998; M. Ramírez & Castañeda, 1974). During the past 12 years, positive psychology has become an established specialty with substantial gains made in theoretical and scientific knowledge that influences therapeutic ideology and deemphasizes psychopathology (Park & Peterson, 2008; Seligman & Csikszentmihalyi, 2000b; Seligman, Steen, Park, & Peterson, 2005; W. B. Walsh, 2003). The relevance of a paradigm shift from a disease model to a strengths perspective is evident in the publication of four special journal issues dedicated to strengths-based therapeutic methods and postulates (Fouad, 2006; Galassi, Griffin, & Akos, 2008; Seligman & Csikszentmihalyi, 2000a). In addition, a new strengths-based counseling model, hope therapy (Chang & Banks, 2007; Snyder, 1994), has been developed, and several books have been published on strengths-based counseling (Snyder & Lopez, 2002; Ungar, 2006; W. B. Walsh, 2003).

Multicultural scholars, however, argue that optimal functioning needs to be understood from a cultural framework, because culture defines the constructs of happiness and well-being (Leong & Wong, 2003; D. W. Sue & Constantine, 2008). For Latinas/os, optimal functioning may be a function of the interaction between personal, cultural, and universal features (P. Arredondo, 2002a; Leong, 1996), with close attention given to how worldviews define happiness (D. W. Sue & Constantine, 2008). Cultural values associated with social relatedness, cooperation, appreciation, family cohesion, family loyalty and obligation, and spirituality may define optimal functioning for some Latinas/os. For instance, when a clinician gives a *regalito* (a small gift) to a young Latino child at the end of a counseling or testing session, the child will commonly express gratitude but may also ask the clinician for a gift for his or her siblings. In this context, sharing a gift with siblings may be more satisfying than receiving a gift given the allocentric socialization that instills loyalty, cooperation, and obligation toward the family unit. Thus, the collectivist value of *familismo* (familism, feelings about family relatedness) fulfills a greater sense of well-being than earning an individual recognition per se.

Lack of cultural competence can result in the misinterpretation of cultural values as character flaws or weaknesses (Knight, Bernal, Garza, Cota, & Ocampo, 1993; D. W. Sue & Sue, 2003). Similarly, neglect or lack of knowledge of cultural strengths may lead the clinician to fall into the psychopathology trap, an automatic response based in part on the influence of abnormal psychology and diagnostic training. For example, a Latina mother may seek more information about a counselor's work with her child. The clinician may misread the mother's behaviors as intrusive and overcontrolling. This problem creates a cycle of negative perceptions that may lead the clinician to misinterpret maternal behaviors as a barrier to treatment rather than as a parent's desire to be active on behalf of her child. Framing cultural values as deficits may also become a form of a microaggression (D. W. Sue et al., 2007), and dismissing cultural strengths can contribute to counseling attrition and a perception of therapeutic oppression. On other occasions, therapists overwhelmed with the complex, multistressor predicaments of clients may overlook personal, cultural, or familial strengths.

Another aspect of a strengths-based model is the conceptualization of presenting problems from a developmental perspective. A stage in the life span (e.g., becoming a parent) or a specific life event (e.g., divorce) presents unique incidents that can be addressed in counseling without relying on a disease model. A developmental framework provides the clinician with a blueprint of stages that allow for the resolution of problems through a focus on the acquisition of adaptive skills. Family therapists (B. Carter & McGoldrick, 2005b) utilize a life-cycle model to address family transitions such as marriage, parenting, death, and the like, whereas developmental psychologists frame individuals' conflicts within life-span stages. Much caution should be exercised when using a life-span developmental process designed for the mainstream population. Because of their divergent cultural systems, Latinas/os do not follow the same sequence or expected time frame as individuals with Euro-American values (Santiago-Rivera et al., 2002). Useful stage task-based frameworks based on ethnic identity (A. S. Ruiz, 1990), bicultural development (A. M. Padilla, 1994, 2006), and bilingual development (E. E. García & Náñez, 2011) exist and should be an integral component of Latino-centered counseling competence.

In addition, the use of a developmental perspective assists the provider in selecting alternative interventions. Psychoeducational research has demonstrated that Latinas/os are motivated to seek information (Parra Cardona et al., 2009) and that psychoeducational interventions are beneficial for Latinas/os. Furthermore, a developmental and life-cycle approach may be nonthreatening, reduce mental health stigma, address relevant psychocultural stressors, facilitate group support, and be cost effective.

Personal and Cultural Assets

Scholars estimate that 10% of therapeutic change is attributed to technique (Beutler, as cited in Consoli & Jester, 2005), whereas 45% is attributed to what the client actually brings to the therapeutic territory (Bohart, as cited in Consoli & Jester, 2005). A Latino-centered, strengths-based counseling approach relies then on the 45% of personal and cultural assets as key elements of successful outcomes. For instance, determination, perseverance, and fortitude during tumultuous events are signs of resilience that need to be recognized. Therefore, an understanding of two processes is essential in therapy: (a) risk factors and psychocultural stressors and (b) personal, cultural protective factors. These different processes can coexist independently but can also interact and complement each other. (Also see Chapter 7.)

Furthermore, Park and Peterson (2008) defined a strengths-based counseling approach as one that focuses on the identification of character attributes and life satisfaction. In their research they found that characteristics of the heart and those associated with social relatedness (e.g., love, hope, gratitude, self-control) are linked to a better sense of well-being than character strengths of the head(e.g., creativity, critical thinking), which are manifested individually. These findings are congruent with core Latino values that emphasize collectivism and social relatedness (e.g., *personalismo* [a focus on the person and the relationship with the person or persons], *familismo, simpatía* [friendly nature], *cariño* [affection, caring]), interpersonal respect and self-control (e.g., *respeto* [respect], *controlarse* [conscious self-control], *aguantarse* [conscious tolerance, self-control]), gratitude (e.g., *agradecimiento* [appreciation, gratefulness], gift giving), and trust (e.g., *confianza* [trust, familiarity], *intimidad* [emotional intimacy]). Likewise, character assets associated with bravery, humor, kindness (e.g., *amabilidad* [kindness] relates to *simpatía, personalismo; caballerismo* [gallantry] relates to kindness, bravery, and protectiveness), spirituality (e.g., *espiritualidad* [spirituality], *fé* [faith], *esperanza* [hope]), and appreciation of beauty are positive mediators in recovery from trauma, medical problems, and other psychological disorders (Park & Peterson, 2008; Peterson, Park, & Seligman, 2006).

Resiliency and Protective Factors

A strengths-based orientation demands an understanding of the risk factors that Latinas/os experience as well as an appreciation of personal and cultural protective factors. The interplay between adversity and protective factors that results in positive adaptation is known as *resilience*. That is, protective factors counteract the effects of stressors. A systematic literature review by Cardoso and Thompson (2010) concluded that significant resilience was evident among immigrant Latinas/os based on family strengths, cultural factors, and community supports. Immigration per se was not a "risk factor for negative outcome" (p. 261), but the negative experiences surrounding immigration became stressors, compromising immigrants' psychological functioning. Prolonged exposure to an aversive environment increases probabilities for discrimination and family deterioration (Viruell-Fuentes, 2007). Hence, a strong accumulation of "cultural capital" (Trueba, as cited in Cardoso & Thompson, 2010, p. 260), ethnic pride, biculturalism, bilingualism, traditions, spirituality, and collectivist worldviews have also been identified as protective factors that foster resiliency (Cardoso & Thompson, 2010; Hull, Kilbourne, Reece, & Husaini, 2008; Umaña-Taylor & Updegraff, 2007). Resiliency has been empirically supported to relate to the following protective factors: siblings (Alfaro & Umaña-Taylor, 2010; B. Kao, Romero-Bosch, Plante, & Lobato, 2012), hopeful perspectives (Stoddard & Garcia, 2011), family involvement (Kopelowicz et al., 2003; R. Pérez, Araujo Dawson, & Suárez-Orozco, 2011), ethnic identity (Umaña-Taylor & Guimond, 2012), *familismo* (Ayón, Marsiglia, & Bermudez-Parsai, 2010), bilingualism (Bialystok, 2011; E. E. García & Náñez, 2011), and biculturalism (Hull et al., 2008).

These protective elements thus are interrelated with personal and cultural assets. Bilingual skills and bicultural perspectives are linked to ethnic identity. For example, a byproduct of reinforcing biculturalism, and, if applicable, bilingualism, solidifies important components of Latino ethnic identity. Among these components are the capacity for cognitive flexibility and academic success, optimum neurological functioning, problem-solving skills, and protective variables against degenerative brain diseases (Bialystok, 2011; E. E. García & Náñez, 2011). Professionals who work with Latino children and adolescents in particular must address these processes and seek opportunities to nourish ethnic identity, as Latino ethnic identity correlates positively with academic success (Conchas, 2001), educational and personality development (Umaña-Taylor, Gonzales-Backen, & Guimond, 2009; Umaña-Taylor & Guimond, 2012), mental health functioning (Alegria et al., 2007), and health outcomes (Cavazos-Rehg, Zayas, & Spitznagel, 2007).

Similarly, Cardoso and Thompson (2010) reported that Latino core values are substantiated elements linked to optimal functioning that can be defined as protective factors. *Familismo*, collectivism, social support, *personalismo*, *fatalismo* (fatalism), and spirituality protect Latinas/os from stressors (Cardoso & Thompson, 2010). Compared to White and African American groups with a history of suicide attempts, Latinas/os had higher scores on survival and coping beliefs, family obligation values, and moral objections related to spiritual beliefs that positively mediated a reduction in suicide attempts (Oquendo et al., 2005). Having a supportive family and kinship network and beliefs about family cohesion and interdependence creates a safe ecology for facing life-cycle tasks, overcoming depression (R. Pérez et al., 2011), and protecting children who face adversity (Leidy, Guerra, & Toro, 2012). Similarly, Puerto Rican adolescents with a supportive family and adherence to cultural values were more prone not to lie to their mothers (Villalobos & Smetana, 2012). The socialization of children with collectivist values has also been identified with higher levels of optimism and social empathetic attitudes (Segal,

Gerdes, Mullins, Wagaman, & Androff, 2011). Hence, treatments that strengthen family values and family interdependence are not only culturally grounded but also efficacious over the long term.

From a broader perspective, one's culture of origin can also support and protect. Alegria and associates (2007) found that Latino children who immigrate before age 6 tend to have higher rates of depression as adults. Exposure to the native culture facilitates the attainment of a strong primary language foundation, and an extended family circle during the formative years strengthens critical developmental tasks. Language proficiency requires 6 to 7 years to develop; however, many U.S.-born Latino children disrupt the course of language development when they are introduced to an English-only educational experience prior to age 7, if in a Spanish-speaking dominant home. Therefore, counseling that defines goals based on culture-centered protective factors facilitates adaptation (Villalba, 2007) and fortifies human development processes.

Cultural Meaning in Latino Therapy

Therapeutic discourse that relies on cultural values facilitates cultural meaning. Because language is a symbolic cognitive process, utilizing cultural language (e.g., *familismo, confianza, respeto, cariño, fatalismo,* machismo, *personalismo*) creates an ambiance of conceptual clarity in communication with clients. For example, a Latina professional with work-related problems with her supervisor could be empowered by her self-control and *respeto* toward her superior, despite the negative circumstances. Through *respeto* she can learn in therapy assertive skills that can be congruent with Latina gender role socialization (Comas-Díaz, 1988). Similarly, utilizing cultural concepts such as *familismo* and caballerismo or the positive face of machismo (Arciniega, Anderson, Tovar-Blank, & Tracey, 2008; Falicov, 2010) can affirm a Latino male client's patience when he is coping with disagreements with his in-laws. Thus, integrating cultural labels in the therapeutic dialogue allows for a mutually understanding choice of language between client and therapist.

Because constructivism is defined by culture, the inclusion of these cultural elements in the therapeutic narrative facilitates awareness and insight, which are important preconditions to change (P. Arredondo et al., 2008; Santiago-Rivera et al., 2002; Torres-Rivera et al., 2002). The integration of Latino popular wisdom, *dichos,* legends, *cuentos,* music, art, literature, and poetry (Bracero, 1998; J. Cervantes, 2010; Costantino et al., 1988; Gallardo, 2009; Santiago-Rivera et al., 2002; Zúñiga, 1991, 1992) affirms meaning. Other examples of empowering strategies include utilizing familial rituals of well-being (Santiago-Rivera et al., 2002), reframing personally damaging attributions into culturally workable cognitions (Szapocznik et al., 1997), focusing on systemic strengths (Gallardo-Cooper & Zapata, 2013), and incorporating healing preferences (J. Cervantes, 2010; Comas-Díaz, 2000, 2006b, 2012). How many times have counselors heard a client remark, "Oh, I remember my *abuelita* (grandmother) used to say that *dicho!*" Yet cultural meaning is often overlooked in general practice, perhaps because of a counselor's lack of cultural knowledge and psychocultural therapeutic skills.

Table 10.1 depicts an adaptation of W. B. Walsh's (2003) empowering strengths-based approach to family therapy. This model can be applied to various formats of therapeutic intervention and can provide an opportunity to assess and utilize personal, systemic, and cultural assets.

The Consideration of Situational and Contextual Interpretations

According to W. B. Walsh (2003), current counseling ideologies endorse the person–environment interaction as a central therapeutic paradigm to promote optimal

Table 10.1
Strengths-Based Family Therapy With Latinos

Resiliency Process	Component	Relevant Areas to Target in Therapy With Latinos
Belief systems	Making meaning from adversity	1. Approach the crisis as a family affair in which all members share in the experience, rely on their inter-relatedness, and can contribute to the resolution ("shared challenge"). Focus on *familismo* to address immigration history, the adaptation process, prejudice, language barriers, parent–child conflict, and family conflict. 2. Normalize adversity and contextualize problems: define the family's life stage crisis, reframe generational conflicts as cultural events, affirm emotional reactions and different styles of emotional expression, justify reactions, defocus away from pathology. 3. Reframe the crisis or problem as a manageable event, *Si se puede* [Yes, it can be done! Yes, we can do it!]. Explore explanatory attributions: *fatalismo,* spiritual attributions, psychocultural explanations for problems (e.g., *nervios* [nerves] due to immigration trauma), *dichos* with positive messages.
	Positive outlook	1. Communicate hope and optimism. 2. Identify and affirm strengths, including personal, family, and cultural strengths; spirituality; and adaptive beliefs. Identify strengths of the native and host cultures. 3. Reinforce perseverance, persistence, and action despite stressors and cultural adaptations. 4. Identify what can and cannot be changed; reframe what cannot be changed and focus on manageable elements: address issues of loss (loss of status, family separations, country-of-origin family and traditions) as well as focus on the here and now to solve present problems, utilize *fatalismo* as a way of coping with what cannot be changed.
	Transcendence and spirituality	1. Seek purpose and existential understanding. 2. Explore sources of *fortaleza interna* (inner strength). 3. Explore healing practices, spirituality, faith, folk healing, rituals, prayers, alternative spiritual beliefs and practices (*curanderismo* [healing practices], *espiritismo* [spiritualism], Santería), and church membership. 4. Provide inspiration: envision new possibilities, promote social action, model coping strategies, empower with a social justice orientation and social justice solutions, provide models. 5. Identify transformations: lessons learned from adversity, gains, *No hay mal que por bien no venga* (There is always an upside to a downside).
Organizational patterns	Flexibility	1. Assist with adaptations, reorganization, and changes in family structure and dynamics: gender roles expectations, working families, shared responsibilities. 2. Maintain stability and continuity through crisis: seek connections with country of origin and extended family, support preferred healing practices and rituals, seek out healers and elders in community who provide continuity of coping mechanism.

(Continued)

Table 10.1 *(Continued)*
Strengths-Based Family Therapy With Latinos

Resiliency Process	Component	Relevant Areas to Target in Therapy With Latinos
Organizational patterns *(Continued)*	Flexibility *(Continued)*	3. Provide authoritative leadership: be an active therapist, give advice, model communication and coping strategies, advocate for clients, educate, seek out resources in the community. 4. Consider alternative medicine methods (*la botánica* [botanical, folk healing store where natural healing medication can be purchased], folk healing practices). 5. Provide ecological therapeutic interventions.
	Connectedness	1. Identify the members of the family network. 2. Strengthen family solidarity and support (*familismo*). 3. Reinforce values of *respeto*, boundaries, tolerance with differences and hierarchical organization. 4. Encourage reconciliation and reconnections with family members, social networks, and extended family members.
	Social and economic resources	1. Include extended family and *compadrazco* (kinship) in the therapeutic process for support and generalization of positive effects. 2. Seek out supportive networks in the community, for example churches, agencies, and institutions that are linguistically and culturally sensitive. 3. Explore assistance with logistics to ensure compliance with treatment: transportation, flexible appointment schedules, child care, in-home services. 4. Engage in client advocacy. 5. Incorporate ecological interventions and community mentors (e.g., *promotoras*).

Source. Adapted from the family resilience model (F. Walsh, 2006).

functioning. The collectivist worldview embedded in the culture further supports the fact that Latinas/os cannot be understood in a vacuum, disengaged from their daily contexts and important relationships. This perspective is influenced by Bronfenbrenner's (1979; Bronfenbrenner & Morris 1998) ecological model of human development, heretofore discussed. The model serves as a useful blueprint for understanding the Latino-centered ecological orientation relevant in counseling. His model depicts the individual's personal attributes as dependent on surrounding systems: the microsystem (e.g., family, friends, workplace, church, neighborhood, school), the mesosystem (e.g., the interplay between microsystems), the exosystem (e.g., political factors, public policies), and the macrosystem (e.g., culture, values, socioeconomic factors). These systems and multiple contexts influence the development of the individual across his or her life span. An ecological orientation views environmental stressors as influential determinants of psychological inertia. For instance, a client's psychological symptoms may be associated with situational (P. Arredondo, 2006; W. B. Walsh, 2003), sociohistorical (Comas-Díaz, 1987, 2000), institutional (Hill & Torres, 2010; Hipólito-Delgado & Lee, 2007), or community (Cardoso & Thompson, 2010) factors or a combination of these factors.

A commitment to familial systems also requires an ecological conceptualization of presenting problems (P. Arredondo, 2006; Boyd-Franklin, & Bry, 2000; Falicov, 2007, 2009; Gallardo et al., 2009; McGoldrick et al., 2005a; McGoldrick & Hardy, 2008; Santiago-Rivera et al., 2002; Szapocznik & Kurtines, 1993). Comas-Díaz (2006a, 2006b) posited that the collectivist orientation of Latinas/os defines the self in relation to others. In contrast, an individualist perspective relies on personal attributes, self-reliance, and mastery of the environment to define the self. Central to this view is the role of the *familia* as a powerful institution with lasting influence throughout an individual's life span (Santiago-Rivera et al., 2002). Considering the values of *familismo,* many Latinos maintain close connections with extended family members even when they are geographically apart because the *familia* continues to influence personal well-being. In particular, a healthy and supportive family network continues to impart long-term positive influence. Because for most Latinas/os the construct of the *familia* is broad and flexible, the clinician needs to assess early in treatment the client's definition of the family and the membership status of individuals in the family circle (Gallardo-Cooper & Zapata, 2013). Assessing the power of these relationships and the inclusion of these members in therapy may prove to be a commanding intervention. It is also worth noting that family composition changes over time. Deceased or disenfranchised family members may be substituted with new *compadres* (people in kinship roles such as godfather, godmother, and other relationships that are considered close and/or special) who are close friends, surrogate *padrinos/madrinas* (godparents), and relatives through association (e.g., *tíos políticos,* or uncles who are not blood related). Intracontinental and intercontinental mobility generate systemic changes, and time influences change across generations (Fernández, 2001).

Likewise, given the fundamental role of family among Latinas/os, family therapy as a treatment modality has cultural fit (P. Arredondo, 2006; Bean et al., 2001; Cardemil & Sarmiento, 2009; Falicov, 1998; Gallardo, 2009; Garcia-Preto, 2005; Santiago-Rivera et al., 2002; Smith & Montilla, 2007). The involvement of family-fortified treatment effects in investigations of evidence-based cultural adaptations (Uttal, 2006; Weisman, 2005) and is effective in filial therapy with children and their parents (Garza & Watts, 2010). But some Latinas/os may seek individual counseling and not family therapy, even when the problem revolves around family and relationship issues. Individual sessions may transition into family therapy, but other clients may choose individual therapy for a variety of reasons, including in circumstances of high levels of acculturation or limited family accessibility. In these circumstances it is critical to consider the impact the family has on the individual. If the family is not involved in vivo, its presence is (clearly) sensed in the session as an alter ego.

Individual therapy can be conducted with a systemic orientation (Comas-Díaz, 2006b) as well as an ecological orientation (Cerezo, O'Neil, & McWhirter, 2009). Some presenting problems may also be more suitable for family therapy than individual therapy (e.g., generational conflicts, substance abuse, family discord, adolescent problems, and/or stress due to the chronic medical or psychiatric problems of one member of the family). The clinician must be able to recognize the relevance of the family and adapt the various modes of treatment deemed clinically necessary (e.g., parents and children seen jointly or separately).

With regard to family therapy modalities, Latino families have benefited from a variety of approaches (Bermúdez, Kirkpatrick, Hecker, & Torres-Robles, 2010; Falicov, 1998; Gallardo-Cooper & Zapata, 2013; Minuchin, Colapinto, & Minuchin, 2007; Szapocznik et al., 1997). What is critical is how the clinician assesses the family's cultural framework to fit the family intervention. Judicious clinical decisions should be exercised about the suitability of successfully researched methods across Latino subgroups. For instance, a Florida migrant population from Honduras differs from a South Florida clientele with two to three generations of residence in the United States and a different socioeconomic status. Given the heterogeneity of Latinas/os, cultural adaptations of counseling methods require ecological validity through the careful alteration of specific population and individual characteristics (e.g., acculturation level, language, sexual orientation, socioeconomic status), contextual factors, and psychocultural stressors (Bernal, Jiménez-Chafey, et al., 2009; Bernal & Sáez-Santiago, 2006; Bernal, Sáez-Santiago, et al., 2009; Domenech Rodríguez et al., 2011).

An illustration of this involves the application of the Bicultural Effectiveness Training Program, developed for a Cuban American population in Miami, with a Mexican family in the Midwest (Acevedo-Polakovich & Gering, 2009). This application utilized a clinical model for culturally responsive therapy, the Latina/o Skills Identification Stage Model developed by Gallardo and associates (2009) and discussed in Chapter 9. Accommodations were made to fit the Bicultural Effectiveness Training Model for use with a Mexican family and its adolescent son, who was experiencing acculturation-related conflicts, by systematically considering each component of the six Latina/o Skills Identification Stage Model domains: connecting with clients (e.g., Latino communication style, respect for parental roles, *platicar* [small talk, informal light conversation], language preference, education about the therapy process), assessment (e.g., presenting problems, family history), facilitating awareness, setting goals, instigating change, and feedback and accountability. Note that the authors changed the title of the provider from "clinical psychologist" to "counselor" because in that particular community, psychologists were linked to the stigma of *enfermedad mental* (mental illness) or *locura* (craziness). Logistical accommodations were made, and the family's history and idiosyncratic features were included in the 12-session psychoeducational intervention.

A more expansive contextual approach includes the larger ecological field of schools, neighborhoods, agencies, institutions, and sociopolitical factors. These external systems may be sources of support or stress. The Latina/o-sensitive counselor may ask the following: What is the role of the school when it comes to the presenting problems and the solutions? What are the family's health and mental health resources? What sociopolitical elements exacerbate the presenting problem? What agencies, religious organizations, or community sources can provide support? Within this perspective, ecologically oriented clinicians also consider sociopolitical conditions such as the increasing anti-immigration agenda in Arizona, Alabama, Georgia, and other parts of the country. Substandard living arrangements, violent neighborhoods, and homelessness create unsafe environments in which to raise children and place undue pressures on family functioning. Recent immigrants with limited English proficiency may require a broader umbrella of community services, as their needs are likely more expansive than those of more acculturated or mainstream residents (Gallardo-Cooper & Zapata, 2013).

It is also important to recognize that Latino-sensitive agencies and churches can provide effective relief during financially fragile circumstances (Uttal, 2006), and institutions have enhanced the well-being of marginalized populations (Cardoso & Thompson, 2010). Empirical research has demonstrated that community-based interventions may prove more effective with Latinas/os than client-centered approaches (Parra Cardona et al., 2012; Uttal, 2006; Weisman, 2005) and that homogenous Latino neighborhoods encourage better health practices at a grassroots level (Cagney, Browning, & Wallace, 2007). Latinas/os tend to respond favorably to group interventions because of their allocentric worldviews and preference for social support (P. Hernández, 2002).

Including contributing environmental factors in therapy can result in a more flexible counseling format. *Counseling without walls* is a term that could be applicable to the Latino-centered clinician who wants to respond with an ecological approach. Although Latinos tend to view mental health providers as experts, many prefer an informal format with interventions. Nevertheless, the stigma of mental illness or of seeing a mental health clinician continues to be a barrier to treatment utilization in many Latino communities (Aguilera & López, 2008; Alegría et al., 2002; Y. C. Padilla & Villalobos, 2007), compromising service delivery, especially in terms of traditional 1-hour sessions. Homes, community centers, schools (Hipólito-Delgado & Lee, 2007; Reyes & Elias, 2011; Villalba, 2007a), and places of prayer are suitable settings for interventions for some specific populations. Engaging in such interventions is also an opportunity for the clinician to become an integral part of the Latino community and develop *confianza* with its members (Gallardo-Cooper & Zapata, 2013).

Spirituality and Healing Practices

Guidelines for multicultural counseling and practice give credence to the fact that the client's belief system supports spiritual and healing practices (American Psychological Association, 2003; J. Cervantes, 2010; Comas-Díaz, 1981, 2003, 2006b, 2012; Pedersen, 1997b; Santiago-Rivera et al., 2002; D. W. Sue & Sue, 2003). This position contrasts with early historical views that spirituality and religion precipitated psychopathology, passivity, and denial (Jenkins & Pargament, as cited in Simoni, Martone, & Kerwin, 2002). Because the purpose of therapy is to relieve discomfort and because psychological pain is cultural-bound, involving the client's healing orientation ensures a holistic and integrative counseling approach, strengthens the therapeutic alliance, and facilitates a positive outcome.

Both therapy and spiritual systems of healing are driven by *esperanza* (hope) and *fortaleza interna* (inner strength), two highly valued virtues for generations of Latinas/os facing adversity. Healing beliefs organize cognitive schemata and affective reactions as well as motivate behaviors. Therefore, the use of a holistic counseling approach that includes mind–body processes allows understanding of person-specific dynamics and guides strategic interventions (J. Cervantes, 2010; Comas-Díaz, 2006a, 2006b, 2012; Vasquez, 1994).

Spirituality is a broad construct that includes humanistic values, religious affiliation, and beliefs in a higher power. Although often associated with an affiliation to the Catholic Church, Latinas/os also follow other Christian religions, Buddhism, Judaism, and Islam (Santiago-Rivera et al., 2002; D. W. Sue & Sue, 2003), as mentioned in Chapter 1. The evangelical movement in particular is growing significantly among Latino communities. Judeo-Christian, African, and indigenous beliefs amalgamate in the practice of *curanderismo* (healing practices), Santería, *espiritísmo* (spiritualism), and other indigenous spiritual orientations. Sustaining these healing traditions throughout generations reinforces familial and cultural continuity (Comas-Díaz, 2006b) and provides healing options when mainstream health services are inaccessible (Gomez-Beloz & Chavez, 2001). Yet Mexican Americans with health coverage continue to use *curanderismo* for less severe medical problems (Hoogasian & Lijtmaer, 2010), suggesting that these healing practices are strongly embedded in cultural beliefs. Healing rituals also give individuals psychological relief when faced with adversity (Comas-Díaz, 2012), and prayer is commonly practiced as a coping mechanism (Gillum & Griffith, 2010). In Miami, for instance, the county courts have a special team to clean sacrificed animal parts, handmade dolls and figurines, colored eggs (with judges' and prosecutors' names on them), and other symbols left in corridors when Santería followers face litigation problems (Booth, 1995). The Miami Police Department also provides training on ritualistic crime investigation to educate public servants about beliefs and rituals of Santería (Clary, 2008). Even Latina/o atheists and agnostics hold existential ideological guidelines regarding the purpose of life (Martínez-Taboas, Varas-Díaz, López-Garay, & Hernández-Pereira, 2011) and underlying sociopolitical positions that become opportunities for therapeutic interventions. Although typically not volunteered in therapy, spiritual and existentialist preferences need to be explored in therapy to avoid a tunnel vision counseling orientation.

Parallels Between Healing Practices and Counseling

Ethnocultural healing rituals, nonetheless, have similarities with therapeutic processes. Comas-Díaz (2012) compared the parallel processes between *espiritismo* and therapy. In her analysis, *espiritismo* is more responsive to Latino cultural values than traditional therapy because of the involvement of the family, the use of familiar healing traditions (rituals, prayers, possession of spirits, and *remedios* [prescriptions]), and the use of a culturally and linguistically congruent communication style. Instead of placing responsibility for presenting problems and their resolution on the client as is typically expected in therapy, *espiritismo* conceptualizes problems and solutions externally from a spiritual development perspective instead of perspective on problem reduction. As individuals become stronger spiritually, problems dissipate. Rituals that include deceased significant others reinforce interconnectedness with the collective and reinforce the reliance on a cosmic afterlife or an external dimension of locus of control (Comas-Díaz, 2006a). Adherence to these beliefs may also be influenced by the cultural construct of *fatalismo*, defined as the belief that one cannot have full control of life events.

Similarly, Hoogasian and Lijtmaer (2010) saw parallels between the practice of *curanderismo* and counseling methods. Complementary similarities include the affirmation and involvement of significant relationships (i.e., reinforcement of the network of family and friends). *Curanderismo* integrates present and deceased significant loved ones (i.e., it is a systemic intervention that includes grief processes and family supportive involvement), uses symbols for intuitive connections, and provides experiences of change through the manipulation of symbols (i.e., multisensorial and cognitive-symbolic interpretations that lead to the release of personal pain to an object). Thus, merging the structures of indigenous ceremonies and therapeutic exercises solidifies the client's belief system and recovery. One of the author's (Gallardo-Cooper's) most flattering pieces of recognition came from an older Mexican American man who told her at the end of a family therapy session, "I feel good that I came to see my *curandera*."

We must add that these indigenous healing practices are similar to therapy in that they are based on (a) a trusting relationship between the provider and the client, (b) a purpose to reduce pain, (c) an affective or enlightening state, (d) a ceremonial ritual, (e) some form of payment for services, (f) homework exercises or *remedios*, and (g) the provision of *consejos* (advice).

Alternative Cultural Healing Beliefs

Eliciting spiritual and healing beliefs from the client can be difficult because some Latinas/os do not readily volunteer this information, especially when it concerns nontraditional healing practices. Amulets, bracelets, necklaces, and other symbols (e.g., the ring or amulet of an Indian chief with feather dressing, bead jewelry) are symbols that alert the clinician to explore spiritual beliefs. Noticing a Peruvian client's bracelet of the Black Jesus (Cristo de Pachacamillas) can stimulate a spiritual dialogue. Some mental health practitioners have healing and spiritual symbols in their offices (Bracero, 1998; J. Cervantes, 2010; Comas-Díaz, 2006b) that facilitate dialogue with clients about divergent healing beliefs. These symbols communicate opportunities for divergent healing beliefs in therapy. If it is necessary for the therapy, one of us (Gallardo-Cooper) discloses to clients about her aunt's *espiritista* practice to facilitate further disclosure and to provide reassurance about her openness to alternative healing practices.

Other healing rituals to explore are the *despojos, limpias,* and *baños de plantas* (cleansings) that are often practiced with children and adults with a combination of Catholic symbols and prayers. Many Latino babies are protected from evil spirits or *mal de ojo* (evil eye) by wearing an *azabache* (black onyx) amulet. For many Latinas/os, endorsing alternative healing beliefs is not in conflict with their distinctive religious affiliations. Many Latinas/os support a general belief in spirits and negative forces that stem from *el maligno* (the evil one, negative forces). These rituals, which are reflections of cultural traditions, blend well with Christian beliefs (i.e., beliefs in an afterlife, the devil, forgiveness, baptismal cleansing of sins, and the Holy Spirit). Another important spiritual source is the *botánica* (a store that sells botanical remedies, candles, and religious products). This community resource continues to be a popular source for magico-spiritual healing products that are often incorporated into health practices (Gomez-Beloz & Chavez, 2001) and currently considered alternative medicine (Mikhail, Wali, & Ziment, 2004; Trangmar & Díaz, 2008).

Linguistic Manifestations of Spirituality

Spanish idioms embedded in communication contain spiritual messages. Most Latinos have an underlying belief in a higher power, even if they do not practice a particular religion. *Vaya con Díos* (Go with God), *Qué Dios te ampare* (May God protect you), and *Que la Virgen te cubra con su manto* (May the Virgin Mary protect you by covering you with her robe) are but a few messages Latinos commonly use. Social encounters may start or end with a blessing (Comas-Díaz, 2006a; Santiago-Rivera et al., 2002). Even among adults, a greeting or farewell to an elder may automatically make a request for a blessing (*Déme su bendición* [Give me your blessing]). From an early age Puerto Ricans are taught to greet elders and parents with a *bendición* (blessing) and not with a typical "How are you?" Elders respond with *Qué Dios te bendiga* (May God bless you) to all requests for blessings. Even a response to a greeting may include the phrase *Estoy bien, gracias a Dios* (I'm fine, thanks be to God). As evidenced by these examples, at either a conscious or unconscious level, Latinas/os communicate the existence of a higher power, and for others these sociolinguistic rituals reinforce cultural values, such as the hierarchical order in relationships and the use of *respeto*. Often attributions reflect a belief in miracles (Comas-Díaz, 2006b; Yakushko & Espin, 2010), God's punishment for diseases (Mikhail et al., 2004), supernatural powers (Gallardo, Yeh, Trimble, & Parham, 2012; Ortiz & Davis, 2008), faith healing (Ortiz & Davis, 2008), the power of prayer (Reyes-Ortíz, Rodriguez, & Markides, 2009), and veneration to a higher power (Bermúdez & Bermúdez, 2002).

Fatalismo

Fatalismo (fatalism) is an important cultural value in spiritual therapeutic work. Falicov (1998) stated that many Latinos view themselves as unable to change fate and take a wait-and-see position or do not push to control a situation over which they may have minimal to no control. Individuals whose worldviews are consistent with *fatalismo* may seem to reflect a passive disposition toward life with an expectation that the future has been preplanned and life vicissitudes are out of their control (*Qué sea lo que Dios quiera* [Let it be God's will]). Others may engage in risky behaviors with no sense of responsibility for their actions, as if a higher power had predetermined life outcomes or had assigned them a life script. Of course, acceptance of *fatalismo* does not necessarily have a negative connotation, nor does it have to be seen as a "cop out" to accepting responsibility.

Health care and prevention, understandably, can be compromised by this belief system. High levels of *fatalismo* have been associated with poor follow-up preventive medicine and adherence to treatment. However, others have demonstrated that *fatalismo* is a complex, misunderstood construct. Latinas have been demonstrated to act proactively and assume a responsible position with their preventive health care (Flórez et al., 2009), and others believe that personal and institutional discrimination may mask fatalism, as women cannot find their way to proper health care with psychosocial barriers (Abraído-Lanza et al., 2007).

In previous chapters, we addressed the impact of *fatalismo*. This worldview is linked to religious beliefs in that health or psychosocial problems may stem from a perspective that problems are a punishment from God, a spiritual trial, or a process of reconciliation and healing for sins committed. Antshel (2002) reported that a chronic disease may be perceived as a *castigo divino* (a holy punishment). The Latino values of *sobreponerse* (overcoming the problem), *aguantarse* (persistence), *controlarse* (self-control and self-restraint), and *no pensar* (not thinking about the problem, denial) are often viewed as coping styles (Añez et al., 2008). However, some believe that these behaviors are linked to *fatalismo* and are negative coping mechanisms that can lead to depression and increased stigmatization of mental health services (Caplan et al., 2011).

Fatalismo, nevertheless, can be counteracted with a spiritual *dicho: Dios dice ayúdate, que yo te ayudaré* (God says help yourself and I will help you). This *dicho* can lead to cognitive shifting and motivation to take action, such as *Tengo que poner de mi parte* (I have to cooperate or I have to help myself) or *Tienes que poner de tu parte* (You have to do your part to start helping yourself). *Fatalismo* can also be the driving force in a deep spiritual belief that reflects a positive coping mechanism of acceptance and letting go. This position is similar to that of other collectivist-oriented ethnic minority groups, such as the Chinese, who have the proverb "Some problems have no solution." Someone with an individualist orientation may look down on the value of *fatalismo* because the individual is not using self-reliance and personal attributes to control his or her future. Yet depending on the circumstances, *fatalismo* may be the healthiest position because it enables one to accept life's unchangeable predicaments with *fortaleza interna* (inner strength). In these instances this prayer of St. Theresa is useful for Christian clients:

> May today there be peace within.
> May you trust God that you are exactly where you are meant to be.
> May you not forget the infinite possibilities that are born of faith.
> May you use those gifts that you have received,
> And pass on the love that has been given to you.
> May you be content knowing you are a child of God.
> Let this presence settle into your bones,
> and allow your soul the freedom to sing, dance, praise and love.
> It is there for each and every one of us.
> (http://catholicfire.blogspot.com/2010/12/prayer-of-saint-teresa-of-avila.html)

Christianity-Based Interventions

Christian rituals and ceremonies often function as coping mechanisms during periods of distress. Given the large number of Latino Catholics, an understanding of common religious rituals deepens a clinician's understanding of clients' attributions and beliefs. When therapists expand their knowledge of spiritual rituals, they may also expand their repertoire of spiritual interventions, thereby providing a counseling experience that is meaningful to Latina/o clients. Mexican and other Latin American populations engage in *juramentos*, or pledges to the Virgin Mary, Christ, or a particular saint, as a strategy for self-control. These spiritual practices have been successful with Mexican men who make a vow to La Virgen de Guadalupe to abstain from substance abuse (Cuadrado & Lieberman, 2011). *Promesas* (promises) have similar healing effects. The individual promises a hardship for a petition. For instance, a woman may wear a basic tunic and not use makeup for a year to request the medical recovery of a family member. *Testimonios* (giving witness) have also been used successfully with Christian groups as a form empowering self-disclosure, typically reflecting overcoming adversity with a message of faith and triumph. *Novenas* (prayers that last 9 days or 9 weeks) and services of *sanación* (healing services) are also often practiced as petitions and intercessory prayers. *Sanación* may imply healing of the soul or the body, with the former reinforcing a positive state of mental health when faced with hardships. Religious retreats and religious classes are also common options for increasing spirituality and *fortaleza* (strength).

In family therapy, praying the rosary at home with the family has been used as a powerful strategic intervention that reinforces family cohesion through spirituality (Arciniega et al., 2010). Another useful family intervention is altar making. Bermúdez and Bermúdez (2002) directed families to arrange a table with important personal objects or artifacts. Through the use of a narrative therapy approach, altar making facilitates the resolution of grief and bereavement issues, strengthens collaboration between family members, and solidifies blended families. Similarly, affirming *bendiciones* (blessings) and being thankful in the therapeutic discourse can have an empowering effect by refocusing on the positive attributes of situations and personal assets.

Prayers continue to be important to Latinas/os. Veneration to both canonized and folk saints has been commonly practiced for generations in the context of indigenous healing (Ortiz & Davis, 2008). Some popular saints include San Martín de Porres, a Peruvian *mulato* saint from the 16th century. He is the patron of medical staff, health problems, and racial conflicts. San Judas Tadeo is the patron saint of impossible causes and unemployment, whereas San Antonio de Padua is the patron for those seeking a partner and lost objects or causes. Among Cubans, San Lázaro is a very popular saint and is often linked to Santería beliefs. Many of his followers light candles daily and place them in a common area in the home. This ritual undoubtedly reinforces the family's spiritual beliefs and healing practices.

In Mexico, grief and loss are addressed by celebrating the Día de los Muertos (Day of the Dead), a day for remembering loved ones who have passed away. Rather than engaging in mourning, Latinas/os create altars with pictures or other memorabilia of the deceased. The family may spend the night at the cemetery by the deceased, adorn the crypt, and bring food to share with others.

Folk healing practices are also important rituals and beliefs. One of the authors (Gallardo-Cooper) worked with a Latin American family whose adolescent daughter suffered from significant anxiety and severe gastrointestinal problems. During the course of the therapy the mother volunteered that she had begun the *sanación de la palabra* (the healing of the word) used in her native country. Because her daughter had an *empacho* (stomach problems), the mother began the ritual of "taking out the *empacho*" (taking away the *empacho*) through a back massage with occasional mild pinching while repeating the words *Todo el empache se va, todo el empache ser irá* (All stomachaches will be gone, all stomachaches will fade). For this mother, doing something dissipated her sense of helplessness, exemplified her support for her daughter, and reinforced the mother–daughter bond. Rituals can be powerful and can encourage empowerment and mental health.

Counselors should consider how cultural and healing practices can complement Western-style interventions in counseling. The sound of a drum, a chant, a relaxation and visualization exercise, and a prayer are healing practices for Latinas/os that often evoke affective content and insight. For many Latinos, a specific ritual or ceremonial process seems culturally expected. Individuals who are used to this experience and format will expect a similar process in therapy. There is room in the counseling process to include community healers, priests, ministers, rabbis, and other religious leaders (Comas-Díaz, 2006b; Gallardo, 2009; Santiago-Rivera et al., 2002). However, there is a need to train clinicians on the role of spirituality in counseling and how to be comfortable when introducing spirituality into the therapeutic process (J. Cervantes, 2010).

Avoiding Addressing Spirituality in Counseling

Clinicians may avoid addressing spirituality in therapy for many reasons. First, Hoogasian and Lijtmaer (2010) posited that Western-trained mental health professionals avoid addressing spiritual beliefs in therapy because of their own perceived religious conflicts and biases. Western training promotes self-reliance as a treatment objective, whereas reliance on a higher power is perceived as a personal deficit. Second, misperceptions about devil worshiping and therapists' own religious conflicts or biases also create discomfort when, for example, clinicians are faced with African and nontraditional spiritual beliefs. Third, many clinicians are not trained in how to integrate clients' spirituality and healing beliefs into therapy (J. Cervantes, 2010). Fourth, pastoral counseling and clinical counseling are perceived as two separate specialties that should not be mixed. Fifth, some clinicians continue to devalue the role of the community healer as a respectable mental health resource. When providers have biases that stem from spiritual conflicts, professional consultation is required to determine their suitability for working with individuals with other healing belief systems. Counseling supervision may also be required for those clinicians who want to integrate spirituality into therapy and to address possible personal biases.

Social Justice Directives

Many Latinas/os, as well as other ethnic minority groups in the United States, have their share of painful experiences from discrimination, prejudice, and oppression. These experiences have both psycho-historical ramifications (Comas-Díaz, Lykes, & Alarcón, 1998) and present-day manifestations (Szalacha et al., 2003) that impact on mental health. Some Latinas/os emigrate to escape political and economical oppression, racism, heterosexism, sexism, and classism, among many other things. They seek freedom, fair living conditions, and opportunities to grow in all areas by fulfilling their dreams. There is a belief among immigrants, for example, that by working hard they can attain the American Dream and that the message on the Statue of Liberty—"Give me your tired, your poor, your huddled masses yearning to breathe free" (Lazarus, 1883)—can be realized in the United States of America. This sense of self-efficacy may explain immigrants' resilience when faced with institutional, social, and personal discrimination. Their motivation to struggle diminishes the more time they spend in the United States, in a phenomenon known as the Latino paradox. With time discriminatory experiences are internalized, and the American Dream vanishes (P. Arredondo, 1986; Arredondo-Dowd, 1981; Gallardo-Cooper & Zapata, 2013).

Unfortunately, these internalized processes become embedded in individuals' cognitive and affective structures as well as passed on to other generations, disempowering their sense of human agency and well-being both in the present and in the future. Having a majority or recognized mainstream status during the formative years yields a very different set of privileged experiences compared to membership in an ethnic minority group. Latinas/os who are privileged in their country of origin may experience discrimination for the first time in the United States, whereas those who were marginalized in their home country, particularly due to socioeconomic status, continue to be exposed to a web of negative and oppressive experiences when they arrive on U.S. soil. Privilege is also reflected in immigration status; for example, consider the case of those who come with political asylum (in which arrival and adaptation is facilitated by public policies) versus unauthorized Latina/o immigrants.

A social justice therapeutic orientation specifically addresses these psychocultural stressors, or experiences that cause much pain, distrust, and alienation. This position has its roots in liberation psychology, a therapeutic model from Latin America developed to improve the living conditions of those who suffer from classism, racism, sexism, and political oppression. Ignacio Martín-Baró, a Spanish Jesuit priest who earned a PhD in social psychology at the University of Chicago (Aron & Corne, 1996), and Paulo Freire (1982), a Brazilian educator, are the two major figures of this movement. Martín-Baró's fervent drive to help the oppressed led to his assassination by a right-wing militia in El Salvador in 1989. He dismissed traditional American mainstream individualist counseling theories because of their lack of ecological validity with the psychological realities of Latin Americans. As a social psychologist aware of rigid systems of political and economic oppression, he believed that psychological empowerment could only be attained through grassroots group interventions and a collectivist orientation. Maintaining a neutral position as a provider, he claimed, was not a moral or ethical position to hold when working with the oppressed. Comas-Díaz (2000) seconded this position as she urged ethnopolitical psychologists to follow a moral commitment to promote freedom in others.

> The psychosocial transformation advocated by Martín-Baró included empowering the people and developing their citizenship capacities while fostering the construction of different social identities based on assertiveness, self-confidence, pride in one's work and achievements, and their own critical capacity. That transformation was also intended to strengthen democracy and empower civil society. (Montero, 2007, p. 524)

Freire's (1982) ideology in his classic book *Pedagogy of the Oppressed* also contributed to the movement with the concept of conscientization. The term refers to human transformation through the development of critical awareness, insight, and understanding of the self in relation to oppressive forces. Conscientization energizes the individual to reject oppression and its concomitant negative consequences. Individuals who are oppressed and marginalized are unable to act because of a fear of expressing thoughts and preferences, but these fears can be eliminated through knowledge and awareness and the ability to experience, act on, and maintain freedom (Montero, 2007). The concept of power also needs to be understood as it relates to class, gender, race, education, and the like. Although feminist psychology has contributed to a greater understanding of the power differential, particularly with respect to gender differences (Moane, 2010; Todd, 2011), liberation psychology expands empowerment through social and community praxis.

Social justice methods are varied. Todd (2011) reviewed the empirical contributions of liberation psychology and found support for methods of advocacy, consciousness raising, community and neighborhood organization, education about public policy, and development of community coalitions. These methods can be implemented in institutions or large-impact interventions (Hipólito-Delgado & Lee, 2007; Villalba, 2007a), in groups with a systemic orientation (P. Hernández et al., 2009), and during therapy.

An example of a large-impact social justice intervention provided in an institution is a school-based empowerment program developed by Hipólito-Delgado and Lee (2007). The goals of their program are to empower minority students through the practice of activism, social action, positive ethnic identity, self-advocacy, and critical consciousness. This program has different facets, including Latina groups with students (i.e., consciousness-raising groups, skills training in leadership and social action), system changes (e.g., curriculum changes, ethnic studies courses), support for students in social action participation (e.g., student government), and community involvement (e.g., leaders as models, parent groups, community resources, community member groups).

Another example of a multifamily therapy group approach with community support is the cultural context model (Almeida, 2003; P. Hernández, 2002; P. Hernández et al., 2005; P. Hernández et al., 2009). The objectives of this structured intervention are to induce collective consciousness and social action through the development of "cultural circles" (Hernández et al., 2009, p. 98; see also Freire, 1982) or groups of community support. Family therapists and community sponsors work together during the implementation of the program so that community support continues with families once the program concludes. Couples and family therapy sessions may be augmented services but are not the primary intervention. Through cultural narratives and group self-disclosure individuals reach conscientization, a sense of their sociopolitical contexts, and empowerment. This is what Comas-Díaz (2000) referred to as the therapist "bearing witness" (p. 1321), listening to testimonies of political and social oppression.

A final social justice approach is implemented during the therapeutic process. Missed subtle cultural messages of discrimination and prejudice are what Comas-Díaz (2012) referred to as "missed empathetic opportunities" (p. 139). When these unintentional clinical errors occur, the effectiveness of therapy is compromised. Also, paying attention to clients' experiences of microaggressions (D. W. Sue et al., 2007) is critical in therapeutic discourse.

Counselor Advocacy

The principles of social justice require the operationalization of advocacy as an important component of a social justice approach. Advocacy can be conducted during the session or in the community. For instance, the counselor or community mentor can accompany the client to a health agency when he or she is not receiving adequate care, modeling for the client the skills needed to face unfairness, discrimination, and other institutional and staff psychocultural barriers. One of the authors (Arredondo) led a psychoeducational group for Latina immigrants to guide their self-advocacy skills. Information about where to access friendly health care services locally and where to go when they had utility problems in their homes were just two things the women sought. The sessions also included role-playing, demonstrating for the women how to communicate in ways that accomplished their objectives. That is, self-advocacy can be taught and mentored.

The ACA (American Counseling Association) Advocacy Competencies, which were developed by leaders in social justice counseling, are an essential reference tool for counseling professionals (Lewis, Arnold, House, & Toporek, 2002). Similar to Bronfenbrenner's (1979; Bronfenbrenner & Morris, 1998) ecological model, the competencies illustrate the interconnections of interventions at individual, community, and societal levels and the role counselors play in applying social justice principles.

Concluding Thoughts

In this chapter, we have delineated therapeutic frameworks that contribute to a sagacious, judicious, and responsive Latino-centered approach to counseling. All models discussed are empowering and strengths based, two important clinical elements in work with Latinas/os. Although a variety of methods are available, we emphasize the need to integrate culture, relational factors, communication synchronization, and practice accommodations with Latina/o clients. Because research and practice with Latinos is growing exponentially (Santiago-Rivera, Cardemil, Prieto, & Romero, 2012), we underscore the need for continued professional development in Latino culture, use of culturally grounded strategies, reliance on evidence-based findings, and on Latino-specific data as essential drivers of efficacious practice.

• • •

Chapter 11

Ethics and Organizational Cultural Competencies

Querer es poder.

Where there is a will, there is a way.

(Sellers, Nelson, & Soto, 1994, p. 62)

• • •

Objectives

- To examine the ethical basis for multicultural competence with Latino populations.
- To understand the role that multicultural counseling competence has played in counselor education.
- To examine resources and Latino-focused professional organizations.

Sabías que/Did you know that . . .

- According to an assessment of multicultural publications by Ponterotto, Fingerhut, and McGuiness (2012), "Multicultural Counseling Competencies and Standards: A Call to the Profession" (D. W. Sue, Arredondo, & McDavis, 1992) is the most cited article on multicultural competencies of all time.
- Multiculturalism is often considered the fourth force in psychology after psychoanalysis, behaviorism, and humanistic psychology.

• • •

Case Scenario

Carlos had always wanted to work with the Latino community. Unfortunately, both his graduate and undergraduate training had occurred in small college towns with very few Latinos. Although he had been bilingual since birth, Carlos had little occasion to use Spanish in a professional setting. He felt that his counseling training had been excellent and that he had grown as a therapist and social advocate. Recently he had moved back home to take a job at a Hispanic-Serving Institution as a counselor educator. Carlos was excited at the opportunity that faced him but also nervous about applying the general skills he had learned to the Latino population. He worried about his ability to practice, conduct research, and reach out to the local community. Carlos was in need of guidance, but at his new job he received a great deal of support but little guidance. He wondered how he could balance being an ethical professional and an agent of change. Fortunately a colleague recommended that he join several professional organizations that focused on Latino issues, and through this membership he was able to access a wealth of resources, information, and support.

Like Carlos, most counselors are not prepared to work with specific cultural or linguistic ethnic minority populations. Professional training programs that offer specialized training with Latino populations are rare but do exist. Our Lady of the Lake in San Antonio, Texas, is a Hispanic-Serving Institution that offers specialized linguistic and cultural training suited to the Latino population. The Chicago School of Professional Psychology has a Latino studies concentration in the master's counseling program. Several other universities, such as the University of Miami, Pepperdine, and Montclair State University, offer certificates in working with Latino populations. The graduates of such programs report that this training is invaluable in their work with the Latino population (Biever et al., 2004).

However, most mental health professionals do not have the opportunity to receive this type of specific training during graduate school and must seek out additional guidance, training, supervision, and mentorship after graduation. This chapter focuses on several resources and the places both Latinos and those interested in working with Latinos can find them.

Ethics

Ethics codes may vary in specificity across organizations and mental health specialties, but most of these entities share similar ethical values. For example, Gibson and Mitchell (2008) compared the ethics codes of different mental health organizations in their text *Introduction to Counseling and Guidance*. They found that mental health practitioners, regardless of specialty, share a desire to help clients in an ethical manner, want to prevent harm to clients, and want to ensure that practitioners practice within their scope of competence.

Professional organizations historically assumed that the types of training and policies that they espoused were universal. However, counselors soon realized that their profession was culturally encapsulated (Wrenn, 1962), and a dedicated group of professionals worked both within and apart from professional counseling and psychology organizations to promote the idea of multicultural counseling competence. Multiculturally competent practice cannot be considered aside from ethics because multicultural competent practice *is* ethical practice. As we have said before, all counseling is multicultural.

American Counseling Association (ACA)

ACA is the largest organization in the world that exclusively represents professional counselors, with a membership topping 52,000 in 2013. ACA is the current-day descendant of several professional groups that began with the American Personnel and Guidance Association in 1952. The *ACA Code of Ethics* (ACA, 2005), which is currently under revision, highlights the importance of respect for diversity and multicultural competence. A commitment to diversity is at the forefront and permeates the *ACA Code of Ethics*. Section C.5. prohibits discrimination, but Section F.11. elaborates the commitment to multicultural competence in counselor education and training programs. The *ACA Code of Ethics* reads as follows:

- *F.11.a. Faculty Diversity.* Counselor educators are committed to recruiting and retaining a diverse faculty.
- *F.11.b. Student Diversity.* Counselor educators actively attempt to recruit and retain a diverse student body. Counselor educators demonstrate commitment to multicultural/diversity competence by recognizing and valuing diverse cultures and types of abilities students bring to the training experience. Counselor educators provide appropriate accommodations that enhance and support diverse student well-being and academic performance.
- *F.11.c. Multicultural/Diversity Competence.* Counselor educators actively infuse multicultural/diversity competency in their training and supervision practices. They actively train students to gain awareness, knowledge, and skills in the competencies of multicultural practice. Counselor educators include case examples, role-plays, discussion questions, and other classroom activities that promote and represent various cultural perspectives (ACA, 2005).

In addition, Standard G.1.g. addresses multicultural/diversity considerations in research. The *ACA Code of Ethics* also has a remarkable addition not found in many ethics codes: a glossary of terms. For example, the glossary defines *multicultural/diversity competence* as "a capacity whereby counselors possess cultural and diversity awareness and knowledge about self and others, and how this awareness and knowledge is applied effectively in practice with clients and client groups" (p. 20). In addition, it defines *multicultural/diversity counseling* as "counseling that recognizes diversity and embraces approaches that support the worth, dignity, potential, and uniqueness of individuals within their historical, cultural, economic, political, and psychosocial contexts" (p. 20).

The *ACA Code of Ethics* is available on the ACA website (www.counseling.org) in Spanish as well as English (go to http://www.counseling.org/Resources/aca-code-of-ethics.pdf for the English version and http://www.counseling.org/docs/ethics/etica_espanol.pdf?sfvrsn=2 for the Spanish version). The translation was led by Dr. María del Pilar Grazioso Rodríguez, director of the master's in mental health counseling program with the Universidad del Valle, Guatemala City, Guatemala. She and a team of her graduates, all active within ACA, took on the monumental task of preparing a culturally and linguistically congruent document.

The *ACA Code of Ethics* is exemplary because of its overt and infused commitment to multicultural competence, which is clearly identified as an ethical issue. ACA arrived at this commitment through the work of several dedicated individuals on developing multicultural competence. D. W. Sue, Arredondo, and McDavis formalized the multicultural competence movement within ACA in 1992 with the publication of their seminal article "Multicultural Counseling Competencies and Standards: A Call to the Profession" in the flagship *Journal of Counseling & Development* and also in the *Journal of Multicultural Counseling and Development*. The *Journal of Multicultural Counseling and Development* is the journal of the Association for Multicultural Counseling and Development (AMCD), whose president at the time, Dr. Thomas Parham, commissioned the Multicultural Counseling Competencies writing committee.

The seminal D. W. Sue et al. (1992) article that unveiled the Multicultural Counseling Competencies is the most cited *Journal of Counseling & Development* article of all time according to the International Science Index Web of Science database

(Nevels, Delgado-Romero, & Heesacker, 2012). Over that same time, the effects of the multicultural competence movement on training, service provision, research, and service have been profound. For example, a review of counseling journals found that of the new classics in counseling and counseling psychology, 36.7% deal with multiculturalism compared to 0% when Heesacker, Heppner, and Rogers (1982) examined classics 3 decades ago (Nevels et al., 2012).

After the initial publication of the Multicultural Counseling Competencies (P. Arredondo et al., 1996) many people worked hard to further the issue of multicultural competence. Perhaps no other person is more readily identified with refining, operationalizing, and advocating for the adoption and development of the Multicultural Counseling Competencies than Patricia Arredondo. Arredondo chaired an AMCD Professional Standards Committee that produced a document with 119 explanatory statements for the 31 competencies (P. Arredondo et al., 1996). She also introduced the dimensions of personal identity model (P. Arredondo et al., 1996) and the concept of multiple or collective identities and multiple contexts. Arredondo was the first Latina president of ACA and was designated a living legend by ACA. Her persistent leadership, along with the work of other multicultural counseling competence advocates, led to the adoption of the Multicultural Counseling Competencies by the ACA Governing Council and the explosion of empirical and theoretical work on multicultural competence.

American Psychological Association (APA)

Unlike ACA, APA has a broad membership that includes both clinical (e.g., clinical, counseling, school) and nonclinical (e.g., social, developmental, biological) specialties in psychology. APA was founded in 1892 and boasts 150,000 members, affiliates, and students. APA refers to "diverse, multicultural" contexts in its mission statement and has social justice, diversity, and inclusion embedded in its core values. APA's (2002a) *Ethical Principles of Psychologists and Code of Conduct* ethics code consists of aspirational principles and enforceable standards. Principle D (Justice) makes reference to fairness, equality, and bias; and Principle E (Respect for People's Rights and Dignity) specifically requires that psychologists respect individual and role differences based on factors such as race, ethnicity, and culture. According to Standard 2.01 (Boundaries of Competence), psychologists are required to obtain the necessary competence to work with diverse populations. Standard 3.01 (Unfair Discrimination) prohibits discrimination. The ethics code also addresses the use of appropriate assessments in Section 9.02 (Use of Assessments).

To bring elements of the Multicultural Counseling Competencies to APA, a joint task force of APA Divisions 17 (Society of Counseling Psychology), 35 (Society for the Psychology of Women), and 45 (Society for the Psychological Study of Ethnic Minority Issues) was cochaired by Arredondo and Nadya Fouad. This task force led to the creation of a document that was approved as policy by the APA Council of Representatives in 2002. *Guidelines on Multicultural Education, Training, Research, Practice, and Organizational Change for Psychologists* (APA, 2002b) provides six guidelines for psychologists to follow for their personal development as well as to guide their education and training, research, practice, and organizational development. These guidelines are currently being reviewed and updated. The guidelines encourage psychologists to attend to multiculturalism and diversity both generally and specifically. For example, Guideline 2 states that "Psychologists are encouraged to recognize the importance of multicultural sensitivity/responsiveness, knowledge, and understanding about ethnically and racially different individuals" (p. 385). In terms of research, Guideline 4 reads, "Culturally sensitive psychological researchers are encouraged to recognize the importance of conducting culture-centered and ethical psychological research among persons from ethnic, linguistic, and racial minority backgrounds" (p. 388).

Other Professional Associations

Both the Multicultural Counseling Competencies (P. Arredondo et al., 1996) and *Guidelines on Multicultural Education, Training, Research, Practice, and Organizational Change for Psychologists* (APA, 2002b) are broad documents that cover multiculturalism in general for a large group of professionals. The following professional groups focus on issues related to all ethnic groups and specifically Latinos:

- *Association for Multicultural Counseling and Development (AMCD).* AMCD publishes a highly regarded journal, the *Journal of Multicultural Counseling and Development.* Abstracts of articles published in this journal appear in both English and Spanish. AMCD has a dedicated Latino focus through its Latinas/os Concerns subgroup, known as LATNET (Latino Network). Since 1996, there have been four Latina/o presidents of AMCD: Patricia Arredondo, Bernal Baca, Robert Davison-Aviles, and Edil Torres-Rivera.
- *Counselors for Social Justice (CSJ).* Like AMCD, CSJ is a division of ACA. CSJ publishes the *Journal for Social Action in Counseling and Psychology.* Azara Santiago-Rivera and Edil Torres-Rivera, past-presidents of CSJ, are leaders in the Latino counseling movement.
- *Society for the Psychological Study of Ethnic Minority Issues.* Division 45 of APA publishes a prestigious journal founded by Latina scholar Lillian Comas-Díaz, *Cultural Diversity and Ethnic Minority Psychology.* The presidency of Division 45 rotates among four major ethnic groups, and Patricia Arredondo, Eduardo Morales, Manuel Casas, and Luis Vásquez are all Latina/o past-presidents of Division 45.
- *National Latina/o Psychological Association (NLPA).* In 1979, the National Hispanic Psychological Association was established. The association waned in the late 1990s with little to no national participation. With encouragement from Latina/o professionals, one of the authors (Arredondo) helped establish NLPA in 2002. This active organization, the premier association for Latina/o psychologists, now boasts more than 50% student membership (Chavez-Korell, Delgado-Romero, & Illes, 2012). NLPA publishes the *Journal of Latina/o Psychology,* whose founding editor is Azara Santiago-Rivera, a past-president of CSJ. Although composed of many psychologists, the membership of NLPA is inclusive of many disciplines in mental health. Many of the association's members hold membership in ACA and hold leadership roles in the AMCD Latina/o Concerns group. NLPA does not have an ethics committee or a separate ethics code, but discussions about these topics are active in the organization. Currently the association invokes APA's ethical guidelines for its members.
- *Council of National Psychology Associations for the Advancement of Ethnic Minority Interests (CNPAAEMI).* In 2013, APA allied itself with psychological associations representing racial/ethnic minority interests to form CNPAAEMI. This council, with representation from the Asian American Psychological Association, NLPA, the Association of Black Psychologists, Division 45, and the Society of Indian Psychologists, sponsors a leadership development program for ethnic minority psychologists and has disseminated publications on ethnic minority interests. Its 2009 publication

Psychology Education and Training From Culture-Specific and Multiracial Perspectives includes a section that specifically addresses training and teaching strategies for work with Latinos. CNPAAEMI has also released *Guidelines for Research in Ethnic Minority Communities* (2000) and *Psychological Treatment of Ethnic Minority Populations* (2003).

- *Latina Researchers Network.* This network, established in 2012 and led by Professor Silvia Mazzula of John Jay College of Criminal Justice, has quickly become both a physical and virtual gathering space for Latina professionals and students interested and engaged in research with Latinas across the life span. At its first conference in May 2012, more than 200 senior professors and graduate students were in attendance. The network has a focus on interdisciplinary research and inquiry into many of the topics discussed in this book, particularly from a strengths perspective. Its web page is quickly becoming a rich source of resources (www.latinaresearchers.com).

- *Sociedad Interamericana de Psicología (SIP).* This organization is dedicated to psychology in North, Central, and South America and the Caribbean. Founded in 1951, SIP meets for biennial congresses (e.g., in Guatemala in 2009, Colombia in 2011, Brazil in 2013, and Peru in 2015). The official languages of SIP are Spanish, English, Portuguese, and French. SIP publishes the *Interamerican Journal of Psychology,* whose editor, Professor Edil Torres-Rivera, is a counselor educator and former president of CSJ.

- *National Board for Certified Counselors (NBCC).* NBCC provides national certifications that recognize individuals who have voluntarily met standards for general and specialty areas of counseling practice. Embedded in its code of ethics are 95 directives; Directive 26 specifies that National Certified Counselors will demonstrate multicultural competence.

- *Council for Accreditation of Counseling and Related Educational Programs (CACREP).* CACREP accredits master's and doctoral programs in counselor education. These programs align with ACA's mission of advancing the profession of counseling and excellence in the training and education of professional counselors, and graduates of CACREP programs are eligible for licensure in their respective states and for consideration for National Certified Counselor status. CACREP's standard for social and cultural diversity includes statements about cultural diversity and multicultural competence.

Other Training Resources

The resources in Appendix B demonstrate the growth in interest in working effectively with Latino clients among counseling and education fields. Latino mental health service providers have collaborated on research, task forces, and working groups to increase the number of training programs and educational agencies committed to preparing multiculturally competent service providers. The ethical responsibility is now placed in training programs to utilize these resources in training.

There are also other resources available to counselors that are not focused specifically on mental health but contain a wealth of relevant information. Long-standing advocacy organizations such as the National Council of La Raza (www.nclr.org) provide a great deal of education and information about the U.S. Latino population. The Pew Hispanic Center (www.pewhispanic.org) conducts and commissions studies on a wide range of topics relevant to the Latino population, such as demography, education, economics, and health. Their research-based publications are exceptionally relevant to counseling professionals because of their focus on contextual issues and factors related to Latinos. Reports of the Pew Hispanic

Center are not only timely and highly specific to Latinos across the life span but relevant to individuals of all ethnic groups.

Research institutes such as the Julian Samora Research Institute (JSRI; www.jsri.msu.edu) at Michigan State University and the Institute for Latino Studies at Notre Dame provide information about the U.S. Latino population that is rich in context. For example, JSRI publishes demographic, research, and statistical reports about Latinos in the Midwest and across the nation. JSRI also has research and outreach initiatives that target the needs of the Latino community in the areas of economic development, education, and families and neighborhoods.

At times professional organizations decide to focus on Latino issues as a part of their broader mission. For example, the Society for the Psychological Study of Social Issues (www.spssi.org) published an entire issue of the *Journal of Social Issues* (vol. 66, no. 1, 2010) on research theory and policy related to how Latinos are transforming the United States (J. F. Casas & Ryan, 2010, Levy, 2010). The issue is available for free online (http://onlinelibrary.wiley.com/doi/10.1111/josi.2010.66.issue-1/issuetoc) and includes a comprehensive examination of issues relevant to Latinos, including ethnic identity and intergroup relations within the United States, improvements to educational outcomes among Latina/o youth, cultural adaptations and negotiations of transitions among Latina/o adults, and social policy implications.

Several health organizations are focused primarily on the U.S. Latino population. For example, the National Hispanic Medical Association (www.nhmamd.org) formed the National Hispanic Health Professionals Leadership Network. This network consists of health care groups such as the Hispanic American Allergy and Asthma Association, Hispanic Dental Association, Latino Caucus of the American Public Health Association, Latino Health Communications, Latinos & Hispanics in Dietetics and Nutrition, National Association of Hispanic Nurses, National Forum for Latino Healthcare Executives, National Latino Behavioral Health Association, and NLPA. The network meets during the annual National Hispanic Medical Association conference and aims to create a synergy among Latino-focused health care organizations (Delgado-Romero, Espino, Werther, & González, 2012). Information on the network as well as many other resources on Latino health issues can be found at www.hispanichealth.info.

Several organizations and resources are focused on Latina/o education, such as the Hispanic Scholarship Fund (www.hsf.net), the American Association of Hispanics in Higher Education (www.aahhe.org), the *Journal of Hispanic Higher Education* (http://www.sagepub.com/journals/Journal201513), and Excelencia in Education (www.edexcelencia.org). Each provides research and advocacy related to Latinas/os in the United States. Many government organizations also provide information on Latinos, such as the U.S. Census Bureau (www.census.gov) and the White House Initiative on Educational Excellence for Hispanics (http://www2.ed.gov/about/inits/list/hispanic-initiative/index.html). *Winning the Future: Improving Education for the Latino Community* (2011) is one such comprehensive report.

Concluding Thoughts

As we have said before, all counseling is multicultural counseling. Freud was no more culture free than Comas-Díaz is. The difference is that Comas-Díaz recognizes and owns her cultural influences as a Puerto Rican American of mixed national and racial heritage (Comas-Díaz, 2012), whereas Freud thought he was discovering universal principles. Given the advanced state of research and professional action regarding multicultural competence, there is no excuse for a counselor to claim that he or she does not have access to information about multiculturalism generally and Latino issues specifically. This chapter has discussed the ethical imperatives found in major mental health organizations and supplemented that discussion with a vast array of professional resources. Clearly, an ethical counselor is one who knows where to access resources to best serve his or her clients, students, and community. Consider the final scenario as another example of the dilemmas students face when their professors are not up to date on the intersection of ethics and cultural competencies.

Case Scenario

Elena enrolled in a CACREP-accredited master's program in counseling at a state university. It was her dream to become a school counselor and to work in the high school she had attended in South Texas. She had done her homework and knew that CACREP-accredited programs would prepare her to become a licensed professional counselor. Yet about a month into her coursework, Elena began to feel uneasy. All she read about were examples of White counselors working with White students. Moreover, the class was required to watch the "Gloria" (a White, middle-aged woman) tapes, and she wondered what these had to do with school counseling, especially in Latino neighborhood high schools. (The "Gloria" tapes are demonstrations of three types of counseling by renowned psychotherapists—Fritz Perls, Albert Ellis, and Carl Rogers. Each conducts a session with a client, Gloria, from his respective theoretical perspective.) Elena finally got up the nerve to ask her professor what Gloria had to do with counseling in 2013. Her professor responded that these were classic tapes, ones that he and his professor had also watched in training. He also reminded her that she was in a theories class, not a multicultural counseling class, where issues of gender, race, and sexual orientation were discussed. As far as Elena was concerned, the therapists in the tapes were unethical and sexist in their treatment of the client, Gloria. In her multicultural counseling class Elena was learning about barriers to culturally competent practice. Her professor certainly was not making any connections to multicultural counseling competencies in his theories class.

Ethical standards and multicultural guidelines are in place for many reasons, and it behooves counselor educators to discuss them in all courses. It is insufficient to teach a required ethics course and then not make connections to ethics in courses on psychological testing or clinical practice with Latinos. Elena's professor is in a position of power in relation to her, and thus he has influence on her performance outcomes. The glibness in his comments about multicultural counseling and theories classes exposes his cultural blinders and their impact on Elena and other students. All counselor educators must be mindful of how their teaching and attitudes about coursework and people can bias or offend others.

Students like Elena are socioculturally astute, aware of the different "-isms" that persist in society and prepared to ask questions and even question authority. Counselor educators must take advantage of the rich resources available to adapt their classes to reflect contemporary issues and practices. The future of the counseling profession is now, and we discuss the implications of this further in Chapter 12. In the meantime, consider the following Multicultural Counseling Competencies (P. Arredondo et al., 1996):

- Culturally skilled counselors possess knowledge about their social impact on others. (p. 60)
- Culturally skilled counselors can recognize in counseling or teaching relationships when and how their attitudes, beliefs, and value are interfering with providing the best service to clients [students]. (p. 58)

• • •

Chapter 12

The Future of Latina/o–Centered Counseling

La ambición nunca se llena.

Ambition never has its fill.

(Sellers, Nelson, & Soto, 1994, p. 42)

• • •

Objectives

- To examine the future of Latino-centered counseling.
- To identify future directions for teaching, clinical practice, research, and service.
- To examine the future of international Latino counseling.

Sabías que/Did you know that . . .

- Comas-Díaz (2012) speculated that the new generation of Latinos will be *futuristas*, a group that synthesizes Latino and U.S. values into a community-focused society.
- The United States is the second largest Latino nation in the world behind only Mexico in terms of numbers of Latinos (Morales, 2009; U.S. Census Bureau, 2010c).

• • •

Case Scenario

Javier is a counselor educator at the University of Florida in the year 2050. He is 49 years old and a biracial Latino. He remembers the "dire" predictions of a Latino majority population during his youth. He recalls how his school system was transformed into a majority-Latino system in a few years. His high school was 30% Latino when he attended, and the percentage of Latinos is greater now. Javier lives in Florida, where the Latino population has moved upward from Miami. The counselor educator program at the University of Florida is stronger than ever thanks to the Latino Studies certificate. The demographic shift in the United States occurred years earlier than predicted, and now 1 in every 4 people in the United States is Latina/o. This new wave of Latinos is what Comas-Díaz (2012) termed *futuristas*, and they have transformed U.S. society with their numbers, their political activism, and their emphasis on social justice. Javier was part of a group of counselors who advocated for passage of the NEW DREAM Act, which created a pathway to citizenship in the 2030s. Although the Latina/o population is large and active, access to political, educational, and social power has come slowly. With such a large population there are also pervasive social issues that need to be addressed. Javier is proud of his students, who represent a colorful mix of races and ethnicities (the polyculture M. Ramírez, 1998, referred to), and the work they have been able to do to make the educational and juvenile justice systems more sensitive to Latinos. Every counselor has the opportunity to study Spanish, and the majority of students are bilingual. Javier smiles when he remembers his father and his colleagues talking about social justice and raising issues of cultural sensitivity. He thinks they would be proud of what has been achieved.

Reasons for Latina/o-Centered Counseling

Now that you have read most of this book, you will recognize the many reasons why counseling must become more Latina/o centered. First there is the *demographic imperative.* The sheer number of Latinos, larger families than non-White Latino families, high birth rates, and a lower average age of parents mean that the future of the United States is tied to the Latino population. Pick any point in the future, and there will be a growing Latino majority. In some geographic locations and cities, this is already true. However, numbers alone do not ensure social justice for the disenfranchised: Consider the case of South Africa, where a small minority oppressed a numerical majority for many years.

The 2012 Presidential election was a watershed moment in U.S. history on several dimensions: the influence of Latino voters in reelecting President Barack Obama, the approval of gay marriage in three states, and legalization of the use of marijuana for medical purposes in two states. Of eligible Latino voters, 71% voted in 2012 compared to 67% in 2008. The Latino turnout was overwhelmingly Democratic.

Another reason why counseling must become more Latina/o centered has to do with *counselor self-interest and survival.* Demographic changes mean that the market for clinical services, research, and outreach will need to address Latino issues to survive and thrive economically and to stay relevant in society. Latinos represent a growing economic market, and so far mostly politicians and beer companies have capitalized on this fact. There is a great deal of need among this population, as well as a great deal of money to be made. Most counselors recoil at the thought of an *economic imperative of Latino-centered counseling,* but the reality is that if counseling is not relevant, then it is obsolete. Counselors and counselor educators require an income, and they must balance economic realities with the desire to provide pro bono work and to be credible as culturally competent counselors sought after by community agencies and others in a position to make referrals (i.e., physicians, attorneys, other counselors).

Most counselors prefer to consider the *ethical imperative of Latino-centered counseling* (Delgado-Romero, 2003), that is, the notion that counselors are bound by ethics to address the needs of society, especially those who are marginalized or underrepresented. Thus, counselors and mental health professionals must ensure social justice to stay true to their ethical principles (Vasquez, 2012). Most counselors are idealistic and are motivated by a genuine desire to help others. The Multicultural

Counseling Competencies (MCC; P. Arredondo et al., 1996; D. W. Sue, Arredondo, & McDavis, 1992) and ACA (American Counseling Association) Advocacy Competencies (Lewis, Arnold, House, & Toporek, 2002) have been developed as a call to action. To engage in ethical practice, counselors should attend to Latinos in a culturally competent manner to prevent harm and malpractice and to benefit them.

Regardless of the motivation, counselors will soon have to deal with new sociocultural and demographic realities if they are not doing so now. This transformation of society has affected and will continue to affect the racial dynamics, politics, and power sharing that define the country. In other words, everything is changing, and counselors should be prepared to help address and foster that change in positive directions. Otherwise oppressive policies coupled with growing Latino and multiple-heritage populations will result in a negative future for all U.S. citizens. Counselors can be at the vanguard of positive change nationally, directing the flow of educational, correctional, and social policies to ensure a better future society and well-being for all. In this chapter, we focus on some specific areas in which counselors can have an impact now and in the future.

Training

Training counselors who are competent to work with and for the Latina/o population is vital. Training should be focused on teaching competencies and intervention methods specific to this community. Santiago-Rivera, Arredondo, and Gallardo-Cooper (2002) built on the MCC to develop Latina/o-specific competencies. For example, within the domain of counselors' awareness of their own cultural values and biases, the MCC state that culturally competent mental health providers do not just believe that self-awareness of one's culture and sensitivity to one's own cultural heritage is important. They also recognize when they themselves hold attitudes, beliefs, and values that encourage actions that show respect and valuing of difference as well as demonstrate devaluing or disrespect of differences. To this Santiago-Rivera et al. (2002) added "as this relates to clients, peers, instructors, and others in the community of Latino heritage" (p. 16). The MCC further state that mental health providers must acknowledge the basis for discomfort with dissimilarity between themselves and clients with regard to race, ethnicity, and culture (P. Arredondo et al., 1996). To this was added "and can describe those specific to individuals of Latino heritage based on real experiences and/or stereotypes they may hold" (Santiago-Rivera et al., 2002, p. 16). Further, counselors must know their hot buttons.

Within the domain of counselors' awareness of the client's worldview, the MCC stipulate that culturally competent mental health providers have specific information and knowledge about the various groups with whom they work and also have an understanding of and an ability to describe "the historical point of contact with dominant society for various ethnic groups" (P. Arredondo et al., 1996, p. 64). The Latina/o-specific competencies add that this includes Latinos of various nationalities, including Mexican, Puerto Rican, and Cuban (Santiago-Rivera et al., 2002). It is suggested that culturally competent counselors have knowledge of and understand the impact of sociopolitical pressure on the lives of Latinos, including how "immigration issues, poverty, racism, stereotyping and powerlessness may affect self-esteem and self-concept in the counseling process" (P. Arredondo et al., 1996, p. 65); it is further suggested that mental health providers understand the impact of language differences (Santiago-Rivera et al., 2002).

Within the domain of culturally appropriate intervention strategies, the MCC suggest that counselors who are culturally competent can provide explicit examples of ways they might "use intrinsic help-giving networks from a variety of client communities" (P. Arredondo et al., 1996, p. 68). Santiago-Rivera et al. (2002) added that counselors should also be able to include networks for Latino clients and from different educational and socioeconomic backgrounds. In terms of assessment instruments, the MCC mention that culturally competent practitioners understand the potential bias in these instruments and use procedures and interpretations in a way that acknowledges the linguistic and cultural characteristics of their clients (P. Arredondo et al., 1996). The Latina/o-specific competencies add that when working with Latino clients, counselors ask about language preferences and encounters with standardized testing, review the relevance of testing norms, explain how the results from a test will be used, gain supervision from culturally competent practitioners, and know the limits of interpreters and tests that are translated (Santiago-Rivera et al., 2002).

It is also noted that counselors working with the Latino population

> 1) [Can] understand the concepts and terms of *personalismo* [the valuing of personal relationships, preference for personal interactions], *familismo* [the importance of immediate and extended family ties], *respeto* [respect], *dignidad* [dignity], and *orgullo* [pride] and their meaning for relationship building with clients of Latino heritage; 2) [Can] recognize the role of spirituality and formalized religion for individual Latino clients; 3) Can determine the counseling approach that may be most suitable for the individual client based on the presenting issues(s) and expected outcomes from counseling, previous experience in counseling, levels of acculturation, migration issues, gender role socialization, socioeconomic status, educational attainment, language proficiency (e.g., level of English-language-speaking ability), and ethnic/racial identity status; 4) Can describe their own level of ethnic/racial identity as it may facilitate or impede the counseling alliance with individuals of varying Latino heritage and phenotype; 5) Can identify and modify approaches to be culturally effective. (Santiago-Rivera et al., 2002, p. 17)

Derived from feminist and multicultural approaches to counseling, Goodman et al. (2004) proposed a set of principles that could guide counseling psychologists in counseling and social justice work. We suggest that these can be modified as a Latina/o-specific set of principles that counselors can implement. Vital are ongoing self-examination and exploration in which counselors face their own stereotypes and biases toward Latinas/os, recognition of how sociohistorical and sociopolitical forces affect counselors' own and Latinas/os' multiple identities, and recognition of the role that power plays in the therapeutic relationship in work with Latinas/os. Counselors are encouraged to share power with their Latina/o clients through shared decision making. Counselors should be cognizant of the power differentials inherent in the relationship when they work with Latinas/os. Counselors also need to make a commitment to giving voice to Latinas/os, who have traditionally been marginalized and oppressed. One way this may occur is through the use of narrative approaches. Furthermore, counselors can engage in consciousness raising by helping their Latina/o clients understand how their presenting issues may be tied to historical, social, cultural, and political influences. In addition, it is vital that counselors help identify Latina/o clients' strengths, skills, and abilities as well as help Latina/o clients recognize their own competence, power, and ability to create and implement solutions to their problems. Finally, counselors should intentionally help provide access to resources for Latinas/os. A number of training videos exist that can be used to educate counselors to work with Latinas/os. Some recommended videos are listed in Appendix B.

Just as Latina/o-specific counseling competencies are important, so too are advocacy competencies. Ratts, D'Andrea, and Arredondo (2004) suggested the evolution of multicultural counseling toward social justice counseling, in which the counselor moves from merely understanding the oppressive experiences of marginalized groups to actively working to create social equity for these populations. The Advocacy Competencies (Lewis et al., 2002) encourage counselors to act with and on behalf of their clients from the individual level all the way through the macrolevel (e.g., the public arena and social policy). We believe it is very important that training also focus on developing competencies of social justice advocacy with and for Latinas/os.

Examples of Culturally Relevant Training Programs

There is a clear need to increase the Latino mental health education and training workforce, which is alarmingly small (Delgado-Romero, Espino, Werther, & González, 2012), and build the infrastructure for Latino mental health. This workforce includes not only Latino mental health workers but also culturally and linguistically competent counselors from all backgrounds. Delgado-Romero and colleagues (2012) found that bilingual mental health workers face many barriers, including inadequate training in bilingual assessment and therapy (Biever et al., 2004), a lack of resources, a lack of accreditation criteria, outdated agency policies, and exploitation (P. Arredondo, Shealy, Neale, & Winfrey, 2004; Rivas, Delgado-Romero, & Ozambela, 2005). Although programs may espouse a generalist training in multicultural work, very few programs offer specific and culturally relevant training and practicum experience in working with Latino mental health needs. Yet here we share some examples of programs from across the country and Spanish-speaking countries that do offer mental health training for work with Latino populations.

Perhaps the most prominent such program is the Psychological Services for Spanish Speaking Populations program at Our Lady of the Lake University in San Antonio, Texas. This program is accredited by the American Psychological Association and is designed to train bilingual (English/Spanish) master's and doctoral students (Biever et al., 2002). The program includes coursework such as professional and technical Spanish, language and psychological variables in interviews and assessments with Latinos, Spanish-language professional communication skills, sociocultural foundations of counseling Mexicans and Mexican Americans, culture-specific family development processes across cultures, theories of multicultural counseling, and Latino psychology. Students also can complete practicum training in Mexico, which provides an experience of cultural immersion.

Platt (2012) described a Mexico City immersion program that has been offered for 9 years through the California School of Professional Psychology, Alliant International University. This program offers both language and cultural immersion in Mexico (the country of origin of 65% of U.S. Latinos). The program's philosophical base is Freire's (1970) critical pedagogy, liberation psychology, self of the therapist, culture as shared stories, and Spanish-language education as cultural training. The program operationalizes this philosophy through labs, classes, and cultural immersion experiences. Platt reported several participants' perceptions of the immersion experience. For example, one participant stated the following:

> I have a greater understanding of what are some of the core cultural values. The program gave me an opportunity to interact with so many different types of people from elite academics to minimum wage earning laborers. It was great to be able to get so many perspectives on what their everyday lives are like from their perspective and not the stereotypical perspective promulgated by the media and other uninformed sources. (p. 361)

The Mexico City immersion program is unique in that the immersion experience is intentionally used to further participants' own awareness of self and culture as well as increase the complexity of clinicians' conceptualizations of Latino clients.

In 2012, Pepperdine University established the Center for Latina/o Communities and the program Aliento (breath). The center is founded on the principles of Gustavo Gutiérrez's liberation theology and Ignacio Martín-Baró's liberation psychology. The mission of the center is to educate, advocate, and empower Latinas/os and those professionals who work with diverse Latina/o communities. The center is dedicated to training future mental health professionals, conducting outreach to Latina/o communities, and conducting research. Aliento opened in 2013, and plans for an immersion experience, perhaps in Argentina, are still under way (M. Gallardo, personal communication, November 4, 2012; see also http://aliento.pepperdine.edu/). Clearly specific Latino-centered cultural and linguistic training needs to move from the fringes to the mainstream of counselor education.

The School Counseling program at the University of Houston–Clear Lake has been the recipient of four grants from the Office of English Language Acquisition to train Spanish-speaking teachers to become school counselors. Under the direction of Dr. Cheryl Sawyer, the program had graduated 99 bilingual counselors as of 2012 and selected another 35 to receive full scholarships for the 2013 academic year. As part of the grant, the program hosts annual conferences for teachers and counselors from the Houston–Galveston area (www.uhcl.edu/soe/BCCON). The focus is on improving the education of English language learners in the region, the majority of whom are from Spanish-speaking countries. The initiative is also supported by the Texas Counselors for Social Justice.

The Universidad del Valle in Guatemala City has partnered with many counselor educators as part of its unique master's in mental health counseling program. The program, which began in 2004, is grounded in multicultural competencies and social justice principles. Two of the authors (Arredondo and Gallardo-Cooper) have taught in the program (in Spanish), which enrolls primarily women with bilingual and bicultural experiences. One of us was asked to teach multicultural counseling; however, all of the textbooks were written with a focus on U.S. groups. Considering this unacceptable, the instructor (Arredondo) purchased books on indigenous cultures in Guatemala that were much more relevant to a multicultural course. She was able to blend information about Guatemalan worldviews with the U.S. multicultural counseling models. Because the counseling students had not previously looked inward, the course proved illuminating and challenging as well. This example is meant to suggest that counselor educators need more than just Spanish language skills to teach counseling in a Spanish-speaking country.

A feature of the Universidad del Valle program is the practicum and research experience. Students journey to the Mayan highlands and other parts of the country, home primarily to more than 26 indigenous groups who do not speak Spanish as their first language. There they become learners while attempting to identify ways to provide empowerment-based interventions for children, adolescents, and families. The program leader, Dr. María del Pilar Grazioso Rodríguez, a leader in ACA, is intentional about the preparation of indigenous community members. The counseling program has expanded to another Universidad del Valle campus (Sololá) in a highly populated indigenous region of the country. Because of its location, individuals can travel to the campus in less time than it takes to get to the capital. The master's program in Sololá has taken on a train-the-trainer orientation. That is, students take their culturally informed counseling skills back to their respective communities and teach them to others. Slowly they are creating a network of local providers who can be considered trustworthy because they speak the indigenous language.

Research

Counselors and counselor educators can contribute to culturally sensitive research concerning Latinos either directly (e.g., through dissertations and ongoing programs of research), indirectly (e.g., through service as journal editors or editorial board members), or as informed consumers of research. As we have outlined in the previous chapters, Latino-centered research is quickly emerging with increased outlets and sophistication. When conducting or evaluating research, counselors should keep in mind national heritage differences among Latinas/os as well as the following factors.

Context

As we have stated many times in this book, there is a great deal of within-group diversity in the Latina/o population. The use of panethnic or generic terms such as *Hispanic* or *Latina/o* does not provide a rich enough understanding of the population and can lead to misleading results. At a minimum, Latinos should be described in research according to salient variables such as educational attainment, acculturation status, immigration history, generation in the United States, country of origin, and region of the country where they reside or their ancestors settled. Researchers need to be increasingly specific about who the Latinas/os in their research are (e.g., Dominicans, Hondurans, Puerto Ricans) and test for generalizability rather than assuming it. At the same time, researchers need to be aware that a panethnic term like *Latino* can sometimes be adopted by second- and third-generation Latinos to represent who they are (U.S. Latinos) versus the country of origin of their parents or grandparents. Thus, the issue of identity should be examined in the proper and relevant context. Latinos may provide interesting and useful data when asked to describe themselves versus when asked to check a predefined category.

When one of the authors (Arredondo) was teaching a course on counseling Latinos to graduate students, she gave an assignment that required students to interview Latino adults. Many students chose friends or family members because they had become curious about issues of identity as discussed in the course. Through these interviews, students learned about how and why individuals self-identified as Mexican Americans, Mejicanos, Hispanics, and Chicanos. The students discovered that there is a great deal of within-group variance in identity that is often lost under the general term *Mexican*.

Underlying Assumptions

Researchers make many assumptions when conducting research, some implicit and some explicit. With regard to research with Latinos, several assumptions are harmful to Latinos and may produce inaccurate research. First, there is an assumption that research on Latinos must focus on deficits or pathology. This assumption leads to research that reaffirms negative and stereotypical views of Latinos and overlooks the roles that strengths and resilience play in optimal Latino functioning (Capielo, Mann, Nevels, & Delgado-Romero, in press; Santiago-Rivera et al., 2002). Second, there is an assumption that racial/ethnic comparisons are necessary and meaningful. Latina/o research results do not necessarily need to be compared to findings for White populations, as this sets up the dynamic of Whites as the norm. Any Latino outcomes should be interpreted through a variety of relevant comparisons (e.g., the national average).

Third, the instruments used in research must be appropriate for the Latino population; using instruments that are not validated with the Latino population is risky, as most norm groups for instruments are White, middle-class populations. Latinos may have different conceptualizations of psychological constructs that are culturally based (e.g., womanism vs. feminism; see E. Schwartz & Delgado-Romero, 2010), and using instruments based on the majority culture is not ethical practice. Fourth, language issues must be given thoughtful consideration. This involves technical concerns (e.g., translation and back-translation of instruments) as well as methodological ones (e.g., At what point do quantitative researchers translate an interview that is conducted in Spanish? Does the translation occur before or after analysis?).

Fifth, counselors should be aware that often ethnic/cultural research is held to a different standard than research with majority-White populations. S. Sue (1999) stated that psychology's overemphasis on internal as opposed to external validity has hindered the development of ethnic minority research. He suggested that all research studies address issues of external validity and explicitly specify the populations to which the findings are applicable (e.g., immigrants from Central America vs. Mexico, and time and context of immigration). He also noted that the use of qualitative and ethnographic methods should be valued in ethnic minority research and that the psychological meaning of ethnicity or race be examined in research.

Finally, Latino research should involve the cooperation of and benefit the Latino community. As a collectivist culture, Latinos are not socialized toward individual gain, and therefore the concept of giving back to (rather than exploiting) the Latino community should be considered. In addition to compensating participants, researchers might consider working with community brokers to provide psychoeducational services to the community in exchange for help with research participation.

In community research conducted in Milwaukee, an advisory board must approve the plans of university faculty (Chavez-Korell, Rendón, et al., 2012). Chavez-Korell described her approach for planning such a project. She usually approaches an agency with a research idea first. The shared discussion addresses why the work is important and how the agency and the participants will benefit. Then "we usually select measures together and revise all research questions/approaches/etc. together. Once the agency approves my final full proposal, then I submit to the [institutional review board] or apply for the grant" (personal communication, October 19, 2012).

Chavez-Korell et al. (2012) studied how to reduce barriers to the treatment of depression among Latino elders. Elders are not often the focus of Latino research, which makes this a very unique study. The study describes the importance of culture-centered engagement and the participation of family members. The publication was authored by representatives of two agencies plus Chavez-Korell, who is from the University of Wisconsin–Milwaukee, and shows how many resources researchers have to bring together to conduct ethical and culture-centered community-based research.

Evidence–Based Practice (EBP) and Research

The movement for EBP originated in the medical field. Psychologists extended the notion of EBP into clinical practice and research. One consistent criticism (Coleman & Wampold, 2003; Quintana & Atkinson, 2002) was the lack of cultural considerations in EBP and the assumption that EBP would be universally effective. That is, EBPs were developed without Latino samples and without Latino cultural considerations in mind. This oversight meant that EBP itself was culturally biased toward White populations. Bernal and Domenech Rodríguez (2012) examined cultural adaptations of EBP and proposed a model and process by which one could adapt an EBP to a cultural group. The results were unequivocal in that research demonstrated that culturally adapted interventions were more efficacious than treatment as usual and unmodified versions of EBP with cultural groups. However, they also found that there are differences in treatment with Latina women and Latino men and indicate that this is a new research pursuit.

In Chapters 9 and 10, we discussed the adequacy of culturally adapted EBPs and alternative practices. For example, indigenous therapeutic interventions facilitated by *curanderas* (healers), *espiritístas* (spiritualists), and *santeros* (spiritual healers) were discussed. It is essential to keep in mind that an individual's worldview and beliefs about getting well will influence his or her orientation to healing practices, be they Western or indigenous.

Other examples of evidence-based research and practice were discussed by Aldarondo and Becker (2011). They described a collaboration that promotes the human rights and well-being of unaccompanied immigrant minors in South Florida through the Immigrant Children Legal and Service Partnership. The collaboration brings together a number of partners—agencies and universities, including the University of Miami School of Education—to address the severity of the children's issues holistically. Aldarondo and Becker noted how important it is to work with the minors from a strengths versus deficit framework and to acknowledge the children's resiliency in the midst of trauma and uncertainty. Aldarondo also leads a migrant worker research partnership initiative that focuses on "both the help-seeking behaviors and the educational achievement in migrant worker families" (personal communication, November 2, 2012). These examples highlight the necessity of partnerships, the need to work from a social justice and positivist perspective, and the need for sociocultural and systemic approaches that benefit children and migrant workers.

Teaching

As we have stated many times throughout this book, general multicultural courses are only the starting point in teaching counselors to work effectively with Latino populations. The first decade of the 21st century saw a rise in the number of courses on Latina/o or Chicano/a issues in psychology and counseling. The National Latina/o Psychological Association (NLPA; www.nlpa.ws) is currently compiling a resource page for those who teach Latino mental health to share information across the nation. Clearly a stand-alone course in Latino psychology is not sufficient to establish competence. Thus, we advocate that Latino cultural sensitivity be infused throughout the curriculum. For example, in a history course counselors could learn about the history of Latino psychology (A. M. Padilla & Olmedo, 2009) and the development of Latino-focused organizations such as NLPA (Chavez-Korell, Delgado-Romero, & Illes, 2012). The value of bilingualism is also important to discuss. "The Cognitive Benefits of Being Bilingual" (Marian & Shook, 2012) suggests the power of bilingualism over the lifetime, particularly as it affects the brain's functioning.

Practica and internship placements are also a part of learning, and clinical teaching (supervision) must also be sensitive to Latino cultural and language issues. For example, it is not ethical for a monolingual English speaker to supervise the clinical work of a supervisee that is conducted in Spanish. NLPA has released the first draft of a predoctoral internship guide that highlights programs that offer training with Latino populations. This guide was initiated and compiled by NLPA students in an effort to identify those agencies with specific Latino training opportunities. At this point the directory is simply a listing of training opportunities reported by directors of training, but in the future it is possible that it will also highlight training that is culturally competent. It is our hope that counselor training programs in areas with large Latino populations will create specific training and practice opportunities that are culturally responsive and effective. One example of this is the work of Professor Melanie Domenech Rodríguez of Utah State University, who combines her research in culturally adapted, empirically supported treatments with training and service components.

Culturally Relevant Supervision

It is important that counselors-in-training receive appropriate supervision of their work with the Latina/o population. Existing theories of multicultural supervision can be specifically modified to address this population. Carney and Kahn (1984) developed a stage model of multicultural supervision. The primary task in Stage 1 is to facilitate the supervisees' exploration of ways in which both they and their clients have been impacted by their group memberships. Thus, supervisors help their supervisees consider their Latina/o client's multiple group memberships and how they may impact his or her lived experiences. We would suggest that this means that supervisors facilitate discussions about sociopolitical and historical factors that contribute to social injustice and marginalization, exploring the roles of power and privilege both within the supervisory relationship as well as in the counseling relationship. This might mean taking on various roles, as suggested in Chen's (2005) discriminant-type model, including teacher, counselor, supervisor, and advocate.

Various tasks are involved in Stage 2 of Carney and Kahn's (1984) model of multicultural supervision. Again, we can modify them to be specific to Latinas/os. Supervisors help supervisees become more familiar with Latina/o ethnic-racial identity theories, help identify stages of Latina/o identity development, discuss ways of interacting at various stages of Latina/o identity development, and foster awareness of and confidence in using Latina/o-specific interventions. Throughout these stages it is vital for counselors to increase their awareness of their own ethnic-racial identity as it interacts within the counseling and supervisory relationships.

In Stage 3 supervisors acknowledge the dilemmas supervisees face in wanting to work in a culturally responsive manner yet also feeling stymied by their limited professional training in working with Latinas/os. In this stage, supervisors need to support supervisees' frustration and provide opportunities for them to acquire new, culturally responsive Latina/o-specific counseling skills. In Stage 4, supervisees develop professional identities as multicultural counselors with expertise in working with the Latina/o population. Supervisors help supervisees develop a thorough understanding of the intersection of various contextual factors as they inform both their own experiences and professional identity as well as those of their Latina/o clients. In Stage 5, supervisees advocate for the rights of Latinas/os, and supervisors play the role of consultant.

Continuing Education

Continuing education for counselors and mental health workers can be used to teach culturally sensitive skills to counselors and counselor educators. At the ACA Annual Conference & Expo, there has been an increase in the number of Pre-Conference Learning Institutes and regular conference programs that address Latinas/os. Some of these programs have been delivered exclusively in Spanish. ACA President Dr. Judy Lewis had a track for Spanish-language programming during the 2001 Annual Conference & Expo in San Antonio. This was a first for ACA.

Faculty at the University of Wisconsin–Milwaukee have developed a graduate certificate program and noncredit programming in multicultural knowledge. ACA members led by Patricia Arredondo have prepared this online programming, which includes modules for counseling and working with Latinos and other groups, including the lesbian, gay, bisexual, transgender, and queer/questioning population and multiracial/multiple-heritage individuals and families (www.sce.uwm.edu). We encourage counselors to invest time, effort, and money into building their skills with the Latino population.

Opportunities for continuing education about Latinos take place at all ACA conferences and other regional and national conferences, but perhaps it is time to create a centralized calendar of these conferences. ACA is the most likely hub for cataloging annual conferences and other Latino-specific education and training programs.

Counselor educators and agency supervisors are also encouraged to use training tapes available through ACA, the American Psychological Association, and Microtraining Associates (see Appendix B). These resources contain valuable debriefing of the cultural competence elements of the encounters they highlight.

Service

The need for culturally sensitive services for the Latino population far exceeds the ability of counselors to provide such services. Counselors are encouraged to donate some services on a pro bono basis, and we suggest that service to the Latino population is worthy of these efforts. Although counselors might initially be inclined to provide clinical services, many Latino communities and families might be better served by psychoeducation, prevention work, and advocacy efforts with local government. Efforts that focus on the community are likely to have a more widespread effect than efforts that focus on a single client or family. For example, obesity has become a national problem, and Latino children and adolescents are particularly at risk. Instead of seeing an individual client, a counselor might have more impact working in a Latino cultural center, a church, or an after-school program to develop or implement a culturally responsive obesity prevention program (Sánchez-Johnsen, Hogan, Wilkens, & Fitzgibbon, 2008) or advocate for healthier lunches at Latino elementary schools. Systemic service offers several benefits. Counselors can get out of their offices and interact with the community, which prevents burnout or isolation. Also, this type of service is interdisciplinary by nature, and counselors may have a chance to interact with other professionals interested in the Latino community, such as lawyers, nurses, social workers, elected officials, and the police. These types of interactions may lead to some productive synergy that benefits the greater community.

Equity in the Mental Health Workplace

One interesting issue on the mental health landscape is the equity of Latinos and bilingual counselors. From 2002 to 2012, one of the authors (Delgado-Romero) has asked bilingual counselors whether their bilingual ability is rewarded in the workplace. The answer is almost always no. Although being bilingual and multicultural is prized, it is not often rewarded. Far from it! Bilingual individuals may be relegated to dealing with very difficult cases and may become the point person for Latino issues. This type of work has the potential for high turnover or burnout. In a survey of Latino psychologists and counselors, Clouse and Delgado-Romero (2008) found that many are the only Latinos in their workplace and that they experience high levels of emotional exhaustion, which is the first stage of burnout. Moreover, one cannot overlook the negative political biases against bilingual education since the early 1970s. In many states, particularly those with large Latino populations, such as Arizona and California, there has been anti-bilingual education legislation. This is counterproductive for counselors who know that speaking Spanish will be an asset to their effectiveness and ethical practice.

We hope that in the future bilingual and bicultural competence, especially competence gained in formal training programs, will be valued and rewarded across different work settings. ACA and its Association for Counselor Education and Supervision, Association for Multicultural Counseling and Development, and Counselors for Social Justice divisions can become the national leaders in preparing future bilingual and bicultural counselors and counselor educators. To this end, ACA can establish an office that leads the way in counseling Latino initiatives as an imperative of both self-interest and professional leadership.

International Aspects of Counseling

Counselors may work with international Latin Americans, both in Latin America and as international students in the United States. Delgado-Romero and Sanabria (2007) reviewed the counseling implications of working with international Latin American students in the United States. Counselors are likely to encounter international Latin Americans, as they make up 12% of international students. International Latin Americans may not identify with U.S. Latinos and may have little desire to acculturate to U.S. Latino culture, especially if their plans are to return to their home country. Often foreign Latino students are of different social classes and are not necessarily eager to mingle with domestic Latino students. Of course, this varies from campus to campus. That being said, foreign Latino students are subject to the same stressors as other international students and students in general.

Mental health education and training differs in Latin America (with the exception of Puerto Rico) compared to the United States. Mental health professionals usually specialize in their professions in the last 2 years of undergraduate study, and doctoral degrees in psychology are relatively rare. It is also important to know about titling differences. After 5 years of study, undergraduate students in psychology in Latin American are titled *licensiados*. This does not mean "licensed," as is the case in the United States, where students must sit for the licensed professional counselor exam. However, in Latin America *licensiados* may open a clinical practice. That being said, the number of psychologists in Latin America is growing, and estimates indicate that in the near future there will actually be more psychologists in Brazil than in the United States (Delgado-Romero, 2009).

Counselors are encouraged to read the *International Handbook of Cross-Cultural Counseling: Cultural Assumptions and Practices Worldwide* (Gerstein, Heppner, Ægisdóttir, Leung, & Norsworthy, 2009) and *Counseling Around the World: An International Handbook* (Hohenshil, Amundson, & Niles, 2013). The latter includes chapters devoted to culture-centered counseling practices as well as perspectives on mental health in several Spanish-speaking countries, including Argentina, Ecuador, Guatemala, Honduras, and Venezuela. The Gerstein et al. (2009) handbook contains a chapter on the status of counseling in Colombia (Delgado-Romero, Delgado Polo, Ardila, & Smetana, 2009).

Sociedad Interamericana de Psicología (SIP) is the psychological association for North, Central, and South America and the Caribbean (see also Chapter 11). The objective of SIP is to develop the behavioral sciences in the Western hemisphere, to further international understanding by using a broader conceptualization of cultural differences and communicating across national boundaries, and to promote research and academic and professional exchanges among the different nations of the American continent (see http://sipsych.org/index.php/es/). Counselors are encouraged to attend the SIP congress to gain an Interamerican perspective on counseling, to explore the host country and city, and to learn about other international counseling and mental health associations.

What do counselors gain from international perspectives? First, international travel and dialogue with international colleagues can counteract the effects of U.S. provincialism. The U.S. mental health system and literature tend to ignore the other 95% of the world's population, and international travel can help expand counselors' horizons. Second, exposure to different governments; standards of living; religious and spiritual traditions; concepts of gender, race, and ethnicity; foods; and other aspects of culture can help counselors understand their own culture better as well as increase awareness of and empathy for their international clients. Finally, international travel and collaboration can help break the ethnocentric encapsulation that Wrenn (1962) wrote about. If counselors can abandon socialized notions of U.S. superiority, they might then engage in a productive cross-national dialogue that may lead to mutual benefit.

Considerations for Various Settings: Knowledge Matters

Throughout this book, we have introduced different scenarios with implications for counselors in a range of settings. As professionals, counselors move from student, to professional, to specialist, and then on to advanced roles with more responsibilities. The Latino-centered counseling competencies (Santiago-Rivera et al., 2002) are essential guidelines that everyone should follow. We have also prepared a brief set of knowledge points that summarize the topics across the different chapters and hope that these will be informative to counseling professionals.

Knowledge Points for School Personnel

Counselors in K–12 schools have perhaps the most encounters with Latino students. Are there more elementary school-age Latino children now than there were 10 years ago? How has this changed school practices with parents? With so many newcomers, perhaps some adults do not speak English fluently. Counselors can play a role in recommending interpreter services or identifying resources to assist with cross-cultural encounters.

As we have noted, 1 out of every 4 children younger than 18 in the United States is of Latino heritage, and 92% are U.S. citizens (Pew Hispanic Research Center, 2012). Schools in cities with the highest number and percentage of Latinos, such as Houston, San Diego, and Chicago, may have a majority-minority student population. Moreover, in certain counties in Kansas and Oklahoma there is a concentration of Latinos with implications for K–12 schools and other county services.

The median age is 27.6 years for Latinas/os and 36.6 years for non-Latinos (Pew Hispanic Research Center, 2012). Latino parents may be younger than non-Hispanic parents and may be immigrants or nonimmigrants; assumptions cannot be made. Another factor school counselors must consider is a family's socioeconomic situation. The 2009 recession had a particularly adverse affect on Latino families. "More Latino children are living in poverty—6.1 million in 2010—than children of any other racial or ethnic group. This marks the first time in U.S. history that the single largest group of poor children is not white" (M. H. López & Velasco, 2011, p. 4).

Knowledge Points for Counselors in College Settings

With an increase in the number of Latinos going to college, counselors in college counseling and career centers need to be prepared to support many first-generation college students, particularly at community colleges and public universities. From a cost perspective, these types of institutions are more accessible to families with limited incomes. Of course, some families with more wealth may send their children to private or Ivy League institutions. The majority of students, however, will likely attend public institutions. All institutions, from community colleges to graduate education institutions, have to anticipate an increase in the enrollment of Latino students. Many will be first-generation college students, although they may be second- or third-generation family members. All colleges want to retain students and see them graduate. Latina/o students may present with issues similar to those of other college students their age or in their socioeconomic situation. However, counselors might also need to be aware of specific cultural factors or the socioeconomic background and educational achievement of the students' parents and other family members. Many Latino children attend schools that do not necessarily provide the best preparation for college. Counselors should remember this instead of blaming a client who is failing his or her general education requirements. Any counselor can uncover where a student went to high school or community college or the educational attainment of a student's parents in the relationship-building process with the student. An ethnic match is not needed to work with Latina/o college students; rather, cultural competency preparation will guide responsive and ethical practice.

If a university is in a mid-sized city in the Midwest, are the Latinos newcomers or long-time residents and citizens? For example, northwest Wisconsin is home to many Mexican-heritage families who arrived more than 50 years ago to work in the agricultural industry. Although some families migrated south in the winter to follow the crop harvest, others stayed and worked in the service industry, bought homes, and have children and grandchildren representing third and fourth generations. Clearly, not all Latinos in Wisconsin are immigrants, but some are. Counselor educators and administrators need to become informed about the local population, the diversity within the population, and the histories of these families.

Knowledge Points for Counselor Educators

Chicago has long been among the top 10 cities and metropolitan areas with a high Latino population; it currently ranks fifth. The total population of the city is 2,695,598 (Census 2010), and the Latino population is 778,662 (U.S. Census Bureau, 2010c). In Chicago, there are Puerto Rican and Mexican neighborhoods. Family members may grow up there and remain, whereas others may move to a Chicago suburb and not have the same amount of daily contact with other Puerto Ricans and Mexican-heritage neighbors. Counselor educators in the Chicago metropolitan area and in cities like New York, Houston, and Phoenix (other cities in the top 10) must bring these data to their counseling students as knowledge relevant to culturally competent preparation. The same can be said for college counseling personnel and school counselors. Counselors need to know their students and families beyond prevailing stereotypes. For example, long-term residents of Latino heritage may be monolingual English speakers and not speak Spanish at all.

Knowledge Points for Community Counselors and Administrators

Community-based agencies that deliver a range of services, including mental health counseling, must be prepared to attend to the Latino clientele at several levels.

The southern states of Alabama and South Carolina, where the Latino population has grown the fastest in recent years, are likely to be more challenged than other states to meet the needs of an increased number of Latino clients. If an agency operates on a fee-for-service basis and is located in a neighborhood where low-income Latinos reside, Latinos may seek out services at this agency.

The 2009 recession affected Latinos disproportionately, with net worth falling dramatically from $18,359 in 2005 to $6,235 in 2009 (Kochhar, Fry, & Taylor, 2011). A more recent report indicated that "from 2005–2009, inflation-adjusted wealth fell by 66% among Hispanic households and 53% among Black households, compared with just 16% among White households" (P. Taylor, Kochhar, Fry, Velasco, & Motel, 2011, p.14). First-time homeowners were especially affected. Is the agency prepared to address economic issues and payment for services sensitively and without judgment?

Are providers prepared to work with monolingual Spanish speakers, bilingual families, and/or culture-bound presenting issues (such as *nervios* [jitters, nerves])? Agencies must have a cultural and language competency framework in place to guide practices, and counselors need to be prepared to work with a range of clients and families who speak Spanish or perhaps even an indigenous language. This may provide unique opportunities for collaboration with medical personnel to better attend holistically to individuals' overall health.

Knowledge Points for Counselors Working With Military Personnel and Veterans

Counselors who work within the Veterans Administration system treat active military personnel, veterans, and/or their families. How Latinos in the military cope with trauma or other issues may be related to their cultural values and religion. The context for counseling will determine whether individual or family services can be provided.

For some undocumented Latinos, serving in the military is seen as a pathway to citizenship as well as a means of preparation for a career. Counselor sensitivity in this regard is essential, and counselors also must be knowledgeable about the pressures on veterans to provide for their families on their discharge from military service.

Knowledge Points for Counselors in Private Practice

With more Latinos graduating from college (although the percentage is still very low, 13% nationally; Fry & Lopez, 2012), career counseling is becoming a helpful intervention. Counselors need to be mindful of barriers experienced by some Latinas/os in the workplace (e.g., color barriers) and of issues that may arise from a client being the only Latina/o in the workplace. Stereotypes often portray Latinos as suitable for primarily service roles. This bias is one counselors need to address for themselves when engaged in career counseling. Latinos who have not graduated from college may experience anxiety and disappointment. Although 89% of Latinos say that college education is important for life success, only 48% report that they themselves plan to pursue a college degree (M. H. López, 2009). It is also important to keep in mind that students may not enter college or persist in higher education because of poor preparation in high school, economics, a lack of mentorship, and family responsibilities (see Chapter 5).

At the same time, counselors in private practice may see college-educated clients who are experiencing performance anxiety because of a normal learning curve in the workplace and/or because they are expected to represent all Latinas/os, for example. Thus, the focus on career counseling may become secondary to helping a client learn strategies to manage difficult workplace challenges.

Concluding Thoughts

The rationale for providing these knowledge points for counselors is to describe the multidimensionality of Latinas/os and the complex context that surrounds individuals, families, specific Latino ethnic groups, and growing communities. The obvious point is that counselors in various roles will have to become knowledgeable about Latinas/os, particularly those in their geographic location. Textbook knowledge is insufficient.

• • •

Culture–Centered Clinical Interview–Revised

Name _____ Date _____

Date of Birth _____ Gender _____

Ethnicity _____ Race _____

Marital Status:

Single ☐   Married ☐   Divorced ☐   Separated ☐   Widowed ☐

Present in Interview_____

Referral _____

Review With Client:

Counseling Process ☐   Consent ☐   Confidentiality ☐

Presenting Problem *(Complaints, behaviors, symptoms)*

- Duration of problem, symptoms
- Stressors
- Precipitating events
- Attributions/explanatory cognitions of problem/illness/condition
  (Client's statement)

Counseling/Psychological/Psychiatric History
(Dates, providers, testing results, findings)

Help-Seeking History *(Dates, providers, results)*

Counseling Objectives *(As expressed by client)*

- Objectives
- Help-seeking style fit

Medical History *(Past and present diagnoses, hospitalization, medications)*

Developmental History *(If applicable)*

Educational and Vocational *(Past and current functioning)*

Family History *(Past and current structure; mental illness/substance abuse)*

Family Kinship Network *(Who are family members?)*

Social Functioning and Relationships *(History and current functioning)*

Primary Social Network: Same Ethnicity ☐   Mixed ☐   Other ☐
Work/school: Coworkers_____   Supervisors _____
Leisure Activities: _____

Cultural Dimensions

Place of Nativity _____   Generation _____
Status _____   Places of Residence _____

Acculturation Level

Integrated ☐   Assimilated ☐   Marginalized ☐   Rejecting ☐
Native Culture Contacts: High ☐   Moderate ☐   Low ☐

Immigration History

- Premigration
- Precipitating Events
- Migration Experience
- Postmigration

Language Dimensions

Language Spoken During Interview _____

Preferred Language _____

First Language_____   Read ☐   Write ☐

Second Language_____   Read ☐   Write ☐

   At What Age Introduced? _____

   How?_____

Language Spoken at Home _____

Language Spoken at Work _____

Language of Self-Talk, Prayer _____

Language of Emotions _____

Code-Switching ☐   Themes Associated With Code-Switching: _____

Sociopolitical Dimensions

- Ethnic Identity
- Acculturative Stress
- Other Sources of Stress

Residency ☐   Immigration ☐   Vocational/Educational ☐   Language ☐
Legal ☐   Oppression ☐   Racism ☐   Prejudice ☐   Economics ☐
Gender ☐   Ethno-support ☐   Familial ☐   Marital ☐ Other ☐ _____

Spiritual Dimensions/Religion _____

Practicing ☐   Nonpracticing ☐

Church Name/Spiritual Guide _____

Folk Healer_____

Spiritual Attributions_____

Substance Abuse Assessment *(History, frequency, current use, drug preferences)*

Risk Assessment

Suicide

☐ History _____

☐ Current _____

Violence

☐ History _____

☐ Current _____

Victim

☐ History _____

☐ Current _____

Perpetrator

☐ History _____

☐ Current _____

Assets and Barriers to Treatment

Personal Strengths_____

Cultural Strengths _____

Barriers_____

Community Resources_____

Observations During Interview

Clinical and Cultural Impressions

Culture-Bound Syndromes

Cultural Formulation *(DSM)*

Preliminary Diagnoses

Axis I

Axis II

Axis III

Axis IV

Initial Treatment Plan
- Individual
- Systemic Ecological
- Referral
- Cultural Accommodations

Risk Plan

_____

Provider

_____

Date

Source. Adapted from Gallardo-Cooper (2001a).

Appendix B

Latino
Mental Health Resources

Acosta, H., Guarnaccia, P. J., & Martinez, I. (2003). *Model mental health program for Hispanics.* Mercerville: New Jersey Mental Health Institute.

> This report based on case examples gives an overview of steps that can be taken to improve the quality and access of mental health services for Latinos.

American Counseling Association (Producer). (2004). *Professional counseling's living legends, presented by American Counseling Association* [Motion picture]. (Available from the American Counseling Association, 5599 Stevenson Ave., Alexandria, VA 22304)

> This video features five individuals recognized as Living Legends at the 2004 American Counseling Association Conference & Expo, which was hosted by then-president Mark Pope. Individuals were recognized for their leadership and scholarship in major areas of counseling. The legends and their areas of expertise are Jon Carlson (marriage and family counseling), Albert Ellis (cognitive behavior therapy), Gerald Glasser (reality therapy), John Krumboltz (vocational counseling), and Patricia Arredondo (multicultural counseling).

American Counseling Association (Producer). (2006). *La Conmovisión de Latinos/as en la Consjería/Latino worldviews in counseling, hosted by Patricia Arredondo and Jon Carlson* [Motion picture]. (Available from the American Counseling Association, 5599 Stevenson Ave., Alexandria, VA 22304)

> The first and only training video in Spanish. Patricia Arredondo moderates a discussion with two counselors demonstrating work with clients in Spanish.

American Psychological Association. (2005). *Counseling Latina/Latino clients with Patricia Arredondo.* [Motion picture]. (Available from American Psychological Association, 750 First St. NE, Washington, DC 20002-4242)

> In this training video, Patricia Arredondo provides a mock counseling scenario with a client who is Latina. The session is hosted by Jon Carlson.

American Psychological Association. (2012). *Crossroads: The psychology of immigration in the new century.* Retrieved from http://www.apa.org/topics/immigration/executive-summary.pdf

> This report was commissioned by Melba Vasquez, the first Latina and first woman of color to be elected president of the American Psychological Association. The report was one of her presidential priorities.

Andres-Hyman, R. C., Ortiz, J., Anez, L. M., Paris, M., & Davidson, L. (2006). Culture and clinical practice: Recommendations for working with Puerto Ricans and other Latinas/os in the United States. *Professional Psychology, 37,* 694–701.

> This article articulates clinical practices based on the literature on working with people of Hispanic heritage, with an emphasis on urban Puerto Ricans.

Arredondo, P. (2005). *Counseling Latina/Latino clients* [Multicultural counseling video series]. (Available from the American Psychological Association, 750 First St. NE, Washington, DC 20002-4242)

> This video provides guidelines for Latino-centered counseling as well as includes a session in which a therapist is working with a Latino client.

Aviera, A. (n.d.). *Culturally sensitive and creative therapy with Latino clients.* Retrieved from http://search.apa.org/search?query=working%20with%20latinos

> This is a brief statement on some culturally sensitive interventions and guidelines for working with Latino clients.

Bandy, T., & Moore, K. (2011). *What works for Latino/Hispanic children and adolescents: Lessons from experiential evaluations of programs and interventions* [Fact sheet]. Washington, DC: Child Trends.

> This document briefly outlines the researchers' findings on what works for Latina/o kids in six outcome areas: substance use, academic achievement, reproductive health and sexuality, physical health and nutrition, externalizing behavior, and social skills.

Buki, L. P., & Piedra, L. M. (Eds.). (2009). *Creating infrastructure for Latino mental health.* New York, NY: Springer.

> This book discusses an interdisciplinary approach to understanding Latino mental health and systemic barriers.

Center for Advanced Studies in Child Welfare. (2010). *Latino cultural guide: Building capacity to strengthen the well-being of immigrant families and their children: A prevention strategy.* Minneapolis: University of Minnesota School of Social Work.

> This brief offers research-based tips for working with Latino immigrants.

Council of National Psychology Associations for the Advancement of Ethnic Minority Interests. (2000). *Guidelines for research in ethnic minority communities.* Washington, DC: American Psychological Association. Available at www.apa.org/pi/oema/resources/cnpaaemi-guidelines.pdf

> This resource provides separate guidelines for researching ethnic groups, including Latinos.

Council of National Psychology Associations for the Advancement of Ethnic Minority Interests. (2009). *Psychology education and training from culture-specific and multiracial perspectives.* Washington, DC: American Psychological Association.

> This resource provides separate guidelines for training ethnic groups, including Latinos. It is authored by members of ethnic minority psychological associations themselves, including the National Latina/o Psychological Association.

McNeill, B. W., & Cervantes, J. M. (Eds.). (2008). *Latina/o healing traditions: Mestizo and indigenous perspectives.* New York, NY: Routledge.

> This book identifies and discusses indigenous and ancestral healing among Latinos.

Microtraining Associates (Producer). (1993). *Cultural consideration for working more effectively with Latin Americans* [Motion picture]. (Available from Microtraining Associates, 25 Burdette Ave., Framingham, MA 01702)

> Four mock counseling sessions with Latino clients are demonstrated in English. Moderator Patricia Arredondo discusses Latino values at the beginning and end of the sessions and debriefs the mock counseling sessions with the therapist and client actors. This training tape promotes Latino-specific competencies (awareness, knowledge, and skills) for counselors.

Microtraining Associates (Producer). (1994). *Specifics of practice for counseling with Latinas/os* [Motion picture]. (Available from Microtraining Associates, 25 Burdette Ave., Framingham, MA 01702)

> This lecture touches on Latino historical factors, issues for immigrants, Latino values, and issues faced by contemporary Latinas/os. The lecture, given by Patricia Arredondo, promotes Latino-specific knowledge building.

Microtraining Associates (Producer). (1999). *Innovative approaches for culture-specific counseling* [Motion picture]. (Available from Microtraining Associates, 25 Burdette Ave., Framingham, MA 01702)

> This five-part series provides demonstrations of counseling with persons and families of African American, Asian, Latina/o, Native American, and multiracial heritage. Designed to promote multicultural and culture-specific competencies, the sessions are cohosted by Patricia Arredondo and Allen Ivey.

Microtraining Associates (Producer). (2002). *Mujeres Latinas—Santas y marquesas* [Motion picture]. (Available from Microtraining Associates, 25 Burdette Ave., Framingham, MA 01702)

> Patricia Arredondo delivers her American Psychological Association Division 45 presidential address dedicated to Latina women. She provides a historical discussion of Latina gender socialization and how this influences women's self-identity, perceptions of opportunities, and ways to lead as informed by religion and protocols of high expectations.

Microtraining Associates (Producer). (2004). *Contemporary counseling with Latinos* [Motion picture]. (Available from Microtraining Associates, 25 Burdette Ave., Framingham, MA 01702)

> Patricia Arredondo delivers a contemporary discussion of Latinas/os in the United States informed by 2000 Census data and changes in U.S. society. It is an updated version of the lecture in the 1994 training video *Specifics of Practice for Counseling With Latinas/os.*

Microtraining Associates (Producer). (2008). *Counseling with immigrants* [Motion picture]. (Available from Microtraining Associates, 25 Burdette Ave., Framingham, MA 01702)

> A lecture that promotes cultural competency for working with immigrants in counseling settings. Patricia Arredondo discusses models for the immigration process and the emotions that result from such a major process of loss and change. The discussion touches on acculturative stress, intergenerational differences in immigrant families, and the awareness- and knowledge-based competencies required for effective counseling practices.

Microtraining Associates (Producer). (2008). *Team-BAS (basic attending skills)* [Motion picture]. (Available from Microtraining Associates, 25 Burdette Ave., Framingham, MA 01702)

> Team-BAS is built upon the microtraining model in counseling. This version is in Spanish and English.

Munsey, C. (2009). *Working with Latino clients.* Retrieved from http://www.apa.org/gradpsych/2009/11/latino-clients.aspx

> This article offers guidelines to help training programs better prepare students to work with Latino clients.

Office of Ethnic Minority Affairs, American Psychological Association. (n.d.). *Resources and publications.* Retrieved from http://www.apa.org/pi/oema/resources

> This website contains many resources, including some that specifically address Latino concerns, such as guidelines for working with linguistically diverse populations and research in ethnic minority communities.

Organista, K. C. (2007). *Solving Latino psychosocial and health problems: Theory, practice, and populations.* Hoboken, NJ: Wiley.

> This book offers best practices for working with Latinos on psychological and health issues.

Ramírez, M. (1998). *Multicultural/multiracial psychology: Mestizo perspectives in personality and mental health.* Northvale, NJ: Jason Aronson.

> This book offers a look at assessment and psychology from a mestizo vantage point.

Rice-Rodriguez, T., & Boyle, D. (2007). *Culturally competent practice with Latino families.* Retrieved from http://dfcs.dhr.georgia.gov/DHR-DFCS/DHR_DFCS-Edu/Files/Latino%20Module%201%20participant%20guide%204-25-07.pdf

> This training manual for child welfare workers developed for the Georgia Division of Family and Children's Services contains an overview of practices that people in human services can use in work with Latino families.

Velasquez, R. J., Arellano, L. M., & McNeill, B. W. (2004). *The handbook of Chicana/o psychology and mental health.* New York, NY: Routledge.

> This book presents a comprehensive look at the psychology of the Chicano experience.

Villarruel, F. A., Carlo, G., Grau, J. M., Azmitia, M., Cabrera, N. J., & Chahin, T. J. (Eds.). (2009). *Handbook of U.S. Latino psychology: Developmental and community-based perspectives.* Thousand Oaks, CA: Sage.

> This book discusses the psychological developments and adaptations of Latinos in America.

Workgroup on Adapting Latino Services. (2008). *Adaptation guidelines for serving Latino children and families affected by trauma* (1st ed.). San Diego, CA: Chadwick Center for Children and Families.

> This document offers guidelines for making regular trauma programs more culturally relevant.

Yancey, G. (2003). *Who is White? Latinos, Asians, and the new Black/nonBlack divide.* Boulder, CO: Lynne Rienner.

> This book explores the Whitening of racial groups other than Blacks.

References

Abalos, D. T. (2002). *The Latino male: A radical redefinition.* Boulder, CO: Lynne Rienner.

Abraído-Lanza, A. F., Viladrich, A., Flórez, K. R., Céspedes, A., Aguirre, A. N., & De La Cruz, A. A. (2007). Commentary: Fatalismo reconsidered: A cautionary note for health-related research and practice with Latino populations. *Ethnicity & Disease, 17,* 153–158.

Acevedo-Polakovich, I. D., & Gering, C. (2009). Case illustration: Evidenced-based practice with Latina/o adolescents and families. In M. Gallardo, C. J. Ych, J. E. Trimble, & T. Parham (Eds.), *Culturally adaptive counseling skills: Demonstrations of evidence-based practices* (pp. 113–125). Thousand Oaks, CA: Sage.

Acosta-Belén, E., & Sjostrom, B. R. (1988). *The Hispanic experience in the United States: Contemporary issues and perspectives.* New York, NY: Praeger.

Adeponle, A. B., Thombs, B. D., Groleau, D., Jarvis, E., & Kirmayer, L. J. (2012). Using the cultural formulation to resolve uncertainty in diagnoses of psychosis among ethnoculturally diverse patients. *Psychiatric Services, 63*(2), 147–153.

Aguilera, A., & López, S. (2008). Community determinants of Latinos' use of mental health services. *Psychiatric Services, 59,* 408–413.

Alarcón, R. D. (2009a). Culture, cultural factors and psychiatric diagnosis: Review and projections. *World Psychiatry, 8,* 131–139.

Alarcón, R. D. (2009b). Hacia nuevos sistemas de diagnóstico: Proceso, preguntas y dilemas [Towards new diagnostic systems: Process, questions and dilemmas]. *Revista de Psiquiatría y Salud Mental, 3*(2), 37–39.

Alarcón, R. D., Alegría, M., Bell, C. C., Boyce, C., Kirmayer, L. J., Lin, K. M., . . . Wisner, K. L. (2002). Beyond the funhouse mirrors: Research agenda on culture and psychiatric diagnosis. In D. Kupfer, M. B. First, & D. E. Regier (Eds.), *A research agenda for* DSM-V (pp. 219–282). Washington, DC: American Psychiatric Association.

Aldarondo, E., & Becker, R. (2011). Promoting the well-being of unaccompanied immigrant minors. In L. Buki & L. Piedra (Eds.), *Creating infrastructures for Latino mental health.* New York, NY: Springer.

Alegría, M., Atkins, M., Farmer, E., Slaton, E., & Stelk, W. (2010). One size does not fit all: Taking diversity, culture and context seriously. *Administration and Policy in Mental Health and Mental Health Services Research, 37*(1–2), 48–60.

Alegría, M., Canino, G., Ríos, R., Vera, M., Calderón, J., Rusch, D., & Ortega, A. N. (2002). Mental health care for Latinos: Inequalities in use of specialty mental health services among Latinos, African Americans, and non-Latino Whites. *Psychiatric Services, 53,* 1547–1555.

Alegría, M., Canino, G., Shrout, P. E., Woo, M., Duan, N., Vila, D., . . . Meng, X. (2008). Prevalence of mental illness in immigrant and non-immigrant U.S. Latino groups. *American Journal of Psychiatry, 165,* 359–369.

Alegría, M., Shrout, P. E., Torres, M., Lewis-Fernández, R., Abelson, J. M., Powell, M., . . . Canino, G. (2009). Lessons learned from the clinical reappraisal study of the Composite International Diagnostic Interview with Latinos. *International Journal of Methods in Psychiatric Research, 18*(2), 84–95.

Alegria, M., Shrout, P. E., Woo, M., Guarnaccia, P., Scribney, W., Polo, A., . . . Canino, G. (2007). Understanding differences in past year psychiatric disorders for Latinos living in the U.S. *Social Science & Medicine, 65,* 214–230.

Alemán, E. (2009). Through the prism of critical race theory: "Niceness" and Latina/o leadership in the politics of education. *Journal of Latinos & Education, 8,* 290–311.

Alemán, E., & Alemán, S. (2010). "Do latin@ interests always have to 'converge' with White interests?": (Re)claiming racial realism and interest-convergence in critical race theory praxis. *Race, Ethnicity and Education, 13*(1), 1–21.

Alexandre, P. K., Martins, S., & Richard, P. (2009). Disparities in adequate mental health care for past-year major depressive episodes among Caucasian and non-Hispanic youth. *Psychiatric Services, 60,* 1365–1371.

Alfaro, E., & Umaña-Taylor, A. (2010). Latino adolescents' academic motivation: The role of siblings. *Hispanic Journal of Behavioral Sciences, 32,* 549–570.

Almeida, R. V. (2003). Creating collectives of liberation. In L. B. Silverstein & T. J. Goodrich (Eds.), *Feminist family therapy: Empowerment in social context* (pp. 293–305). Washington, DC: American Psychological Association. doi:10.1037/10615-022

Altarriba, J. (2002). Bilingualism: Language, memory and applied issues. *Online Readings in Psychology and Culture, 4*(2). http://dx.doi.org/10.9707/2307-0919.1034

Altarriba, J., & Santiago-Rivera, A. L. (1994). Current perspectives on using linguistic and cultural factors in counseling the Hispanic client. *Professional Psychology: Research and Practice, 25,* 388–397.

Alvarado, G. C. (2011). *Best practices in the special education evaluation of students who are culturally and linguistically diverse, revised 2011.* Retrieved from http://www.educationeval.com/files/Best_Practices_2011.pdf

Alvarez, A. N., & Helms, J. E. (2001). Racial identity and reflected appraisals as influences on Asian Americans' racial adjustment. *Cultural Diversity and Ethnic Minority Psychology, 7,* 217–231.

Alvarez McHatton, P. (2007). Listening and learning from Mexican and Puerto Rican single mothers of children with disabilities. *Teacher Education and Special Education, 30,* 237–248.

American Counseling Association. (2005). *ACA code of ethics.* Alexandria, VA: Author.

American Enterprise Institute. (2011). *2011 annual report.* Washington, DC: Author.

American Psychiatric Association. (2000). *Diagnostic and statistical manual of mental disorders* (4th ed., text rev.). Washington, DC: Author.

American Psychological Association. (2002a). *Ethical principles of psychologists and code of conduct.* Washington, DC: Author.

American Psychological Association. (2002b). *Guidelines on multicultural education, training, research, practice, and organizational change for psychologists.* Washington, DC: Author.

American Psychological Association. (2003). Guidelines on multicultural education, training, research, practice, and organizational change for psychologists. *American Psychologist, 58,* 377–402. doi:10.1037/0003-066X.58.5.377

American Psychological Association Presidential Task Force on Evidence-Based Practice. (2006). Evidenced-based practice in psychology. *American Psychologist, 61,* 271–285.

Anderson, E. R., & Mayes, L. C. (2007). Race/ethnicity and internalizing disorders in youth: A review of the literature. *Clinical Psychology Review, 30,* 338–348.

Andrade, R. (1992). Machismo: A universal malady. *Journal of American Culture, 15*(4), 33–41.

Añez, L., Silva, M., Paris, M., & Bedregal, L. (2008). Engaging Latinos through the integration of cultural values and motivational interviewing principles. *Professional Psychology: Research and Practice, 39*(2), 153–159.

Anti-Latino hate crimes spike in California. (2011, Winter). *Intelligence Report, 144.* Retrieved from http://www.splcenter.org/get-informed/intelligence-report/browse-all-issues/2011/winter/anti-latino-hate-crimes-spike-in-cali#.UYcSD-JVH0WZ

Antshel, K. M. (2002). Integrating culture as a means of improving treatment adherence in the Latino population. *Psychology, Health, & Medicine, 7,* 435–449.

Anzaldúa, G. (1987). *Borderlands/La frontera: The new mestiza.* San Francisco, CA: Aunt Lute Books.

Arbona, C., & Nora, A. (2007). The influence of academic and environmental factors on Hispanic college degree attainment. *Review of Higher Education, 30,* 247–269.

Arciniega, G., Anderson, T. C., Tovar-Blank, Z. G., & Tracey, T. G. (2008). Toward a fuller conception of machismo: Development of a traditional machismo and caballerismo scale. *Journal of Counseling Psychology, 55*(1), 19–33. doi:10.1037/0022-0167.55.1.19

Arciniega, G. M., Gallardo-Cooper, M., Santana-Pellicier, A., Tovar-Blank, Z. G., Poloskov, E., & Estrada, F. (2010, March). *Exemplary practices and clinical applications of Latino counseling competencies.* Learning Institute at the ACA 2010 Conference & Expo, Pittsburgh, PA.

Arciniega, G. M., Tovar-Gamero, Z. G., & Sand, J. (2004, February). *Machismo and marianismo: Definitions, instrumentation, and clinical relevance.* Workshop presented at the Relevance of Assessment and Culture in Evaluation Conference, Tempe, AZ.

Arias, E. (2010). United States life tables by Hispanic origin. *Vital and Health Statistics, 2*(152). Retrieved from http://www.cdc.gov/nchs/data/series/sr_02/sr02_152.pdf

Aron, A., & Corne, S. (Eds.). (1996). *Ignacio Martín-Baró: Writings for a liberation psychology.* Cambridge, MA: Harvard University Press.

Arredondo, G. F., Hurtado, A., Klahn, N., Nájera-Ramírez, O., & Zavella, P. (2003). Introduction: Chicana feminisms at the crossroads: Disruptions in dialogue. In G. F. Arredondo, A. Hurtado, N. Klahn, O. Nájera-Ramírez, & P. Zavella (Eds.), *Chicana feminisms: A critical reader* (pp. 1–18). Durham, NC: Duke University Press.

Arredondo, P. (1986). Immigration as an historical moment leading to an identity crisis. *Journal of Counseling & Human Services, 1,* 79–87.

Arredondo, P. (2002a). Counseling individuals from specialized marginalized and underserved groups. In P. Pedersen, J. G. Draguns, W. J. Lonner, & J. E. Trimble (Eds.), *Counseling across cultures* (5th ed., pp. 233–250). Thousand Oaks, CA: Sage.

Arredondo, P. (2002b). Mujeres Latinas: Santas y marquesas. [Latina women: Saints and royalty.] *Cultural Diversity & Ethnic Minority Psychology, 8*(4), 308–319.

Arredondo, P. (2006). Multicultural competencies and family therapy strategies with Latino families. In R. L. Smith & E. Montilla (Eds.), *Counseling and family therapy with Latino populations: Strategies that work* (pp. 77–95). New York, NY: Routledge.

Arredondo, P. (2010). Pathways to cultural malpractice: Shortcomings in professional psychology education and training programs. *Professional Psychology: Research and Practice, 41*(3), 217–218.

Arredondo, P. (2011). The "borderlands" experience for women of color as higher education leaders. In J. L. Martin (Ed.), *Women as leaders in education* (pp. 275–298). Santa Barbara, CA: Praeger.

Arredondo, P., & Castellanos, J. (2003). Latinas and the professoriate: An interview with Patricia Arredondo. In J. Castellanos & L. Jones (Eds.), *The majority in the minority: Expanding the representation of Latina/o faculty, administrators, and students in higher education* (pp. 221–239). Sterling, VA: Stylus.

Arredondo, P., & Castillo, L. G. (2011). Latina/o student achievement: A collaborative mission of professional associations of higher education. *Journal of Hispanic Higher Education, 10,* 6–17. doi:10.1177/1538192710391907

Arredondo, P., & Glauner, T. (1992). *Personal dimensions of identity model.* Boston, MA: Empowerment Workshops.

Arredondo, P., Psalti, A., & Cella, K. (1993). The woman factor in multicultural counseling. *Counseling and Human Development, 25*(8), 1–8.

Arredondo, P., & Santiago-Rivera, A. (2000). *Latino dimensions of personal identity (adapted from Personal Dimensions of Identity Model).* Unpublished manuscript.

Arredondo, P., Shealy, C., Neale, M., & Winfrey, L. L. (2004). Consultation and interprofessional collaboration: Modeling for the future. *Journal of Clinical Psychology, 60,* 787–800.

Arredondo, P., Toporek, M. S., Brown, S., Jones, J., Locke, D. C., Sanchez, J., & Stadler, H. (1996). Operationalization of the Multicultural Counseling Competencies. *Journal of Multicultural Counseling and Development, 24,* 42–78.

Arredondo, P., Tovar-Blank, Z. G., & Parham, T. A. (2008). Challenges and promises of becoming a culturally competent counselor in a sociopolitical era of change and empowerment. *Journal of Counseling & Development, 86*(3), 261–268.

Arredondo-Dowd, P. (1981). Personal loss and grief as a result of immigration. *The Personnel and Guidance Journal, 59*(6), 376–378.

Arreola, S. G. (2010). Latina/o childhood sexuality. In M. Asencio (Ed.), *Latina/o sexualities: Probing powers, passions, practices and policies* (pp. 48–61). New Brunswick, NJ: Rutgers University Press.

Artenstein, I. (Producer), & Arau, S. (Director). (2004). *A day without a Mexican* [Motion picture]. United States: Eye on the Ball Films.

Asencio, M., & Acosta, K. (2010). Mapping Latina/o sexualities: Research and scholarship. In M. Asencio (Ed.), *Latina/o sexualities: Probing powers, passions, practices and policies* (pp. 1–12). New Brunswick, NJ: Rutgers University Press.

Aviera, A. (1996). "Dichos" therapy group: A therapeutic use of Spanish language proverbs with hospitalized Spanish-speaking psychiatric patients. *Cultural Diversity and Mental Health, 2*(2), 73–87.

Ayón, C., Marsiglia, F. F., & Bermudez-Parsai, M. (2010). Latino family mental health: Exploring the role of discrimination and familismo. *Journal of Community Psychology, 38,* 742–756.

Azmitia, M., & Brown, J. R. (2002). Latino immigrant parents' beliefs about the "path of life" of their adolescent children. In J. M. Contreras, K. A. Kerns, & A. M. Neal-Barnett (Eds.), *Latino children and families in the United States: Current research and future directions* (pp. 77–106). Westport, CT: Praeger.

Baker-Ericzén, M. J., Connelly, C. D., Hazen, A. L., Dueñas, C., Landsverk, J. A., & Horwitz, S. M. (2012). A collaborative care telemedicine intervention to overcome treatment barriers for Latina women with depression during the perinatal period. *Families, Systems, & Health, 30*(3), 224–240. doi:10.1037/a0028750

Bamford, K. W. (1991). Bilingual issues in mental health assessment and treatment. *Hispanic Journal of Behavioral Sciences, 13*(4), 377–390.

Battle, J. J. (1997). Academic achievement among Hispanic students from one-versus dual-parent households. *Hispanic Journal of Behavioral Sciences, 19,* 156–166.

Bauer, A. M., & Alegría, M. (2010). Impact of patient language proficiency and interpreter service use on the quality of psychiatric care: A systematic review. *Psychiatric Services, 61,* 765–773.

Bauer, A. M., Chen, C. N., & Alegría, M. (2010). English language proficiency and mental health service use among Latino and Asian Americans with mental disorders. *Medical Care, 48,* 1097–1104.

Baumrind, D. (1966). Effects of authoritative parental control on child behavior. *Child Development, 37,* 887–907.

Baxter, R. (n.d.). *USA Patriot Act facts uncovered.* Retrieved from http://general-law.knoji.com/u-s-a-patriot-act-facts-uncovered/

Bean, R. A., Perry, B., & Bedell, T. M. (2001). Developing culturally competent marriage and family therapists: Guidelines for working with Hispanic families. *Journal of Marital & Family Therapy, 27,* 43–54.

Berkel, C., Knight, G. P., Zeiders, K. H., Tein, J. Y., Roosa, M. W., Gonzales, N. A., & Saenz, D. (2010). Discrimination and adjustment for Mexican American adolescents: A prospective examination of the benefits of culturally related values. *Journal of Research on Adolescence, 20,* 893–915.

Bermúdez, J. M., & Bermúdez, S. (2002). Altar making with Latino families: A narrative therapy perspective. *Journal of Family Psychotherapy, 13,* 329–347. doi:10.1300/J085v13n03_06

Bermúdez, J. M., Kirkpatrick, D. R., Hecker, L., & Torres-Robles, C. (2010). Describing Latinos families and their help-seeking attitudes: Challenging the family therapy literature. *Contemporary Family Therapy, 32*(2), 155–172.

Bernal, G. (2006). Intervention development and cultural adaptation research with diverse families. *Family Process, 45,* 143–152.

Bernal, G., & Domenech Rodríguez, M. (2009). Advances in Latino family research: Cultural adaptations of evidence-based interventions. *Family Process, 48*(2), 169–178.

Bernal, G., & Domenech Rodríguez, M. (2012). *Cultural adaptations: Tools for evidenced-based practice with diverse populations.* Washington, DC: American Psychological Association.

Bernal, G., Jiménez-Chafey, M., & Domenech Rodríguez, M. (2009). Cultural adaptation of treatments: A resource for considering culture in evidence-based practice. *Professional Psychology: Research and Practice, 40*(4), 361–368.

Bernal, G., & Sáez-Santiago, E. (2006). Culturally centered psychosocial interventions. *Journal of Community Psychology, 34*(2), 121–132. doi:10.1002/jcop.20096

Bernal, G., Sáez-Santiago, E., & Galloza-Carrero, A. (2009). Evidence-based approaches to working with Latino youth and families. In F. A. Villarruel, G. Carlo, J. M. Grau, M. Azmitia, N. J. Cabrera, & T. J. Chahin (Eds.), *Handbook of U.S. Latino psychology: Developmental and community-based perspectives* (pp. 309–328). Thousand Oaks, CA: Sage.

Bernal, G., & Scharró-del-Río, M. R. (2001). Are empirically supported treatments valid for ethnic minorities? Toward an alternative approach for treatment research. *Cultural Diversity and Ethnic Minority Psychology, 7*(4), 328–342. doi:10.1037/1099-9809.7.4.328

Berry, J. W. (1980). Acculturation as varieties of adaptation. In A. Padilla (Ed.), *Acculturation: Theory, models and findings* (pp. 9–25). Boulder, CO: Westview Press.

Berry, J. W. (1997). Immigration, acculturation, and adaptation. *Applied Psychology, 46*, 5–68.

Berry, J. W. (2003). Conceptual approaches to acculturation. In K. Chung, P. B. Organista, & G. Marín (Eds.), *Acculturation advances in theory, measurement and applied research* (pp. 17–37). Washington, DC: American Psychological Association.

Beutler, L. E., Consoli, A., & Lane, G. (2005). Systematic treatment selection and prescriptive psychotherapy. In J. Norcross & M. R. Goldfried (Eds.), *Handbook of psychotherapy integration* (pp. 121–143). New York, NY: Oxford University Press.

Bialystok, E. (2011). Reshaping the mind: The benefits of bilingualism. *Canadian Journal of Experimental Psychology, 65*, 229–235.

Biever, J. L., Castaño, M. T., de la Fuentes, C., González, C., Servín-López, S., Sprowls, C., & Tripp, C. G. (2002). The role of language in training psychologists to work with Hispanic clients. *Professional Psychology: Research and Practice, 33*, 330–336.

Biever, J. L., Castaño, M. T., González, C., Levy-Navarro, R., Sprowls, C., & Verdinelli, S. (2004). Spanish-language psychotherapy: Therapists' experiences and needs. *Advances in Psychology Research, 29*, 157–182.

Blustein, D. L. (2006). *The psychology of working: A new perspective for career development, counseling, and public policy.* Mahwah, NJ: Erlbaum.

Blustein, D. L. (2008). The role of work in psychological health and well-being: A conceptual, historical, and public policy perspective. *American Psychologist, 63*(4), 228–240. doi:10.1037/0003-066X.63.4.228

Booth, W. (1995, July 2). God help us all at Miami Courthouse: A chicken in every spot. *The Washington Post*, p. F1.

Borrayo, E. A., Goldwaser, G., Vacha-Haase, T., & Hepburn, K. W. (2007). An inquiry into Latino caregivers' experience caring for older adults with Alzheimer's disease and related dementias. *Journal of Applied Gerontology, 26*, 486–505.

Bowe, J. (2007). *Nobodies.* New York, NY: Random House.

Bracero, W. (1998). Intimidades [Intimacies]. *Cultural Diversity and Mental Health, 4*(4), 264–277.

Bradford, D. T., & Muñoz, A. (1993). Translation in bilingual psychotherapy. *Professional Psychology: Research and Practice, 24*(1), 52–61.

Bray, I. (n.d.). *Asylum or refugee status: Who is eligible?* Retrieved from http://www.nolo.com/legal-encyclopedia/asylum-or-refugee-status-who-32298.html

Bronfenbrenner, U. (1979). *The ecology of human development: Experiments by nature and design* (1st ed.). Cambridge, MA: Harvard University Press.

Bronfenbrenner, U., & Morris, P. A. (1998). The ecology of developmental processes. In W. Damon & R. M. Lerner (Eds.), *Handbook of child psychology: Vol. 1. Theoretical models of human development* (5th ed., pp. 993–1028). Hoboken, NJ: John Wiley.

Brooks, A. J., Stuewig, J., & Lecroy, C. W. (1998). A family based model of Hispanic adolescent substance abuse. *Journal of Drug Education, 28*, 65–86.

Brown, A., & Delgado, E. A. (2010, November). *Psychology degree programs at Hispanic serving institutions.* Poster presented at the National Latina/o Psychological Association Conference. San Antonio, TX.

Bullock, K. (2005). Ahora le voy a cuidar mis nietos: Rural Latino grandparents raising grandchildren of alcohol and other drug abusing parents. *Alcoholism Treatment Quarterly, 23*, 107–130.

Bureau of Justice. (2009). *Prisoners in 2009.* Retrieved from http://www.bjs.gov/index.cfm?ty=pbdetail&iid=2232

Bureau of Labor Statistics. (2011, September 14). *Earnings and employment by occupation, race, ethnicity, and sex, 2010.* Retrieved from http://www.bls.gov/opub/ted/2011/ted_20110914.htm

Bureau of Labor Statistics. (2012a, August). *Labor force characteristics by race and ethnicity, 2011.* Retrieved from http://bls.gov/cps/cpsrace2011.pdf

Bureau of Labor Statistics. (2012b, September). *National Hispanic Heritage Month.* Retrieved from http://bls.gov/spotlight/2012/hispanic_heritage/pdf/hispanic_heritage_bls_spotlight.pdf

Burnam, M. A., Telles, C. A., Karno, M., Hough, R. L., & Escobar, J. I. (1987). Measurement of acculturation in a community population of Mexican Americans. *Hispanic Journal of Behavioral Sciences, 9*(2), 105–130.

Burns, K. Novick, L. (Producers), & Ward, G. C. (Writer). (2007). *The war* [Documentary]. United States: Public Broadcasting Service.

Byler, C. G. (2013). *Fatal injuries to Hispanic/Latino workers.* Retrieved from http://www.bls.gov/opub/mlr/2013/02/art2full.pdf

Cabrera, N. J., Aldoney, D., & Tamis-LeMonda, C. S. (2013). Latino fathers. In N. J. Cabrera & C. S. Tamis-LeMonda (Eds.), *Handbook of father involvement: Multidisciplinary perspectives* (2nd ed., pp. 244–260). New York, NY: Routledge.

Cabrera, N. J., & Bradley, R. H. (2012). Latino fathers and their children. *Child Development Perspectives, 6,* 232–238.

Cabrera, N., Ryan, R., Mitchell, S., Shannon, J., & Tamis-LeMonda, C. (2008). Low-income, nonresident father involvement with their toddlers: Variation by fathers' race and ethnicity. *Journal of Family Psychology, 22,* 643–647.

Cabrera, N., Shannon, J., Rodríguez, V. J., & Lubar, A. (2009). Early intervention programs: The case of Head Start for Latino children. In F. A. Villarruel, G. Carlo, J. M. Grau, M. Azmitia, N. J. Cabrera, & T. J. Chahin (Eds.), *Handbook of U.S. Latino psychology: Developmental and community-based perspectives* (pp. 251–266). Thousand Oaks, CA: Sage.

Cabrera, N., Shannon, J., West, J., & Brooks-Gunn, J. (2006). Parental interactions with Latino infants: Variation by country of origin and English proficiency. *Child Development, 77,* 1190–1207.

Cagney, K. A., Browning, C. R., & Wallace, D. M. (2007). The Latino paradox in neighborhood context: The case of asthma and other respiratory conditions. *American Journal of Public Health, 97,* 919–925.

Calzada, E. J., Brotman, L. M., Huang, K. Y., Bat-Chava, Y., & Kingston, S. (2009). Parent cultural adaptation and child functioning in culturally diverse, urban families of preschoolers. *Journal of Applied Developmental Psychology, 30,* 515–524.

Canino, G. (2004). Are somatic symptoms and related distress more relevant in Hispanic/Latino youth? Some methodological considerations. *Journal of Clinical Child and Adolescent Psychology, 33,* 272–275.

Canino, G., & Alegría, M. (2008). Psychiatric diagnosis—Is it universal or relative to culture? *Journal of Child Psychology and Psychiatry, 49*(3), 237–250.

Cano, M. A., & Castillo, L. G. (2010). The role of enculturation and acculturation on Latina college student distress. *Journal of Hispanic Higher Education, 9*(3), 221–231.

Canul, K. H. (2003). Latina/o cultural values and the academy: Latinas navigating through the administrative role. In J. Castellanos & L. Jones (Eds.), *The majority in the minority: Expanding the representation of Latina/o faculty, administrators, and students in higher education* (pp. 167–175). Sterling, VA: Stylus.

Capielo, C., Mann, L., Nevels, B., & Delgado-Romero, E. (in press). Multicultural considerations in measurement and classification of positive psychology. In L. Edward & J. T. Pedrotti (Eds.), *Perspectives on the intersection of multiculturalism and positive psychology.* New York, NY: Springer.

Caplan, S., Paris, M., Whittemore, R., Desai, M., Dixon, J., Alvidrez, J., . . . Scahill, L. (2011). Correlates of religious, supernatural and psychosocial causal beliefs about depression among Latino immigrants in primary care. *Mental Health, Religion, & Culture, 14,* 589–611.

Cardemil, E. V., & Sarmiento, I. (2009). Clinical approaches to working with Latino adults. In F. A. Villarruel, G. Carlo, J. M. Grau, M. Azmitia, N. J. Cabrera, & T. J. Chahin (Eds.), *Handbook of U.S. Latino psychology: Developmental and community-based perspectives* (pp. 329–345). Thousand Oaks, CA: Sage.

Cardoso, J., & Thompson, S. (2010). Common themes of resilience among Latino immigrant families: A systematic review of the literature. *Families in Society, 91*(3), 257–265.

Carlson, V. J., & Harwood, R. L. (2003). Attachment, culture, and the caregiving system: The cultural patterning of everyday experiences among Anglo and Puerto Rican mother–infant pairs. *Infant Mental Health Journal, 24*(1), 53–73.

Carney, C. G., & Kahn, K. B. (1984). Building competencies for effective cross-cultural counseling: A developmental view. *The Counseling Psychologist, 12,* 111–119.

Carson, E. A., & Sabol, W. J. (2011). *Prisoners in 2011.* Retrieved from http://www.bjs.gov/index.cfm?ty=pbdetail&iid=4559

Carter, B., & McGoldrick, M. (2005a). Coaching at various stages of the life cycle. In B. Carter & M. McGoldrick (Eds.), *The expanded family life cycle: Individual, family and social perspectives* (3rd ed., pp. 436–454). Boston, MA: Allyn & Bacon.

Carter, B., & McGoldrick, M. (Eds.). (2005b). *The expanded family life cycle: Individual, family and social perspectives.* New York, NY: Allyn & Bacon.

Carter, R. T., & Cook, D. A. (1992). A culturally relevant perspective for understanding the career paths of visible racial/ethnic group people. In H. D. Lea & Z. B. Leibowitz (Eds.), *Adult career development: Concepts, issues, and practice* (pp. 192–217). Alexandria, VA: National Career Development Association.

Casas, J. F., & Ryan, C. S. (2010). How Latinos are transforming the United States: Research, theory, and policy. *Journal of Social Issues, 66,* 1–10.

Casas, J. M., Wagenheim, B. R., Banchero, R., & Mendoza-Romero, J. (1994). Hispanic masculinity: Myth or psychological schema meriting clinical consideration. *Hispanic Journal of Behavioral Sciences, 16,* 315–331. doi:10.1177/07399863940163009

Castellanos, J., Gloria, A. M., & Kamimura, M. (Eds.). (2006). *The Latina/o pathway to the Ph.D.: Abriendo caminos.* Sterling, VA: Stylus.

Castellanos, J., & Jones, L. (Eds.). (2003). *The majority in the minority: Expanding the representation of Latina/o faculty, administrators, and students in higher education.* Sterling, VA: Stylus.

Castillo, L. G., Conoley, C. W., Choi-Pearson, C., Archuleta, D. J., Van Landingham, A., & Phoummarath, M. J. (2006). University environment as a mediator of Latino ethnic identity and persistence attitudes. *Journal of Counseling Psychology, 53,* 267–271. doi:10.1037/0022-0167.53.2.267

Castillo, L. G., López-Arenas, A., & Saldivar, I. M. (2010). The influence of acculturation and enculturation on Latino high school students' decision to apply to college. *Journal of Multicultural Counseling and Development, 38,* 88–98.

Castro Martín, T., Martín García, T., & Dolores Puga González, D. (2008). Matrimonio vs. unión consensual en Latinoamérica: Contrastes desde una perspectiva de género [Marriage vs. consensual unions in Latin America: Contrasts from a gender perspective]. In *III Conferencia de la Asociación Latinoamericana de Población. Córdoba, Argentina* [Third Congress of the Latin American Population Association].

Cauce, A. M., & Domenech-Rodríguez, M. (2002). Latino families: Myths and realities. In J. M. Contreras, K. A. Kerns, & A. M. Neal-Barnett (Eds.), *Latino children and families in the United States: Current research and future directions* (pp. 3–26). Westport, CT: Praeger.

Cavazos-Rehg, P. A., Zayas, L. H., & Spitznagel, E. L. (2007). Legal status, emotional well-being and subjective health status of Latino immigrants. *Journal of the National Medical Association, 99,* 1126–1131.

Centers for Disease Control and Prevention. (2012a). *Diagnosed diabetes by race/ethnicity, sex, and age.* Retrieved from http://www.cdc.gov/diabetes/statistics/prev/national/menuage.htm

Centers for Disease Control and Prevention. (2012b). *Health, United States, 2011: With special feature on socioeconomic status and health.* Retrieved from http://www.cdc.gov/nchs/data/hus/hus11.pdf

Cerezo, A., O'Neil, M., & McWhirter, B. (2009). Counseling Latina/o students from an ecological perspective: Working with Peter. *Journal of College Counseling, 12,* 170–181.

Cervantes, J. (2010). Mestizo spirituality: Toward an integrated approach to psychotherapy for Latina/os. *Psychotherapy: Theory, Research, Practice, Training, 47,* 527–539.

Cervantes, J. M., & Lechuga, D. M. (2004). The meaning of pain: A key to working with Spanish-speaking patients with work-related injuries. *Professional Psychology: Research and Practice, 35*(1), 27–35.

Cervantes, R. C., & Cordova, D. (2011). Life experiences of Hispanic adolescents: Developmental and language considerations in acculturation stress. *Journal of Community Psychology, 39,* 336–352.

Chang, E., & Banks, K. (2007). The color and texture of hope: Some preliminary findings and implications for hope theory and counseling among diverse racial/ethnic groups. *Cultural Diversity and Ethnic Minority Psychology, 13*(2), 94–103.

Chapa, T., & Acosta, H. (2010). *Movilizandonos por nuestro futuro: Strategic development of a mental health workforce for Latinos.* Washington, DC: U.S. Department of Health and Human Services, Office of Minority Health, and the National Resource Center for Hispanic Mental Health.

Chávez, D. (2001). *Loving Pedro Infante.* New York, NY: Farrar, Straus & Giroux.

Chavez, L. M., Shrout, P. E., Alegría, M., Lapatin, S., & Canino, G. (2010). Ethnic differences in perceived impairment and need for care. *Journal of Abnormal Child Psychology, 38,* 1165–1177.

Chavez-Korell, S., Delgado-Romero, E. A., & Illes, R. (2012). The National Latina/o Psychological Association: Like a phoenix rising. *The Counseling Psychologist, 40,* 675–684.

Chavez-Korell, S., Rendón, A. D., Beer, J., Rodriguez, N., Garr, A. D., Pine, C. A., . . . Malcolm, E. (2012). Improving access and reducing barriers to depression treatment for Latino elders: Un nuevo amanecer (a new dawn). *Professional Psychology: Research and Practice, 43*(3), 217–226.

Chavira, V., López, S. R., Blacher, J., & Shapiro, J. (2000). Latina mothers' attributions, emotions, and reactions to the problem behaviors of their children with developmental disabilities. *Journal of Child Psychology and Psychiatry, 41*(2), 245–252.

Chen, E. C. (2005). Racial-cultural training for supervisors: Goals, foci and strategies. In R. T. Carter (Ed.), *Handbook of racial-cultural psychology and counseling: Vol. 2. Training and practice* (pp. 168–188). Hoboken, NJ: Wiley.

Chrisler, J., & Smith, C. (2004). Feminism and psychology. In M. A. Paludi (Ed.), *Praeger guide to the psychology of gender* (pp. 271–292). Westport, CT: Praeger.

Chung, K. M., & Akutsu, P. D. (2002). Acculturation among ethnic minority families. In K. M. Chung, P. B. Organista, & G. Marín (Eds.), *Acculturation: Advances in theory, measurement, and applied research* (pp. 95–119). Washington, DC. American Psychological Association.

Chung, K. M., Organista, P. B., & Marín, G. (Eds.). (2003). *Acculturation: Advances in theory, measurement, and applied research.* Washington, DC: American Psychological Association.

Clary, M. (2008, July 17). Mysterious controversial: Santeria sacrifices protected humane animal killings permitted in ceremonies are permitted under U.S. Constitution. *Sun Sentinel,* p. B.1.

Clouse, S., & Delgado-Romero, E. (2008, October). *Language, training, and burnout experiences of Spanish speaking therapists.* Poster presented at the Cultural Competency Conference, Georgia State University, Atlanta.

Coleman, H. L. K., & Wampold, B. E. (2003). Challenges to the development of culturally relevant, empirically supported treatment. In D. B. Pope-Davis, H. L. K. Coleman, W. Ming-Lui, & R. L. Toporek (Eds.), *Handbook of multicultural competencies in counseling and psychology* (pp. 227–246). Thousand Oaks, CA: Sage.

Coltrane, S., Parke, R. D., & Adams, M. (2004). Complexity of father involvement in low-income Mexican American families. *Family Relations, 46,* 109–121.

Comas-Díaz, L. (1981). Puerto Rican espiritismo and psychotherapy. *American Journal of Orthopsychiatry, 51,* 636–645. doi:10.1111/j.1939-0025.1981.tb01410.x

Comas-Díaz, L. (1987). Feminist therapy with mainland Puerto Rican women. *Psychology of Women Quarterly, 11,* 461–474.

Comas-Díaz, L. (1988). Mainland Puerto Rican women: A sociocultural approach. *Journal of Community Psychology, 16*(1), 21–31.

Comas-Díaz, L. (1994). An integrated approach. In L. Comas-Díaz & B. Greene (Eds.), *Women of color: Integrating ethnic and gender identities in psychotherapy* (pp. 287–318). New York, NY: Guilford Press.

Comas-Díaz, L. (1996). LatiNegra: Mental health issues of African Latinas. In M. P. P. Root (Ed.), *The multiracial experience: Racial borders as the new frontier* (pp. 167–190). Thousand Oaks, CA: Sage.

Comas-Díaz, L. (2000). An ethnopolitical approach to working with people of color. *American Psychologist, 55,* 1319–1325.

Comas-Díaz, L. (2001). Hispanics, Latinos, or Americanos: The evolution of identity. *Cultural Diversity and Ethnic Minority Psychology, 7,* 115–120.

Comas-Díaz, L. (2003). The Black Madonna: The psychospiritual feminism of Guadalupe, Kali, and Monserrat. In L. B. Silverstein & T. J. Goodrich (Eds.), *Feminist family therapy: Empowerment in social context* (pp. 147–160). Washington, DC: American Psychological Association.

Comas-Díaz, L. (2006a). Cultural variation in the therapeutic relationship. In C. Goodheart, A. Kazdin, & R. J. Sternberg (Eds.), *Evidence-based psychotherapy: Where practice and research meet* (pp. 81–105). Washington, DC: American Psychological Association.

Comas-Díaz, L. (2006b). Latino healing: The integration of ethnic psychology into psychotherapy. *Psychotherapy: Theory, Research, Practice, Training, 43,* 436–453. doi:10.1037/0033-3204.43.4.436

Comas-Díaz, L. (2012). *Multicultural care: A clinician's guide to cultural competence.* Washington, DC: American Psychological Association.

Comas-Díaz, L., Lykes, M. B., & Alarcón, R. D. (1998). Ethnic conflict and the psychology of liberation in Guatemala, Peru, and Puerto Rico. *American Psychologist, 53,* 778–792.

Conchas, G. (2001). Structuring failure and success: Understanding the variability in Latino school engagement. *Harvard Educational Review, 71,* 475–504.

Consoli, A. J., & Jester, C. M. (2005). A model for teaching psychotherapy theory through an integrated structure. *Journal of Psychotherapy Integration, 15,* 358–373.

Constantine, M. G., Gloria, A. M., & Barón, A. (2006). Counseling Mexican American college students. In C. C. Lee (Ed.), *Multicultural issues in counseling: New approaches to diversity* (pp. 207–222). Alexandria, VA: American Counseling Association.

Contreras, J. M. (2004). Parenting behaviors among mainland Puerto Rican adolescent mothers: The role of grandmother and partner involvement. *Journal of Research on Adolescence, 14,* 341–368.

Contreras, J. M., Mangelsdorf, S., Rhodes, J., Diener, M., & Brunson, L. (1999). Parent-child interaction among Latina adolescent mothers: The role of the family and social support. *Journal of Research and Adolescence, 9,* 417–439.

Contreras, J. M., Narang, D., Ikhlas, M., & Teichman, J. (2002). A conceptual model of the determinants of parenting among Latina adolescent mothers. In J. M. Contreras, K. A. Kerns, & A. M. Neal-Barnett (Eds.), *Latino children and families in the United States: Current research and future directions* (pp. 155–177). Westport, CT: Praeger.

Corcoran, J. (2000). Solution-focused family therapy with ethnic minority clients. *Crisis Intervention, 6*(1), 5–12.

Corcoran, J., & Pillai, V. (2009). A review of the research on solution-focused therapy. *British Journal of Social Work, 39*(2), 234–242.

Cordova, D., Huang, S., Pantin, H., & Prado, G. (2012). Do the effects of a family intervention on alcohol and drug use vary by nativity status? *Psychology of Addictive Behaviors, 26,* 655–660. doi:10.1037/a0026438

Correa, V. I., Bonilla, Z. E., & Reyes-MacPherson, M. E. (2011). Support networks of single Puerto Rican mothers of children with disabilities. *Journal of Child Family Studies, 20,* 66–77.

Costantino, G., Malgady, R. G., & Rogler, L. H. (1986). Cuento therapy: A culturally sensitive modality for Puerto Rican children. *Journal of Consulting and Clinical Psychology, 54,* 639–645. doi:10.1037/0022-006X.54.5.639

Costantino, G., Malgady, R., & Rogler, L. (1988). Folk hero modeling therapy for Puerto Rican adolescents. *Journal of Adolescence, 11*(2), 155–165.

Council of Graduate Schools. (2008). *Data sources: Graduate enrollment by race/ethnicity, 1996 to 2006—Special analysis from the graduate enrollment and degrees survey report.* Washington, DC: Author.

Council of National Psychology Associations for the Advancement of Ethnic Minority Interests. (2000). *Guidelines for research in ethnic minority communities.* Washington, DC: American Psychological Association. Available at www.apa.org/pi/oema/resources/cnpaaemi-guidelines.pdf

Council of National Psychology Associations for the Advancement of Ethnic Minority Interests. (2003). *Psychological treatment of ethnic minority populations.* Washington, DC: Association of Black Psychologists.

Council of National Psychology Associations for the Advancement of Ethnic Minority Interests. (2009). *Psychology education and training from culture-specific and multiracial perspectives.* Washington, DC: Author.

Cox, C. B., Brooks, L. R., & Valcarcel, C. (2000). Culture and caregiving: A study of Latino grandparents. In C. B. Cox (Ed.), *To grandmother's house we go and stay: Perspectives on custodial parents* (pp. 218–232). New York, NY: Springer.

Cuadrado, M., & Lieberman, L. (2011). The Virgin of Guadalupe as an ancillary modality for treating Hispanic substance abusers: Juramentos in the United States. *Journal of Religion and Health, 50,* 922–930.

Cuellar, I., Arnold, B., & Maldonado, R. (1995). Acculturation Rating Scale for Mexican Americans–II: A revision of the original ARSMA Scale. *Hispanic Journal of Behavioral Sciences, 17*(3), 275–304.

Cuéllar, I., Harris, L., & Jasso, R. (1980). An acculturation scale for Mexican American and clinical populations. *Hispanic Journal of Behavioral Sciences, 2,* 199–221.

Cummins, J. (1984). *Bilingualism and special education: Issues in assessment and pedagogy.* Clevedon, England: Multilingual Matters.

D'Andrea, M., & Arredondo, P. (2000, April). Convergence of multiple identities presents new challenges. *Counseling Today, 42,* pp. 12, 40.

D'Angelo, E., Llerena-Quinn, R., Shapiro, R., Colon, F., Rodriguez, P., Gallagher, K., & Beardslee, W. (2009). Adaptation of the preventive intervention program for depression for use with predominantly low-income Latino families. *Family Process, 48*(2), 269–291.

Dass-Brailsford, P. (2012). Culturally sensitive therapy with low-income ethnic minority clients: An empowering intervention. *Journal of Contemporary Psychotherapy, 42,* 37–44.

Dávila, A. (2001). *Latinos Inc.: The marketing and making of a people.* Berkeley: University of California Press.

Day, S. X., & Rottinghaus, P. (2008). The healthy personality. In W. B. Walsh (Ed.), *Counseling psychology and optimal human functioning* (pp. 1–13). Mahwah, NJ: Erlbaum.

De Shazer, S. (1985). *Keys to solution in brief therapy.* New York, NY: Norton.

Deci, E. L., & Ryan, R. M. (1985). *Intrinsic motivation and self-determination in human behavior.* New York, NY: Plenum.

Deci, E. L., & Ryan, R. M. (2000). The "what" and "why" of goal pursuits: Human needs and the self-determination of behavior. *Psychological Inquiry, 11,* 227–268.

Delgado-Romero, E. A. (2001). Counseling a Hispanic/Latino client—Mr. X. *Journal of Mental Health Counseling, 23*(3), 207–221.

Delgado-Romero, E. A. (2003). Ethics and the multicultural competencies. In D. B. Pope-Davis, H. L. K. Coleman, W. M. Liu, & R. L. Toporek (Eds.), *Handbook of multicultural competencies in counseling and psychology* (pp. 313–346). Thousand Oaks, CA: Sage.

Delgado-Romero, E. A. (2009, February). *Latinos and higher education: The case of psychology.* Invited address at the Cross-Cultural Winter Roundtable conference for Psychology and Education at Teachers College, New York, NY.

Delgado-Romero, E. A., Delgado Polo, E. E., Ardila, R., & Smetana, C. (2009). After la violencia: The psychology profession in Colombia. In L. H. Gerstein, P. P. Heppner, S. Ægisdóttir, S.-M. A. Leung, & K. L. Norsworthy (Eds.), *International handbook of cross-cultural counseling: Cultural assumptions and practices worldwide* (pp. 369–374). Thousand Oaks, CA: Sage.

Delgado-Romero, E. A., Espino, M., Werther, E., & González, M. J. (2012). Building infrastructure through training of bilingual mental health providers. In L. P. Buki & L. M. Piedra (Eds.), *Haciendo camino al andar: Creating infrastructures for Latino mental health* (pp. 99–116). New York, NY: Springer.

Delgado-Romero, E. A., Flores, L., Gloria, A., Arredondo, P., & Castellanos, J. (2003). Developmental career challenges for Latina/o faculty in higher education. In J. Castellanos & L. Jones (Eds.), *The majority in the minority: Expanding the representation of Latina/o faculty, administrators, and students in higher education* (pp. 257–283). Sterling, VA: Stylus.

Delgado-Romero, E. A., Galván, N., Maschino, P., & Rowland, M. (2005). Race and ethnicity: Ten years of counseling research. *The Counseling Psychologist, 33,* 419–448.

Delgado-Romero, E. A., & Hernandez, C. A. (2002). Empowering Hispanic students through student organizations: Competencies for faculty advisors. *Journal of Hispanic Higher Education, 2,* 144–157.

Delgado-Romero, E. A., Hernandez, C. A., & Montero, H. (2004). Mapping the development of Hispanic/Latino(a) student organizations: A model at the University of Florida. *Journal of Hispanic Higher Education, 3,* 237–253.

Delgado-Romero, E. A., Manlove, A., Manlove, J., & Hernandez, C. A. (2007). Controversial issues in the recruitment and retention of Latino/a faculty. *Journal of Hispanic Higher Education, 6,* 1–18.

Delgado-Romero, E. A., Matthews, P. H., & Paisley, P. O. (2007). A school counseling conference focused on the emerging Latino/a populations: A model in the state of Georgia. *Journal of Hispanic Higher Education, 6,* 209–221.

Delgado-Romero, E. A., Rojas, A., & Shelton, K. L. (2007). Immigration history and therapy considerations with Hispanics from Cuba, Central and South America. In C. Negy (Ed.), *Cross-cultural psychotherapy: Toward a critical understanding of diverse client populations* (2nd ed., pp. 133–160). Reno, NV: Bent Tree Press.

Delgado-Romero, E. A., & Sanabria, S. (2007). Counseling international students from Latin America and the Caribbean. In H. Singaravelu & M. Pope (Eds.), *A handbook for counseling international students in the United States* (pp. 155–172). Alexandria, VA: American Counseling Association.

DeNavas-Walt, C., Proctor, B. D., & Smith, J. C. (2012). *Income, poverty and health insurance in the United States: 2011.* Retrieved from http://www.census.gov/prod/2012pubs/p60-243.pdf

Devine, K. A., Holbein, C. E., Psihogios, A. M., Amaro, C. M., & Holmbeck, G. N. (2012). Individual adjustment, parental functioning, and perceived social support in Hispanic and non-Hispanic White mothers and fathers with spina bifida. *Journal of Pediatric Psychology, 37,* 769–778.

Díaz, E., Miskemen, T., Vega, W., Gara, M., Wilson, D. R., Lesser, I., . . . Strakowski, S. (2009). Inconsistencies in diagnosis and symptoms among bilingual and English-speaking Latinos and Euro-Americans. *Psychiatric Services, 60,* 1379–1382.

Díaz McConnell, E., & Delgado-Romero, E. A. (2004). Panethnic options and Latinos: Reality or methodological construction? *Sociological Focus, 37*(4), 297–312.

Diaz-Strong, D., Gómez, C., Luna-Duarte, M. E., & Meiners, E. R. (2011). Purged: Undocumented students, financial aid policies, and access to higher education. *Journal of Hispanic Higher Education, 10,* 107–119.

Domenech Rodríguez, M., Baumann, A., & Schwartz, A. (2011). Cultural adaptation of an evidence based intervention: From theory to practice in a Latino/a community context. *American Journal of Community Psychology, 47*(1–2), 170–186.

Domenech Rodríguez, M. M., Donovick, M. R., & Crowley, S. L. (2009). Parenting styles in a cultural context: Observations of "protective parenting" in first-generation Latinos. *Family Process, 48*(2), 195–210.

Dovidio, J. F., Gluszek, A., John, M. S., Ditlmann, R., & Lagunes, P. (2010). Understanding bias toward Latinos: Discrimination, dimensions of difference, and experience of exclusion. *Journal of Social Issues, 66,* 59–78.

Downs, A., Martin, J., Fossum, M., Martinez, S., Solorio, M., & Martinez, H. (2008). Parents teaching parents: A career and college knowledge program for Latino families. *Journal of Latinos & Education, 7*(3), 227–240.

DREAM Act. (n.d.). Retrieved from http://en.wikipedia.org/wiki/DREAM_Act

Duany, J., & Silver, P. (2010). The "Puerto Ricanization" of Florida: Historical background and current status. *Centro Journal, 22*(1), 4–31.

Eamon, M. K., & Mulder, C. (2005). Predicting antisocial behavior among Latino young adolescents: An ecological systems analysis. *American Journal of Orthopsychiatry, 75*(1), 117–127.

Eamranond, P. P., Davis, R. B., Phillips, R. S., & Wee, C. C. (2009). Patient-physician language concordance and lifestyle counseling among Spanish-speaking patients. *Journal of Immigrant and Minority Health, 11,* 494–498.

Eitle, D. (2005). The moderating effects of peer substance use on the family structure-adolescent substance use association: Quantity versus quality of parenting. *Addictive Behaviors, 30,* 963–980.

Ennis, S. R., Ríos-Vargas, M., & Albert, N. G. (2011, May). *The Hispanic population: 2010.* Retrieved from the U.S. Census Bureau website: http://www.census.gov/prod/cen2010/briefs/c2010br-04.pdf

Erikson, E. H. (1963). *Childhood and society.* New York, NY: Norton.

Erikson, E. H. (1964). *Insight and responsibility.* New York, NY: Norton.

Espín, O. (1994). Feminist approaches. In L. Comas-Díaz & B. Greene (Eds.), *Women of color: Integrating ethnic and gender identities in psychotherapy* (pp. 265–286). New York, NY: Guilford Press.

Espín, O. (1998). *Women crossing boundaries: A psychology of immigration and transformations of sexuality.* New York, NY: Routledge.

Essoyan, S. (2012, January 4). *Hispanic population growing in Hawaii.* Retrieved from http://www.Hispanicbusiness.com/2012/1/4/Hispanic_population_growing_in_hawaii.htm

Estrada, F., Rigali-Oiler, M., Arciniega, G. M., & Tracey, T. (2011). Machismo and Mexican American men: An empirical understanding using a gay sample. *Journal of Counseling Psychology, 58,* 358–367.

Everson, S. A., Maty, S. A., Lynch, J. W., & Kaplan, G. A. (2002). Epidemiologic evidence for the relation between socioeconomic status and depression, obesity, and diabetes. *Journal of Psychosomatic Research, 53,* 891–895.

Ewing Marion Kauffman Foundation. (2013). *America's new immigrant entrepreneurs: Then and now.* Retrieved from http://www.kauffman.org/infographic-americas-new-immigrant-entrepreneurs-then-and-now.aspx

Excelencia in Education. (2011). *Fast facts.* Retrieved from http://www.edexcelencia.org/research/fast-facts

Fairlie, R. W. (2012, March). *Kauffman index of entrepreneurial activity: 1996-2011.* Kansas City, MO: Kauffman Foundation.

Falicov, C. (1998). *Latino families in therapy: A guide to multicultural practice.* New York, NY: Guilford Press.

Falicov, C. J. (2007). Working with transnational immigrants: Expanding meanings of family, community, and culture. *Family Process, 46,* 157–171.

Falicov, C. J. (2008). Transnational journeys. In M. McGoldrick & K. V. Hardy (Eds.), *Re-visioning family therapy: Race, culture and gender in clinical practice* (2nd ed., pp. 25–38). New York, NY: Guilford Press.

Falicov, C. J. (2009). On the wisdom and challenges of culturally attuned treatments for Latinos. *Family Process, 48,* 292–309.

Falicov, C. (2010). Changing constructions of machismo for Latino men in therapy: "The devil never sleeps." *Family Process, 49*(3), 309–329.

Fernández, J. M. (2001). *La familia puertorriqueña: Ayer y hoy.* [The Puerto Rican family: Yesterday and today]. San Juan, Puerto Rico: Editorial Edil.

Field, L. D., Korell-Chavez, S., & Rodríguez, M. M. D. (2010). No hay rosas sin espinas: Conceptualizing Latina-Latina supervision from a multicultural developmental supervisory model. *Training and Education in Professional Psychology, 4*(1), 47–54.

Fields, J. (2003). *Children's living arrangements and characteristics: March 2002* (Current Population Report No. P20-547). Washington, DC: U.S. Census Bureau.

Figueroa, M. A., González, K. P., Marín, P., Moreno, J. F., Navia, C. N., & Pérez, L. X. (2001). Understanding the nature and context of Latina/o doctoral student experiences. *Journal of College Student Development, 42,* 563–580.

Flores, G. (2005). The impact of medical interpreter services on the quality of health care: A systematic review. *Medical Care Research and Review, 62*(3), 255–299.

Flores, G. (2006). Language barriers to health care in the United States. *New England Journal of Medicine, 355,* 229–231.

Flores, L. Y., Mendoza, M., Ojeda, L., He, Y., Rosales Meza, R., Medina, V., . . . Varvel, S. (2011). A qualitative inquiry of Latino immigrants' work experiences in the Midwest. *Journal of Counseling Psychology, 58,* 522–536.

Flores, L. Y., & O'Brien, K. M. (2002). The career development of Mexican American adolescent women: A test of social cognitive career theory. *Journal of Counseling Psychology, 49,* 14–27.

Flores, L. Y., Ojeda, L., Huang, Y., Gee, D., & Lee, S. (2006). The relation of acculturation, problem-solving appraisal, and career decision-making self-efficacy to Mexican American high school students' educational goals. *Journal of Counseling Psychology, 53,* 260–266.

Flores, L. Y., Ramos, K., & Kanagui, M. (2010). Applying the cultural formulation approach to career counseling with Latinas/os. *Journal of Career Development, 37,* 411–422.

Flores, L. Y., Robitschek, C., Celebi, E., Andersen, C., & Hoang, U. (2010). Social cognitive influences on Mexican Americans' career choices across Holland's themes. *Journal of Vocational Psychology, 76,* 198–210.

Flores, L. Y., Spanierman, L. B., Armstrong, P. I., & Velez, A. D. (2006). Validity of the Strong Interest Inventory and Skills Confidence Inventory with Mexican American high school students. *Journal of Career Assessment, 14,* 183–202.

Flórez, K. R., Aguirre, A. N., Viladrich, A., Céspedes, A., De La Cruz, A. A., & Abraído-Lanza, A. F. (2009). Fatalism or destiny? A qualitative study and interpretative framework on Dominican women's breast cancer beliefs. *Journal of Immigrant and Minority Health, 11*(4), 291–301.

Fontes, L. A. (2008). *Interviewing clients across cultures: A practitioner's guide.* New York, NY: Guilford Press.

Fortuna, L. R., Porche, M. V., & Alegría, M. (2009). A qualitative study of clinicians' use of the cultural formulation model in assessing posttraumatic stress disorder. *Transcultural Psychiatry, 46,* 429–450.

Fouad, N. (2006). Major contribution. *The Counseling Psychologist, 34*(2).

Fouad, N. A., & Byars-Winston, A. M. (2004). Work: Cultural perspectives on career choices and decision making. In R. T. Carter (Ed.), *Handbook of racial-cultural psychology and counseling, theory, research, and practice* (pp. 232–255). Hoboken, NJ: Wiley.

Freire, P. (1970). *Pedagogy of the oppressed.* Harmondsworth, England: Penguin.

Freire, P. (1982). *Pedagogy of the oppressed.* New York, NY: Continuum.

Freudenberg, N., Daniels, J., Crum, M., Perkins, T., & Richie, B. E. (2005). Coming home from jail: The social and health consequences of community reentry for women, male adolescents, and their families and communities. *American Journal of Public Health, 95,* 1725–1736.

Fry, R. (2010). *Hispanics, high school dropouts and the GED.* Retrieved from the Pew Hispanic Center website: http://www.pewhispanic.org/files/reports/122.pdf

Fry, R. (2011). *Hispanic college enrollment spikes, narrowing gaps with other groups.* Retrieved from the Pew Hispanic Center website: http://www.pewhispanic.org/files/2011/08/146.pdf

Fry, R., & Lopez, M. H. (2012). *Hispanic student enrollments reach new highs in 2011.* Retrieved from the Pew Hispanic Center website: http://www.pewhispanic.org/files/2012/08/Hispanic-Student-Enrollments-Reach-New-Highs-in-2011_FINAL.pdf

Fuligni, A. J., Witkow, M., & Garcia, C. (2005). Ethnic identity and the academic adjustment of adolescents from Mexican, Chinese, and European backgrounds. *Developmental Psychology, 41,* 799–811.

Fuller, B., & García Coll, G. (2010). Learning form Latinos: Contexts, families, and child development. *Developmental Psychology, 46,* 559–565.

Fuller-Thompson, E., & Minkler, M. (2007). Central American grandparents raising grandchildren. *Hispanic Journal of Behavioral Sciences, 29,* 5–18.

Galassi, J. P., Griffin, D. A., & Akos, P. (2008). Strengths-based school counseling and the ASCA National Model. *Professional School Counseling, 12,* 176–181. doi:10.5330/PSC.n.12.176.2010

Gallardo, M. (2009). Therapists as cultural architects and systemic advocates: Latina/o skills identification stage model. In M. Gallardo, C. J. Yeh, J. E. Trimble, & T. Parham (Eds.), *Culturally adaptive counseling skills: Demonstrations of evidence-based practices* (pp. 77–112). Thousand Oaks, CA: Sage.

Gallardo, M., Johnson, J., Parham, T., & Carter, J. (2009). Ethics and multiculturalism: Advancing cultural and clinical responsiveness. *Professional Psychology: Research and Practice, 40,* 425–435.

Gallardo, M. E., Parham, T. A., Trimble, J. E., & Yeh, C. J. (2012). Understanding the skills identification stage model in context. In M. E. Gallardo, C. J. Yeh, J. E. Trimble, & T. A. Parham (Eds.), *Culturally adaptive counseling skills: Demonstrations of evidence-based practices* (pp. 1–20). Thousand Oaks, CA: Sage.

Gallardo, M. E., Yeh, C. J., Trimble, J. E., & Parham, T. A. (Eds.). (2012). *Culturally adaptive counseling skills: Demonstrations of evidence-based practices.* Thousand Oaks, CA: Sage.

Gallardo-Cooper, M. (2001a). *Culture-centered clinical interview.* Unpublished manuscript.

Gallardo-Cooper, M. (2001b, March). *The Latino parent-child relationship across the life-span.* Learning Institute presented at the meeting of the American Counseling Association, San Antonio, TX.

Gallardo-Cooper, M. (2008). Bilingual counseling. In F. T. L. Leong, H. E. A. Tinsley, & S. H. Lease (Eds.), *Encyclopedia of counseling: Vol. 2. Personal and emotional counseling* (pp. 1022–1024). Thousand Oaks, CA: Sage.

Gallardo-Cooper, M., Arciniega, G. M., Santana-Pellicer, A., Estrada, E., Tovar, Z., & Grazioso de Rodríguez, M. (2006). *Latino Competencies Task Force.* Alexandria, VA: American Counseling Association.

Gallardo-Cooper, M., Arciniega, G. M., Santana-Pellicer, A., Tovar-Blank, Z., & Estrada, E. (2012, March). *Latino-centered supervision.* Learning institute at the annual conference of the American Counseling Association, San Francisco, CA.

Gallardo-Cooper, M., & Zapata, A. L. (2013). Multicultural family therapy. In F. T. L. Leong (Ed.), *APA Handbook of multicultural psychology: Vol. 2. Applications and training* (pp. 499–525). Washington, DC: American Psychological Association.

Galvan, N. (2012, October). *Latinas/os behind bars: Opportunities for intervention and empowerment.* Paper presented at the 5th Biennial Conference of the National Latina/o Psychological Association, New Brunswick, NJ.

Gándara, P. (2006). Strengthening the academic pipeline leading to careers in math, science, and technology for Latino students. *Journal of Hispanic Higher Education, 5*(3), 222–237.

Garcia, G. (2012). *Some like it hot: Hispanics and the American melting pot.* Retrieved from http://www.nationaljournal.com/thenextamerica/perspectives/some-like-it-hot-hispanics-and-the-american-melting-pot-20120517

García, E. E., & Náñez, J. E. (2011). *Bilingualism and cognition: Informing research, pedagogy, and policy.* Washington, DC: American Psychological Association.

García, E. E., & Scribner, K. P. (2009). Latino pre-K-3 education: A critical foundation. In F. A. Villarruel, G. Carlo, J. M. Grau, M. Azmitia, N. J. Cabrera, & T. J. Chahin (Eds.), *Handbook of U.S. Latino psychology: Developmental and community-based perspectives* (pp. 267–289). Thousand Oaks, CA: Sage.

García Coll, C. G., & Pachter, L. M. (2002). Ethnic and minority parenting. In M. H. Bornstein (Ed.), *Handbook of parenting: Vol. 2. Biology and ecology of parenting* (pp. 189–209). Mahwah, NJ: Erlbaum.

Garcia-Preto, N. (1996). Latino families: An overview. In M. McGoldrick, J. Giordano, & J. Pearce (Eds.), *Ethnicity and family therapy* (pp. 141–154). New York, NY: Guilford Press.

Garcia-Preto, N. (2005). Latino families: An overview. In M. McGoldrick, J. Giordano, & N. Garcia-Preto (Eds.), *Ethnicity and family therapy* (3rd ed., pp. 153–165). New York, NY: Guilford Press.

Garland, B. E., Spohn, C., & Wodahl, E. J. (2008). Racial disproportionality in the American prison population: Using the Blumstein method to address the critical race and justice issue of the 21st century. *Justice Policy Journal, 5*(2), 1–42.

Garza, Y., & Bratton, S. (2005). School-based child-centered play therapy with Hispanic children: Outcomes and cultural consideration. *International Journal of Play Therapy, 14*(1), 51–80.

Garza, Y., & Watts, R. (2010). Filial therapy and Hispanic values: Common ground for culturally sensitive helping. *Journal of Counseling & Development, 88,* 108–113.

Generation ñ. (n.d.). Retrieved from http://generation-ntv.com/about

Germán, M., Gonzales, N. A., & Dumka, L. (2009). Familism values as a protective factor for Mexican-origin adolescents exposed to deviant peers. *Journal of Early Adolescence, 29*(1), 16–42.

Gerstein, L. H., Heppner, P. P., Ægisdóttir, S., Leung, S.-M. A., & Norsworthy, K. L. (Eds.). (2009). *International handbook of cross-cultural counseling: Cultural assumptions and practices worldwide.* Thousand Oaks, CA: Sage.

Gibson, R. L., & Mitchell, M. (2008). *Introduction to counseling and guidance* (7th ed.). Upper Saddle River, NJ: Pearson.

Gil, A. G., & Vega, W. A. (1996). Two different worlds: Acculturation stress and adaptation among Cuban and Nicaraguan families. *Journal of Social and Personal Relationships, 13,* 435–456.

Gil, M. R., & Vázquez, C. I. (1996). *The Maria paradox: How Latinas can merge old world traditions with new world self-esteem.* New York, NY: Putnam.

Gillum, F., & Griffith, D. M. (2010). Prayer and spiritual practices for health reasons among American adults: The role of race and ethnicity. *Journal of Religion and Health, 49*(3), 283–295.

Gladding, S. T. (2002). *Family therapy: History, theory and practice.* Upper Saddle River, NJ: Merrill Prentice Hall.

Gloria, A. M. (1997). Chicana academic persistence: Creating a university-based community. *Education and Urban Society, 30,* 107–121.

Gloria, A. M., & Castellanos, J. (2003). Latina/o and African American students at predominantly White institutions: A psychosociocultural perspective of cultural congruity, campus climate, and academic persistence. In J. Castellanos & L. Jones (Eds.), *The majority in the minority: Expanding the representation of Latina/o faculty, administrators, and students in higher education* (pp. 71–92). Sterling, VA: Stylus.

Gloria, A. M., & Castellanos, J. (2012). Desfios y bendiciones: A multiperspective examination of the educational experiences and coping responses of first-generation college Latina students. *Journal of Hispanic Higher Education, 11*(1), 82–99.

Golash-Boza, T. (2006). Dropping the hyphen? Becoming Latino(a)-American through racialized assimilation. *Social Forces, 85,* 27–55.

Goldsmith, A., & Diette, T. (2012). *Exploring the link between unemployment and mental health outcomes.* Retrieved from http://www.apa.org/pi/ses/resources/indicator/2012/04/unemployment.aspx

Gomez-Beloz, A., & Chavez, N. (2001). The botánica as a culturally appropriate health care option for Latinos. *Journal of Alternative & Complementary Medicine, 7,* 537–546.

Gonzalez, N. A., Fabrett, F. C., & Knight, G. P. (2009). Acculturation, enculturation, and the psycho-social adaptation of Latino youth. In F. A. Villarruel, G. Carlo, J. M. Grau, M. Azmitia, N. J. Cabrera, & T. J. Chahin (Eds.), *Handbook of U.S. Latino psychology: Developmental and community-based perspectives* (pp. 115–134). Thousand Oaks, CA: Sage.

González-Ramos, G., Zayas, L. H., & Cohen, E. V. (1998). Child-rearing values of low-income, urban Puerto Rican mothers of preschool children. *Professional Psychology Research and Practice, 29*(4), 377–382.

Goodman, L. A., Liang, B., Helms, J. E., Latta, R. E., Sparks, E., & Weintraub, S. R. (2004). Training counseling psychologists as social justice agents: Feminist and multicultural perspectives in action. *The Counseling Psychologist, 32,* 793–837.

Gorman-Smith, D., Tolan, P. H., Henry, D. B., & Florsheim, P. (2000). Patterns of family functioning and adolescent outcomes among urban African American and Mexican American families. *Journal of Family Psychology, 14,* 436–457.

Gould, S. J. (1994). The geometer of race. *Discover, 15*(11), 65–69.

Grau, J., Azmitia, M., & Quattlebaum, J. (2009). Parenting, relational, and developmental processes. In F. A. Villarruel, G. Carlo, J. M. Grau, M. Azmitia, N. J. Cabrera, & T. J. Chahin (Eds.), *Handbook of U.S. Latino psychology: Developmental and community-based perspectives* (pp. 153–169). Thousand Oaks, CA: Sage.

Griner, D., & Smith, T. (2006). Culturally adapted mental health intervention: A meta-analytic review. *Psychotherapy: Theory, Research, Practice, Training, 43,* 531–548.

Guarnaccia, P. J., Lewis-Fernandéz, R., Pincay, I. M., Shrout, P., Guo, J., Torres, M., . . . Alegría, M. (2010). Ataque de nervios as a marker of social and psychiatric vulnerability: Results from the NLAAS. *International Journal of Social Psychiatry, 56*(3), 298–309.

Guarnaccia, P. J., & Rodríguez, O. (1996). Concepts of culture and their role in the development of culturally competent mental health services. *Hispanic Journal of Behavioral Sciences, 18,* 419–443.

Guarnaccia, P. J., & Rogler, L. H. (1999). Research on culture-bound syndromes: New directions. *American Journal of Psychiatry, 156,* 1322–1327.

Guerin, P. J. (Ed.). (1976). *Family therapy: Theory and practice.* New York, NY: Gardner Press.

Guilamo-Ramos, V., Dittus, P., Jaccard, J., Johansson, M., Bouris, A., & Acosta, N. (2007). Parenting practices among Dominican and Puerto Rican mothers. *Social Work, 52*(1), 17–30.

Guinn, B., & Vincent, V. (2002). A health intervention on Latina spiritual well-being constructs: An evaluation. *Hispanic Journal of Behavioral Sciences, 24*(3), 379–391.

Gushue, G. V., Clarke, C. P., Pantzer, K. M., & Scanlan, K. R. (2006). Self-efficacy, perceptions of barriers, vocational identity, and the career exploration behavior of Latino/a high school students. *The Career Development Quarterly, 54,* 307–317.

Gutiérrez y Muhs, G., Flores-Niemann, Y., González, C. G., & Harris, A. P. (Eds.). (2012). *Presumed incompetent: The intersections of race and class for women in academia.* Logan: Utah State University Press.

Guyll, M., Madon, S., Prieto, L., & Scherr, K. C. (2010). The potential roles of self-fulfilling prophecies, stigma consciousness, and stereotype threat in linking Latino/a ethnicity and educational outcomes. *Journal of Social Issues, 66,* 113–130.

Gzesh, S. (2006, April). *Central Americans and asylum policy in the Reagan era.* Retrieved from http://www.migrationinformation.org/USfocus/display.cfm?id=384

Halgunseth, L. C., Ispa, J. M., & Rudy, D. (2006). Parental control in Latino families: An integrated review of the literature. *Child Development, 77,* 1282–1297.

Handlin, O. (1951). *The uprooted*. Boston, MA: Little, Brown.

Hardy, K. V., & Laszloffy, T. A. (1995). The cultural genogram: Key to training culturally competent family therapists. *Journal of Marital and Family Therapy, 21*(3), 227–237.

Haro, R., & Lara, J. F. (2003). Latinos and administrative positions in American higher education. In J. Castellanos & L. Jones (Eds.), *The majority in the minority: Expanding the representation of Latina/o faculty, administrators, and students in higher education* (pp. 167–175). Sterling, VA: Stylus.

Hartman, A. (1995). Diagrammatic assessment of family relationships. *Families in Society, 76*(2), 111–122.

Harwood, R., Leyendecker, B., Carlson, V., Asencio, M., & Miller, A. (2002). Parenting among Latino families in the US. In M. H. Bornstein (Ed.), *Handbook of parenting: Vol. 2. Biology and ecological perspectives* (2nd ed., pp. 21–46). Mahwah, NJ: Erlbaum.

Heesacker, M., Heppner, P. P., & Rogers, M. E. (1982). Classics and emerging classics in counseling psychology. *Journal of Counseling Psychology, 29*, 400–405.

Helms, J. E. (Ed.). (1990). *Black and White racial identity: Theory, research and practice*. Westport, CT: Greenwood Press.

Helms, J. E., & Cook, D. A. (1999). *Using race and culture in counseling and psychotherapy: Theory and process*. Needham Heights, MA: Allyn & Bacon.

Henriksen, R. C., & Paladino, D. A. (2009). Identity development in a multiple heritage world. In R. C. Henriksen & D. A. Paladino (Eds.), *Counseling multiple heritage individuals, couples, and families* (pp. 25–43). Alexandria, VA: American Counseling Association.

Hernandez, M., & McGoldrick, M. (2005). Migration and the life cycle. In B. Carter & M. McGoldrick (Eds.), *The expanded family life cycle: Individual, family, and social perspectives* (3rd ed., pp. 169–184). New York, NY: Pearson.

Hernández, P. (2002). Resilience in families and communities: Latin American contributions from the psychology of liberation. *The Family Journal: Counseling and Therapy for Couples and Families, 10*, 334–343.

Hernández, P., Almeida, R., & Dolan-Del Vecchio, K. (2005). Critical consciousness, accountability, and empowerment: Key processes for helping families heal. *Family Process, 44*(1), 105–119.

Hernández, P., Siegel, A., & Almeida, R. (2009). The cultural context model: How does it facilitate couples' therapeutic change? *Journal of Marital & Family Therapy, 35*(1), 97–110.

Herrera, R. (2003). Notes from a Latino graduate student at a predominantly White university. In J. Castellanos & L. Jones (Eds.), *The majority in the minority: Expanding the representation of Latina/o faculty, administrators, and students in higher education* (pp. 111–126). Sterling, VA: Stylus.

Hill, N. E., Bush, K. R., & Roosa, M. W. (2003). Parenting and family socialization strategies and children's mental health: Low income Mexican American and Euro American mothers and children. *Child Development, 74*, 180–204.

Hill, N. E., & Torres, K. (2010). Negotiating the American dream: The paradox of aspirations and achievement among Latino students and engagement between their families and school. *Journal of Social Issues, 66*(1), 95–112. doi:10:1111/j.1540-4560.2009.01653.x

Hipólito-Delgado, C., & Lee, C. (2007). Empowerment theory for the professional school counselor: A manifesto for what really matters. *Professional School Counseling, 10*(4), 327–332.

Ho, M. K. (1987). *Family therapy with ethnic minorities*. Newbury Park, CA: Sage.

Hochschild, J. L. (2003). Social class in public schools. *Journal of Social Issues, 59*, 821–840.

Hofferth, S. L. (2003). Race/ethnic differences in father involvement in two-parent families: Culture, context, or economy? *Journal of Family Issues, 24*(2), 185–216.

Hofstede, G. (1980). *Culture's consequences: International differences in work-related values.* Newbury Park, CA: Sage.

Hohenshil, T. H., Amundson, N. E., & Niles, S. G. (Eds.). (2013). *Counseling around the world: An international handbook.* Alexandria, VA: American Counseling Association.

Holley, L. C., Salas, L. M., Marsiglia, F. F., Yabiku, S. T., Fitzharris, B., & Jackson, K. F. (2009). Youths of Mexican descent of the Southwest: Exploring differences in ethnic labels. *Children & Schools, 31*, 15–26.

Hoogasian, R., & Lijtmaer, R. (2010). Integrating curanderismo into counselling and psychotherapy. *Counselling Psychology Quarterly, 23*(3), 297–307.

Houben, L. M. (2012). *Counseling Hispanics through loss, grief, and bereavement.* New York, NY: Springer.

Hughes, M. T., Valle-Riestra, D. M., & Arguelles, M. E. (2008). The voices of Latino families raising children with special needs. *Journal of Latinos & Education, 7*(3), 241–257.

Hull, P., Kilbourne, B., Reece, M., & Husaini, B. (2008). Community involvement and adolescent mental health: Moderating effects of race/ethnicity and neighborhood disadvantage. *Journal of Community Psychology, 36*, 534–551.

Humes, K. R., Jones, N. A., & Ramírez, R. R. (2011). *Overview of race and Hispanic origin: 2010* (Publication No. C2010BR-02). Retrieved from the Pew Hispanic Center website: http://www.census.gov/prod/cen2010/briefs/c2010br-02.pdf

Hurtado, A. (1997). Understanding multiple group identities: Inserting women into cultural transformations. *Journal of Social Issues, 53*, 299–328.

Hurtado, A., & Sinha, M. (2006). Differences and similarities: Latina and Latino doctoral students navigating the gender divide. In J. Castellanos, A. M. Gloria, & M. Kamimura (Eds.), *The Latina/o pathway to the Ph.D.: Abriendo caminos* (pp. 149–168). Sterling, VA: Stylus.

Hwang, W. (2006). Acculturative family distancing: Theory, research, and clinical practice. *Psychotherapy: Theory, Research, Practice, Training, 43*, 397–409.

Hwang, W. C., & Wood, J. J. (2009). Acculturative family distancing: Links with self-reported symptomatology among Asian Americans and Latinos. *Child Psychiatry and Human Development, 40*, 123–138.

Ibarra, R. A. (2003). Latina/o faculty and the tenure process in cultural context. In J. Castellanos & L. Jones (Eds.), *The majority in the minority: Expanding the representation of Latina/o faculty, administrators, and students in higher education* (pp. 207–220). Sterling, VA: Stylus.

Ibrahim, A. B., & Goodwin, J. R. (1986). Perceived causes of success in small business. *American Journal of Small Business, 11*(2), 41–50.

Inclán, J. E. (1990). Understanding Hispanic families: A curriculum outline. *Journal of Strategic and Systemic Therapies, 9*, 64–82.

Ispa, J. M., Fine, M. A., Halgunseth, L. C., Harper, S., Robinson, J., Boyce, L., . . . Brady-Smith, C. (2004). Maternal intrusiveness, maternal warmth, and mother-toddler relationship outcomes: Variations across, low-income ethnic and acculturation groups. *Child Development, 75*, 1613–1631.

Jones, A. (2004). Latinos in the military, 1946-present. In J. Phillips Resch (Ed.), *Americans at war: Society, culture, and the homefront.* New York, NY: Macmillan Reference.

Jordan, M. (2011, July 15). U.S. news: Births fuel Hispanic gains—Immigration is no longer the main factor behind a surging Latino population. *Wall Street Journal*, pp. A3-3.

Jordan, M. (2012, September 24). Migrants' cash keeps flowing home. *Wall Street Journal*, p. A16.

Jordan, M., & Kesling, B. (2012, August 15). Illegal immigrants flock to youth program. *Wall Street Journal, 259*(191), p. A2.

Kanter, R. M. (1979). *The tale of "O": On being different* [Video]. Goodmeasure.

Kao, B., Romero-Bosch, L., Plante, W., & Lobato, D. (2012). The experiences of Latino siblings of children with developmental disabilities. *Child: Care, Health and Development, 38,* 545–552.

Kao, H. F. S., & Travis, S. S. (2005). Effects of acculturation and social exchange on the expectations of filial piety among Hispanic/Latino parents of adult children. *Nursing & Health Sciences, 7*(4), 226–234.

Keller, J. H. (2006). *Síndromes culturales: Nervios y susto en Guatemala* [Cultural syndromes: Anxieties and fears in Guatemala]. Unpublished manuscript, Department of Psychology, Universidad de Guatemala, Guatemala. Retrieved from http://www.coedu.usf.edu/zalaquett/cic/sc.htm

Kiang, L., Perreira, K. M., & Fuligni, A. J. (2011). Ethnic label use in adolescents from traditional and non-traditional immigrant communities. *Journal of Youth and Adolescence, 40,* 719–729.

Kirmayer, L. J. (2001). Cultural variations in the clinical presentation of depression and anxiety: Implications for diagnosis and treatment. *Journal of Clinical Psychiatry, 62,* 22–30.

Kluckhohn, C., & Stodtbeck, F. (1961). *Variations in value orientations.* Oxford, England: Row, Peterson.

Knight, G. P., Bernal, M. E., Garza, C. A., Cota, M. K., & Ocampo, K. A. (1993). Family socialization and the ethnic identity of Mexican-American children. *Journal of Cross-Cultural Psychology, 24*(1), 99–114.

Kochhar, R. (2012). *The demographics of the jobs recovery: Employment gains by race, ethnicity, and gender and nativity.* Retrieved from the Pew Hispanic Center website: http://www.pewHispanic.org/files/2012/03/PHC-Labor-report-FINAL_3-21-12.pdf

Kochhar, R., Fry, R., & Taylor, P. (2011). *Hispanic household wealth fell by 66% from 2005 to 2009.* Retrieved from the Pew Hispanic Center website: http://www.pewHispanic.org/2011/07/26/the-toll-of-the-great-recession/

Kopelowicz, A., Zárate, R., Smith, V., Mintz, J., & Liberman, R. (2003). Disease management in Latinos with schizophrenia: A family-assisted, skills training approach. *Schizophrenia Bulletin, 29*(2), 211–227.

Lakes, K., López, S. R., & Garro, L. C. (2006). Cultural competence and psychotherapy: Applying anthropologically informed conceptions of culture. *Psychotherapy: Theory, Research, and Practice, 43,* 380–396.

Landale, N. S., & Oropesa, R. S. (2007). Hispanic families: Stability and change. *Annual Review of Sociology, 33,* 381–405.

La Roche, M., D'Angelo, E., Gualdron, L., & Leavell, J. (2006). Culturally sensitive guided imagery for allocentric Latinos: A pilot study. *Psychotherapy: Theory, Research, Practice, Training, 43,* 555–560.

Latino/a Education Network Service. (n.d.). *Historical background.* Retrieved from http://palante.org/History.htm

Lazarus, E. (1883). *The new colossus.* Retrieved from http://www.nps.gov/stli/historyculture/upload/new%20colossus%20for%20displaypage2.pdf

Lee, R. M., & Liu, H. T. T. (2001). Coping with intergenerational family conflict: Comparison of Asian American, Hispanic, and European American college students. *Journal of Counseling Psychology, 48,* 410–419.

Leidy, M., Guerra, N., & Toro, R. (2012). Positive parenting, family cohesion, and child social competence among immigrant Latino families. *Journal of Latina/o Psychology, 1*(S), 3–13.

Leong, F. (1996). Toward an integrative model for cross-cultural counseling and psychotherapy. *Applied & Preventive Psychology, 5*(4), 189–209.

Leong, F. T. L., Kohout, J., Smith, J., & Wicherski, M. (2003). A profile of ethnic minority psychology: A pipeline perspective. In G. Bernal, J. E. Trimble, A. K. Burlew, & F. T. L. Leong (Eds.), *Handbook of racial and ethnic minority psychology* (pp. 76–99). Thousand Oaks, CA: Sage.

Leong, F., & Wong, P. (2003). Optimal human functioning from cross-cultural perspectives: Cultural competence as an organizing framework. In W. B. Walsh (Ed.), *Counseling psychology and optimal human functioning* (pp. 123–150). Mahwah, NJ: Erlbaum.

Levy, S. R. (Ed.). (2010). Latinos [Special issue]. *Journal of Social Issues, 66*(1).

Lewin, K. (1935). *A dynamic theory of personality: Selected papers.* New York, NY: McGraw-Hill.

Lewis, J. A., Arnold, M. S., House, R., & Toporek, R. L. (2002). *ACA advocacy competencies.* Retrieved from http://www.counseling.org/Resources/Competencies/Advocacy_Competencies.pdf

Lewis-Fernández, R., & Díaz, N. (2002). The cultural formulation: A method for assessing cultural factors affecting the clinical encounter. *Psychiatric Quarterly, 73,* 271–295.

Lewis-Fernández, R., Gorritz, M., Raggio, G. A., Peláez, C., Chen, H., & Guarnaccia, P. J. (2010). Association of trauma-related disorders and dissociation with four idioms of distress among Latino psychiatric outpatients. *Culture, Medicine and Psychiatry, 34*(2), 219–243.

Lewis-Fernández, R., Hinton, D. E., Patterson, E. H., Hofmann, S. G., Craske, M. G., Stein, D. J., . . . Liao, B. (2011). Culture and anxiety disorders: Recommendations for *DSM V. Focus: Psychiatry Online, 9*(1), 351–368.

Lipman, F. J. (2006). Taxing undocumented immigrants: Separate, unequal and without representation. *Harvard Latino Law Review, 9,* 1–58.

Llamas, J. D., & Morgan Consoli, M. (2012). The importance of familia for Latina/o college students: Examining the role of familial support in intragroup marginalization. *Cultural Diversity and Ethnic Minority Psychology, 18*(4), 395–403. doi:10.1037/a0029756

Lockhead, C. (2006, May 21). Give and take across the border—1 in 7 Mexican workers migrates—Most send money home. *San Francisco Chronicle,* p. 21.

Logan, J. R. (2003). *How race counts for Hispanic Americans.* Albany, NY: Lewis Mumford Center for Comparative Urban and Regional Research.

Lopez, E. M. (2001). Guidance of Latino high school students in mathematics and career identity development. *Hispanic Journal of Behavioral Sciences, 23*(2), 189–207.

López, M. H. (2009). *Latinos and education: Explaining the attainment gap.* Washington, DC: Pew Hispanic Center.

López, M. H., & Cohn, D. (2011). *The toll of the great recession: Childhood poverty among Hispanics sets record, leads nation.* Washington, DC: Pew Hispanic Center.

López, M. H., & Light, M. T. (2009). *A rising share: Hispanics and federal crime.* Washington, DC: Pew Hispanic Center.

Lopez, M. H., & Livingston, C. (2009). *Hispanics in the criminal justice system: Low confidence, high exposure.* Washington, DC: Pew Hispanic Center.

López, M. H., Livingston, G., & Kochhar, R. (2009). *Hispanics and the economic downturn: Housing woes and remittance cuts.* Retrieved from the Pew Hispanic Center website: http://www.pewHispanic.org/2009/01/08/Hispanics-and-the-economic-downturn-housing-woes-and-remittance-costs

López, M. H., & Velasco, G. (2011). *Childhood poverty among Hispanic sets record, leads nation.* Retrieved from the Pew Hispanic Center website: http://www.pewHispanic.org/2011/09/28/childhood-poverty-among-Hispanics-sets-record-leads-nation/

Loukas, A., Suizzo, M. A., & Prelow, H. M. (2007). Examining resource and protective factors in the adjustment of Latino youth in low income families: What role does maternal acculturation play? *Journal of Youth Adolescence, 36*, 489–501.

Luna, I., de Ardon, E., Lim, Y., Cromwell, S., Phillips, L., & Russell, C. K. (1996). The relevance of familism in cross-cultural studies of family caregiving. *Western Journal of Nursing Research, 18*(3), 267–283.

Magaña, S. (1999). Puerto Rican families caring for an adult with mental retardation: Role of familism. *American Journal on Mental Retardation, 104*, 466–482.

Magaña, S., Seltzer, M. M., & Krauss, M. W. (2004). Cultural context of caregiving: Differences in depression between Puerto Rican and non-Latina White mothers of adults with mental retardation. *Mental Retardation, 42*, 466–482.

Magaña, S., Seltzer, M. M., Krauss, M. W., Rubert, M., & Szapocznik, J. (2002). Well-being and family role strains among Cuban American and Puerto Rican mothers of adults with mental retardation. *Journal of Human Behavior in the Social Environment, 5*(3–4), 31–55.

Magaña, S., & Smith, M. J. (2006). Psychological distress and well-being of Latina and non-Latina White mothers of youth and adults with an autism spectrum disorder: Cultural attitudes toward coresidence status. *American Journal of Orthopsychiatry, 76*, 346–357.

Magilvy, J. K., Congdon, J. G., Martinez, R. J., Davis, R., & Averill, J. (2000). Caring for our own: Health care experiences of rural Hispanic elders. *Journal of Aging Studies, 14*(2), 171–190.

Maldonado, C., & Farmer, E. I. (2007). Examining Latinos involvement in the workforce and postsecondary technical education in the United States. *Journal of Career and Technical Education, 22*(2), 26–40.

Maldonado-Torres, S. E. (2011). Differences in learning styles of Dominican and Puerto Rican students: We are Latinos from the Caribbean; our first language is Spanish, however; our learning preferences are different. *Journal of Hispanic Higher Education, 10*(3), 226–236.

Malgady, R. G., Costantino, G., & Rogler, L. H. (1984). Development of a thematic apperception test ({temas}) for urban Hispanic children. *Journal of Consulting and Clinical Psychology, 52*, 986–996. doi:10.1037/0022-006X.52.6.986

Malgady, R. G., Rogler, L. H., & Costantino, G. (1987). Ethnocultural and linguistic bias in mental health evaluation of Hispanics. *American Psychologist, 42*(3), 228–234.

Malgady, R. G., Rogler, L. H., & Costantino, G. (1990). Culturally sensitive psychotherapy for Puerto Rican children and adolescents: A program of treatment outcome research. *Journal of Consulting and Clinical Psychology, 58*, 704–712. doi:10.1037/0022-006X.58.6.704

Malott, K. M. (2009). Investigation of ethnic self-labeling in the Latina population: Implications for counselors and counselor educators. *Journal of Counseling & Development, 87*, 179–185.

Mapp, K. L. (2003). Having their say: Parents describe why and how they are engaged in their children's learning. *School Community Journal, 13*(1), 35–64.

Maramba, G. G., & Nagayama Hall, G. C. (2002). Meta-analyses of ethnic match as a predictor of dropout, utilization, and level of functioning. *Cultural Diversity and Ethnic Minority Psychology, 8*(3), 290–297.

Marcos, L. R. (1973). The effect of interview language on the evaluation of psychopathology. *American Journal of Psychiatry, 130*, 549–553.

Marcos, L. (1994). The psychiatric examination of Hispanics: Across the language barrier. In R. G. Malgady & O. E. Rodriguez (Eds.), *Theoretical and conceptual issues in Hispanic mental health* (pp. 144–154). Melbourne, FL: Krieger.

Marcos, L. R., & Trujillo, M. (1981). Culture, language, and communicative behavior: The psychiatric examination of Spanish-Americans. In R. P. Duran (Ed.), *Latino language and communicative behavior* (pp. 187–194). Newark, NJ: Ablex.

Marcos, L. R., & Urcuyo, L. (1979). Dynamic psychotherapy with the bilingual patient. *American Journal of Psychotherapy, 33*, 331–338.

Marian, V., & Shook, A. (2012). *The cognitive benefits of being bilingual.* Retrieved from http://dana.org/news/cerebrum/detail.aspx?id=39638

Marín, B. V., & Gómez, C. A. (1997). Latino culture and sex: Implications for HIV prevention. In J. G. Garcia & M. C. Zea (Eds.), *Psychological intervention and research with Latino populations* (pp. 73–93). Boston, MA: Allyn & Bacon.

Marín, G., & Gamba, R. J. (2002). Acculturation and changes in cultural values. In K. M. Chung, P. B. Organista, & G. Marín (Eds.), *Acculturation: Advances in theory, measurement, and applied research* (pp. 83–93). Washington, DC: American Psychological Association.

Marín, G., & Marín, B. V. (1991). *Research with Hispanic populations.* Newbury Park, CA: Sage.

Martin, J. A., Hamilton, B. E., Ventura, S. J., Osterman, M., Wilson, E. C., & Mathews, T. J. (2012). Births: Final data for 2010. *National Vital Statistics Reports, 61*(1). Retrieved from http://www.cdc.gov/nchs/data/nvsr/nvsr61/nvsr61_01.pdf#table16

Martinez, S., & Cervera, Y. (2012). Fulfilling educational aspirations: Latino students' information seeking patterns. *Journal of Hispanic Higher Education, 11*, 388–402.

Martínez-Taboas, A., Varas-Díaz, N., López-Garay, D., & Hernández-Pereira, L. (2011). What every psychologists practitioner should know about atheist people and atheism. *Revista Interamericana de Psicologia, 45*(2), 203–210.

Maslow, A. (1950). *Self-actualizing people: A study of psychological health.* New York, NY: Grune & Stratton.

Masud-Piloto, F. R. (1988). *With open arms: Cuban migration to the United States.* Totowa, NJ: Rowman-Littlefield.

Matos, M., Torres, R., Santiago, R., Jurado, M., & Rodríguez, I. (2006). Adaptation of parent-child interaction therapy for Puerto Rican families: A preliminary study. *Family Process, 45*(2), 205–222.

McDonald, E. J., McCabe, K., Yeh, M., Lau, A., Garland, A., & Hough, R. L. (2005). Cultural affiliation and self-esteem as predictors of internalizing symptoms among Mexican American adolescents. *Journal of Clinical Child and Adolescent Psychology, 34*(1), 163–171.

McGill, R. K., Hughes, D., Alicea, S., & Way, N. (2012). Academic adjustment across middle school: The role of public regard and parenting. *Developmental Psychology, 48*, 1003–1018. doi:10.1037/a0026006

McGoldrick, M. (1992). Ethnicity and the family life cycle. *Family Business Review, 5*(4), 437–459.

McGoldrick, M., & Carter, B. (1998). Self in context: The individual life cycle in systemic perspective. In B. Carter & M. McGoldrick (Eds.), *The expanded life cycle: Individual, family, and social perspectives* (pp. 27–45). Boston, MA: Allyn & Bacon.

McGoldrick, M., Gerson, R., & Shellenberger, S. (1999). *Genograms: Assessment and intervention.* New York, NY: Norton.

McGoldrick, M., Giordano, J., & Garcia-Preto, N. (Eds.). (2005a). *Ethnicity and family therapy.* New York, NY: Guilford Press.

McGoldrick, M., Giordano, J., & Garcia-Preto, N. (2005b). Overview: Ethnicity and family therapy. In M. McGoldrick, J. Giordano, & N. Garcia-Preto (Eds.), *Ethnicity and family therapy* (pp. 1–40). New York, NY: Guilford Press.

McGoldrick, M., & Hardy, K. V. (Eds.). (2008). *Re-visioning family therapy: Race, culture and gender in clinical practice* (2nd ed.). New York, NY: Guilford Press.

McGoldrick, M., & Preto, N. G. (1984). Ethnic intermarriage. *Family Process, 23*(3), 347–364.

McQueen, A., Getz, J., & Bray, J. (2003). Acculturation, substance use, and deviant behavior: Examining separation and family conflict as mediators. *Child Development, 74,* 1737–1750.

Mendez, J. L., Carpenter, J. L., LaForett, D. R., & Cohen, J. S. (2009). Parental engagement and barriers to participation in a community-based preventive intervention. *American Journal of Community Psychology, 44*(1), 1–14.

Mendez, J. L., & Westerberg, D. (2012). Implementation of a culturally adapted treatment to reduce barriers for Latino parents. *Cultural Diversity & Ethnic Minority Psychology, 18*(4), 363–372.

Mendible, M. (Ed.). (2007). *From bananas to buttocks: The Latina body in popular film and culture.* Austin: University of Texas Press.

Messer, S. B., & McWilliams, N. (2003). The impact of Sigmund Freud and the interpretations of dreams. In R. J. Sternberg (Ed.), *The anatomy of impact: What makes the great work of psychology great* (pp. 71–88). Washington, DC: American Psychological Association.

Migration Policy Institute. (2012). *US immigration.* Retrieved from http://www.migrationpolicy.org/research/usimmigration.php

Mikhail, N., Wali, S., & Ziment, I. (2004). Use of alternative medicine among Hispanics. *Journal of Alternative & Complementary Medicine, 10,* 851–859.

Minority Business Development Agency. (n.d.). *Hispanic-owned business growth and global reach.* Retrieved from http://www.mbda.gov/pressroom/news-and-announcements/hispanic-owned-businesses-increased-nearly-44-percent

Minsky, S., Vega, W., Miskimen, T., Gara, M., & Escobar, J. (2003). Diagnostic patterns in Latino, African American, and European American psychiatric patients. *Archives of General Psychiatry, 60,* 637–644.

Minuchin, P., Colapinto, J., & Minuchin, S. (2007). *Working with families of the poor* (2nd ed.). New York, NY: Guilford Press.

Miranda, A. O., Bilot, J. M., Peluso, P. P., Berman, K., & Van Meek, L. G. (2006). Latino families: The relevance of the connection among acculturation, family dynamics and health for family counseling research and practice. *The Family Journal: Counseling and Therapy for Couples and Families, 14*(3), 268–273. doi:10.1177/1066480706287805

Miranda, A. O., & Umhoefer, D. L. (1998). Depression and social interest differences between Latinos in dissimilar acculturation stages. *Journal of Mental Health Counseling, 20,* 159–171.

Mirandé, A. (1988). Que gacho es ser macho: It's a drag to be a macho man. *Aztlan, 17,* 63–89.

Mirandé, A. (1997). *Hombres y machos: Masculinity and Latino culture.* Boulder, CO: Westview Press.

Mize, R. L., & Delgado, G. P. (2012). *Latino immigrants in the United States.* Malden, MA: Polity Press.

Moane, G. (2010). Sociopolitical and political activism: Synergies between feminist and liberation psychology. *Psychology of Women Quarterly, 34,* 521–529.

Mogro-Wilson, C. (2011). Resilience in vulnerable and at-risk Latino families. *Infants and Young Children, 24,* 267–279.

Montalvo, B., & Gutierrez, M. J. (1989). Nine assumptions for work with ethnic minority families. In G. W. Saba, B. M. Karrer, & K. V. Hardy (Eds.), *Minorities and family therapy* (pp. 36–52). New York, NY: Hawthorn Press.

Montero, M. (2007). The political psychology of liberation: From politics to ethics and back. *Political Psychology, 28,* 517–533.

Montilla, R. E., & Medina, F. (2006). *Pastoral care and counseling with Latino/as.* Minneapolis, MN: Fortress.

Morales, E. (2009, August). *Psychology's preparedness in science and practice amid changing multicultural demographics.* Paper presented at the 117th Annual Convention of the American Psychological Association, Toronto, Ontario, Canada.

Moreno, R. (1991). Maternal teaching of preschool children in minority and low status families: A critical review. *Early Childhood Research Quarterly, 6,* 395–410.

Morin, J. L. (2008). Latinas/os and US prisons: Trends and challenges. *Latino Studies, 6,* 11–34.

Motel, S. (2012). *Statistical portrait of Hispanics in the United States, 2010.* Retrieved from the Pew Hispanic Center website: http://www.pewHispanic.org/2012/02/21/statistical-portrait-of-Hispanics-in-the-united-states-2010/

Motel, S., & Patten, E. (2012a, June 27). *Hispanics of Puerto Rican origin in the United States, 2010.* Retrieved from the Pew Hispanic Center website: http://www.pewHispanic.org/files/2012/06/2010-Puerto-Rican-Factsheet.pdf

Motel, S., & Patten, E. (2012b, June 27). *The 10 largest Hispanic origin groups: Characteristics, rankings top counties.* Retrieved from the Pew Hispanic Center website: http://www.pewHispanic.org/files/2012/06/The-10-Largest-Hispanic-Origin-Groups.pdf

Muir, J. A., Schwartz, S. J., & Szapocznik, J. (2004). A program of research with Hispanic and African American families: Three decades of intervention development and testing influenced by the changing cultural context of Miami. *Journal of Marital and Family Therapy, 30*(3), 285–303.

Mullinix, K., Garcia, A., Lewis-Lorentz, A., & Qazi, J. (2006). Latino views of agriculture, careers and education: Dispelling the myths. *NACTA Journal, 50*(2), 2–11.

Mulvaney-Day, N. E., Earl, T. R., Díaz-Linhart, Y., & Alegría, M. (2011). Preferences for relational style with mental health clinicians: A qualitative comparison of African American, Latino and non-Latino White patients. *Journal of Clinical Psychology, 67*(1), 31–44.

Muñoz, S. M., & Guardia, J. R. (2009). Nuestra historia y futuro (our history and future): Latino/a fraternities and sororities. In C. L. Torbenson & G. Parks (Eds.), *Brothers and sisters: Diversity in college, fraternities and sororities* (pp. 104–132). Cranbury, NJ: Associated University Presses.

Murguía, J. (2011, April). Hispanic values are American values. *Wall Street Journal, 257*(93), pp. A11.

National Coalition of Hispanic Health and Human Services Organizations. (1986). *Delivering preventive health care to Hispanics: A manual for providers.* Washington, DC: Author.

National Council of La Raza. (2011). *We needed the work: Latino worker voices in the new economy.* Retrieved from http://issuu.com/nclr/docs/jobquality_web?mode=window&backgroundColor=%23222222

National Council of La Raza. (2012, April 17). *Tax day a reminder that Latino workers are paying their fare share of taxes.* Retrieved from http://www.nclr.org/index.php/about_us/news/news_releases/tax_day_a_reminder_that_latino_workers_are_paying_their_fare_share_of_taxes/

Navarro, R. L., Flores, L. Y., & Worthington, R. L. (2007). Mexican American middle school students' goal intentions in mathematics and science: A test of social cognitive career theory. *Journal of Counseling Psychology, 54,* 320–335.

Nazario, S. (2007). *Enrique's journey.* New York, NY: Random House.

Nevels, B. J., Delgado-Romero, E., & Heesacker, M. (2012, August). *Citation patterns in articles published in three counseling psychology journals.* Poster presented at the 120th Annual Convention of the American Psychological Association, Orlando, FL.

Niemann, Y. F., & Dovidio, J. (2005). Affirmative action and job satisfaction: Understanding underlying processes. In Y. F. Neimann & G. Maruyama (Eds.), *The Journal of Social Issues, Special Issue: Inequities in Higher Education: Issues and Promising Practices in a World Ambivalent About Affirmative Action, 61*(3), 507–523.

Nieto-Phillips, J. M. (2008). *The language of blood: The making of Spanish-American identity in New Mexico, 1880's-1930's.* Albuquerque: University of New Mexico Press.

Nora, A., & Cabrera, A. F. (1996). The role of perceptions of prejudice and discrimination on the adjustment of minority students to college. *Journal of Higher Education, 67,* 119–148.

Office of Minority Health. (2012a). *HIV/AIDS and Hispanic Americans.* Retrieved from http://minorityhealth.hhs.gov/templates/content.aspx?lvl=3&lvlID=7&ID=3327

Office of Minority Health. (2012b). *HIV/AIDS data/statistics.* Retrieved from http://minorityhealth.hhs.gov/templates/browse.aspx?lvl=3&lvlID=7

Office of Minority Health. (2012c). *Infant mortality/SIDS data and stat.* Retrieved from http://www.minorityhealth.hhs.gov/templates/browse.aspx?lvl=3&lvlid=8

Office of Minority Health. (2012d). *Obesity and Hispanic Americans.* Retrieved from http://www.minorityhealth.hhs.gov/templates/content.aspx?lvl=3&IvIID=f37&ID=6459

Ojeda, L., Navarro, R. L., Rosales Meza, R., & Arbona, C. (2012). Too Latino and not Latino enough: The role of ethnicity-related stress on life satisfaction. *Journal of Hispanic Higher Education, 11,* 14–28.

Ojeda, L., Piña-Watson, B., Castillo, L. G., Khan, N., Castillo, R., & Leigh, J. (2012). Acculturation, enculturation, ethnic identity, and conscientiousness as predictors of Latino girls' and boys' career decision self-efficacy. *Journal of Career Development, 39,* 208–228.

Oquendo, M., Dragatsi, D., Harkavy-Friedman, J., Dervic, K., Currier, D., Burke, A. K., . . . Mann, J. J. (2005). Protective factors against suicidal behavior in Latinos. *Journal of Nervous and Mental Disease, 193,* 438–443.

Orozco, V. (2003). Latinas and the undergraduate experience: No estamos solas! In J. Castellanos & L. Jones (Eds.), *The majority in the minority: Expanding the representation of Latina/o faculty, administrators, and students in higher education* (pp. 127–137). Sterling, VA: Stylus.

Ortiz F. A., & Davis, K. G. (2008). Latina/o folk Saints and Marian devotions popular religiosity and healing. In W. McNeill & J. M. Cervantes (Eds.), *Latina/o healing practices: Mestizo and indigenous perspectives* (pp. 29–62). New York, NY: Taylor & Francis.

Ortiz Salgado, S. (2009). Case illustration: Implementation and application of Latina/o cultural values in practice. In M. Gallardo, C. J. Yeh, J. E. Trimble, & T. Parham (Eds.), *Culturally adaptive counseling skills: Demonstrations of evidence-based practices* (pp. 127–154). Thousand Oaks, CA: Sage.

Padilla, A. M. (1994). Bicultural development: A theoretical and empirical examination. In R. G. Malgady & O. Rodriguez (Eds.), *Theoretical and conceptual issues in Hispanic mental health* (pp. 20–51). Melbourne, FL: Krieger.

Padilla, A. M. (2006). Bicultural social development. *Hispanic Journal of Behavioral Sciences, 28,* 467–497.

Padilla, A. M., & Olmedo, E. O. (2009). Synopsis of key persons, events and associations in the history of Latino psychology. *Cultural Diversity & Ethnic Minority Psychology, 15,* 363–373.

Padilla, Y. C., & Villalobos, G. (2007). Cultural responses to health among Mexican American women and their families. *Family & Community Health, 30,* S24–S33.

Pan, E. L., & Farrell, M. P. (2006). Ethnic differences in the effects of intergenerational relations on adolescent problem behavior in U.S. single-mother families. *Journal of Family Issues, 27,* 1137–1158.

Paniagua, F. A. (2005). *Assessing and treating culturally diverse clients: A practical guide* (3rd ed., Vol. 4). Thousand Oaks, CA: Sage.

Pappas, G., & Guajardo, M. (1997). Ethnic diversity as a measurement of quality in higher education. *Latinos in Colorado: A Profile of Culture, Changes, and Challenges, 5,* 19–22.

Parham, T. A. (2002). Counseling models for African Americans: The what and how of counseling. In T. A. Parham & T. M. J. Parham (Eds.), *Counseling persons of African descent: Raising the bar of practitioner competence* (pp. 100–118). Thousand Oaks, CA: Sage.

Parham, T. A., & Parham, T. M. J. (Eds.). (2002). *Counseling persons of African descent: Raising the bar of practitioner competence.* Thousand Oaks CA: Sage.

Parham, T. A., White, J. L., & Ajamu, A. (1999). *The psychology of Blacks* (3rd ed.). Upper Saddle River, NJ: Prentice-Hall.

Park, N., & Peterson, C. (2008). Positive psychology and character strengths: Application to strengths-based school counseling. *Professional School Counseling, 12*(2), 85–92.

Parke, R. D., Coltrane, S., Duffy, S., Buriel, R., Dennis, J., & Powers, J. (2004). Economic stress, parenting, and child adjustment in Mexican American and European American families. *Child Development, 75,* 1632–1652.

Parra-Cardona, J. R., Córdova, D., Jr., Holtrop, K., Villarruel, F. A., & Wieling, E. (2008). Shared ancestry, evolving stories: Similar and contrasting life experiences described by foreign-born and U.S. born Latino parents. *Family Process, 47,* 157–172.

Parra Cardona, J., Domenech Rodríguez, M., Forgatch, M., Sullivan, C., Bybee, D., Holtrop, K., . . . Bernal, G. (2012). Culturally adapting an evidence-based parenting intervention for Latino immigrants: The need to integrate fidelity and cultural relevance. *Family Process, 51*(1), 56–72. doi:10.1111/j.1545-5300.2012.01386.x

Parra Cardona, J., Holtrop, K., Córdova, D. R., Escobar-Chew, A., Horsford, S., Tams, L., . . . Fitzgerald, H. (2009). "Queremos aprender": Latino immigrants' call to integrate cultural adaptation with best practice knowledge in a parenting intervention. *Family Process, 48*(2), 211–231.

Parsons, F. (1909). *Choosing a vocation.* Boston, MA: Houghton Mifflin.

Passel, J. S. (2006). *The size and characteristics of the unauthorized migration population in the US: Estimates based on the March 2005 Current Population Survey.* Washington, DC: Pew Hispanic Center.

Passel, J. S., & Cohn, D. (2008). *U.S. population projections: 2005-2050.* Retrieved from the Pew Hispanic Center website: http://www.pewHispanic.org/files/reports/85.pdf

Passel, J. S., & Cohn, D. (2011). *Unauthorized immigrant population: National and state trends, 2010.* Retrieved from the Pew Hispanic Center website: http://www.pewHispanic.org/files/reports/133.pdf

Passel, J., Cohn, D., & Lopez, M. H. (2011). *Hispanics account for more than half of nation's growth in past decade.* Retrieved from the Pew Hispanic Center website: http://www.pewhispanic.org/2011/03/24/hispanics-account-for-more-than-half-of-nations-growth-in-past-decade/

Passel, J., Livingston, G., & Cohn, D. (2012). *Explaining why minority births now out-number white births.* Retrieved from the Pew Hispanic Center website: http://pewsocialtrends.org/2012/05/17/explaining why-minority-births-now-out-number-white-births

Passel, J., & Taylor, P. (2010). *Unauthorized immigrants and their U.S. born children.* Retrieved from the Pew Hispanic Center website: http://www.pewhispanic.org/files/reports/125.pdf

Passel, J., Wang, W., & Taylor, P. (2010). *One-in-seven new U.S. marriages is interracial or interethnic.* Retrieved from the Pew Hispanic Center website: http://www.pewsocialtrends.org/files/2010/10/755-marrying-out.pdf

Pedersen, P. B. (1997a). The cultural context of the American Counseling Association code of ethics. *Journal of Counseling & Development, 76*(1), 23–28.

Pedersen, P. B. (1997b). *Culture-centered counseling interventions: Striving for accuracy.* Los Angeles, CA: Sage.

Peña, J. B., Kuhlberg, J. A., Zayas, L. H., Baumann, A. A., Gulbas, L., Hausmann-Stabile, C., & Nolle, A. P. (2011). Familism, family environment, and suicide among Latina youth. *Suicide and Life-Threatening Behaviors, 41,* 330–341.

Pérez, R., Araujo Dawson, B., & Suárez-Orozco, C. (2011). Understanding acculturation, depressive symptoms, and the protective role of family involvement among Latino(a) immigrant families. *Journal of Family Social Work, 14,* 429–445.

Pérez, W. (2009). *We are Americans: Undocumented students pursuing the American dream.* Sterling, VA: Stylus.

Pérez Foster, R. (1998). *The power of language in the clinical process: Assessing and treating the bilingual person.* Northvale, NJ: Jason Aronson.

Perreira, K. M., Chapman, M., & Stein, G. L. (2006). Becoming an American parent: Overcoming challenges and finding strengths in new immigrant Latino community. *Journal of Family Issues, 27,* 1383–1414.

Peterson, C., Park, N., & Seligman, M. E. P. (2006). Greater strengths of character and recovery from illness. *Journal of Positive Psychology, 1,* 17–26.

Pew Hispanic Center. (2007). *Changing faiths: Latinos and the transformation of American religion.* Retrieved from http://www.pewHispanic.org/files/reports/75.pdf

Pew Hispanic Center. (2009). *Between two worlds: How young Latinos come of age in America.* Retrieved from http://www.pewhispanic.org/files/reports/117.pdf

Pew Hispanic Center. (2011). *The Mexican American boom: Births overtake immigration.* Retrieved from http://www.pewhispanic.org/files/reports/144.pdf

Pew Hispanic Research Center. (2012). *Pew Hispanic Research Center.* Retrieved from http://www.pewhispanic.org/

Phinney, J. S. (1992). The Multigroup Ethnic Identity Measure: A new scale for use with diverse groups. *Journal of Adolescent Research, 7*(2), 156–176.

Phinney, J. S. (2003). Ethnic identity and acculturation. In K. M. Chung, P. B. Organista, & G. Marín (Eds.), *Acculturation: Advances in theory, measurement, and applied research* (pp. 63–81). Washington, DC: American Psychological Association.

Phinney, J. S., Ong, A., & Madden, T. (2000). Cultural values and intergenerational value discrepancies in immigrant and non-immigrant families. *Child Development, 71,* 528–539.

Pielemeier, K. (2007, February 23). *Rift seen in growing local Latino population.* Retrieved from http://www.post-gazette.com/stories/business/news/rift-seen-in-growing-local-latino-population-473535/

Piedra, L., & Byoun, S. (2012). Vida alegre: Preliminary findings of a depression intervention for immigrant Latino mothers. *Research on Social Work Practice, 22*(2), 138–150.

Platt, J. J. (2012). A Mexico City–based immersion education program: Training mental health clinicians for practice with Latino communities. *Journal of Marital & Family Therapy, 38*(2), 352–364. doi:10.1111/j.1752-0606.2010.00208.x

Pokhrel, P., Unger, J. B., Wagner, K. D., Ritt-Olson, A., & Sussman, S. (2008). Effects of parental monitoring, parent–child communication, and parents' expectation of the child's acculturation on the substance use behaviors of urban, Hispanic adolescents. *Journal of Ethnicity in Substance Abuse, 7*(2), 200–213.

Polo, A. J., Alegría, M., & Sirkin, J. T. (2012). Increasing the engagement of Latinos in services through community-derived programs: The Right Question Project–Mental Health. *Professional Psychology: Research and Practice, 43*(3), 208–216.

Ponterotto, J. G., Fingerhut, E. C., & McGuiness, R. (2012). Legend of the field: Influencial scholars in multicultural counseling. *Psychological Reports, 111*, 364–382.

Portes, P. R. (2005). *Dismantling educational inequity: A cultural-historical approach to closing the achievement gap.* New York, NY: Peter Lang.

Preciado, J., & Henry, M. (1997). Linguistic barriers in health education and services. In J. G. Garcia & M. C. Zea (Eds.), *Psychological interventions and research with Latino populations* (pp. 235–254). Boston, MA: Allyn & Bacon.

President's Advisory Commission on Educational Excellence. (1996). *Our nation on the fault line: Hispanic American education.* Washington, DC: White House Initiative on Educational Excellence for Hispanic Americans.

Preston, J. (2012, August 26). Young and alone, facing court and deportation. *New York Times*, pp. 1, 18.

Price, C. S., & Cuellar, I. (1981). Effects of language and related variables on the expression of psychopathology in Mexican American psychiatric patients. *Hispanic Journal of Behavioral Sciences, 3*(2), 145–160.

Quintana, S. M., & Atkinson, D. R. (2002). A multicultural perspective on principles of empirically supported interventions. *The Counseling Psychologist, 30*(2), 281–291. doi:10.1177/0011000002302005

Rajaram, S. S., & Rashidi, A. (1998). Minority women and breast cancer screening: The role of cultural explanatory models. *Preventive Medicine, 27*, 757–764.

Ramírez, J. R., Crano, W. D., Quist, R., Burgoon, M., Alvaro, E. M., & Grandpre, J. (2004). Acculturation, familism, parental monitoring, and knowledge as predictors of marijuana and inhalant use in adolescents. *Psychology of Addictive Behaviors, 18*(1), 3–11.

Ramírez, M. (1998). *Multicultural/multiracial psychology: Mestizo perspectives in personality and mental health.* Northvale, NJ: Jason Aronson.

Ramírez, M., & Castañeda, A. (1974). *Cultural democracy, bicognitive development, and education.* New York, NY: Academic Press.

Ramírez, M., III, Cox, B. G., & Castañeda, A. (1977). *The psychodynamics of biculturalism* (No. SEE-12/75-FR). Santa Cruz, CA: Systems and Evaluations in Education.

Ratts, M., D'Andrea, M., & Arredondo, P. (2004, September 13). Social justice counseling: "Fifth force" in field. *Counseling Today, 47*(1), pp. 28–30.

Reyes, J., & Elias, M. (2011). Fostering social-emotional resilience among Latino youth. *Psychology in the Schools, 48*, 723–737.

Reyes-Ortíz, C. A., Rodriguez, M., & Markides, K. S. (2009). The role of spirituality healing with perceptions of the medical encounter among Latinos. *Journal of General Internal Medicine, 24*, 542–547.

Rhodes, R. L., Ochoa, S. H., & Ortíz, S. O. (2005). *Assessing culturally and linguistically diverse students: A practical guide.* New York, NY: Guilford Press.

Risdal, D., & Singer, G. H. (2004). Marital adjustment in parents of children with disabilities: A historical review and meta-analysis. *Research and Practice for Persons With Severe Disabilities, 29*(2), 95–103.

Rivas, L., Delgado-Romero, E. A., & Ozambela, K. R. (2005). Our stories: Convergence of the language, professional, and personal identities of three Latino therapists. In L. Wieling & M. Rastogi (Eds.), *Voices of color: First-person accounts of ethnic minority therapists* (pp. 23–41). Thousand Oaks, CA: Sage.

Rivas-Drake, D. (2010). Public ethnic regard and academic adjustment among Latino students. *Journal of Research on Adolescence, 21*, 537–544.

Rivas-Drake, D., & Mooney, M. (2009). Neither colorblind nor oppositional: Perceived minority status and trajectories of academic adjustment among Latinos in elite higher education. *Developmental Psychology, 45*, 642–651. doi:10.1037/a0014135

Rivera-Arzola, M., & Ramos-Grenier, J. (1997). Anger, ataques de nervios, and la mujer Puertorriqueña: Sociocultural considerations and treatment implications. In J. G. García & M. C. Zea (Eds.), *Psychological interventions and research with Latino populations* (pp. 125–141). Boston, MA: Allyn & Bacon.

Rocque, M. (2010). Disproportionate minority discipline: Does race matter? *American Journal of Education, 116*, 557–581.

Rodríguez, C. E. (Ed.). (1997). *Latin looks: Images of Latinas and Latinos in the U.S. media*. Boulder, CO: Westview Press.

Rodríguez, C. E. (2000). *Changing race: Latinos, the census and the history of ethnicity in the United States*. New York: New York University Press.

Rogler, L. H. (1999). Methodological sources of cultural insensitivity in mental health research. *American Psychologist, 54*, 424–433. doi:10.1037/0003-066X.54.6.424

Rogler, L. H. (2000). Implementing cultural sensitivity in mental health research: Convergence and new directions. (Part III: V. Selected Psychometric Issues: VI. Discussion). *Psychline, 3*(3), 5–13.

Rogler, L. H., Malgady, R. G., Costantino, G., & Blumenthal, R. (1998). What do culturally sensitive services mean? The case of Hispanics. In D. Atkinson & G. Morten (Eds.), *Counseling American minorities* (5th ed., pp. 268–279). New York, NY: McGraw-Hill.

Rosselló, J., & Bernal, G. (1999). The efficacy of cognitive-behavioral and interpersonal treatments for depression in Puerto Rican adolescents. *Journal of Consulting and Clinical Psychology, 67*, 734–745. doi:10.1037/0022-006X.67.5.734

Rosselló, J., Bernal, G., & Rivera-Medina, C. (2008). Individual and group CBT and IPT for Puerto Rican adolescents with depressive symptoms. *Cultural Diversity and Ethnic Minority Psychology, 14*(3), 234–245. doi:10.1037/1099-9809.14.3.234

Rosselló, J., Bernal, G., & Rivera-Medina, C. (2012). Individual and group CBT and IPT for Puerto Rican adolescents with depressive symptoms. *Journal of Latina/o Psychology, 1*, 36–51.

Roth, W. D. (2012). *Race migrations: Latinos and the cultural transformation of race*. Stanford, CA: Stanford University Press.

Rounsaville, B. J., Alarcón, R. D., Andrews, G., Jackson, J. S., Kendell, R. E., & Kendler, K. (2002). Basic nomenclature issues for *DSM-V*. In D. Kupfer, M. B. First, & D. E. Regier (Eds.), *A research agenda for DSM-V* (pp. 1–30). Washington, DC: American Psychiatric Association.

Rovira, L. I. (1984). *Spanish proverbs: A survey of Spanish culture and civilization*. Lanham, MD: University Press of America.

Rudolph, B., Chavez, M., Quintana, F., & Salinas, G. (2011). Filial responsibility expectations among Mexican American undergraduates: Gender and biculturalism. *Hispanic Journal of Higher Education, 10*(3), 168–182.

Ruiz, A. S. (1990). Ethnic identity: Crisis and resolution. *Journal of Multicultural Counseling and Development, 18,* 29–40.

Ruiz, E. (2012). Understanding Latina immigrants using relational cultural theory. *Women & Therapy, 35*(1–2), 68–79.

Saenz, V. B., & Ponjuan, L. (2009). The vanishing Latino male in higher education. *Journal of Hispanic Higher Education, 8*(1), 54–89. doi:10.1177/1538192708326995

Saldaina, D. H. (1994). Acculturative stress: Minority status and distress. *Hispanic Journal of Behavioral Sciences, 16*(2), 116–128.

Sánchez, B., Colón, Y., & Esparza, P. (2005). The role of sense of school belonging and gender in the academic adjustment of Latino adolescents. *Journal of Youth and Adolescence, 34,* 619–628.

Sanchez, Y. M. (1997). Families of Mexican origin. In M. K. Degenova (Ed.), *Families in cultural context* (pp. 61–83). Mountain View, CA: Mayfield.

Sánchez-Johnsen, L. A., Hogan, K., Wilkens, L. R., & Fitzgibbon, M. L. (2008). Correlates of problematic eating behaviors in less acculturated Latinas. *Eating Behaviors, 9*(2), 181–189.

Sanchez Korrol, V. (n.d.). *The story of U.S. Puerto Ricans—Part Four.* Retrieved from http://centropr.hunter.cuny.edu/education/puerto-rican-studies/story-us-puerto-ricans-part-four

Sandage, S. J., Hill, P. C., & Vang, H. C. (2003). Toward a multicultural positive psychology: Indigenous forgiveness and Hmong culture. *The Counseling Psychologist, 31,* 564–592.

Sandler, B. R., & Hall, R. (1986). *The campus climate revisited: Chilly for women faculty, administrators and graduate students.* Washington, DC: Association of American Colleges and Universities.

Santiago-Rivera, A. L., & Altarriba, J. (2002). The role of language in therapy with the Spanish-English bilingual client. *Professional Psychology: Research and Practice, 33*(1), 30–38.

Santiago-Rivera, A. L., Arredondo, P., & Gallardo-Cooper, M. (2002). *Counseling Latinos and la familia: A practical guide.* Thousand Oaks, CA: Sage.

Santiago-Rivera, A., Cardemil, E., Prieto, L., & Romero, A. (2012). Welcome to the *Journal of Latina/o Psychology! Journal of Latina/o Psychology, 1,* 1–2.

Santiago-Rivera, A., Kanter, J., Benson, G., Derose, T., Illes, R., & Reyes, W. (2008). Behavioral activation as an alternative treatment approach for Latinos with depression. *Psychotherapy: Theory, Research, Practice, Training, 45*(2), 173–185.

Santiago-Rivera, A., Kanter, J., Busch, A., Rusch, L., Reyes, W., West, P., & Runge, M. (2011). Latino immigrants with depression: An initial examination of treatment issues at a community clinic. *Journal of Immigrant and Minority Health, 13,* 772–779.

Santisteban, D. A., & Mitrani, V. B. (2002). The influence of acculturation processes on the family. In K. M. Chung, P. B. Organista, & G. Marín (Eds.), *Acculturation: Advances in theory, measurement, and applied research* (pp. 95–119). Washington, DC: American Psychological Association.

Santisteban, D. A., Suarez-Morales, L., Robbins, M., & Szapocznik, J. (2006). Brief strategic family therapy: Lessons learned in efficacy research and challenges to blending research and practice. *Family Process, 45*(2), 259–271.

Schutte, O. (2000). Negotiating Latina identities. In J. J. E. Garcia & P. De Greiff (Eds.), *Hispanic/Latinos in the United States: Ethnicity, race, and rights* (pp. 61–76). New York, NY: Rutledge.

Schwartz, E., & Delgado-Romero, E. A. (2010). *Multiple identities: The intersection of womanist identity and ethnicity in Latinas.* Paper presented at the National Latina/o Psychological Association Conference, San Antonio, TX.

Schwartz, S. J., Mason, C. A., Pantín, H., & Szapocznik, J. (2009). Longitudinal relationships between family functioning, and identity development in Hispanic adolescents: Continuity and change. *Journal of Early Adolescence, 29,* 177–211.

Schwartz, S. J., Zamboanga, B. L., & Hernandez Jarvis, L. (2007). Ethnic identity and acculturation in Hispanic early adolescents: Mediated relationships to academic grades, prosocial behaviors, and externalizing symptoms. *Cultural Diversity and Ethnic Minority Psychology, 13,* 364–373.

Sciarra, D. T. (2001). Assessment of diverse family systems. In L. A. Suzuki, J. G. Ponterotto, & P. J. Meller (Eds.), *Handbook of multicultural assessment: Clinical, psychological, and educational applications* (2nd ed., pp. 135–168). San Francisco, CA: Jossey-Bass.

Segal, E., Gerdes, K., Mullins, J., Wagaman, M., & Androff, D. (2011). Social empathy attitudes: Do Latino students have more? *Journal of Human Behavior in the Social Environment, 21,* 438–454.

Seligman, M. E. P., & Csikszentmihalyi, M. (Eds.). (2000a). Positive psychology [Special issue]. *American Psychologist, 55*(1).

Seligman, M., & Csikszentmihalyi, M. (2000b). Positive psychology: An introduction. *American Psychologist, 55*(1), 5–14.

Seligman, M., Steen, T., Park, N., & Peterson, C. (2005). Positive psychology progress: Empirical validation of interventions. *American Psychologist, 60,* 410–421.

Sellers, J. M., Nelson, A. M., & Soto, G. (1994). *Folk wisdom of Mexico/Proverbios y dichos mexicanos.* San Francisco, CA: Chronicle Books.

Sentencing Project. (2003). *Hispanic prisoners in the United States.* Washington, DC: Author.

Shea, M., Cachelin, F., Uribe, L., Striegel, R., Thompson, D., & Wilson, T. (2012). Cultural adaptation of a cognitive behavior therapy guided self-help program for Mexican American women with binge eating disorders. *Journal of Counseling & Development, 90,* 308–318.

Shelton, K., Delgado-Romero, E. A., & Wells, E. M. (2009). Race and ethnicity in empirical diversity-focused research: An 18-year review. *Journal of Multicultural Counseling and Development, 37,* 130–140.

Shin, S. M., Chow, C., Camacho-Gonsalves, T., Levy, R. J., Allen, I. E., & Leff, H. S. (2005). A meta-analytic review of racial-ethnic matching for African American and Caucasian American clients and clinicians. *Journal of Counseling Psychology, 52*(1), 45–56.

Shinnar, R. S. (2007). A qualitative examination of Mexican immigrants' career development: Perceived barriers and motivators. *Journal of Career Development, 33,* 338–375.

Shorris, E. (1992). *Latinos: A biography of the people.* New York, NY: Avon Books.

Silverstein, M., & Chen, X. (1999). The impact of acculturation in Mexican American families on the quality of adult grandchild-grandparent relationships. *Journal of Marriage and Family, 61,* 188–198.

Simoni, J. M., Martone, M. G., & Kerwin, J. F. (2002). Spirituality and psychological adaptation among women with HIV/AIDS: Implications for counseling. *Journal of Counseling Psychology, 49*(2), 139–147.

Singley, C. (2012). *Work fatalities on the rise.* Washington, DC: National Council of La Raza.

Skinner, D. G., Correa, V., Skinner, M., & Bailey, D. B. (2001). The role of religion in the lives of Latino families of young children with developmental delays. *American Journal of Mental Retardation, 106,* 297–313.

Smart, J. F., & Smart, D. W. (1995). Acculturative stress of Hispanics: Loss and challenge. *Journal of Counseling & Development, 73*(4), 390–396.

Smith, R. L., & Montilla, R. E. (Eds.). (2007). *Counseling and family therapy with Latino populations: Strategies that work.* New York, NY: Routledge.

Smithsonian Latino Center. (2012). *Latino patriots in American military history.* Retrieved from http://latino.si.edu/education/latinopatriots.htm

Snyder, C. R. (1994). *The psychology of hope: You can get there from here.* New York, NY: Simon & Schuster.

Snyder, C. R., & Lopez, S. J. (Eds.). (2002). *Handbook of positive psychology.* New York, NY: Oxford University Press.

Solórzano, D., Ceja, M., & Yosso, T. (2000). Critical race theory, racial microaggressions, and campus racial climate: The experiences of African American college students. *Journal of Negro Education, 69,* 60–73.

Solórzano, D. G., & Yosso, T. J. (2001). From racial stereotyping and deficit discourse toward a new critical race theory in teacher education. *Multicultural Education, 9*(1), 2–8.

Soto, J. A., Armenta, B. E., Perez, C. R., Zamboanga, A. J., Umaña-Taylor, A. J., Lee, R. M., . . . Ham, L. S. (2012). Strength in numbers? Cognitive reappraisal and psychological functioning among Latinos in the context of oppression. *Cultural Diversity & Ethnic Minority Psychology, 18,* 384–394.

Sotomayor-Peterson, M., Figueredo, A. J., Christensen, D. H., & Taylor, A. R. (2012). Couples' cultural values, shared parenting, and family emotional climate within Mexican American families. *Family Process, 51,* 218–233.

Southern Poverty Law Center. (2011, May 18). *SPLC wins settlement for Latino man beaten by Georgia police officers.* Retrieved from http://www.splcenter.org/get-informed/news/splc-wins-settlement-for-latino-man-beaten-by-georgia-police-officers#.UapbykA4uE4

Southern Poverty Law Center. (2012, October 30). *SPLC wins record $11.8 million judgment for guestworkers in suit against forestry company.* Retrieved from http://www.splcenter.org/get-informed/news/splc-wins-record-118-million-judgment-for-guestworkers-in-suit-against-forestry-co#.UYcTS5VH0WY

Stacciarini, J. M., O'Keeffe, M., & Mathews, M. (2007). Group therapy for depressed Latina women: A review of the literature. *Issues in Mental Health Nursing, 28,* 473–488.

Steele, C. M. (1997). A threat in the air: How stereotypes shape intellectual identity and performance. *American Psychologist, 52,* 613–629.

Steele, C. M., & Aronson, J. (1995). Stereotype threat and the intellectual test performance of African Americans. *Journal of Personality and Social Psychology, 69,* 797–811.

Stein, D. J., Phillips, K. A., Bolton, D., Fulford, K. W. M., Sadler, J. Z., & Kendler, K. S. (2010). What is a mental/psychiatric disorder? From *DSM-IV* to *DSM-V. Psychological Medicine, 40,* 1759–1765.

Stoddard, S., & Garcia, C. (2011). Hopefulness among non-U.S.-born Latino youth and young adults. *Journal of Child and Adolescent Psychiatric Nursing, 24*(4), 216–222.

Sue, D. W. (1978). World views and counseling. *Personnel and Guidance Journal, 56,* 458–462.

Sue, D. W., Arredondo, P., & McDavis, R. J. (1992). Multicultural counseling competencies and standards: A call to the profession. *Journal of Counseling & Development, 70,* 477–486. doi:10.1002/j.2161-1912.1992.tb00563.x

Sue, D. W., Capodilupo, C. M., Torino, G. C., Bucceri, J. M., Holder, A., Nadal, K. L., & Esquilin, M. (2007). Racial microaggressions in everyday life: Implications for clinical practice. *American Psychologist, 62*(4), 271–286.

Sue, D. W., & Constantine, M. G. (2008). Optimal human functioning in people of color in the United States. In W. B. Walsh (Ed.), *Counseling psychology and optimal human functioning* (pp. 151–169). Mahwah, NJ: Erlbaum.

Sue, D. W., & Sue, D. (2003). *Counseling the culturally diverse: Theory and practice* (4th ed.). New York, NY: Wiley.

Sue, S. (1999). Science, ethnicity, and bias: Where have we gone wrong? *American Psychologist, 54,* 1070–1077.

Sue, S., Zane, N., Nagayama Hall, G. C., & Berger, L. K. (2009). The case for cultural competency in psychotherapeutic interventions. *Annual Review of Psychology, 60,* 525–548.

Suro, R. (2007, November). *The Hispanic family in flux.* Retrieved from the Brookings Institution website: http://www.coloradodads.com/UserFiles/File/11_hispanicfamily_suro.pdf

Suro, R., & Passel, J. (2003). *The rise of the second generation: Changing patterns in Hispanic population growth.* Washington, DC: Pew Hispanic Center.

Suzuki, L., Ponterotto, J., & Meller, P. (2001). Multicultural assessment: Trends and directions revisited. In L. A. Suzuki, J. G. Ponterotto, & P. J. Meller (Eds.), *Handbook of multicultural assessment* (pp. 569–574). San Francisco, CA: Jossey-Bass.

Szalacha, L. A., Erkut, S., Coll, C. G., Alarcón, O., Fields, J. P., & Ceder, I. (2003). Discrimination and Puerto Rican children's and adolescents' mental health. *Cultural Diversity and Ethnic Minority Psychology, 9*(2), 141–155.

Szapocznik, J., Hervis, O., & Schwartz, S. J. (2003). *Brief strategic family therapy for adolescent drug abuse.* Bethesda, MD: National Institute on Drug Abuse.

Szapocznik, J., & Kurtines, W. M. (1993). Family psychology and cultural diversity: Opportunities for theory, research, and application. *American Psychologist, 48,* 400–407. doi:10.1037/0003-066X.48.4.400

Szapocznik, J., Kurtines, W. M., Foote, F., Perez-Vidal, A., & Hervis, O. (1986). Conjoint versus one-person family therapy: Further evidence for the effectiveness of conducting family therapy through one person with drug-abusing adolescents. *Journal of Consulting and Clinical Psychology, 54,* 395–397.

Szapocznik, J., Kurtines, W., Santisteban, D. A., Pantín, H., Scopetta, M., Mancilla, Y., . . . Coatsworth, J. D. (1997). The evolution of structural ecosystemic theory for working with Latino families. In J. García & M. C. Zea (Eds.), *Psychological interventions and research with Latino populations* (pp. 166–190). Boston: Allyn & Bacon.

Szapocznik, J., Kurtines, W. M., Santisteban, D. A., & Rio, A. T. (1990). Interplay of advances between theory, research, and duplication in treatment interventions aimed at behavior problem children and adolescents. *Journal of Consulting and Clinical Psychology, 58,* 696–703.

Szapocznik, J., Santisteban, D., Kurtines, W., Perez-Vidal, A., & Hervis, O. (1984). Bicultural effectiveness training: A treatment intervention for enhancing intercultural adjustment in Cuban American families. *Hispanic Journal of Behavioral Sciences, 6*(4), 317–344.

Szapocznik, J., & Williams, R. A. (2000). Brief strategic family therapy: Twenty-five years of interplay among theory, research, and practice in adolescent behavior problems and drug use. *Clinical Child and Family Psychology Review, 3,* 117–134.

Tafoya, S. (2004). *Shades of belonging: Latinos and racial identity.* Retrieved from the Pew Hispanic Center website: http://www.pewHispanic.org/files/reports/35.pdf

Takushi, R., & Uomoto, J. M. (2001). The clinical interview from a multicultural perspective. In L. A. Suzuki, J. G. Ponterotto, & P. J. Meller (Eds.), *Handbook of multicultural assessment: Clinical, psychological, and educational applications* (pp. 47–66). San Francisco, CA: Jossey-Bass.

Taylor, B. A., Gambourg, M. B., Rivera, M., & Laureano, D. (2006). Constructing cultural competence: Perspectives of family therapists working with Latino families. *American Journal of Family Therapy, 34,* 429–445.

Taylor, P., Gonzalez-Barrera, A., Passel., J., & Lopez, M. H. (2012). *An awakened giant: The Hispanic electorate is likely to double by 2030.* Retrieved from the Pew Hispanic Center website: http://www.pewhispanic.org/2012/11/14/an-awakened-giant-the-hispanic-electorate-is-likely-to-double-by-2030/

Taylor, P., Kochhar, D. R., Fry, R., Velasco, G., & Motel, S. (2011). *Wealth gaps rise to record highs between Whites, Blacks and Hispanics.* Retrieved from the Pew Hispanic Center website: http://www.pewsocialtrends.org/files/2011/07/SDT-Wealth-Report_7-26-11_FINAL.pdf

Taylor, P., Lopez, M. H., Martinez, J. H., & Velasco, G. (2012). *When labels don't fit: Hispanics and their views of identity.* Retrieved from the Pew Hispanic Center website: http://www.pewHispanic.org/files/2012/04/PHC-Hispanic-Identity.pdf

Todd, S. (2011). "That power and privilege thing": Securing Whiteness in community work. *Journal of Progressive Human Services, 22*(2), 117–134.

Torres, V., & Delgado-Romero, E. (2008). Defining Latino/a identity through late adolescent development. In K. L. Kraus (Ed.), *Lenses applying lifespan development theories in action: A case study approach for counseling professionals* (pp. 363–388). Boston, MA: Lahaska Press.

Torres, V., & Zerquera, D. D. (2012). Hispanic serving institutions: Patterns, predictions, and implications for informing policy discussions. *Journal of Hispanics in Higher Education, 11*(3), 259–278.

Torres-Rivera, E., Wilbur, M. P., Maddux, C. D., Smaby, M. H., Phan, L. T., & Roberts-Wilbur, J. (2002). Factor structure and construct validity of the Counselor Skills and Personal Development Rating Form. *Counselor Education and Supervision, 41*(4), 268–278.

Torres-Rivera, E., Wilbur, M. P., Roberts-Wilbur, J., & Phan, L. (1999). Group work with Latino clients: A psychoeducational model. *Journal for Specialists in Group Work, 24,* 383–404.

Toth, J. F., & Xu, X. (1999). Ethnic and cultural diversity in fathers' involvement: A racial/ethnic comparison of African American, Hispanic, and White fathers. *Youth & Society, 31*(1), 76–99.

Trangmar, P., & Díaz, V. A. (2008). Investigating complementary and alternative medicine use in a Spanish-speaking Hispanic community in South Carolina. *Annals of Family Medicine, 6*(Suppl. 1), S12–S15.

Tucker, C. M., Ferdinand, L. A., Mirsu-Paun, A., Herman, K. C., Delgado-Romero, E. A., van den Berg, J. J., & Jones, J. D. (2007). The roles of counseling psychologists in reducing health disparities. *The Counseling Psychologist, 35,* 650–678.

Umaña-Taylor, A., Gonzales-Backen, M. A., & Guimond, A. B. (2009). Latino adolescents' ethnic identity: Is there a developmental progression and does growth in ethnic identity predict growth in self-esteem? *Child Development, 80,* 391–405.

Umaña-Taylor, A. J., & Guimond, A. B. (2012). A longitudinal examination of parenting behaviors and perceived discrimination predicting Latino adolescents' ethnic identity. *Journal of Latino Psychology, 1,* 14–35.

Umaña-Taylor, A., & Updegraff, K. (2007). Latino adolescents' mental health: Exploring the interrelations among discrimination, ethnic identity, cultural orientation, self-esteem, and depressive symptoms. *Journal of Adolescence, 30,* 549–567.

Ungar, M. (2006). *Strengths-based counseling with at-risk youth.* Thousand Oaks, CA: Corwin Press.

Updegraff, K. A., McHale, S. M., Whiteman, S. D., Thayer, S. M., & Delgado, M. Y. (2005). Adolescent sibling relationships in Mexican American families: Exploring the role of familism. *Journal of Family Psychology, 19,* 512–522.

Ure, L. (2009). *Incentives drawing more Latinos to military, Rand study finds.* Retrieved from http://www.cnn.com/2009/US/10/21/latinos.military/

U.S. Census Bureau. (n.d.). *America's families and living arrangements: 2010.* Retrieved from http://www.census.gov/population/www/socdemo/hh-fam/cps2010.html

U.S. Census Bureau. (2009). *Income, poverty, and health insurance coverage in the United States: 2009.* Retrieved from http://www.census.gov/newsroom/releases/archives/income_wealth/cb10-144.html

U.S. Census Bureau. (2010a). *American Community Survey.* Retrieved from http://www.census.gov/acs

U.S. Census Bureau. (2010b). *Census Bureau reports Hispanic-owned businesses increase at more than double the national rate.* Retrieved from http://www.census.gov/newsroom/releases/archives/business_ownership/cb10-145.html

U.S. Census Bureau. (2010c, March). *Overview of race and Hispanic origin: 2010.* Retrieved from http://www.census.gov/prod/cen2010/briefs/c2010br-02.pdf

U.S. Census Bureau. (2012a, February). *Educational attainment in the United States: 2009.* Retrieved from http://www.census.gov/prod/2012pubs/p20-566.pdf

U.S. Census Bureau. (2012b, September). *Income, poverty and insurance coverage in the United States: 2011.* Retrieved from http://www.census.gov/prod/2012pubs/p60-243.pdf

U.S. Citizenship and Immigration Services. (2012). *Consideration of deferred action for childhood arrivals process.* Retrieved from http://www.uscis.gov/portal/site/uscis

U.S. Department of Health and Human Services. (2001). *Mental health: Culture, race, and ethnicity—A supplement to mental health: A report of the Surgeon General.* Retrieved from http://www.surgeon general.gov/library/reports/

U.S. Department of Labor. (2003). *National Agricultural Workers Survey.* Washington, DC: Author.

U.S. Department of Labor. (2012, April). *The Latino labor force at a glance.* Retrieved from http://www.dol.gov/_sec/media/reports/HispanicLaborForce/HispanicLaborForce.pdf

Uttal, L. (2006). Organizational cultural competency: Shifting programs for Latino immigrants from a client-centered to a community-based orientation. *American Journal of Community Psychology, 38*(3–4), 251–262.

Varela, R. E., & Hensley-Maloney, L. (2009). The influence of culture on anxiety in Latino youth: A review. *Clinical Child Family Psychology Review, 12,* 217–233.

Vasconcelos, J. (1925). *La raza cósmica: Misión de la raza iberoamericana* [The cosmic race]. Barcelona, Spain: Agencia Mundial de la Librería.

Vasquez, M. J. T. (1994). Latinas. In L. Comas-Díaz & B. Greene (Eds.), *Women of color: Integrating ethnic and gender identities in psychotherapy* (pp. 114–138). New York, NY: Guilford Press.

Vasquez, M. J. T. (2007). Cultural difference and the therapeutic alliance: An evidence-based analysis. *American Psychologist, 62,* 878–883.

Vasquez, M. J. T. (2012). Psychology and social justice: Why we do what we do. *American Psychologist, 67,* 337–346. doi:10.1037/a0029232

Vazquez-Nuttall, E., Romero-García, I., & de León, B. (1987). Sex roles and perceptions of femininity and masculinity of Hispanic women: A review of the literature. *Psychology of Women Quarterly, 11,* 409–425.

Vega, W. A. (2005). Higher stakes ahead for cultural competence. *General Hospital Psychiatry, 27,* 446–450.

Vega, W. A., & Amaro, H. (1998). Latino outlook: Good health, uncertain prognosis. *Annual Review of Public Health, 15,* 39–67.

Vega, W., Gil, A., Warheit, G., Zimmerman, R., & Apospori, E. (1993). Acculturation and delinquent behavior among Cuban American adolescents: Toward an empirical model. *American Journal of Community Psychology, 21*(1), 113–125.

Vega, W. A., Karno, M., Alegría, M., Alvidrez, J., Bernal, G., Escamilla, M., . . . Loue, S. (2007). Research issues for improving treatment of U.S. Hispanics with persistent mental disorders. *Psychiatric Services, 58*, 385–394.

Verdugo, R. R. (2003). Discrimination and merit in higher education: The Hispanic professoriate. In J. Castellanos & L. Jones (Eds.), *The majority in the minority: Expanding the representation of Latina/o faculty, administrators, and students in higher education* (pp. 241–254). Sterling, VA: Stylus.

Vignoli, J. R. (2005). Unión y cohabitación en América Latina: Modernidad, exclusión, diversidad? [Union and cohabitation in Latin America: Modernity, exclusion, diversity?] *Serie Población y desarrollo.* Retreived from http://www.eclac.org/publications/xml/5/21135/LCL2234e-P.pdf

Villalba, J. A. (2007). Culture-specific assets to consider when counseling Latina/o children and adolescents. *Journal of Multicultural Counseling and Development, 35*, 15–25.

Villalbos, M., & Smetana, J. G. (2012). Puerto Rican adolescents' disclosure and lying to parents about peer and risky activities: Association with teens' perceptions of Latino values. *Journal of Adolescence, 35*(4), 875–885.

Viruell-Fuentes, E. A. (2007). Beyond acculturation: Immigration, discrimination, and health research among Mexicans in the United States. *Social Science & Medicine, 65*, 1524–1535.

Wagner, K. D., Ritt-Olsen, A., Chou, C. P., Pokhrel., P., Duan, L., Baezconde-Garbanati, L., . . . Unger, J. B. (2010). Associations between family structure, family functioning, and substance use among Hispanic/Latino adolescents. *Psychology of Addictive Behavior, 24*, 98–108.

Walker, N., Senger, J. M., Villarruel, F., & Arboleda, A. (2004). *Lost opportunities: The reality of Latinos in the U.S. criminal justice system.* Washington, DC: National Council of La Raza.

Walsh, F. (2006). *Strengthening family resilience* (2nd ed.). New York, NY: Guilford Press.

Walsh, W. B. (2003). Person-environment psychology and well-being. In W. B. Walsh (Ed.), *Counseling psychology and optimal human functioning* (pp. 93–121). Mahwah, NJ: Erlbaum.

Wang, W. (2012). *The rise of intermarriage: Rates, characteristics vary by race and gender.* Retrieved from the Pew Research Center website: http://www.pewsocialtrends.org/files/2012/02/SDT-Intermarriage-II.pdf

Wehrly, B., Kenney, K. R., & Kenney, M. E. (1999). *Counseling multiracial families.* Thousand Oaks, CA: Sage.

Wei, M., Liao, Y. H., Chao, R. C. L., Mallinckrodt, B., Tsai, P. C., & Botello-Zamarron, R. (2010). Minority stress, perceived bicultural competence, and depressive symptoms among ethnic minority college students. *Journal of Counseling Psychology, 57*, 411–422.

Wei, X., & Yu, J. (2012). The concurrent and longitudinal effects of child disability types and health on family experiences. *Maternal and Child Health Journal, 16*(1), 100–108.

Weisman, A. (2005). Integrating culturally based approaches with existing interventions for Hispanic/Latino families coping with schizophrenia. *Psychotherapy: Theory, Research, Practice, Training, 42*(2), 178–197.

Weisman, A. G., Gomes, L. G., & López, S. R. (2003). Shifting blame away from ill relatives: Latino families' reactions to schizophrenia. *Journal of Nervous and Mental Disease, 191,* 574–581.

Whaley, A. L., & Davis, K. E. (2007). Cultural competence and evidence-based practice in mental health services: A complementary perspective. *American Psychologist, 62,* 563–574.

Wiley, S., Deaux, K., & Hagelskamp, C. (2012). Born in the USA: How immigrant generation shapes meritocracy and its relation to ethnic identity and collective action. *Cultural Diversity and Ethnic Minority Psychology, 18*(2), 171–180. doi:10.1037/a0027661

Winning the future: Improving education for the Latino community. (2011, April). Retrieved from http://www.whitehouse.gov/sites/default/files/rss_viewer/WinningTheFutureImprovingLatinoEducation.pdf

Withrow, R. L. (2008). Early intervention with Latino families: Implications for practice. *Journal of Multicultural Counseling and Development, 36,* 245–256.

Woodcock, A., Hernandez, P., Estrada, M., & Schultz, P. W. (2012). The consequences of chronic stereotype threat: Domain disidentification and abandonment. *Journal of Personality and Social Psychology, 103,* 635–646. doi:10.1037/a0029120

World Bank. (2011). *Migration and remittances fact book 2011.* Retrieved from http://econ.worldbank.org/WBSITE/EXTERNAL/EXTDEC/EXTDECPROSPECTS/0,,contentMDK:21352016~pagePK:64165401~piPK:64165026~theSitePK:476883,00.html

Wrenn, C. G. (1962). The culturally encapsulated counselor. *Harvard Educational Review, 32,* 444–449.

Yakushko, O., & Espin, O. M. (2010). The experience of immigrant and refugee women: Psychological issues. In H. Landrine & N. F. Russo (Eds.), *Handbook of diversity in feminist psychology* (pp. 535–558). New York, NY: Springer.

Zamarripa, M. X., Lane, I., Lerma, E., & Holin, L. M. (2011). Self-knowledge and identity in a Mexican American counseling course: A qualitative exploration. *Hispanic Journal of Behavioral Sciences, 33,* 88–104.

Zamarripa, M. X., & Lerma, E. (2013). School-based assessment with Hispanic children and adolescents. In L. Benuto (Ed.), *Guide to psychological assessment with Hispanics* (pp. 335–350). New York, NY: Springer.

Zambrana, R. E. (Ed.). (1995). *Understanding Latino families: Scholarship, policy, and practice.* Thousand Oaks, CA: Sage.

Zane, N., & Mak, W. (2003). Major approaches to the measurement of acculturation among ethnic minority populations: A content analysis and an alternative empirical strategy. In K. M. Chung, P. B. Organista, & G. Marín (Eds.), *Acculturation: Advances in theory, measurement, and applied research* (pp. 39–60). Washington, DC: American Psychological Association.

Zayas, L. H., Borrego, J., & Domenech Rodríguez, M. M. (2009). Parenting interventions and Latino families. In F. A. Villarruel, G. Carlo, J. M. Grau, M. Azmitia, N. J. Cabrera, & T. J. Chahin (Eds.), *Handbook of U.S. Latino psychology: Developmental and community-based perspectives* (pp. 291–307). Thousand Oaks, CA: Sage.

Zayas, L. H., & Rojas-Flores, L. (2002). Learning from Latino parents: Combining etic and emic approaches to designing interventions. In J. M. Contreras, K. A. Kerns, & A. M. Neal-Barnett (Eds.), *Latino children and families in the United States: Current research and future directions* (pp. 233–249). Westport, CT: Praeger.

Zayas, L. H., Torres, L. R., & Cabassa, L. J. (2009). Diagnostic, symptom, and functional assessments of Hispanic outpatients in community mental health practice. *Community Mental Health Journal, 45*(2), 97–105.

Zeiders, K. H., Roosa, M. W., & Tein, J. Y. (2011). Family structure and family processes in Mexican-American families. *Family Process, 50*(1), 77–91.

Zeitlin, J. (2008, April 17). The man who created Generation Ñ: A decade after Newsweek named him tops, Bill Teck is back. *Miami New Times News.* Retrieved from http://www.miaminewtimes.com/2008-04-17/news/the-man-who-made-generation-ntilde/

Zúñiga, M. E. (1991). "Dichos" as metaphorical tools for resistant Latino clients. *Psychotherapy: Theory, Research, Practice, Training, 28,* 480–483. doi:10.1037/0033-3204.28.3.480

Zúñiga, M. E. (1992). Using metaphors in therapy: Dichos and Latino clients. *Social Work, 37*(1), 55–60.

Index

Figures and tables are indicated by f and t following the page number.

M

P

R

T

U